The Printer's Eye

Ukiyo-e from the Grabhorn Collection

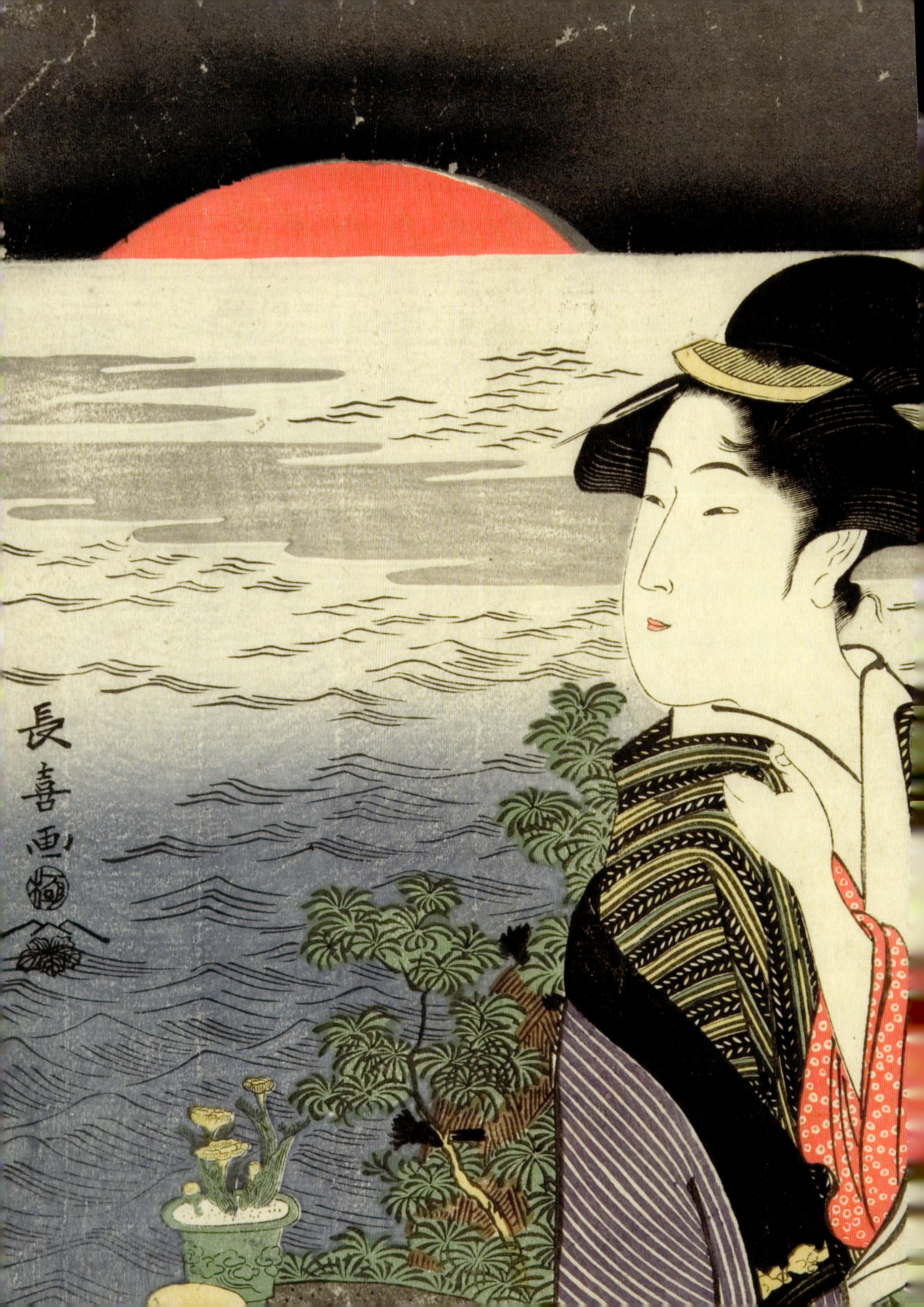

長喜画

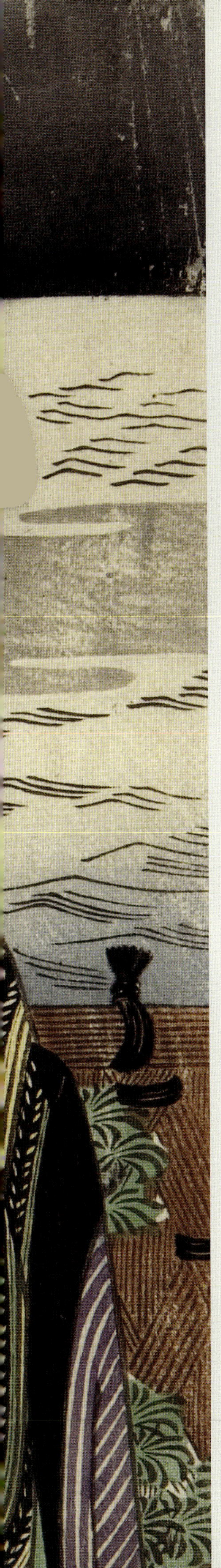

The Printer's Eye

Ukiyo-e from the Grabhorn Collection

Edited by Laura W. Allen and Melissa M. Rinne

Essays by Kobayashi Tadashi, Julia Meech,
Melissa M. Rinne, and David Waterhouse

Entries by Laura W. Allen and Melissa M. Rinne

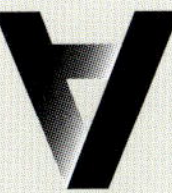

Asian Art Museum

Chong-Moon Lee Center for Asian Art and Culture | San Francisco

ISBN: 978-0-939117-60-4

The Asian Art Museum–Chong-Moon Lee Center for Asian Art and Culture is a public institution whose mission is to lead a diverse global audience in discovering the unique material, aesthetic, and intellectual achievements of Asian art and culture.

This publication was made possible thanks to generous contributions from an Ahmanson Foundation trustee, Lloyd E. Cotsen, and Mrs. Kazuko Imagawa Zolinsky.

Front cover: no. 34 (detail)
Back cover: no. 77 (detail)
Title page: no. 101 (detail)

1 3 5 7 9 8 6 4 2
FIRST PRINTING

Contents

JAY XU

Director's Preface

Ukiyo-e, literally "pictures of the floating world," have captivated viewers worldwide since the late 1800s. How can a museum committed to bringing the cultures of Asia alive to new generations fail to include these examples of the Japanese printmaker's art? Yet until recently, the Asian Art Museum of San Francisco, home to a world-renowned collection of more than 18,000 treasures spanning 6,000 years of history, owned few ukiyo-e prints.

In 2005 this deficiency was happily corrected when we received a momentous donation: more than 130 masterworks of woodblock printing from the collection of Irma Grabhorn. Assembled by her husband Edwin over the course of four decades, the collection includes many rare prints from the eighteenth and nineteenth centuries, among them a number of unique impressions of unparalleled quality and preservation. We are deeply indebted to Irma Grabhorn's nephew, Andreas Fuld, and niece, Katrin Fuld, for offering this outstanding collection to this museum. Credit is also due to Asian Art Museum director emerita Emily Sano and curator emerita Yoko Woodson for facilitating the donation.

I have been privileged to see many of these prints firsthand, and for me, they are not only beautiful and rare but also offer a marvelous lens into late Edo period (1615–1868) society, its customs, fashions, and mores. Until now only a small fraction of the prints has ever been shown or published outside of Japan. Our first objective upon receiving the prints was to publish a catalogue that would introduce them to general readers and scholars.

Our associate curator of Japanese art Melissa M. Rinne began to compile information about the prints in 2011, in collaboration with Laura W. Allen, who has since joined our staff as curator of Japanese art. We hope the catalogue will inspire interest in the collection, provide access to critical data, and offer a framework for future research.

We are grateful to Julia Meech and David Waterhouse, who contributed excellent essays to the catalogue, and to Kobayashi Tadashi for his poignant foreword. Sebastian Izzard, who assisted the museum in acquiring the collection in 2005, graciously spent many hours in storage reviewing the prints and adding to our store of knowledge, as did David Waterhouse and Andreas Marks on separate occasions. Amy Poster, Allen Hockley, Sarah Thompson, and Geoff Dunn were also extremely generous, providing many details about the prints that might otherwise have been missed. Thanks go also to Arion Press director Andrew Hoyem, who shared many personal memories about the Grabhorns and Grabhorn Press. This publication was made possible thanks to generous contributions from an Ahmanson Foundation trustee, Lloyd E. Cotsen, and Mrs. Kazuko Imagawa Zolinsky. We are also thankful for a generous donation from Andrew C. McLaughlin that enabled us to purchase the complete *Ukiyo-e shūka* series for our library.

Members of our museum staff were instrumental in bringing this project to fruition; in particular we want to thank John Stucky, Susie Kantor, and Stephanie Schnorbus, as well as Daniel King, who edited and proofread the manuscript together with Thomas Christensen, who designed and typeset the catalogue, and prepared the index. We are also indebted to several volunteers for their careful efforts: Jane Lurie, Yoshie Wirks, Ayako Sato, Peter Sinton, and Kakehashi Aiko. Finally, our heartfelt thanks to Stacey Jung, who as an undergraduate intern from Harvard University worked tirelessly to help create a database capturing information on all aspects of the prints' history.

KOBAYASHI TADASHI

Foreword: A Treasure Trove of Ukiyo-e Prints

Having admired the Grabhorn Collection from afar for many years, I got my first chance to view these prints in 1978, when I was still in my thirties. As the recipient of a grant from an American organization to conduct a comprehensive research survey of early ukiyo-e print collections in the United States, I traveled around the country viewing prints in numerous museums and private collections. The last stop on this long trip was San Francisco.

Mrs. Irma Grabhorn, who had lost her husband Edwin some years before, had been charged with the protection and keeping of his ukiyo-e collection, and she was known to be very cautious about showing it to scholars, connoisseurs, and, especially, dealers. For this reason, it was quite difficult for me, never having met her before, to be granted an appointment. But thanks to the good graces of a mutual acquaintance in San Francisco, her tightly locked doors were opened to me, and I was invited to meet her one evening. When she first saw me, she appeared rather surprised; nevertheless, she welcomed me warmly. "You are an associate of Dr. Narazaki? But you are so young.... Come in."

 To my great embarrassment, it soon became evident that to break down the iron walls with which Mrs. Grabhorn surrounded herself, the scholar who had introduced me had strategically made liberal use of the name of the eminent ukiyo-e specialist Narazaki Muneshige. I realized very quickly that I had been granted an audience due to this woman's trust in and respect for the great professor, of whom, she had been told, I was a "close friend."

My acquaintance introduced me briefly and, without entering the house, made his excuses, leaving me and the two students accompanying me alone with Mrs. Grabhorn. Perhaps due to the way we had been introduced or perhaps because we had not been invited by Mrs. Grabhorn directly, I was not entirely comfortable with the circumstances surrounding our visit; nonetheless, we were able in this way to enter a treasure trove.

Mrs. Grabhorn's German-accented English and my strongly Japanese-accented English turned out, in fact, to be advantageous for communicating meaning and feelings, and we immediately felt comfortable with one another. We started the evening off with a meal. Because I was a "friend of Dr. Narazaki," she had prepared a special menu for us, which was served in a formal dining room by a waiter in a bowtie. The ease with which I was able to interact with Mrs. Grabhorn was certainly facilitated by my presumed association with Professor Narazaki and by the trust she had in our mutual acquaintance; however, I must also acknowledge to this end the brisk, respectful manner of one of the students, Kamiya Hiroshi, who is now deputy director of the Nagoya City Museum.

After dinner, we began looking at an extraordinary group of masterworks, from primitive prints—including works by Sugimura Jihei, Torii Kiyomasu, and Okamura Masanobu—to images of beauties by Kitagawa Utamaro, Eishōsai Chōki, and others from the golden age of full color prints (*nishiki-e*). She graciously allowed me to view the collection deep into the night, entirely belying her reputation as a difficult person. Instead, I found her to be a delightful woman, with an expansive personality and a deep appreciation for beauty. I especially remember how the walls were decorated with colorful, expressive oils that she had painted herself. I remember thinking to myself how, as her own understanding of these prints developed, she and her husband must have relished their shared love of the collection. I became increasingly certain that this was in fact why she showed such extraordinary concern over the protection of the collection.

In 1995 and 1996, the most beautiful and significant prints from the collection I saw in Mrs. Grabhorn's San Francisco home were brought back to Japan for an exhibition organized by the late Yamaguchi Keizaburō (another eminent print scholar)—a nostalgic experience for me. As there was some uncertainty as to what would happen to the prints after Mrs. Grabhorn passed away, I am delighted that most of the stellar prints shown in Japan are now safely preserved in the Asian Art Museum, a most suitable place for this San Francisco collection. Through this publication and through future exhibitions and research, the Grabhorn treasure trove will finally be made accessible to scholars and lovers of Japanese prints around the world.

Translated by Melissa M. Rinne

MELISSA M. RINNE

The Grabhorn Ukiyo-e Collection at the Asian Art Museum

Early Japanese prints were not initially a strong focus of the Asian Art Museum's collection. Although the City of San Francisco was in possession of a large print collection when the museum opened in 1966, the museum's first administrators dismissed ukiyo-e prints as not being "high art" worthy of the museum's collection. As a result, the city's prints went not to the Asian Art Museum but to the Fine Arts Museums of San Francisco, where they are kept as part of the Achenbach Foundation for Graphic Arts at the Legion of Honor.

By 1965 a selection of Edwin Grabhorn's best prints had been published in four limited edition books printed by the Grabhorn Press for the Book Club of California.[1] Perhaps as a result of the museum's evident lack of appreciation for Japanese prints, Edwin Grabhorn never displayed his own extensive collection at the Asian, nor did he exhibit it publicly elsewhere in San Francisco.

After Grabhorn's death in 1968, Japanese scholars, aware of the collection, decided to feature many of its prints in 1979 as the tenth volume of *Ukiyo-e shūka,* a deluxe series cataloguing major print collections around the world. Eventually Yamaguchi Keizaburō, president of the Japan Ukiyo-e Society, persuaded Grabhorn's widow, Irma, to allow a selection of the best prints to be shown in a traveling exhibition in Japan. The exhibition traveled to four venues from the fall of 1995 to early 1996, as described in Professor Kobayashi Tadashi's foreword. A limited-edition catalogue was produced to accompany the show under the direction of Yamaguchi with brief entries on each print written by Koike Mikiko (then curator of the Shunsen Museum of Art in Kushigata in Yamanashi Prefecture); that publication informs the content of the catalogue entries in the present work.

Following Irma Grabhorn's death in 2003, her nephew in Germany, Mr. Andreas Fuld, inherited the print collection. The family decided to donate the best works from the collection to a museum—but which museum would be the beneficiary was an open question. Dr. Emily Sano, at that time director of the Asian Art Museum, got wind of the family's plans. Together with Dr. Yoko Woodson, then the museum's curator of Japanese art, Sano convinced the family to allow the prints to remain in San Francisco. They were acquired by the museum in 2005.

This catalogue, while far from exhaustive, presents the collection to an English-speaking audience for the first time. We are fortunate to include fine essays by Julia Meech and David Waterhouse, and benefited from the assistance of a number of specialists who looked at the collection and provided insights on individual works. We have done our best to provide basic information about each print, including full transcriptions of titles, signatures, and seals along with publication information and explanations gauged for nonspecialists. We hope thereby to make them accessible to general readers while offering connoisseurs an understanding of the collection's scope, scale, and significance.

The Grabhorn Collection at the Asian Art Museum comprises 136 titles; a number of these are diptychs or triptychs, made up of multiple sheets. This selection includes

---

1   *Figure Prints of Old Japan* (1959); *Landscape Prints of Old Japan* (1960); *Ukiyo-e: The Floating World* (1962); and *Twelve Wood-Block Prints of Kitagawa Utamaro* (1965).

all the prints that were sent to Japan in the 1995 exhibition, with the exception of the works by Hokusai and Hiroshige, which remained with the family.

The collection is significant for several reasons. Because the prints were stored away from light for decades under the Grabhorns' care, many of them are extraordinarily well preserved. Some are the best surviving examples of their kind or the only known impressions of a given design. Standouts are works by Eishōsai Chōki (no. 101), Kitagawa Utamaro (no. 86), Utagawa Toyokuni (no. 114), Katsukawa Shun'ei (no. 60), and Katsukawa Shunkō (no. 61). Also notable are a number of exquisite, Western-influenced landscape prints, including works by Ryūryūkyo Shinsai (no. 122), Yashima Gakutei (nos. 123 and 124), and Utagawa Kuniyoshi (no. 130 and others).

For the Asian Art Museum, this collection not only establishes a superlative foundation for growth in the area of ukiyo-e but also provides an excellent basis for introducing the early history of Japanese prints. The prints range from the earliest decades of Japanese printmaking in the late seventeenth century through the first decades of the nineteenth century. These examples effectively chronicle each phase in the technical development of Japanese printmaking in a representative array of notable artists and styles.

The collection includes many rare monochrome and hand-colored prints as well as several masterpieces from the early phase of color printing. Prints from the 1760s illustrate the emergence of full-color *nishiki-e* prints under Harunobu and his contemporaries, as detailed in David Waterhouse's essay. Others demonstrate the full flowering of color printing—specifically the use of mica, blind-printing, and the representation of intricately patterned, even translucent textiles—in works by Utamaro, Tōshūsai Sharaku, and others in the 1790s. A later development, the use of Prussian blue printing ink, is documented in the early-nineteenth-century landscape prints. We also find changes in paper size from the oversized *ō-ōban* used in the prints by the earliest ukiyo-e artists, to the *hosoban, hashira-e,* and *chūban* prints favored in the early- to mid-eighteenth century, and finally the standardized *ōban* size common in prints of the 1740s and later.

Because of their light sensitivity and fleeting colors, the Grabhorn prints will be exhibited only rarely and will continue to spend most of their time kept safely in archival storage to preserve their brilliant colors for future generations. This catalogue attempts to establish a foundation of basic information to facilitate their understanding, research, and appreciation for years to come.

JULIA MEECH

Edwin Grabhorn

Passionate Printer and Print Collector

A man of many contrasts, Edwin Grabhorn (1889–1968) is variously described as gregarious and outgoing, a bit aloof and shy, discerning and self-confident, arrogant and curmudgeonly, canny and focused—an unpredictable genius who, all agree, left the art world a rich legacy.

The Grabhorn Collection of Japanese prints is known to specialists and those fortunate to see a selection exhibited in 1995 in Japan. In 2003, after the death of the collector's widow, Irma, most of the collection was sold. In 2005, her heirs elected to donate the 216 titles from the 1995 Japan exhibition, minus works by Hokusai and Hiroshige, to the Asian Art Museum.

The collector, Edwin Grabhorn, worked first in Seattle for an uncle who was a music printer. With his younger brother, Robert (1900–1973), Edwin founded the Grabhorn Press in their hometown of Indianapolis around 1915, then moved the press to San Francisco in 1919 (fig. 1). After Edwin moved to San Francisco, he and his first wife divorced, and he married Marjorie ("Mudge") Robertson, the daughter of John W. Robertson. A successful physician who founded the Livermore Sanitarium in Livermore, California—where Robertson Park is named for him—the doctor was also a book collector with a concentration on Edgar Allan Poe. The Grabhorns had one daughter, Mary Ellis (now deceased), who became an illustrator and worked at the press with her father.

Although a modest business, for more than forty years the Grabhorn Press was the most distinguished book printer in California, preeminent in the making of deluxe, limited editions. The brothers' masterpiece is agreed to be Walt Whitman's *Leaves of Grass*, published by Random House in 1930. Grabhorn's peers in the printing world considered Edwin a wholly unpredictable genius. Seemingly everything he touched became a thing of beauty.[1]

The press closed in 1965 (the year after Edwin, then seventy-six, married his third wife, Irma Engel), but Robert joined in partnership with the much younger Andrew Hoyem (b. 1935) in a new printing business. Hoyem, who had worked for the brothers for a year, is today the head of Arion Press, the successor to the Grabhorn Press. In 2000, Arion Press formed the Grabhorn Institute, a nonprofit bookmaking facility located in the Presidio.

ENAMORED BEGINNER

Grabhorn began acquiring Japanese prints around 1925. One of Marjorie's ancestors, the captain of a trading vessel, reportedly returned from a voyage to Yokohama with a Harunobu beauty print. Grabhorn said that what started him collecting Japanese prints was that his wife liked them.[2] Over the years, she kept conscientious records of their purchases in a series of ledger books; she may have helped with the funding, as well.

Describing the inception of his collection, Grabhorn said, "I have always been interested in all forms of the graphic arts. I became enamored with what was to me a new form of pictorial presentation."[3] Like so many American collectors, he and his wife were attracted first to Hiroshige. ("You always come back to Hiroshige," Grabhorn recalled in a wistful moment after Marjorie's death.) "It was the landscapes of Hiroshige that first started us collecting Japanese prints," Marjorie and Edwin wrote in 1962:

The poetry in Hiroshige's interpretation of the different moods of nature opened our eyes to the beauty that

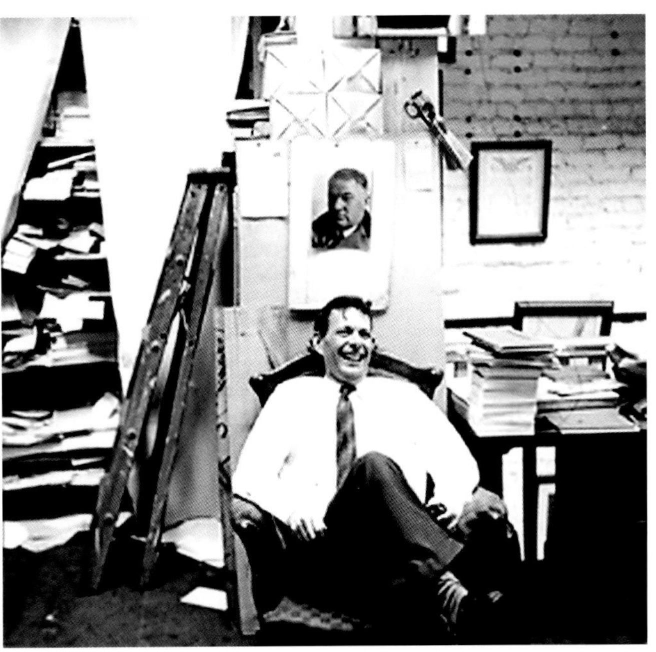

Fig. 1. Edwin Grabhorn at the Grabhorn Press. 1937. *Photo: Marjory Bridge Farquhar.*

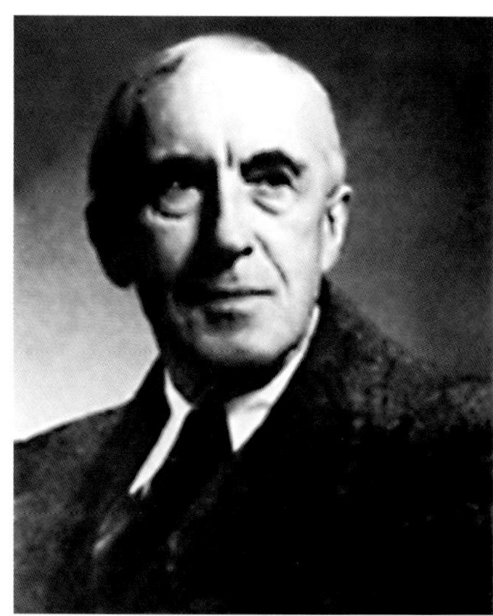

Fig. 2. Judson D. Metzgar. *Courtesy William Green.*

surrounds us in and about San Francisco Bay: the bridges in the rain, the fog on the hills, and the moonlight on the water. The artist speaks a universal language, and Hiroshige was interpreter for us as well as the Japanese.

The next step in our collecting of Japanese prints led us to the great master Hokusai, and from Hokusai to his one-time teacher Shunshō. Thus our collecting instincts seemed to progress backward in point of time, and, as we gradually acquired confidence, we arrived at the very beginning, to those earliest prints that had no color—or, if they did, the color was applied by hand.[4]

INFLUENTIAL CRONY

As early as 1926, Grabhorn, working with somewhat limited capital, was negotiating purchases and trades with the Los Angeles print consultant and dealer Judson D. Metzgar (1869–1958). Over the next thirty years, the two became real cronies (fig. 2). Metzgar had been a lawyer working on a tight budget in Moline, Illinois. He was one of the first Americans to benefit from the sudden rise in print prices in the teens, selling his collection at auction in New York at the peak of the market in 1916, for a record $19,000. By that time, he had already acquired three thousand prints by Hiroshige. He moved to Los Angeles in the 1920s and was much in demand as a senior authority, a successor to his mentor, the great Frederick Gookin (1853–1936) in Chicago, who had assisted collectors of the preceding generation. The last correspondence between Grabhorn and Metzgar, over increasingly complicated print deals, is dated 1958, the year Metzgar died.

DELUXE GRABHORN CATALOGUES

In 1943, the Grabhorn Press printed Metzgar's informative book, *Adventures in Japanese Prints*, for Dawson's Bookshop in Los Angeles. For years, Metzgar had an uneasy dual role with Grabhorn as both vendor of fine prints and supplicant nudging along the printing of this autobiographical account of the Golden Age of print collecting, his magnum opus. (He does not mention Grabhorn in the book.) Metzgar often vetted prints for Grabhorn. Writing to the collector in 1935, he states the case rather baldly: "I wish you would feel free to submit to me any prints you may think of buying. I would be glad to pass on their genuine-

ness which, frankly, you are not able to do."[5] (Grabhorn was actually known to be confident in his own expertise to the point of arrogance.) In those days, California was arid territory for Japanese art aficionados. There were few collectors, and Metzgar regretted the long commute between Los Angeles and San Francisco, though he relished having a "good hot print argument" with Grabhorn.[6]

Grabhorn loaned prints to exhibitions occasionally, and by 1943, he was vice-president of the local Oriental Art Society with headquarters at Mills College. He is described by many of those who knew him as gregarious and outgoing, a man of enormous charisma who liked being the center of attention. He and Marjorie visited The Art Institute of Chicago in 1956 to view the Buckingham print collection with Margaret Gentles, the associate curator of Japanese art, and she complimented him on his "discerning eye."[7] Still, he was known to be antiestablishment; he hated to see prints "buried" in public institutions and reportedly said of museums in general, "Why would you want to go see something you couldn't buy?"[8] His rude humor belied his learning, taste, and sophistication. In 1959, when the Grabhorns set out to produce three deluxe catalogues of their substantial collection (they had some seven hundred prints at the time), the Book Club of California, an organization of book lovers and collectors headquartered on Sutter Street in San Francisco, stepped in and asked to have a small selection of the prints published for its members. The images were reproduced with linoleum blocks cut in Grabhorn's own shop and printed over black-and-white collotype reproductions; the mica-ground prints rendered in this technique are quite impressive.

The first of the three volumes was *Figure Prints of Old Japan*, published in 1959, with an introduction by Harold P. Stern (1922–1977) of the Smithsonian's Freer Gallery of Art in Washington, DC, a few captions by the Japanese print scholar Yoshida Teruji (1901–1972) and substantial additional text by Grabhorn himself. It was published in an edition of four hundred, and featured fifty-two eighteenth-century images of actors and courtesans. The second, *Landscape Prints of Old Japan*, with text by the British authority on ukiyo-e, Jack Hillier (1912–1995), was published in 1960. Hillier, an executive in a fire-insurance company, acted as a consultant in Japanese prints and paintings for Sotheby's, London, and found a client in Edwin Grabhorn. The third volume, *Ukiyo-e: The Floating World*, was published in 1962. Grabhorn's "The Printer to the Reader," his preface to the first volume, reveals a well-grounded understanding of both the materials and the history of the Japanese print. His captions betray a keen enthusiasm for rarity and pride in provenance.

Thanks to these books, Grabhorn was now known to have one of the finest collections in private hands. Hiraki

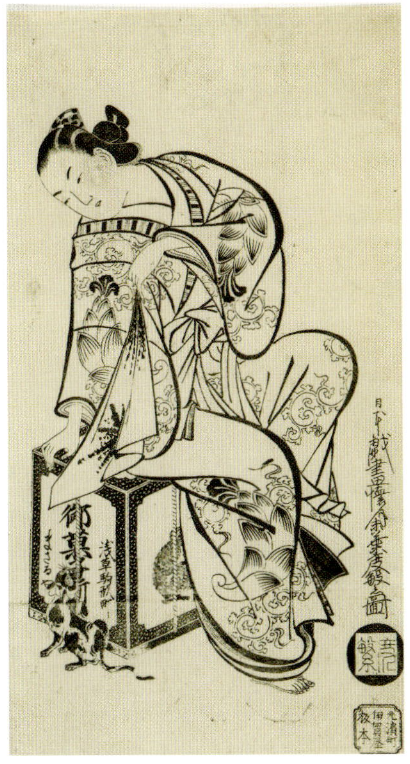
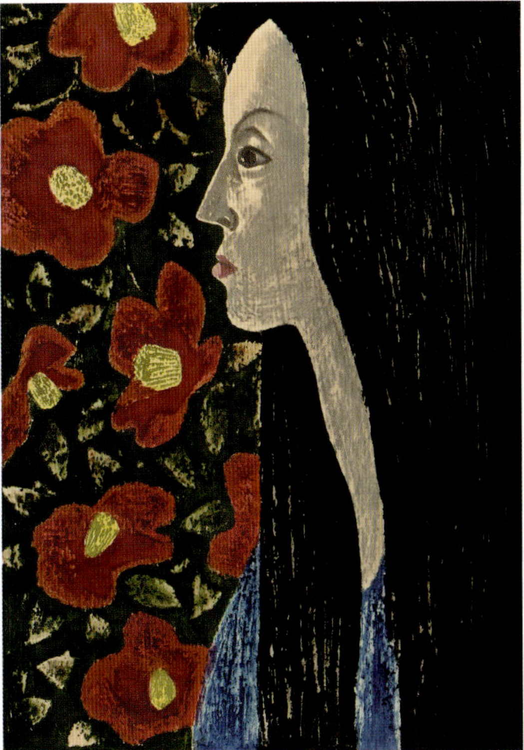
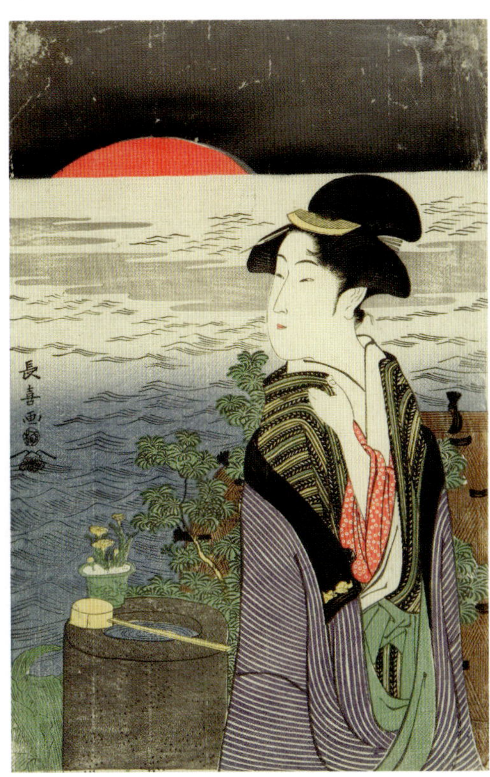

From left: Fig. 3. Kaigetsudō Dohan. *Courtesan playing with a cat* (no. 5). Woodblock print, 22 x 12¼ in. *Asian Art Museum of San Francisco, Gift of the Grabhorn Ukiyo-e Collection,* 2005.100.6. Fig. 4. Saitō Kiyoshi. *Camellia.* 1948. Signed by the artist at the home of Marjorie and Edwin Grabhorn on February 24, 1956. Color woodblock print, 25½ x 19½ in. *Ex. Grabhorn Collection. Courtesy Christie's Images, New York.* Fig. 5. Eishōsai Chōki. *Sunrise on New Year's morning* (no. 101), 1794–1795. Color woodblock print with mica ground, 15 x 9⅞ in. *Asian Art Museum of San Francisco, Gift of the Grabhorn Ukiyo-e Collection,* 2005.100.84.

Shinji, the president of Riccar, a sewing-machine company, and member of the Japan Ukiyo-e Society, was in the process of forming a large print collection and opening his own museum in the Ginza, Tokyo. He tried to buy the entire Grabhorn Collection after seeing these impressive catalogues.[9] In 1964, Margaret Gentles convinced Grabhorn to lend five prints to her exhibition at New York's Asia House Gallery, *Masters of the Japanese Print: Moronobu to Utamaro,* the first such postwar exhibition. (It had been twenty-five years since the great Sharaku exhibition organized by Louis V. Ledoux and Harold G. Henderson for the Museum of Fine Arts, Boston, and elsewhere.) In 1969, Harold Stern chose three superb Chōki and three rare Utamaro for *Master Prints of Japan,* his landmark exhibition at the UCLA Art Galleries in Los Angeles.

HUNTING FOR EARLY PRINTS

Grabhorn bought his eighteenth-century Kaigetsudō Dohan *Courtesan playing with a cat,* one of only three known impressions, for a whopping $3,000 at auction in New York in 1957, at the sale of the Charles Morse (1852–1911) estate (fig. 3). There were two Kaigetsudō prints in the Morse sale, and Grabhorn calls attention to the fact that James Michener, the famous novelist, purchased the other one. The provenance of the Grabhorn print goes back to 1896,

when Ernest Fenollosa (1853–1908), former curator of the Japanese department at the Museum of Fine Arts, Boston cataloged it as the property of Charles Morse in his 1896 exhibition in the Fine Arts Building in New York.[10] In his book, Grabhorn passes on the insider information that when he and Marjorie met the New York dealer William Ketcham in 1937, Ketcham told them that he and Fenollosa had been partners at the time of the 1896 exhibition; he provided the capital, and Fenollosa the prints.

Early eighteenth-century prints represent an obvious strength in the Grabhorn Collection—and the Grabhorns knew it. In her ledger book, Marjorie Grabhorn singled out a large, hand-colored pillar print of a standing courtesan by Nishimura Shigenaga (d. 1756?), purchased in Japan in August 1937 from Satō Shōtarō for more than a thousand dollars, as "the most beautiful print we own." The later prints in the collection, especially the Hiroshiges (many of them from Metzgar), are now considered disappointing in light of the opportunities that prevailed. Surprisingly, the Grabhorns also had major modern works by Onchi Kōshirō (1891–1955), Munakata Shikō (1903–1975) and Saitō Kiyoshi (1907–1997), among others. Saitō visited the Grabhorns during his three-month tour of the United States under the auspices of the State Department and the Asia Foundation. In 1956, he signed a number of his prints in their home (fig. 4).

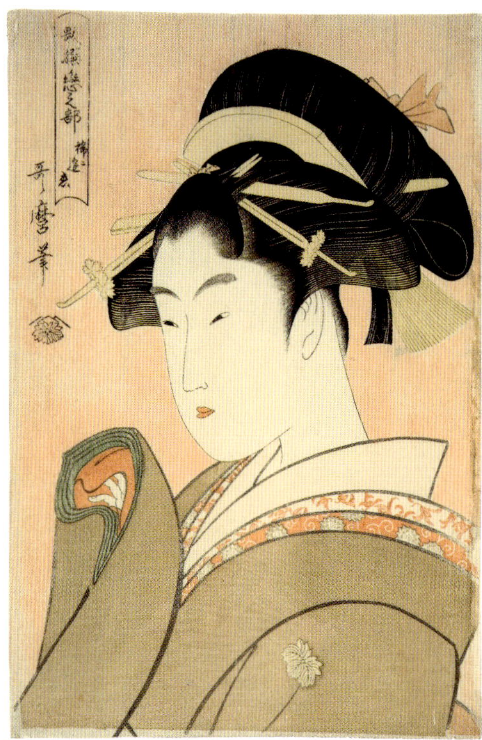

Fig. 6. Kitagawa Utamaro (1754–1806), "Love That Rarely Meets" (*Mare ni au koi*) (no. 78), from the series *Anthology of Poems: The Love Section* (Kasen koi no bu). Woodblock print. *Asian Art Museum of San Francisco, Gift of the Grabhorn Ukiyo-e Collection,* 2005.100.72.

Several prints, including the Chōki New Year's print, the best example in the world, came to the Grabhorns through the Paris dealer Aoyama Saburō, who had purchased them from the widow of Japanophile Gaston Migeon (1861–1930), a former curator at the Louvre (fig. 5). (The Chōki cost $1,350. The date of the purchase is not clear, but it was probably in the 1930s.) The dealer Hayashi Tadamasa (1853–1906) in turn had given them to Migeon as thanks for introductions to the Parisian collectors. Grabhorn wrote in *Figure Prints* that he and Marjorie bought a late eighteenth-century Ippitsu-sai Bunchō actor print on a trip to Kyoto in 1936 for 600 yen—"about $130 at that time." So even in the Depression days, "prints were 'a good investment.'" Grabhorn took advantage of the low prices during the worst years of the Depression, buying at auction at the J. C. Morgenthau and Walpole Galleries in New York. For the most part, prints were sent to him on consignment; he was not a stickler about condition. Price was always an issue—he was most comfortable with prices ranging from $15 to $200. The expensive prints repaid the investment, as many of them are worth a fortune today.

SELECTING ONLY THE BEST

Between 1937 and 1941, when Metzgar was acting as agent for Tod Ford and his brother Freeman, he sold the Grabhorns at least thirty-five prints, including a stunning Utamaro large-head portrait of a courtesan on an apricot mica ground (fig. 6). The asking price for the entire Ford group was $25,000, based on an appraisal by the art critic Sadakichi Hartmann (1867–1944).[11] Grabhorn picked only the best. The Utamaro cost him $200 (the average American earned less than $500 a year at that time) and is today probably worth around half a million dollars. The Ford brothers' father, David Tod Ford, Sr., had been a prominent attorney in Youngstown, Ohio, where he knew Charles Morse, before Morse moved to Evan-

ston in 1891. In 1905, Morse, who was a close confidant of the Detroit industrialist and collector Charles Freer (1854–1919), had brokered the sale of Freer's entire print collection to Ford, by then an invalid widower living in Pasadena, near his elder son, Freeman. Morse bought a portion of the prints from Ford.[12] David Tod Ford and his son Freeman both commissioned work from the architect brothers Greene and Greene, known for their Japanese design elements. The 1907 Freeman A. Ford house on South Grand in Pasadena is one of their masterpieces; it predates the more famous David A. Gamble house by only a year.

Grabhorn could not buy whole collections in the manner of the wealthy Spaulding brothers in Boston, but he cast his net wide. Many important purchases came from the Kyoto print publisher Satō Shōtarō—$1,500 for a mica-ground Sharaku in 1937, for example. (Satō published numerous articles on Hokusai and Hiroshige between 1915 and 1942.) Subsequently, prints came from Mary Thayer, daughter-in-law of the Kansas City print collector Sallie Casey Thayer (1856–1925); Helen Gunsaulus at the Art Institute of Chicago, who sold him duplicates from the Gookin bequest; the Japanese-art dealers Mathias Komor (1909–1984) and Roland Koscherak (1899–1987) in New York (the latter sold him a Bunchō portrait of the teahouse waitress Osen from the Ledoux Collection in 1950 for $350, probably overpriced); Felix Tikotin in Switzerland; Gump's and Daibutsu in San Francisco; the peripatetic Bay Area dealer Harry C. Nail Jr. (1909–1990); Yokoi Kiyoshi of Mayuyama in Tokyo; Alice Boney in Tokyo; and Kegan Paul, Trench and Trubner in London (fig. 7). He paid big prices for yellow-ground Utamaro prints at the 1962 Cartier sale in Paris.

FINDING AN ALLY IN HARRY PACKARD

Harry G. C. Packard (1914–1991) was an American civil engineer living in Tokyo, and is best known for the fine Japanese collection bearing his name that now resides in the Metropolitan Museum of Art (fig. 8). Packard, who had roots in the San Francisco Bay Area, was a knowledgeable, competitive collector and dealer who came to Japanese art through prints. He learned Japanese in naval intelligence during World War II and was buying prints in Tokyo by 1946, but that is another story.[13] Packard and Grabhorn, two curmudgeonly eccentrics, began working together in 1950, and many deals were struck between 1958 and 1962. Packard also helped with the authentication of some prints Grabhorn sent to him in Tokyo (he took the prints to various local authorities) and he enlisted a fellow dealer, Yabumoto Sōshirō (1914–1987), to help sell some of Grabhorn's etchings and lithographs by Degas, Klee, and others.

Packard hoped to have Grabhorn finance a "print hunt" with a big advance ($5,000 might do the trick), adding the familiar refrains about "chance of a lifetime" and "the period

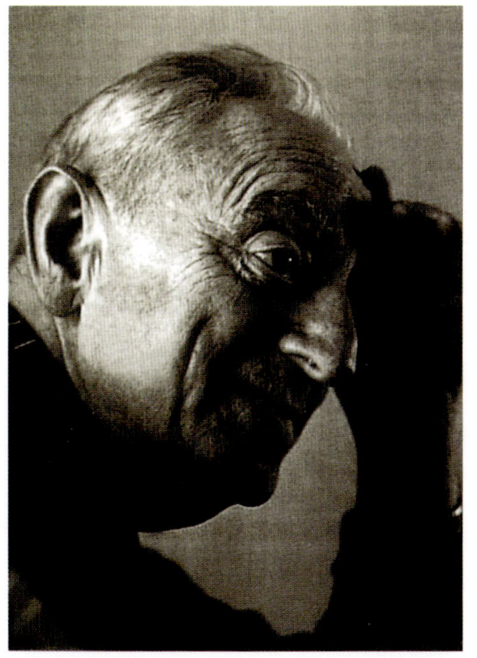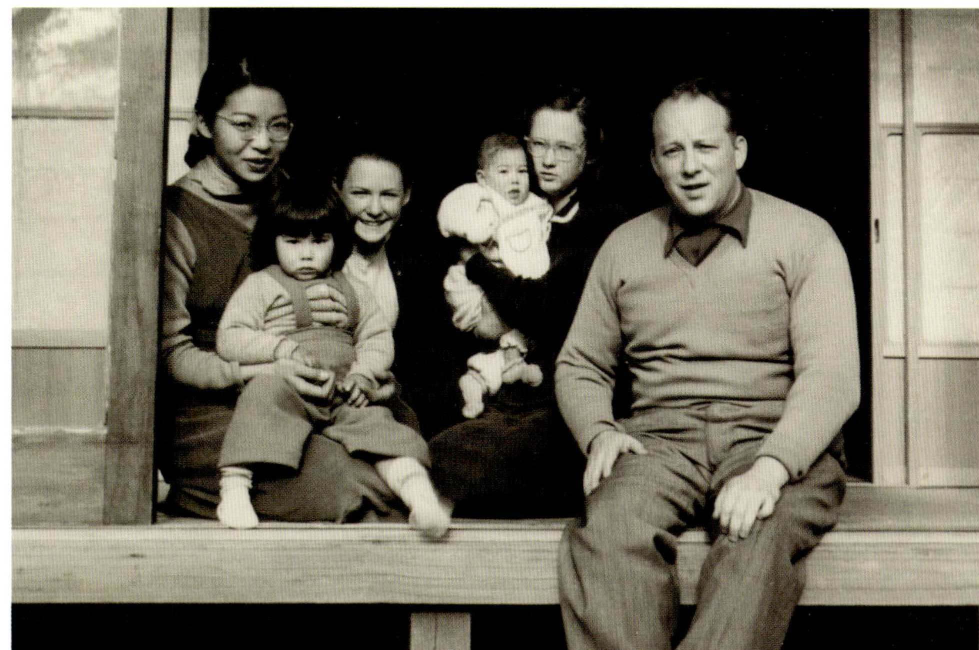

Left to right: Fig. 7. Roland Koscherak in the mid 1970s. *Courtesy Stephen Koscherak.* Fig. 8. Harry Packard with his family (Harry's wife, Carol; and daughters Kim, b. 1953; Catherine, 1941–2005; and Sally Ann, b. 1939, holding baby Chisa, b. 1954) in Kamakura, 1954. *Courtesy David Packard.*

when good prints could be picked up cheaply in Japan is past. It is tough to find really fine things even at high prices."[14] Grabhorn's money, Packard said, would give him first choice of the inventory of the Kyoto dealers Kondō Sentarō (1933–1983) at the Red Lantern Shop on Shinmonzen and of Kawai at the Shōgadō. In Tokyo, Packard made the rounds of the dealers Nishi Saijū (1927–1995) and Kaneko Fusui (1898–1978); Hayashi's widow at Marumiya in Marunouchi; Nakajima at Shōbisha; Yokoi and a host of others.[15] He even offered to approach private collectors such as Shibui Kiyoshi (1899–1992), an ukiyo-e scholar who would not sell cheaply. Over the years, Grabhorn often traded his Californiana for Japanese art, and Packard frequently requested payment in kind in the form of paintings by those West Coast artists. Grabhorn sold early California paintings as a sideline from a gallery in his basement.

Packard frequently invoked the specter of a rival San Francisco collector, Hans Popper (1904–1971). Popper, a Viennese businessman and serious amateur musician, lived in San Francisco following some years spent in Japan selling scrap metal from battle ships salvaged in the Pacific after the war. (His collection of more than three hundred and fifty Japanese prints, including many masterpieces, was sold at Sotheby Parke Bernet, New York, in 1972.) He was often in Japan on business, and Packard would pressure Grabhorn with the news that Popper could buy the best things if Grabhorn did not produce immediate funding for them himself. "I have bad news for you," Packard wrote in July of 1958:

Popper has bought the white mica Utamaro of the "Girl with the Pipe."

I should tell you that I acted as guide and interpreter for Hans during his stay in Japan since we have known each other for over ten years. We visited Kaneko. . . . Kaneko would have sold it to me under ordinary circumstances but several factors were in Popper's favor. 1) He is here and could decide the moment he saw the print whether he wanted to buy it or not. 2) He had the cash, which he paid the morning after Kaneko accepted his offer. I, on the other hand, was acting for you and had to wire you for a decision, which took time. I didn't have the cash and you failed to send it in time.[16]

THE VISIT FROM YOKOI

In 1958, on the eve of the publication of the Grabhorn volume featuring the early prints, Packard wrote to Grabhorn about the possibility of an acquisition of early eighteenth-century prints ("primitives") from Yokoi Kiyoshi (1907–1999) (fig. 9). Yokoi is something of an unsung hero of the Japanese print world. The head of the jewelry department of Mayuyama & Co. in the Imperial Hotel Arcade in Tokyo, he was an important senior staff member and one of the largest shareholders of the company. He also handled ukiyo-e for Mayuyama, both tourist items and high-end. In 1949, for example, Yokoi sold the first of many important prints to the fledgling Minneapolis collector Richard P. Gale (1900–1973), the nephew of Alfred F. Pillsbury. Gale was in Tokyo as a freelance reporter for the Minneapolis *Star* and *Tribune* newspapers. In 1960 he sold Gale three rare actor prints by the enigmatic artist Kabukidō Enkyō (active c. 1796); Gale "later remarked that he mortgaged the family farm in order to acquire these spectacular works."[17] Packard described Yokoi's prices as "just about the highest in the world."[18]

Yokoi would be touring America and could visit Grabhorn

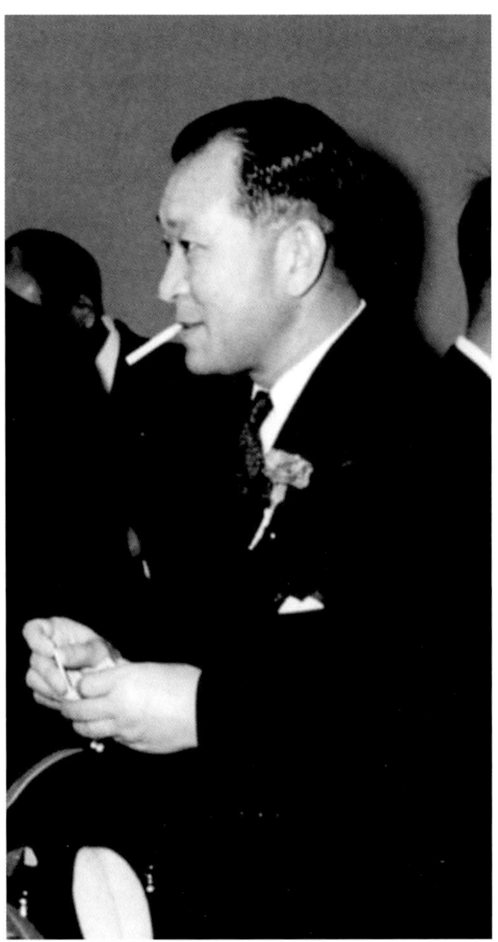

Fig. 9. Yokoi Kiyoshi. Tokyo 1960. *Courtesy Mayuyama & Co.*

in early December 1958. Packard gave instructions in etiquette:

When Yokoi got your letter, his main reaction was one of surprise and even indignation. He remarked that he "didn't know you." He had never heard of you, had no idea of your status as a collector, and thought you had a nerve to abruptly proposition him with an offer. . . . However, . . . Kaneko and I told Yokoi the following about you:

You are one of the world's great publishers of fine books.

You are about seventy, and in poor health. You want at this time to publish a major set of books, namely the Catalogue of the Grabhorn Print Collection.

That, with your ability as a book maker, this Catalogue will remain as one of the great books on Ukiyoe in the West.

That you are very anxious to get started on the first volume on Primitives, but that your primitive collection is not strong enough.

That you are a long time collector of prints and have about 700 prints including some great ones. That you bought from Sato Shotaro before he died, and that I have helped you with the collection since. That all you lack to make a fine book are some good Primitives.

That you are a natural gentleman. That you have no pretense and don't regard yourself as anyone special. But that your books are known the world over. I told Yokoi about the time I went to the Lahore Library in Pakistan and found a display of Grabhorn books in the display case in the center of the entrance.

That you were not an exceedingly rich man because you regarded book making as an art and not a business. That you have enough money to pay him a reasonable price in cash for his prints, if he is willing to sell.

That you asked me to do the research on the book, and that I intend to do a thorough job, enlisting the help of various Japanese print specialists on the various special problems and fields. Yokoi, by the way, respects my knowledge on prints.

That you have been losing sleep about his Primitives. That prints are a life-long passion with you.

These are the very qualities which Japanese respect most in a man, and in an art collector. . . .

Meet Yokoi in San Francisco at plane or train if possible and have him out to your house for dinner. Feed him some of Mudge's good cooking, being sure that it won't ruin his indigestion. Seafood (crab, lobster, clams, oysters, etc.) with some plain cooked rice to take the place of bread might be good. Or maybe some roast chicken, but not steak or lamb.[19]

The Grabhorn ledger books record a payment of $4,000 for a stunning Kaigetsudō Doshin print of a courtesan with a patterned gown and some orange pigment, now in a private collection. It was one of five early prints purchased from Yokoi for $12,000.

CONNOISSEURSHIP

Expertise in Japanese prints is fraught, and there is no collector who has not been fooled at one time or another. In 1958, Grabhorn purchased from Packard what now appears to be a controversial Kaigetsudō Anchi image of a standing courtesan for $2,000, half to be paid in cash and half in nineteenth-century California paintings (fig. 10). It is printed on suitably worm-eaten and soiled old paper, and only one other impression is known. "One of the joys of collecting is the discovery that you possess something unique and are the envy of every other collector in the same field," Grabhorn wrote of this print.[20] Packard acknowledged that, because it had been doubted by Kaneko, he had taken it to three respected authorities for authentication: Nakajima at the Shōbisha, a print gallery founded in the 1920s by Matsuki Kihachirō; Fujikake Shizuya (1881–1958), the editor of the prestigious art journal *Kokka* and a former professor at the University of Tokyo who had specialized in ukiyo-e for more than forty years; and the well-known Tokyo print publisher Watanabe Shōzaburō (1885–1962), a man who had been in the business for more than fifty years, and who affixed a dated certificate of authentication to the verso. Packard said he had acquired the print from a private collector, a Mr. Tase in Yamagata Prefecture to the north of Tokyo, a manufacturer of special silk threads for export to France. James Michener supposedly had offered Packard $3,000 for it.[21] Unfortunately, the hand-colored orange pigment is "wrong." The pigment is like that used in the first decades of the twentieth century by Takamizawa Enji (1870–1927), a collector who made facsimiles as a hobby. Fujikake once confessed that he couldn't tell Takamizawa's creations from original prints.[22] That only two impressions of the Anchi courtesan survive, both with identical hand coloring, may be more than a coincidence.

Some years earlier, in 1951, Metzgar and Margaret Gentles had looked over a group of prints valued at $45,000 that Packard had left temporarily in storage with the collector Avery Brundage (1887–1975) in Chicago. (Grabhorn had introduced Packard to Brundage.) Grabhorn must have asked Metzgar, who was in Chicago on business, to take a look. "Every one of the prints, with the bare exception of one Kisokaido, is a reproduction," Metzgar wrote him. "Yes, every one of them, from Masanobu down to Hiroshige. . . . He is either perfectly ignorant of old Japanese prints or a big rascal."[23] Packard was well aware of the backstabbing. From his perspective, Americans like Metzgar were hampered by never having seen prints in perfect condition; Americans expected fading or brown paper and signs of age.[24] Curiously, however, Packard himself devoted a great deal of energy to having three of Grabhorn's early eighteenth-century prints artfully restored (at Grabhorn's request) at the Adachi Woodblock Studio in Tokyo, using old paper (paper salvaged from "junk prints") and new blocks to replace the missing lower section of each of these large prints.[25]

METICULOUS COLLECTOR

The San Francisco fine print dealer and connoisseur R. E. Lewis (1923–2005) knew Grabhorn for many years—their businesses were located near each other on Sutter Street. Lewis sold him prints ranging from Emil Nolde etchings to Hokusai woodcuts. He thought that Grabhorn and Popper were the only true collectors of ukiyo-e in the city, and vowed he would leave town himself when Grabhorn died (he didn't). He remembered Grabhorn as a collector with a capital "C"—but as a difficult, testy personality with a formidable ego who never got close to people. (Others have suggested that this irascible side was a front for shyness or insecurity.) The only way Lewis could sell a print to Grabhorn was to assure him that it was inferior and not worth the trouble to come see it. Grabhorn would retort, "That's for me to decide, buster," and he'd be over in half an hour. If the dealer bragged about a new consignment, the contrarian Grabhorn might not show up for weeks.

The Grabhorns kept the prints matted and stored in folios covered in green cloth on open shelves in a special print room on the top floor of their home. The folios were meticulously organized according to size, artist, and period. For viewing, Grabhorn liked to set a folio into a V-shaped print stand. Metzgar approved of the way Grabhorn showed the prints "standing in portfolios instead of in drawers or on shelves flat. This is the way the great branch in New York of Yamanaka & Co. used to display them in the early years of the century."[26]

EDWIN AND IRMA

Marjorie Grabhorn died after a long illness in the fall of 1963. Roger Keyes, then a young assistant to R. E. Lewis, and his new bride, Keiko, were invited to stay with Edwin over Christmas that year. Keyes recalls that Grabhorn, who did not drive, had Keiko ferry him to and from assignations with the recently widowed Irma Engel (1906–2003) in the collector's 1940s sedan. He would come back with lipstick on his collar, a bit sheepish but excited, complaining that Irma said she "won't

sleep with me unless I marry her." Edwin married Irma in 1964, and the newlyweds traveled to Japan at least once. But only four years after his marriage to Irma, Edwin Grabhorn died at the age of seventynine. Although their life together was brief, Edwin and Irma seemed to share an affectionate partnership.

O. P. Reed, Jr. (b. 1921), a Los Angeles art dealer with expertise in old-master prints and Japanese woodcuts, had a visit from Edwin and Irma at his small gallery on La Cienaga Boulevard when he was selling the thousands of Japanese prints consigned by the widow of Frank Lloyd Wright (1867–1959). Reed had put aside two groups of choice prints that he sold in 1965–66 to institutions in Los Angeles, but Grabhorn had the pick of the rest. Reed

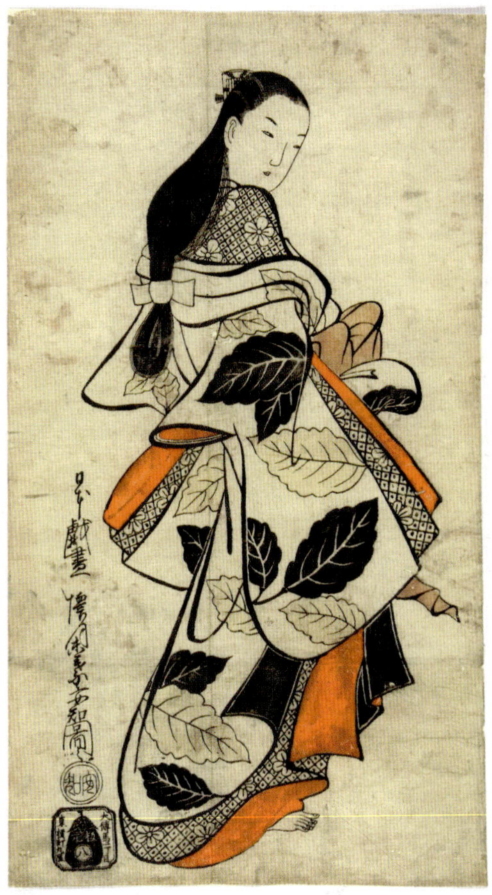

Fig. 10. Style of Kaigetsudō Anchi (active c. 1710–1715). *Courtesan.* Date uncertain. Woodblock print with hand coloring. 21½ x 12 in. *Asian Art Museum of San Francisco, Gift of the Grabhorn Ukiyo-e Collection,* 2005.100.120. This print was not included in the 1995 exhibition of Grabhorn prints sent to Japan, but remains with the collection at the Asian Art Museum as a study piece.

had a separate catalogue sheet for every print and had hired Ling Po (b. 1917), a Chinese architect working for Taliesin Associated Architects, to translate titles and signatures. Prices were listed and had been double-checked by both Harry Packard and the London dealer Roger Bluett. No changes or offers were allowed. According to Reed:

Ed wanted to see my Japanese prints. Irma, always active, examined every corner of my place, picking up framed Dürers, opening each print box, talking, yakking. Ed was a very quiet man, seemed to go inward and not listen to the magpie of an Irma, although they seemed affectionate. He spoke with a simple vocabulary. He was not quick to reply, thought things over and answered with complete sentences like a good editor. His glance was warm. He was a bit aloof but very likable as a man.

Ed sat on my shoddy couch and took each print into two hands and remarked about details, impressing me with his taste and comprehension. He bought some, but I cannot remember which. They could only have been the most superb impressions, as he limited his collection to the best.

Strangely, his patience and authority with young people like my wife and me reminded me of Frank Lloyd Wright. Both were forceful men to whom one listened knowing instinctively what they said was valuable. Neither had to nor needed to show off. Later Ed sent me a large volume about his collection. He and his wife visited a few more times before he died. He was elderly when I met him. Irma and I corresponded, until I ignored her letters when I got involved deeply with a new field, German Expressionism.[27]

Roger Keyes remembers that Grabhorn, a canny and focused collector, was pleased with a couple of Katsukawa Shunkō (1743–1812) portraits of sumo wrestlers that he bought on that trip. Grabhorn, he thought, had been on guard, not wanting to give Reed too many cues.

A LONG LIFE ENDS

Irma Grabhorn died in San Francisco on February 23, 2003, at the age of ninety-seven. Born Irma Leisinger in Badenweiler, Germany, she said she first noticed Japanese prints in Paris in 1926 at the age of twenty, while studying with the French Cubist painter and sculptor André Lhote (1885–1962). She was inspired at the time to buy a small set of Hiroshige Tōkaidō prints, which she treasured for the rest of her life. She also attended the Academy of Arts in Berlin under Karl Hofer (1878–1955). In 1932, Irma married the ophthalmologist Samuel Engel, with whom she emigrated to the United States in 1938, when he was invited to teach in the School of Medicine at Stanford University. The couple settled in San Francisco. Engel, who died in 1960, collected antiquarian books; he and Edwin Grabhorn were well acquainted through the Book Club of California. In 1965, the year after Irma and Edwin married, the Grabhorn Press printed *Twelve Wood-Block Prints of Kitagawa Utamaro* for the Book Club of California. Jack Hillier provided the introduction and modest captions for the reproductions of this series on sericulture, the originals of which Grabhorn had purchased at the Charles Morse sale in 1957 (see nos. 87–98). The ownership of the prints in this volume is attributed on the title page to "The Edwin and Irma Grabhorn Collection," and Irma cut the color blocks for the reproductions herself.

GUARDIAN OF A LEGACY

Although Edwin Grabhorn with his wife Marjorie had spent the best part of a lifetime building one of the great American collections of ukiyo-e prints, Edwin's widow, Irma Grabhorn, was the devoted guardian of this legacy for the next thirty-four years, often obsessive in her desire to circle the wagons and fend off the advances of hopeful curators, rival collectors, art dealers, and auctioneers. Even scholars faced obstacles. She once invited David Waterhouse to catalogue the collection but expected him to do it from the color reproductions made by her husband, not from the originals. Waterhouse recalls that he was invited for lunch with Roger and Keiko Keyes:

> We entered a gloomy concrete front hall which echoed to the sound of classical music; and presently Irma herself made a theatrical entry down the curving staircase. After lunch, she gave us a tour of the house, which had been built about eighty years ago to withstand earthquakes, and was furnished throughout in an antique style. It had cold, prison-like walls and for extra security was divided into sections kept separated by locked doors. It would have made a good set for a Hollywood horror film.[28]

The Grabhorn house on Chestnut Street in San Francisco may have been a pilgrimage site for enthusiasts, but Irma's passion was her own painting. She was quite a good painter, specializing in floral still lifes and portraits; many hundreds filled the spare rooms of her home. Her portrait subjects included her favorites—the scholar Narazaki Muneshige (1904–2001), who founded the Japan Ukiyo-e Society in 1962, and Sebastian Izzard, then head of the Japanese department at Christie's, New York. She insisted that a group of her oil paintings accompany the exhibition of the Grabhorn prints that went to Japan in 1995. That year, the Japan Ukiyo-e Society, in collaboration with the Asahi Shinbun newspaper, organized the first Japanese tour of a selection of the 216 best examples chosen from a collection of nearly a thousand at venues in Tokyo, Osaka, and Nagoya. The catalogue was written by Yamaguchi Keizaburō (1923–2012), professor emeritus at Risshō University, Tokyo, and the director of the Japan Ukiyo-e Society (fig. 11).[29]

The Chicago collector George Mann and his wife, Roberta, once visited Irma at her home in San Francisco. It took the intercession of Roger Keyes, and several telephone calls, to convince her to see them. Mann wanted to visit so that he could compare a particular print with his own, the only other known impression. Mann reports that:

> Apparently she believed that anyone who wanted to see her prints was only interested in buying them and she wasn't prepared to sell.
>
> Roger convinced her of my "honorable" interests and she agreed to bring the print out of the vault and to show it to us after we had lunch at her home. Also in attendance, as I recall, was a young man from Sotheby's. Luncheon was formal but pleasant. She seemed rather shy and wary, at first. Her home was very "old" San Francisco with burgundy velvet drapes covering the windows from the very high ceilings to the floor.
>
> After lunch, she showed us the print, which I studied for about twenty minutes, becoming convinced that hers and mine came from the same blocks. She had no other prints at home but showed us some of the color separations from the volumes published by the Grabhorn Press about the collection. We thanked her profusely for her hospitality and prepared to leave.

When we were at the door, she startled us by almost insisting that we stay longer. It seemed that once we broke the ice, she wanted to spend more time with us. She asked that we come back again the next day, but we couldn't because we were scheduled to leave on a driving trip down the coast. As I recall, she sent us a note the next day. All in all, it was somewhat sad because she seemed so lonely.[30]

In the end Irma Grabhorn left her husband's collection, the last and largest of the early collections of ukiyo-e in private hands, to her sister's children, who live in Germany. The heirs sold the bulk of the prints. As custodian, Irma might have designated a museum as their final resting place. Instead, offended by the brash local museum directors and the many others who approached her after her husband's death, she went into a defensive crouch and determined never to part with her treasures. She stamped her personal seal onto the margin of many of the later prints. Fortunately, at the time the heirs were debating the disposal of the cream of the collection, Emily Sano, then the director of the Asian Art Museum, spoke up forcefully in defense of her institution. As a result, a significant selection, including many masterpieces, has now found a most suitable home in San Francisco.

NOTES

My thanks to Joe Brotherton, Andrew Hoyem, Sebastian Izzard, R. E. Lewis, George Mann, Matsuda Takuji, Geoffrey Oliver, O. P. Reed, Bruce Smith, and David Waterhouse for helping to recreate the story of Edwin and Marjorie Grabhorn and the collection that they formed. It was a relief and a pleasure to find a handful of people who remember Edwin Grabhorn well. Roger Keyes has been at the center of the Japanese print world for almost fifty years, and I am especially grateful for his insights. For an earlier version of this account of Grabhorn, see Julia Meech, "Edwin Grabhorn: Printer and Print Collector," *Impressions* 25 (2003): 55–69. *Impressions* is the journal of the Japanese Art Society of America (www.japaneseartsoc.org).

1   Carl I. Wheat, "Private Presses and Fine Printers of California," *News Notes of California Libraries* 29, no. 3 (July 1934): 94.

2   Carol Packard, "An Interview at the Grabhorn Press," undated typescript interview with Edwin Grabhorn (ca. 1959), Grabhorn Ukiyo-e Collection archives. The preceding reference to Marjorie's ancestor, the sea captain, comes from Harry Packard, "Nihon bijutsu shūshūki" (Diary of a collector of Japanese art), *Geijutsu shinchō* 27, no. 2 (Feb. 1976): 139.

3   Marjorie and Edwin Grabhorn, "The Printer to the Reader," *Figure Prints of Old Japan* (San Francisco: Book Club of California, 1959), n.p.

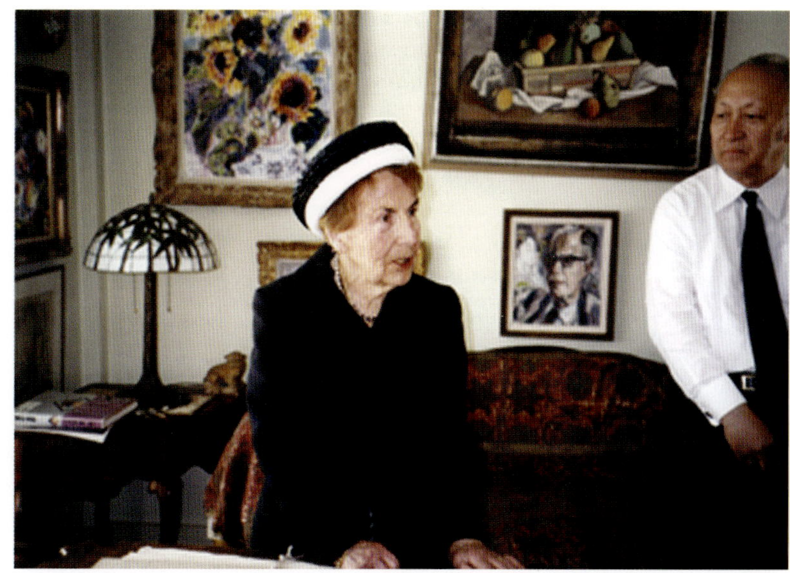

Fig. 11. Irma Grabhorn in her atelier with Yamaguchi Keizaburō. 1995; on the wall behind her, her painting of sunflowers, one of her portraits of Edwin Grabhorn and a painting by Karl Hofer. *Courtesy Yamaguchi Keizaburō.*

4   Marjorie and Edwin Grabhorn, "To the Reader," *Ukiyo-e: The Floating World* (San Francisco: Book Club of California, 1962), n.p.

5   Letter from Judson D. Metzgar to Edwin Grabhorn, Los Angeles, Mar. 11, 1935. Grabhorn Ukiyo-e Collection archives.

6   Letter from Metzgar to Grabhorn, Los Angeles, Feb. 5, 1937. Grabhorn Ukiyo-e Collection archives.

7   Letter from Margaret Gentles to Edwin Grabhorn, Chicago, Oct. 12, 1956. Grabhorn Ukiyo-e Collection archives.

8   Grabhorn makes reference to Kaigetsudō prints "buried" in the Metropolitan Museum of Art in *Figure Prints,* no. 5. The Grabhorn quote is a recollection by Roger Keyes as conveyed to the author on May 7, 2003.

9   Grabhorn received notice of this offer from both Charles H. Mitchell (1910–1986) and Harry G. C. Packard. Letter from Mitchell to Grabhorn, Tokyo, May 16, 1964, and letter from Packard to Grabhorn, Tokyo, Mar. 20, 1964. Grabhorn Ukiyo-e Collection archives. For Mitchell, see H. George Mann, "Osamu Ueda," *Impressions* 33 (2012): 113–117.

10   "Oh, you lucky man," Judson Metzgar wrote him when he heard of this new acquisition, "even if you had to put a mortgage on your home and your business." Letter from Metzgar to Grabhorn, Los Angeles, Dec. 18, 1957. Grabhorn Ukiyo-e Collection archives. For one of the two other known impressions of this print, see Sakamoto Gorō, "Eight Parts Full: A Life in the Tokyo Art Trade," Special issue of *Impressions* (2011), fig. 57. For Fenollosa's 1896 exhibition, see Meech, "The Early Years of Japanese Print Collecting in North America," *Impressions* 25 (2003): 20–22.

11   Letter from Metzgar to Grabhorn, Los Angeles, Dec. 18, 1957. Grabhorn Ukiyo-e Collection archives.

12   Letter from Metzgar to Grabhorn, Los Angeles, Mar. 1, 1937. Grabhorn Ukiyo-e Collection archives. For information about David Tod Ford, Sr., and his sons, I am indebted to Bruce Smith, The Arts and Crafts Press, Olalla, Washington. For the Morse/Ford/Freer transaction, see Judson D. Metzgar, *Adventures in Japanese Prints* (Los Angeles: Grabhorn Press for Dawson's Bookshop, 1943), 74; the matter is also discussed by Freer in correspondence with Charles J. Morse between December 1904 and March 1905, Freer Gallery of Art and Arthur M. Sackler Gallery Archives, Smithsonian Institution, Washington, DC. A ledger book in the Grabhorn Ukiyo-e Collection archives gives the name of the vendor and the price. See also Grabhorn's caption for this Utamaro print in his 1959 *Figure Prints of Old Japan.*

13   Packard, "Nihon bijutsu shūshūki," 136–39. For the story of Harry Packard, see Julia Meech, "Who Was Harry Packard?" *Impressions* 32 (2011): 83–113.

14   Letters from Packard to Grabhorn, Tokyo, June 26 and Aug. 14, 1958. Grabhorn Ukiyo-e Collection archives.

15   For Nishi Saijū, see Narazaki Muneshige, "Tsuitō Nishi Saijūshi" (In memory of Nishi Saijū), *Ukiyo-e Art/Ukiyoe geijutsu* 119 (May 30, 1996): 16–19. For Kaneko Fusui, see Aoki Shinzaburō, "Kono michi hitosuji ukiyo-e no michi—Kaneko Fusui-shi o shinobu" (A life dedicated to ukiyo-e—Remembering Kaneko Fusui), *Ukiyo-e Art/Ukiyoe geijutsu* 58 (Dec. 1978): 22–25; Tsuboi Kyō, "Kaneko Fusui o shinobu" (Remembering Kaneko Fusui), *Kikan ukiyo-e* 75 (Oct. 5, 1978).

16   Letter from Packard to Grabhorn, July 6, 1958. Grabhorn Ukiyo-e Collection archives.

17   Matthew Welch, "Seductive Beauty: Coveting and Collecting Ukyo-e," in Matthew Welch and Yuiko Kimura-Tilford, *Worldly Pleasures, Earthly Delights* (Minneapolis: Minneapolis Institute of Arts, 2011), 19.

18   Letter from Packard to Grabhorn, June 11, 1958. Grabhorn Ukiyo-e Collection archives.

19   Letter from Packard to Grabhorn, Oct. 7, 1958. Grabhorn Ukiyo-e Collection archives.

20   Grabhorn, caption for Kaigetsudō Anchi, *Figure Prints of Old Japan,* pl. 7.

21   Letter from Packard to Grabhorn, Tokyo, June 11, 1958. Grabhorn Ukiyo-e Collection archives.

22   For Takamizawa, see Takahashi Seiichirō, *Traditional Woodblock Prints of Japan,* trans. Richard Stanley-Baker, Heibonsha Survey of Japanese Art, vol. 22, 3rd ed. (New York and Tokyo: Weatherhill and Heibonsha, 1976), 175; and Takamizawa Takako, *Aru ukiyo-eshi no isan: Takamizawa Enji oboegaki* (Legacy of a certain ukiyo-e artist: Notes about Takamizawa Enji) (Tokyo: Tōsho Sensho, 1978), 14.

23   Letter from Metzgar to Grabhorn, Chicago, Feb. 27, 1951. Grabhorn Ukiyo-e Collection archives.

24   Packard, "Nihon bijutsu shūshūki," *Geijutsu shinchō* 27, no. 1 (Jan. 1976): 158–59; and 27, no. 2 (Feb. 1976): 136–40.

25   Letter from Packard to Grabhorn, Tokyo, June 5, 1958. Grabhorn Ukiyo-e Collection archives.

26   Letter from Metzgar to Grabhorn, location unknown, Sept. 18, 1955. Grabhorn Ukiyo-e Collection archives.

27   E-mail communications from O. P. Reed, Jr., to author, May 17 and May 19, 2003. See also O. P. Reed, Jr., "Appraising the Frank Lloyd Wright Collection: A Personal Memoir," *Impressions* 24 (2002): 92–97; and Reed, "To the Editor," *Impressions* 26 (2004): 138.

28   E-mail communication from David Waterhouse to author, Apr. 24, 2003.

29   Yamaguchi Keizaburō, ed. *Gurabuhoon korekushon: Ukiyo-e meihin-ten/Masterpieces of Ukiyo-e from the Irma Grabhorn-Engel Collection,* Tokyo: Bun You Associates, 1995.

30   E-mail communication from George Mann to author, Apr. 20, 2003. For Mann, see H. George Mann, "Passionate Pursuit: My Adventures in Ukiyo-e," *Impressions* 25 (2003): 77–91.

DAVID WATERHOUSE

Figures of Humans and Animals

Some Early Japanese Color Prints from the Grabhorn Collection

The Japanese prints from the Grabhorn Collection in the Asian Art Museum were all produced in Edo (modern Tokyo), which was the seat of government in pre-modern Japan and was already one of the largest cities in the world. The figure prints in the collection, ranging from the late seventeenth to the early nineteenth centuries, are undoubtedly its chief glory. They include important examples of hand-colored prints; *benizuri-e* ("pink-printed pictures"), using two or even three color blocks in addition to the black key block, and a dazzling selection of *nishiki-e* (literally "brocade picture"), which use considerably more color blocks. From the last of these categories, I consider here two groups of prints from the short period between 1765 and 1770, when *nishiki-e* technique and style first reached maturity.

FULL-COLOR PRINTS BY SUZUKI HARUNOBU

The trigger for the development of *nishiki-e* seems to have been celebrations in 1765 for the opening of a new state observatory: groups of Edo aesthetes with close connections to the ruling household commissioned pictorial calendar designs containing half-concealed information about the "large" or "small" months for the year, in the old lunar calendar. Commercial adaptations quickly followed, and over the next century and a half color-printed ukiyo-e, "pictures of the floating world", were turned out in vast numbers by publishers who employed professional block cutters and printers, as well as the artists themselves.

Suzuki Harunobu (1725?–1770), a pivotal figure for the whole history of ukiyo-e, was the first artist to use full-color technique systematically, in prints that were marketed to the Edo public. Often he seems to have acted as his own publisher. He introduced themes that were copied by other ukiyo-e artists well into the nineteenth century; and his work is notable for its sensitivity to design and color, and for its many ingenious and witty allusions to classical Japanese or Chinese poetry, drama, and folklore. We know little about Harunobu's life: his active career lasted less than a decade, from the earlier 1760s to his sudden death in 1770; but he produced well over a thousand single-sheet color print designs, more than two dozen black-and-white illustrated books, as well as two in full color. The largest collection of Harunobu's work is in the Museum of Fine Arts,

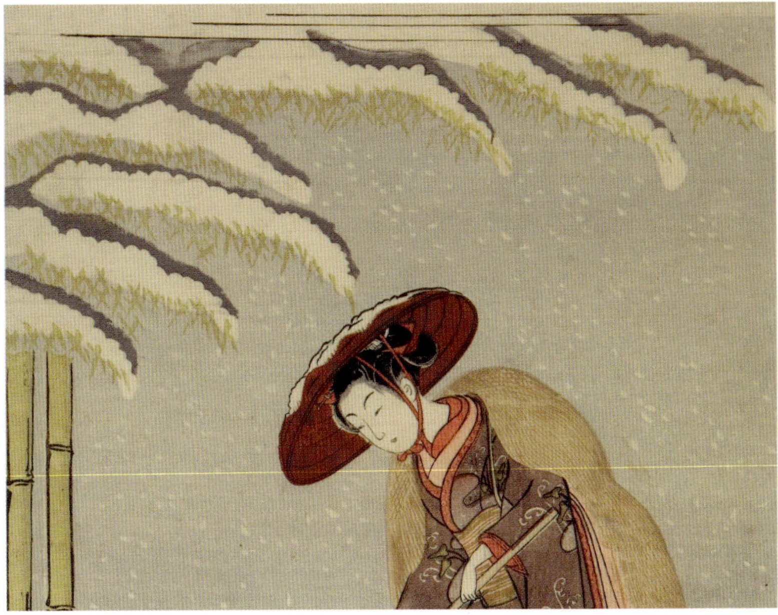

Fig. 1. Suzuki Harunobu (1725?–1770), Snow-covered bamboo, detail from *Mitate* of Meng Zong, one of the Twenty-four Paragons of Filial Piety, 1765. Woodblock print. *Asian Art Museum of San Francisco, Gift of the Grabhorn Ukiyo-e Collection,* 2005.100.26.

Boston, but it is far from complete.[1] In the following commentaries, more detailed consideration is given to prints not represented in the Boston collection.

The earliest Grabhorn Harunobu (*Mitate* of Meng Zong, no. 31) is the second state of a pictorial calendar (*egoyomi*) for 1765. In the first state, the numbers of the large months for the year (2, 3, 5, 6, 8, 10) were indicated by the leaves of the snow-covered bamboo. This print was produced for private circulation. In the second state, made for commercial release, probably the following year, the calendrical marks are obscured (fig. 1).[2] The subject is the same as that of no. 11 by Okumura Masanobu: namely Meng Zong (Mōsō), one of the Chinese Twenty-four Paragons of Filial Piety (*Nijūshikō*). He was devoted to his mother and, with divine help, located for her some bamboo shoots which were buried in snow. Here, however, the part of Mōsō is played by a beautiful girl. As with several other Harunobu prints in the Grabhorn Collection, it is a *mitate*, a witty reinterpretation in contemporary terms of a well-known classical theme. In this instance the allusion is straightforward; but sometimes it is not immediately evident, even to the educated observer.

Another early example ("Returning Sails of the Towel Rack," no. 39) comes from a celebrated set of eight prints, first produced privately for a poetry group led by "Kyosen," the pen name of a well-to-do samurai serving in the Edo Castle guard. The title of this series, *Eight Parlor Views* (Zashiki hakkei), refers to the *Eight Views of Ōmi* (Ōmi hakkei), which had been a stock subject in ukiyo-e since the 1730s, and was constantly being repeated during the rest of the period. In turn, the *Ōmi hakkei* (and accompanying poems about each of them) were based on a standard set of Chinese views, at the confluence of the Xiao and Xiang Rivers, in Hunan Province.

The individual titles of the *Zashiki hakkei* further allude to parodic poems composed in the early eighteenth century. Harunobu's prints make play with these titles and with the poems (which are not themselves quoted). The proper title of the Grabhorn print is "Returning Sails of the Towel Rack" (*Tenuguikake kihan*); the corresponding title in *Ōmi hakkei* is "Returning Sails at Yabase" (*Yabase no kihan*), and in prints of this subject we usually see fishing boats returning to Yabase, on Lake Biwa. However, the *Zashiki hakkei* prints are all set indoors. In the corresponding design the hand towel blowing on its rack does duty for the sails of the boats, while the water-stoup on the verandah suggests Lake Biwa. In a straight *Ōmi hakkei* series published a few years earlier, in *hosoban* ("narrow block") format, Harunobu himself had depicted *Yabase no kihan*, quoting the original (nonparodic) poem.[3] The Grabhorn *Zashiki hakkei* print represents the second state, from which the signature and seal of its commissioning agent Kyosen have been omitted. Often the signature of Harunobu too is absent from his early full-color prints.

Another such unsigned *mitate* print (*Mitate* of the story of Ōta Dōkan, no. 33) alludes to a legend about Ōta Dōkan (1432–1486), the traditional founder of Edo Castle. This story first appeared in a miscellany by Harunobu's contemporary Yuasa Jōzan (1708–1781); it describes how Dōkan, caught in the rain, tried to borrow a straw raincoat from a woman in a small cottage. Without saying a word to him, she held out a branch of flowering yellow roses (*yamabuki*), in allusion to a classical poem that could be translated either as referring to this flower, or as politely expressing regret that she had no raincoat to offer. Harunobu had previously put out a *hosoban* version of this subject, with a similar design. The *chūban* ("medium block") version exists in two states, which show significant differences in the color blocks, though the key block for both is the same. The Grabhorn print belongs to the later one, which probably dates from some time in the nineteenth century.[4]

As Harunobu established a reputation for his color prints, he put out other sets of single-sheet prints, especially on classical themes. In 1765 he had produced a black-and-white illustrated book, which illustrated and quoted one poem each by the Thirty-six Poetic Immortals (*Sanjūrokkasen*), and in 1767–1768 he reused some of the same ideas for an ambitious set of color prints on the same theme. The set was probably issued first as an album, and perhaps with a title sheet; but no such album has survived, and even individual prints are scarce. Since I first identified the set, I have traced all but one design. The Grabhorn Collection has no. 33 from the series, "Ōnakatomi Yoshinobu Ason" (no. 38).[5] According to Edwin Grabhorn, "This lovely print … was brought back from Japan by a tea merchant in the 1890s."[6] It depicts a room in an aristocratic residence, with two ladies warmly clad in court dress: the junior lady brings a tray with a sprig of young pine, while her mistress inscribes a poem. Beyond the verandah a plum tree is in flower; and above the stylized cloud line is a poem by Ōnakatomi Yoshinobu Ason (921–991; fig. 2):

chitose made	A thousand years may
kagireru matsu mo	be its limit, but the pine
kyō yori wa	that is picked out by
kimi ni hikarete	my lord, from today shall see
yorozuyo ya hen	ten thousand ages pass by!

This sycophantic verse was included in the early eleventh-century imperial anthology *Shūi wakashū*, vol. 1 ("Spring"); it is more interesting than appears at first sight. Yoshinobu was the son of the court poet Ōnakatomi Yorimoto (886–958?), and both men are included among the *Sanjūrokkasen*, a list drawn up by Fujiwara Kintō (966–1041). By Harunobu's time it had become customary to assign one poem to each poet. The circumstances surrounding Yoshinobu's poem, written when he was still young, are recounted in *Wallet Story Book* (*Fukuro zōshi*), a collection of anecdotes about court poetry, compiled by yet another court poet, Fujiwara Kiyosuke (1104–77).

In Book 4 of this latter work we learn that Yoshinobu told his father how he had been invited to the Rat Day (*Ne no hi*) ceremony at the residence of Prince Atsumi (Atsumi Shinnō, 843–967), and had presented a poem to the Prince. On the first Rat Day of the year it was the custom, after collecting pine shoots (*komatsu-hiki*) from the countryside, to hold an elegant party for exchanging poems. Prince Atsumi, who became a senior Buddhist monk at Ninnaji in Kyoto, was actually the eighth son of Emperor Uda (Uda Tennō: r. 887–897): a detail of significance in the present context. In answer to his father's question about the poem, Yoshinobu proudly recited it, and said it had been praised by everybody. Yorimoto himself repeated it; then, seizing a pillow lying nearby, he struck his son with it, and upbraided him in strong terms for his brazen stupidity. How would he be able now to

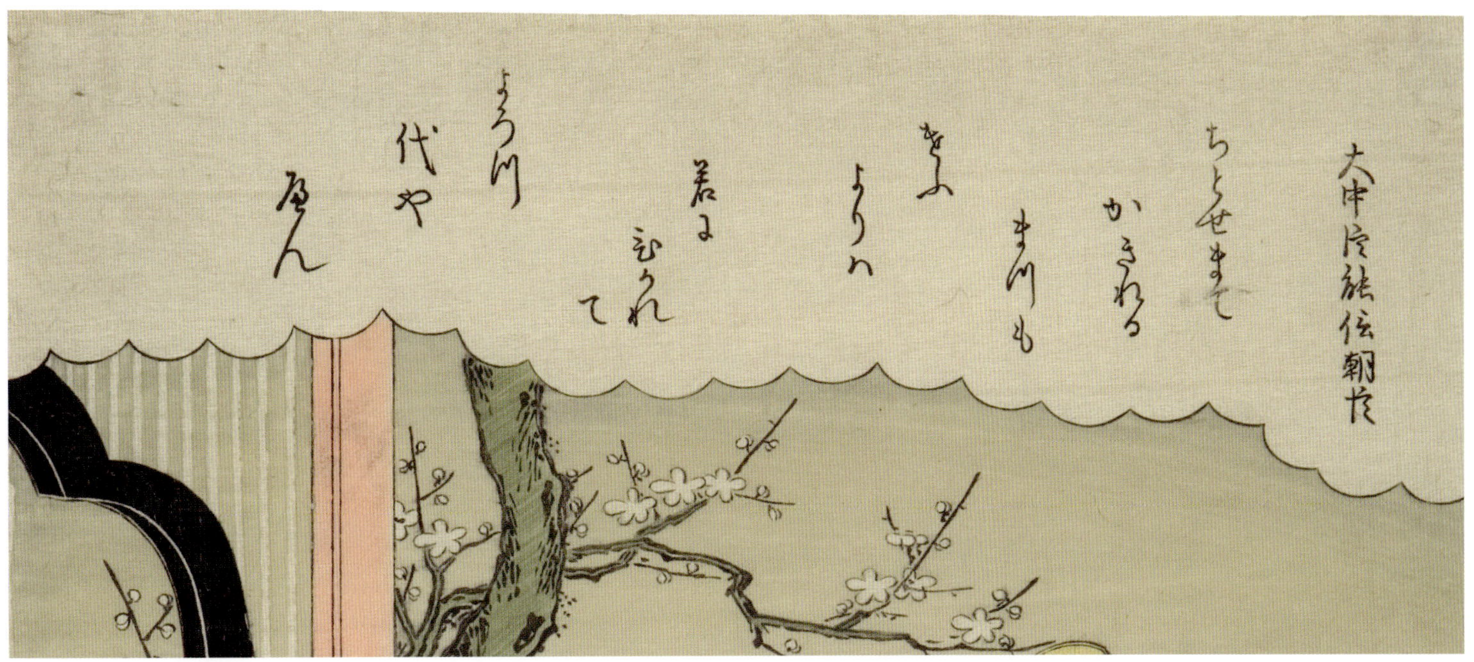

Fig. 2. Detail from Suzuki Harunobu, 1725?–1770, Ōnakatomi Yoshinobu Ason, from an untitled series of Thirty-six Poetic Immortals, 2005.100.33.

compose another poem, if subsequently he was invited for a Rat Day audience with the Emperor himself? Ashamed, Yoshinobu rose from his seat and fled the room.

Hunting Cherry Blossoms (no. 36), a rare print,[7] is a straightforward illustration of another Spring poem from *Shūi wakashū* (vol. 1, no. 50). It reads:

Sakuragari	Hunting cherry blooms,
ame wa furikinu	the rain comes tumbling down: but
onajiku wa	all the same, even
nuru to mo hana no	if we get drenched, we may take
kage ni kakuren	shelter in the flowers' shade.

Many Spring poems praise the beauty of cherry blossoms, lament their evanescence, and liken their falling to rain. The author of this poem is unknown, though it is traditionally associated with the court poet Fujiwara Sanekata (d. 999), and it became well known from a reference to it in *Senjūshō* (late twelfth century), a collection of anecdotes about poetry. We are to imagine that the writer and his companion went out to view cherry blossoms on Higashiyama, near Kyoto. Harunobu has depicted a young couple whose excursion for the same purpose has similarly been interrupted by rain.

Another "hunting" print, of a different kind (Hunting for fireflies, no. 34), depicts young lovers catching fireflies. Harunobu suggests night by printing the entire background in black: a simple but effective device which he employed in several other nighttime scenes. At least two states of this print are known: in another, and probably earlier state (in the Art Institute of Chicago and the Tokyo National Museum), the young man is wearing straw sandals (*waraji*) and leggings, and the insect cage has netting; in the Grabhorn print, and another in the Hiraki Ukiyo-e Museum, he is wearing thonged sandals (*zōri*) and no leggings, and the cage has no netting.

Under the influence of Harunobu, another recurrent theme in ukiyo-e was provided by the "Six Poetic Immortals" (*rokkasen*). This early list derived from the preface, written sometime after 905, to the imperial anthology *Kokin wakashū*. Harunobu had first portrayed the six poets themselves in classical landscape settings, together with their individual poems by them, in an early *hosoban* series from about 1764. In 1768 or 1769 he returned to the subject, this time in full color and in *chūban* format; but the designs are all *mitate*, quoting a poem by each poet, but with contemporary settings and facetious twists. All the prints are rare.[8] The design of Ariwara Narihira (no. 37), from this set, is based on a page in *Ehon chiyomigusa* (1763), a black-and-white book illustrated by the Kyoto artist Nishikawa Sukenobu, from whom Harunobu took ideas for many of his color prints. There are two states of the design, with important differences in the patterning and coloring of several blocks; and the Grabhorn print is probably a later reprint, using the original key block.[9]

The poem on the print comes from *Ise monogatari*, a collection of 125 amorous episodes and associated poems, which is traditionally ascribed to Ariwara Narihira (825–880), though he is not named as the protagonist. In the fourth episode the love-sick courtier, prompted by the sight of plum blossoms outside his house, visits the Western Pavilion, where one year previously a certain lady had been living. Not finding her, he remained plunged in melancholy till the moon went down, and composed the following poem:

tsuki ya aranu	Ah! There is no moon,
haru ya mukashi no	and this spring is not the spring
haru naran	of a time long past:
waga mi hitotsu wa	alone this body of mine
moto no mi ni shite	is as it formerly was.

Harunobu's print, one of his *mitate*, substitutes a girl who is depicted thinking of her absent lover as she gazes out at the moon. Spring flowers on the verandah and on the tree in the garden outside indicate the season.

Harunobu made two sets of *chūban* prints on the theme of the "Six Jewel Rivers" (*Mu Tamagawa*), referring to rivers of that name in six different provinces, and quoting appropriate classical poems. Toward the end of his life he made a pillar-print version, quoting the same poems, and including cartouche portraits of the poets. Two of these prints are in the Grabhorn Collection ("Chōfu Jewel River" no. 41, and "The Cloth-Fulling Jewel River," no. 42), and it happens that both poems (probably not by the poets who are named) allude to cloth: to the beating of it with a fulling mallet, or to the drying of hemp cloth on a hedge.[10] The poem on no. 41 reads:

Tazukuri ya	The hand-woven hemp
sarasu kakine no	cloth drying on the hedge holds
asa tsuyu wo	morning dew like gems
tsuranuki tomenu	strung on threads: this truly is
Tamagawa no sato	the Jewel River Village!

That on no. 42 reads:

matsukaze no	The wind in the pines
oto dani aki wa	makes a sound in autumn which
sabishiki ni	is forlorn enough —
koromo utsu nari	but now they are beating cloth
Tamagawa no sato	in Jewel River Village.

The "Eight Views" provided a linking theme for several sets by Harunobu, including *Fashionable Eight Views of Noh Chants* (*Fūryū utai hakkei*), which makes allusion to Noh plays. Through his connections in samurai circles he developed an informed taste for Noh, as is apparent from clever allusions in some of these prints. In Autumn Moon of Matsukaze (*Matsukaze no shūgetsu*, no. 30), we see the beach at Suma, its lonely pine tree and two girls, who represent the spirits of Murasame and Matsukaze.[11] Centuries earlier, they were romantically entangled with the exiled courtier Ariwara Yukihira; and Matsukaze is holding his hunting cloak and court hat. In a *chūban* design of much the same date Harunobu depicted Murasame and Matsu-

kaze more literally, in their role as gatherers of salt, and quoting the poem around which the play unfolds.

Three other Harunobu prints deserve mention, for their own sake and as illustrations of recurrent motifs in his work. No. 32 is one of a number that make fun of Taoist Immortals: in this case, Qin Gao (*Kinkō*).[12] Several Japanese books from the eighteenth century depict Qin Gao on the back of a carp; but Harunobu's immediate source for this *mitate* is a double page from Okumura Masanobu's black-and-white album *Ehon Edo-e sudare byōbu* (n.d.), depicting a courtesan seated as Qin Gao on the back of a giant carp, and reading a love letter. Harunobu's earliest version of this subject was a calendar print for 1765; and he did several others, in various formats. The underlying conceit is that beautiful courtesans possess and can confer on others the secret of immortality. Qin Gao supposedly lived for more than two hundred years, and one day announced to his disciples that he was going to the bottom of the river to fetch the Dragon King's son. He presently reappeared, riding on the back of a carp; but after a month again vanished beneath the waves.

Another of Harunobu's favorite subjects, made famous almost single-handedly by him, was the tea-stall proprietor Kagiya Osen (Osen of the Kagiya serving tea in front of Kasamori Shrine, no. 35). In 1768 she became the talk of the town and, along with a handful of other stall owners, such as Moto-Yanagiya Ofuji (*cf.* Torii Kiyomitsu I, The Actor Segawa Kikunojō as the Young Woman of the Yanagiya, no. 23), was much celebrated in ukiyo-e, as well as on the stage and in popular literature. Osen's stall, near the entrance gate of the Kasamori Inari Shrine in the Yanaka district, was a *mizu-chaya*, serving hot tea to thirsty pilgrims. In 1770 she married a junior samurai who worked as a superintendent of gardens at Edo Castle, and we may guess that Kyosen or another well-placed friend helped to arrange this. The couple had a large family, and Osen died in 1827. Her fame lived on, but the original Kasamori Inari Shrine no longer exists, and the exact location of her stall was identified only in modern times. The Grabhorn print is one of Harunobu's best-known depictions of Osen, seen here serving tea to a samurai visitor.[13]

Lastly, Boys Sumo Wrestling, no. 40, a charming and apparently unique full-color *hosoban*, depicts boy sumo wrestlers. The boy in the red loincloth, with a determined expression on his face, grips his opponent round the back and behind his lower leg, stepping forward to throw him off balance. The technical name for this sumo throw is *susotori*, literally "taking the skirt." The other boy, wearing a spotted loincloth, defends by wrapping his right hand round the attacker's neck, while holding his loincloth at the rear. The technical name for this defense is *kubinage*. Behind them is a third boy, who acts as the referee, brandishing a fan with the crest badge (*mon*) of the Kabuki actor Ichikawa Danjūrō; and a grassy bank with flowers.

Stylistically this print can be dated to about 1769. No other impression has surfaced; but the figures of the two wrestlers were repeated by Harunobu almost exactly from an earlier print by him: a three-color horizontal *ōban* ("large block") composition with seven boys, including a different referee and four spectators, and a background of trailing wisteria.[14] This print, dating from the early 1760s, was published by "Tomita," who also published actor prints by Harunobu datable to late 1762 and early 1763, and used the triangular trademark previously used by Urokogataya Magobei (Rikakudō). Harunobu depicted boy wrestlers in two other single-sheet prints, in which the referee is a woman;[15] as well as in a 1763 black-and-white book, which depicts another group of seven boys (one carrying his baby brother), and in which the referee is similarly holding a fan with the crest badge of Ichikawa Danjūrō.[16] However, the closest parallel to the Grabhorn print is a full-color *chūban*, with two boy wrestlers and a boy referee, against a similar background of a grassy bank with flowers. Even the faces of the boys are similar, and it is possible they were actual boys known to Harunobu. Only the poses are different; and the throw is a dangerous two-handed leg grab (*ashitori*). This equally rare print, in the former Takahashi collection, is of much the same date, or slightly earlier.[17]

TACHIBANA MINKŌ AND THE "FOXES' WEDDING" SERIES

The artist Tachibana Minkō, whose exact dates are unknown, was originally an embroiderer, but in the later 1760s he became known for his attractive book illustrations in ukiyo-e style. His studio name (*gō*) was Gyoku-juken, and his personal name (*na*) was Masatoshi. Saitō Gesshin (1804–1878)[18] suggested that he was originally from Kyoto or Ōsaka; in Edo he seems to have moved in the same circles as Harunobu and his friends. Minkō's best book, *Iro-e shokunin burui* (2 vols. Edo: Uemura Tōsaburō and Sawa Isuke, 1770; 2nd ed. 1784) contains a collection of "mad poems" (*kyōka*), with full-color illustrations of various occupations. The text for this book was partly contributed by Harunobu's friend and supporter Ōta Nanpo (1749–1823), and the blocks were cut by Okamoto Shōgyo, who cut blocks also for Harunobu and was an associate of Harunobu's friend Hiraga Gennai (1728–1780). Both Nanpo and Gennai were samurai with a pronounced taste for the demi-monde; and they wrote at great length about it, often using pen-names. Other books illustrated by Minkō were *Sayo shigure* (5 vols., 1765), a comic novelette by "Mubō"; *Kakuchū kitan* (1

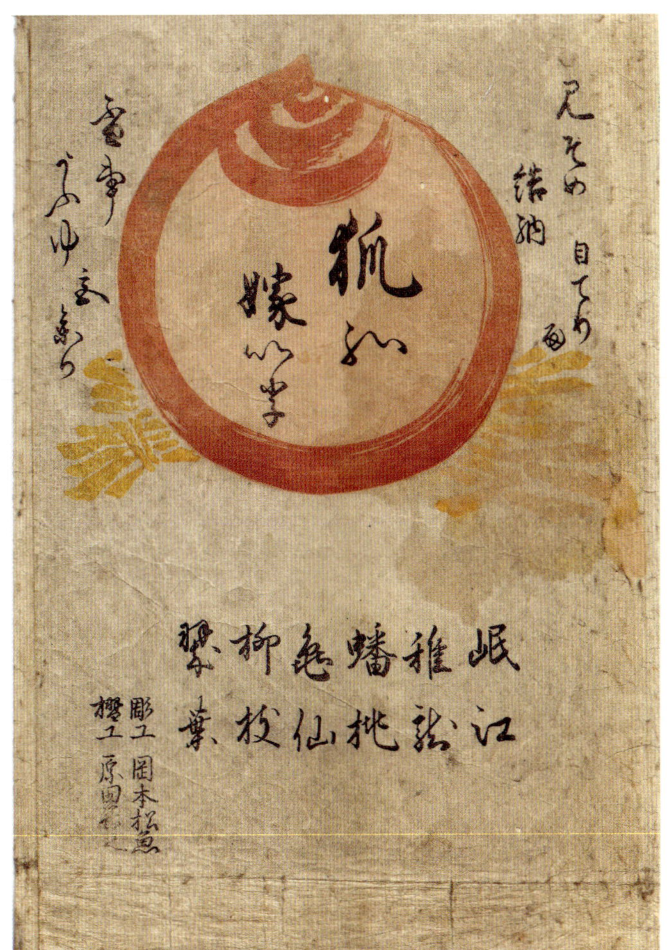

Fig. 3. Front of wrapper for the series *The Foxes' Wedding,* by Suzuki Harunobu. *Courtesy Mr. and Mrs. Harlow Niles Higinbotham.*

vol., 1769), a novelette about courtesans (text by "Usuoka Sensei"); and two readers, *Otsuya sōshi* (5 vols., 1771), and *Misao sōshi* (5 vols., 1771; text by "Tankaishi").

In 1765 a remarkable set of six prints was produced for a group of connoisseurs led by Minkō. It takes for its light-hearted theme the successive stages of a wedding between humanoid foxes, from the first meeting of the couple at a Shinto shrine, to the subsequent presentation of their baby at the shrine. The date is known from the third and sixth prints in the series, since (like Harunobu's prints of the same kind) they are at the same time pictorial calendars for 1765, with characters identifying the year by name, and by the numbers of the "large" (*dai*) or "small" (*shō*) months for that year in the old lunar calendar. The prints, in a small horizontal *chūban* format, use the new full-color *nishiki-e* technique, with special printing effects. This set must have been produced in very few impressions; it is now extremely rare, and it has not previously been described accurately or in detail. The Grabhorn Collection has a complete set of six (nos. 24–29); another set, including also a title wrapper, is in the collection of Dr. Harlow Higinbotham;[19] what is apparently a third set, lacking the title wrapper (fig. 3), was formerly in the collection of Baron Walter von

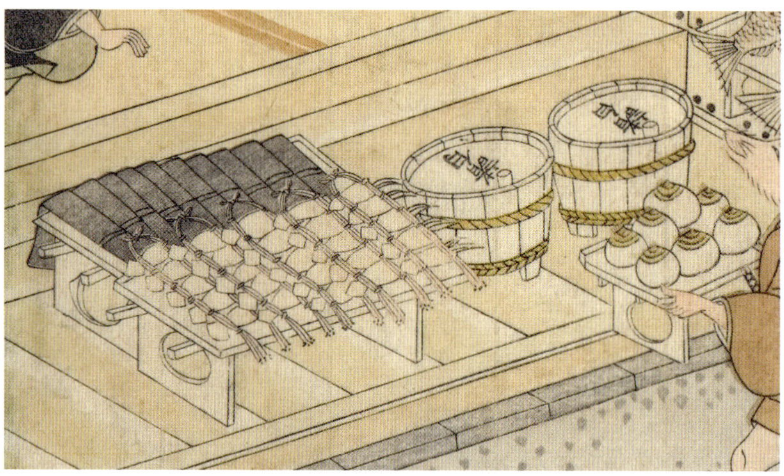

Fig. 4. Detail from Tachibana Minkō, "Betrothal Gifts," from the series *The Foxes' Wedding*, 2005.100.24.2.

Heymel (1878–1914);[20] and there is a variant of the third print (discussed below) in the Art Institute of Chicago.[21]

In the center of the wrapper is a printed design with a large circular "treasure jewel" (*hōshu*) and a sheaf of rice (*inaho*). Scattered across the wrapper are inscriptions, also printed, which give the title of the set, the titles of the individual prints, the fanciful pen names of the six connoisseurs (who are otherwise unknown), and the names of the block cutter and printer who worked for them, as follows:

Kitsune no yome-iri:
Misome, Yuinō, Hideri-ame, Sakazuki-goto, Ubuyu, Miya-mairi
Minkō, Chiryū, Hantō, Kisen, Ryūshi, Suiyō
chōkō Okamoto Shōgyo, shōkō Harada Yoshiyuki

The Fox's Taking of a Bride:
First Meeting, Exchange of Gifts, Rain When the Sun Is Shining, Sake Cup Ceremony, First Bathing [of the Infant], Visit to the Shrine
"Min River," "Child Dragon," "Gnarled Peach Tree," "Turtle Immortal," "Willow Branch," "Emerald Green Leaves"
block cutter Okamoto Shōgyo, printer Harada Yoshiyuki

The individual prints bear red seals of the various members of the group, in a slightly different order than that of the wrapper. Minkō's seal appears on *Hideri-ame*, the third print in the sequence; but since he was a professional artist, and since the set is unified in style and conception, we may guess that the contribution of other members of the group was mainly financial. However, they probably applied their seals individually: on one of the Higinbotham prints the seal is upside down, and it is unlikely that Harada Yoshiyuki would make such a mistake, or leave it uncorrected. There are minor differences between the Grabhorn and Higinbotham impressions, which are noted below, and, as mentioned previously, the

third print exists in a variant state, showing small differences in coloring and in some of the color blocks (for example, there are more lines to indicate driving rain). This variant state also has a new signature, *aru motome ni ōjite Minkō kore wo tsukuru* ("In accordance with a certain request, Minkō made this"); there is a new seal, which is imperfectly legible but may read *Naiso Ōtei*; and at the right-hand side of the paper, outside the design, there is a new inscription, *chōkō Yamaguchi Bokuyō* ("block cutter Yamaguchi Bokuyō"). This block cutter is not known from any other of the pictorial calendars of the period, but we may suppose that he was brought in to redo some of the color blocks for this special edition. Similarly, the printer Harada Yoshiyuki is not known from any other source.

In "First Meeting" (*Misome*, no. 24), the first print of *Kitsune no yome-iri*, we see the introduction of the fox couple to each other, within the misty precincts of an Inari shrine (the type of Shinto shrine especially associated with magic foxes). As the bride-to-be passes by, accompanied by her mother and a maidservant, a go-between (*nakōdo*) draws their attention to a young male fox who is resting nearby on the bench of a *mizu-chaya*, smoking a pipe, with his servant squatting behind him. The bride-to-be wears the long-sleeved *furisode* of an unmarried woman, with a pattern of flaming jewels (*hōshu*) and a crest badge (*mon*) with the character *tama* ("jewel") in a circle; the *mon* on the male fox's outer kimono appears to contain a *hōshu*. All the figures have approximations to human hair styles of the period; and the three male figures wear samurai swords. Only their long snouts and ears, and the bushy tail of the servant, betray their real nature. The connoisseur's seal, *Hantō*, "Gnarled Peach Tree," refers to the peach tree of the Taoist Queen Mother of the West (Xi Wang Mu), which produces fruit once in three thousand years.

In "Betrothal Gifts" (*Yuinō*, no. 25), the bride and her mother watch through a lattice as three bushy-tailed servants of the bridegroom arrive (on an auspicious day) and unload gifts from a large black-lacquered tray. The latter is attached with rods to a carrying pole, and the cloth covering it is decorated with three flaming *hōshu*; the gifts include dried cuttlefish (*surume*), dried bonito (*katsuobushi*), sea-bream (*tai*), and large round rice cakes (*kagami-mochi*: in the shape of *hōshu*), all arranged on ceremonial tray stands (*sanbō*); two large barrels of *sake* (labelled *morohaku*, "all white"); and no doubt also dowry money (fig. 4). Inside the house, evidently belonging to a prosperous family, the gifts are being received by the bride's father, in front of a large screen with a black lacquer frame. Multicolored chrysanthemums are depicted on this screen, in allusion to the tale of a noble in love with a beautiful girl who reverted to her fox shape when she slept beside chrysanthemums. The crest badge on the father's kimono is a key (*kagi*), in reference to the role of foxes in Inari

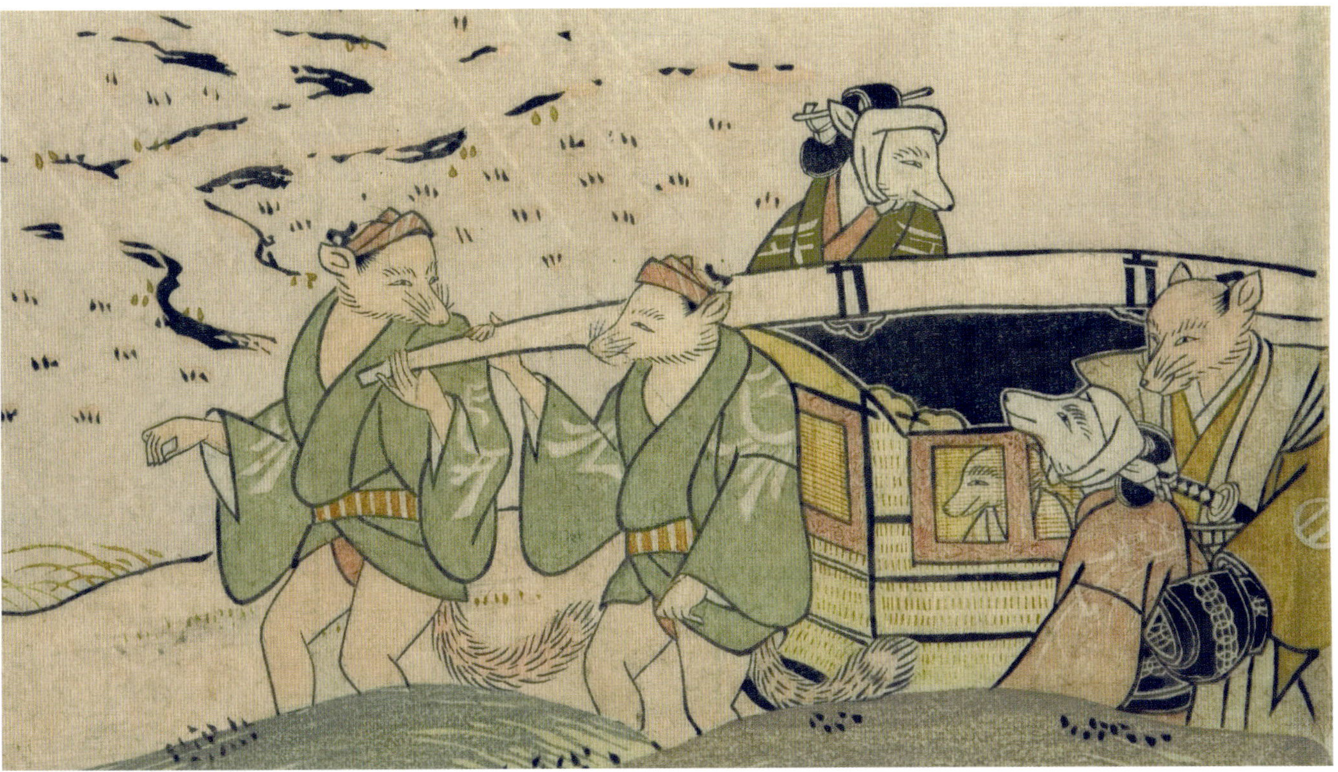

Fig. 5. Detail from Tachibana Minkō, "Rain When the Sun Is Shining," from the series *The Foxes' Wedding,* 2005.100.24.3.

worship as protectors of the rice granary, or "warehouse of treasure" (*takara no kura*); that on the kimono of the other male fox (the bridegroom's father?) is a *hōshu*. The connoisseur's seal reads *Chiryū,* "Child Dragon." The seal on the corresponding print in the Higinbotham collection is different, and unfortunately illegible.

In "Rain When the Sun Is Shining" (*Hideri-ame,* no. 26), the bride is being carried in a closed palanquin (*norimono*) to the groom's house, accompanied by her parents and a female attendant. Traditionally this ceremony occurred in early evening (around 6:00 p.m.), and through mist we see the sun setting behind distant hills. However, it is also raining (hence the title of the print); and it is at such times that foxes' weddings are said to take place. The print is at the same time a clever pictorial calendar: crest badges on the father's surcoat identify the year-period, *Meiwa;* the year "2" (*ni*) is shown by another crest badge on his sleeve; and on the maid-servant's kimono the date is spelled out more fully as "year two" (*ninen*), namely 1765 (fig. 5). The coats of the bearers specify the short months of the year: first, fourth, seventh, ninth, eleventh and twelfth; the stripes on their sashes further echo two of the months (fourth, seventh). The design on the mother's red kimono includes a *kagi.* The connoisseur's seal reads *Minkō no in,* "Seal of Minkō."

In "Nuptial Sake Cup Ceremony" (*Sakazuki-goto,* no. 27), the bride and groom are seated on either side of an "island tray" (*shimadai*) adorned with symbols of longevity: a pine tree, a crane and a turtle. Two attendants prepare to pour *sake* for the couple from a decorated kettle and a long-handled ladle (*chōshi*), in the "3-3-9 times" (*san-san-ku-do*) wedding ritual. The bride's mother, seated beside her, wears a red kimono and a black outer robe (*uchikake*) decorated with a design of *hōshu* jewels and paper strips (*noshi*) tied to resemble rice ears; the crest badge on the groom's sleeve is a *hōshu;* and the walls of the room are papered with a prominent *hōshu* design. On a Chinese table in the alcove is an incense burner in the form of a lion-dog, and a painting of a white crane. The connoisseur's seal reads *Ryūshi,* "Willow Branch."

In "First Bathing [of the Infant]" (*Ubuyu,* no. 28), a fox midwife is bathing an infant white fox, assisted by two other foxes. In an adjacent room the mother is resting, seated upright, warmly wrapped and covered with a heavy *futon.* A nurse (?) sits beside her and comforts her. Traditionally the room used for child-bearing was small; the mother would sit to give birth, in a special chair; and she would remain upright for twenty-one days afterwards. The design on the *futon* prominently includes a key (*kagi*) with a cord and tassel; the large spirals on the sliding panel between the two rooms appear to be talismanic; the dado bears a chrysanthemum motif (*cf. Yuinō*), and the folding screen behind the bed is appropriately painted with a crane flying over pine and bamboo shoots). Meanwhile, against all the rules, the new father peeps in from behind a curtain decorated with a *hōshu* design. The connoisseur's seal reads *Kisen no in.* On the Higinbotham impression it is upside down, and the register of the pink color block of the mother's *futon* is less exact.

In "Visit to the Shrine" (*Miya-mairi*, no. 29), the bride's family is presenting the baby to the *ujigami*, the local deity of an Inari Shinto shrine, having selected an auspicious day after its birth: which, depending partly on its sex, may be the thirty-second or thirty-third, or even the hundredth day. The large stone trough (*mitarashi*) holding lustral water is emblazoned on the side with a flaming *hōshu*, as well as the date *Meiwa ni, hinoto tori*, "Meiwa 2 [1765], The Bird Year, Wood's Younger Brother" (fig. 6). On a pair of cloth banners hanging above are inscribed the numerals of the large and small months for the year: *dai*: second, third, fifth, sixth, eighth, tenth; and *shō*: first, fourth, seventh, ninth, eleventh, twelfth. The baby is being carried by its nurse, and wears white swaddling clothes with a design of *hōshu* and *kagi*. In procession behind them are a maidservant bearing wrapped gifts (a tobacco pipe and pouch?); the bride's mother and father; and a male servant, who bears a gift (of money?) on a *sanbō*. The bride's father's sleeve has a crest badge of crossed keys (*kagi*). Inside a room of the shrine the fox priest awaits the party, and holds ritual paper fronds (*gohei*) on a stick, with which to bless and purify the child. The Higinbotham impression bears the connoisseur's seal *Suiyō*, which is almost invisible on the Grabhorn print, and was apparently absent from that in the former von Heymel collection.

The Grabhorn set may represent a slightly later state than that in the Higinbotham collection. The colors of the Higinbotham impressions are consistently stronger, and reveal a number of details that are otherwise hard to see. They also show significant differences of coloring and shading, and occasional small differences of pattern. Thus, in *Misome*, the bowls and tobacco pouch on the bench in the Higinbotham impression are patterned, where in the Grabhorn print they are plain. Differences between the connoisseurs' seals and inscriptions on the various sets have been noted above.

In Japan, the folklore associated with foxes has two aspects. Foxes possess magical powers, which they may use either to cause mischief, or for the benefit and protection of mankind. In the latter capacity they are intimately connected with the worship of Inari-sama, the Shinto god of rice; and there are countless Inari shrines throughout the country, the best-known and oldest being the Fushimi Inari Taisha complex centred on Mt. Inari in the southern outskirts of Kyoto. Edo too was dotted with small Inari shrines (such as that of Kagiya Osen); but many of these have since disappeared.

It is noteworthy that in *Misome*, *Yuinō*, and *Miya-mairi* the bride's father and mother are depicted respectively as brown and white foxes. Fushimi Inari Taisha dates from the early eighth century; and in the ninth century a pair of foxes, brown and white, had come from Funaoka-yama, a hill in the northern part of Kyoto. They made their den near the shrine, and came to be regarded as messengers of Inari-sama. In front of the Rōmon, the entrance to the main shrine, is a pair of large stone fox images: of these, the female holds in its mouth exactly the type of key (*kagi*) which is depicted on the mother's *futon* in *Ubuyu*, as a crest badge (*mon*) on her father's sleeve (in *Yuinō* and *Miya-mairi*), and in the design of her mother's kimono (in *Hideri-ame*); the male holds a globular jewel (*hōshu*, or *tama*), as depicted in several of the prints (as well as on the Higinbotham wrapper), sometimes singly, sometimes as a repeated motif, and as the bridegroom's family *mon* (in *Misome*, *Yuinō*, *Sakazuki-goto*, and *Ubuyu*). The *kagi* and *tama* came to be associated with fox worship, as yin and yang symbols respectively; and pairs of protective fox images are commonly found at Inari shrines. The *kagi* is the key of the rice granary or other storehouse (*kura*), while the *tama* represents wealth. Often, under Buddhist influence, flames may rise from it (*cf. Ubuyu*), or three jewels will be shown (*cf. Yuinō*). A further legend connects the white crane painting in the alcove of *Sakazuki-goto* with Fushimi Inari Taisha. According to the *Yamashiro no kuni fudoki* (713), Hata no Iroku, having become wealthy in rice, was using rice cakes (*mochi*) as archery targets; when one of them suddenly turned into a white crane (*hakuchō*) and flew off. Rice grew at the top of the mountain where it lodged; and in recognition of the event Iroku set up a shrine to the Rice God Inari.[22]

The *Foxes' Wedding* series created by Minkō and his colleagues contains many witty and ingenious allusions. It would have been intended for exchange between them, and could also have been used as a New Year gift to other friends. If Minkō was originally from the Kansai region, he would have known Fushimi Inari Taisha (then known by simpler names, such as Inari Jinja) at first hand. Some ideas for the prints could have come from the work of the Kyoto artist Nishikawa Sukenobu (1671–1750), whose many illustrated books were used as a quarry by Harunobu and other Edo artists. For example, Sukenobu's *Ehon masu kagami* (3 vols. Kyoto: Kikuya Kihei, 1748) includes in vol. 2 a double-page illustration of a bride being borne in a *norimono* to the bridegroom's house; and in vol. 3 a double-page scene of childbirth and the washing of the newborn baby.

Sukenobu's book was certainly used by Harunobu, who in about 1769 adapted Minkō's idea for a series of seven horizontal *chūban* prints, depicting a human marriage ceremony. This series too originally had a title wrapper, from which we know its title, "Carriage for the Marriage Ceremonies of a Chaste Maid" (*Konrei nishiki misao-guruma*).[23] The sequence and details are slightly different: the first meeting of the couple takes place at the tea stall of Sakaiya Osode, who sold *Yamato-cha* by a shrine in the precincts of Asakusa-dera, and Harunobu omits the final visit to the shrine; but there are close parallels, and he would certainly have been aware of the earlier project.

Minkō may have taken ideas from other sources, as yet unidentified. For example Torii Kiyomitsu, in his *Ne no hijiri no yurai* (n.d.), vol. 1, fol. 3a, depicts a newborn

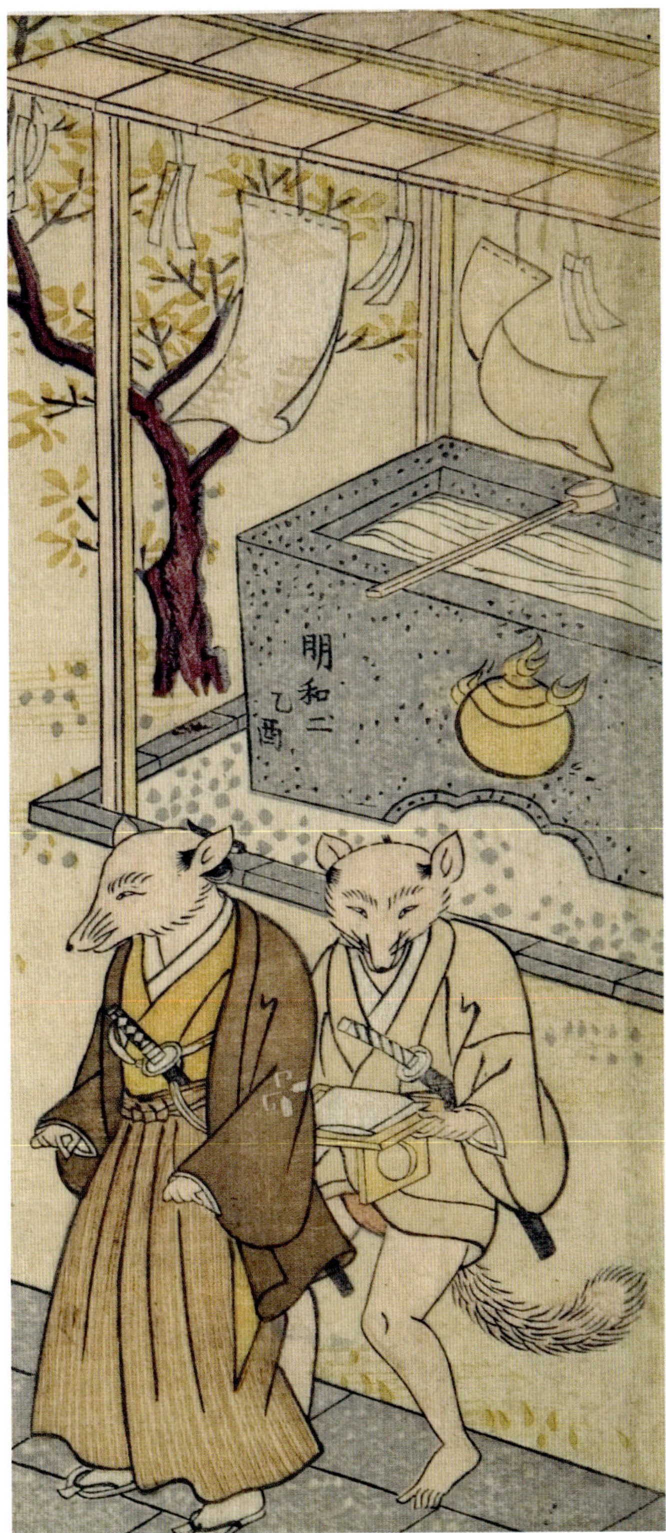

Fig. 6. Detail from Tachibana Minkō, "The First Meeting," from the series *The Foxes' Wedding*, 2005.100.24.1.

human baby being washed in a similar tub and with a similar water pot. Under influences from theater and from popular literature, the theme of the Foxes' Wedding seems to have taken on a life of its own by the mid eighteenth century, and it was occasionally treated by other ukiyo-e artists, including Utagawa Toyoharu (1735–1814), and (in the nineteenth century) Katsushika Hokusai (1760–1849),

Utagawa Kuniyoshi (1797–1861) and Utagawa Yoshitora (active 1830s–c. 1888). Toyoharu treated the subject of the bride's departure in *uki-e* style, with receding perspective.[24] His print, dating from the 1770s, was published by Iwatoya Genpachi; and is entitled (on the right-hand side) *Uki-e: Kitsune no yome-iri*, "Floating Picture: The Fox's Taking of a Bride." Like Harunobu's corresponding print, it depicts a night scene with a *norimono* and buildings; and elements in it were obviously influenced by him as well as by Minkō. It may be significant that Toyoharu himself was originally from the Kansai region. Lord Redesdale, in his celebrated *Tales of Old Japan*, first published in 1871,[25] briefly retells "The Foxes' Wedding," with woodcut illustrations by an anonymous Japanese artist; and in modern times there has even been a Japanese manga version.[26] The idea of a Foxes' Wedding seems to have deep roots in Japanese folklore, taking different forms in different parts of the country.[27] Elsewhere in the world there are countless stories of magic foxes, and analogous legends that connect strange weather with the nuptial rites of animals: but to consider these ramifications would take us too far afield.[28]

NOTES

1   A detailed English-language catalogue of this collection, by the present author, will soon be published under the title *The Harunobu Decade: A Catalogue of Woodcuts by Suzuki Harunobu and His Followers in the Museum of Fine Arts, Boston* (Leiden: Hotei Publishing, forthcoming 2013).

2   There are specimens of the first state in the Bibliotèque Nationale and the former Vever collection. At least six other specimens of the second state have survived: for details and additional commentary, see *The Harunobu Decade*, no. 73.

3   There is a specimen of the first state of this print in the University Art Museum, Berkeley (1919.342).

4   For additional details, see *The Harunobu Decade*, nos. 22, 145, and 146.

5   There are other specimens at Berkeley; in the Östasiatiska Museet, Stockholm; and in two private collections. Boston lacks this print; but in *The Harunobu Decade* I discuss the series in detail and describe most of the other designs (nos. 194–215).

6   Marjorie and Edwin Grabhorn, *Figure Prints of Old Japan* (San Francisco: Book Club of California, 1959), *ad* no. 27.

7   The only other known specimen is in the Metropolitan Museum: 2771; illus. Alan Priest, *Japanese Prints from the Henry L. Phillips Collection* (New York, 1947), pl. v.

8 For references to other prints of the set, see *The Harunobu Decade*, no. 349.

9 For a comparison between the two states, see Jack Hillier, *Suzuki Harunobu: An Exhibition of His Colour-Prints and Illustrated Books on the Occasion of the Bicentenary of His Death in 1770* (Philadelphia: Philadelphia Museum of Art), nos. 111 and 112.

10 For details of the two *chūban* series, see *The Harunobu Decade*, nos. 164 and 317; and for the *hashira-e* series, no. 562. Source references for the poems on the two Grabhorn prints are given under nos. 319 and 166 respectively.

11 There are other specimens in the Minneapolis Institute of Arts, and in Boston, which has seven of the eight prints from this series. See *The Harunobu Decade*, nos. 335–41. For a translation of *Matsukaze*, see Royall Tyler, *Japanese Nō Dramas* (London, etc.: Penguin Group, 1992), 183–204.

12 There is another specimen in the Metropolitan Museum of Art (1647).

13 There are specimens of this print in several institutional and private collections, including the British Museum, the Tokyo National Museum, the Brooklyn Museum, the Metropolitan Museum, and the Rijksmuseum, Amsterdam.

14 See D. B. Waterhouse, *Harunobu and His Age: The Development of Colour Printing in Japan* (London: Trustees of the British Museum, 1964), no. 12.

15 There are impressions of both prints in the Museum of Fine Arts, Boston (21.4577 and Res.56.5). The earlier of the two dates from 1763–1764; the later one from 1767–1768.

16 *Ehon shogei no nishiki* (1763), vol. 3, fols. 7b–8a.

17 This print is now in the collection at Keiō University. See Chiba-shi Bijutsukan, ed., *Seishun no ukiyo-eshi Suzuki Harunobu—Edo no kararisuto tōjō* (Chiba: Chiba-shi Bijutsukan; Hagi: Yamaguchi Kenritsu Hagi Bijutsukan, Uragami Kinenkan, 2002), cpl. 221.

18 In *Zōho ukiyo-e ruikō* (1844), a series of notes added to *Ukiyo-e ruikō*, the oldest biographical compendium of *ukiyo-e* artists. (See Yura Tetsuji, ed., *Sōgō Nihon ukiyo-e ruikō* (Tokyo: Gabundō, 1979), p. 116.) This theory has been followed by later writers, both Japanese and Western. It is not directly supported; but the prolific book illustrator Tachibana Morikuni (1679–1748) was from Ōsaka.

19 I am indebted to Dr. Higinbotham for allowing me to study his prints, and for supplying excellent images of them. In modern times the first appearance of this set, together with the wrapper, was probably at the sale of the collection of W. O. Danckwerts KC (William Otto Adolph Julius Danckwerts, 1853–1914) in London in 1914: see *A Valuable and Extensive Collection of Japanese Colour Prints, Formed by the Late W. O. Danckwerts, Esq., K. C. …* (London: Sotheby, Wilkinson & Hodge, 21 July 1914), lot 44. According to a brief report in *The New York Times* (22 July 1914) it fetched the highest price of the sale ($1,150). On the back of each of the Higinbotham prints is a neatly stamped green cipher, which seems to incorporate the initials "WOD."

20 See *A Choice Collection of Japanese Colour Prints, the Property of Baron Walter von Heymel, of Munich … and a Very Important Old Japanese Album, Containing Forty Prints by Harunobu, the Property of Mrs. A. M. Litchfield* (London: Sotheby, Wilkinson & Hodge, 2 December 1910), lot 25(a) to (f), & pl. III. The photographs, in black-and-white, are small; and the catalogue description is partly incorrect. The photographs were reproduced, without acknowledgment of their source, in Yoshida Teruji's *Harunobu zenshū* (Tokyo: Takamizawa Mokuhan-sha, 1942), pl. 161.

21 Formerly in the collection of Mr. and Mrs. James A. Michener. It is illustrated and described in Margaret O. Gentles, *The Clarence Buckingham Collection of Japanese Prints, Volume II: Harunobu, Koryūsai, Shigemasa, Their Followers and Contemporaries* (Chicago: The Art Institute of Chicago, 1965), p. 169, no. 1.

22 There are later elaborations of the legend, which need not concern us. For this and other details concerning Inari worship and its connexion with foxes I have drawn especially on Nannichi Gimyō, *Inari o tazunete: inari shinkō no yurai to goshintoku* (4th edition. Ōsaka: Bunshindō, 1981), 59–89.

23 The wrapper is apparently no longer extant, but the late Jack Hillier provided me with a photograph of it. I have translated the text and described the entire set in my forthcoming catalogue of the Boston collection, nos. 420–430.

24 See Toyama Usaburō, *The Western-Style Colour Prints in Japan: A Catalogue on Retrospective Works of the Exhibition in Foreign Country, Organised by Nippon Hanga Kyokai / Nihon shoki yōfū hanga shū: kaigai tenrankai zuroku*. Preface by Yone Noguchi (Tokyo: Daiichishobo, 1936), pl. 33. There is an impression of this print in Honolulu (HMA: 16492; ex Michener).

25 *Tales of Old Japan* (2 vols. London: Macmillan and Co.); by Algernon Bertram Freeman-Mitford, 1st Baron Redesdale (1837–1916).

26 See www.mangafox.com/manga/fox_s_wedding.

27 See Karen A. Smyers, *The Fox and the Jewel: Shared and Private Meanings in Contemporary Japanese Inari Worship* (Honolulu: University of Hawai'i Press, 1998).

28 See, for example, Hans-Jörg Uther, "The Fox in World Literature: Reflections on a 'Fictional Animal.'" *Asian Folklore Studies*, vol. 65, no. 2 (2006): 133–160.

Plates

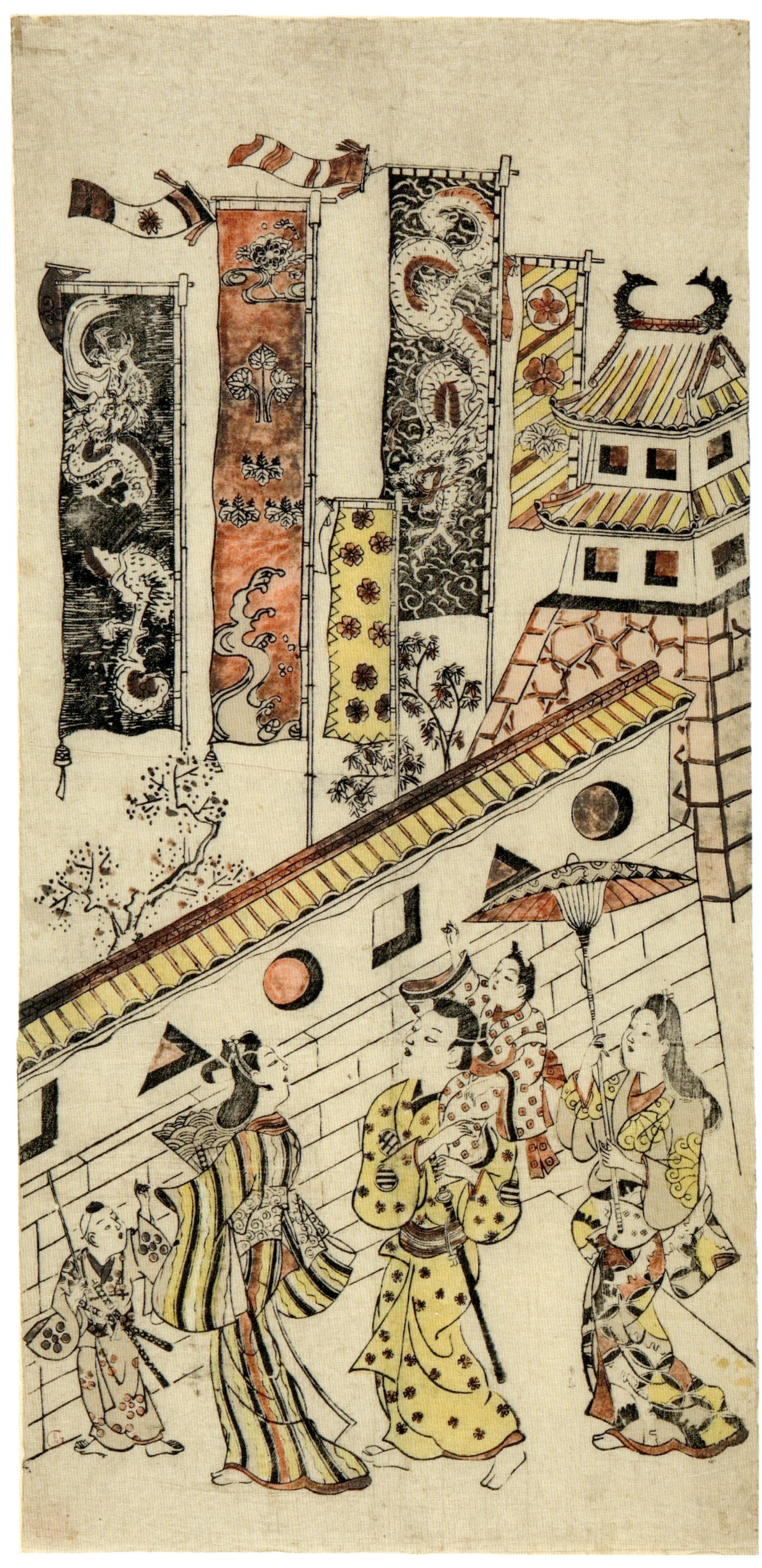

   1   Attributed to Sugimura Jihei, active c. 1681–1698, A Boys' Day outing

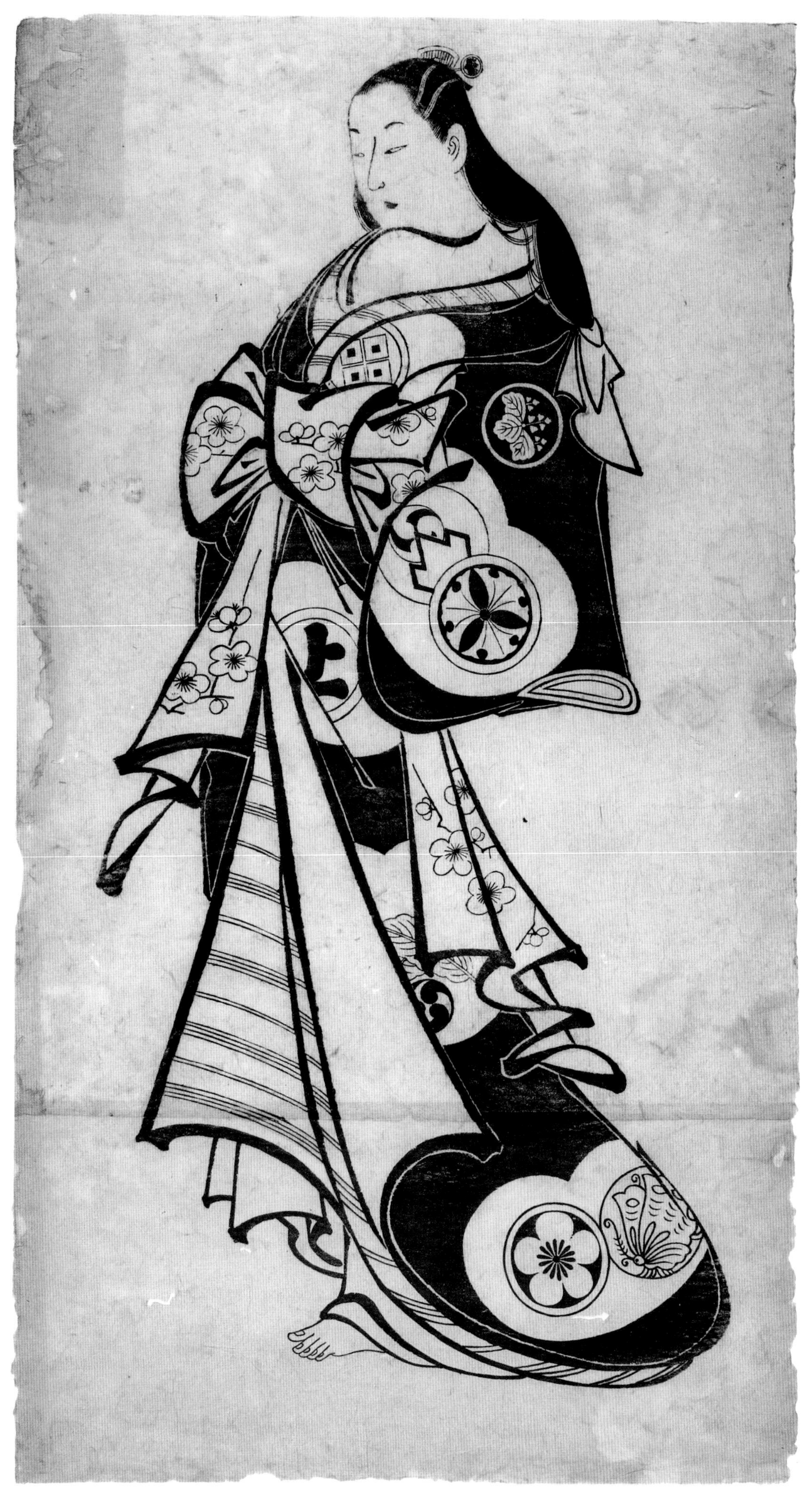

2   Attributed to Torii Kiyonobu I, 1664–1729, A courtesan wearing a robe decorated with actors' crests | *33*

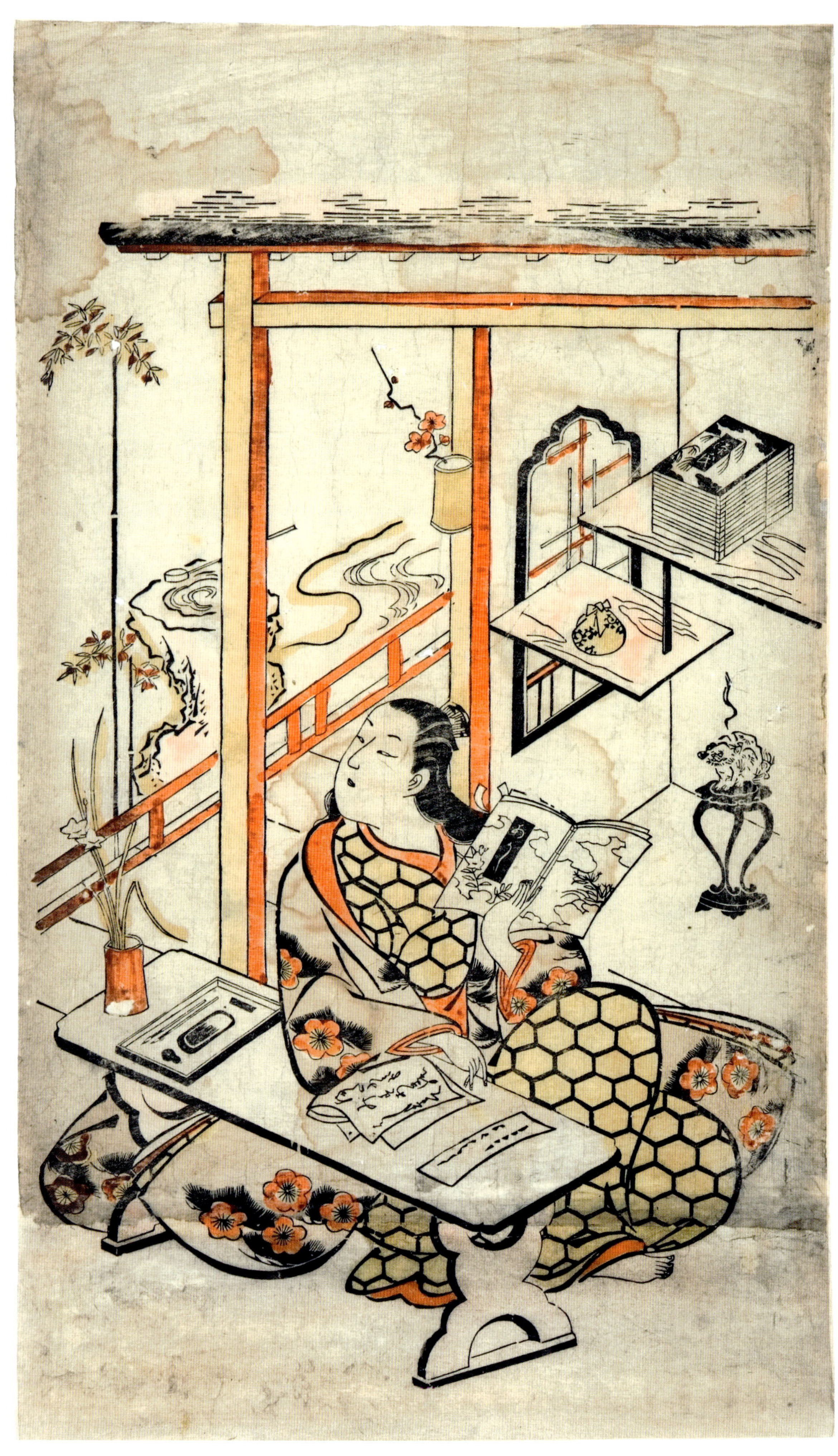

3 Attributed to Torii Kiyomasu I, active c. 1696–1716, Woman reading the "Akashi" chapter of *The Tale of Genji*

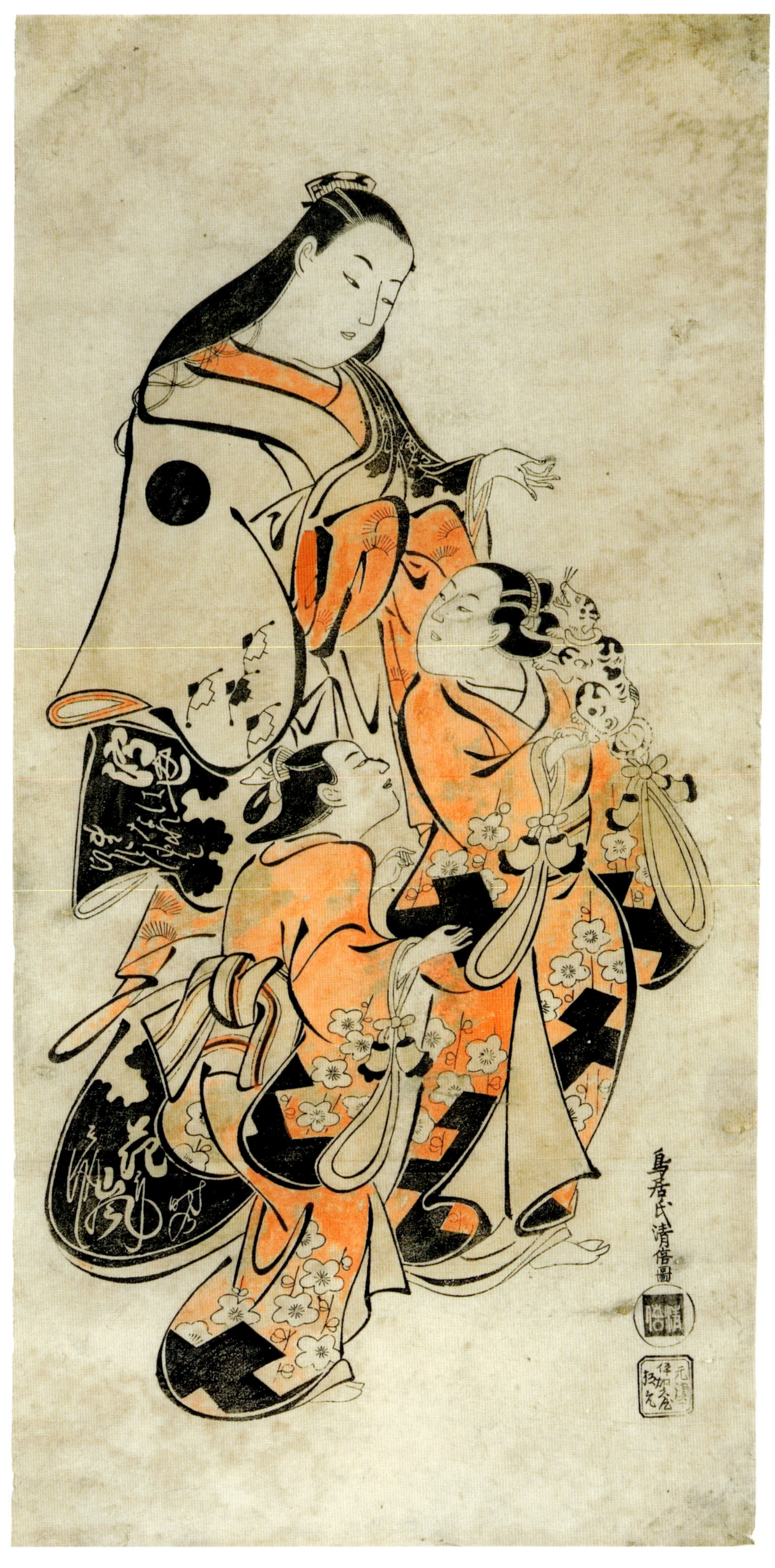

4 Torii Kiyomasu I, active c. 1696–1716, *Courtesan parading with two child attendants*

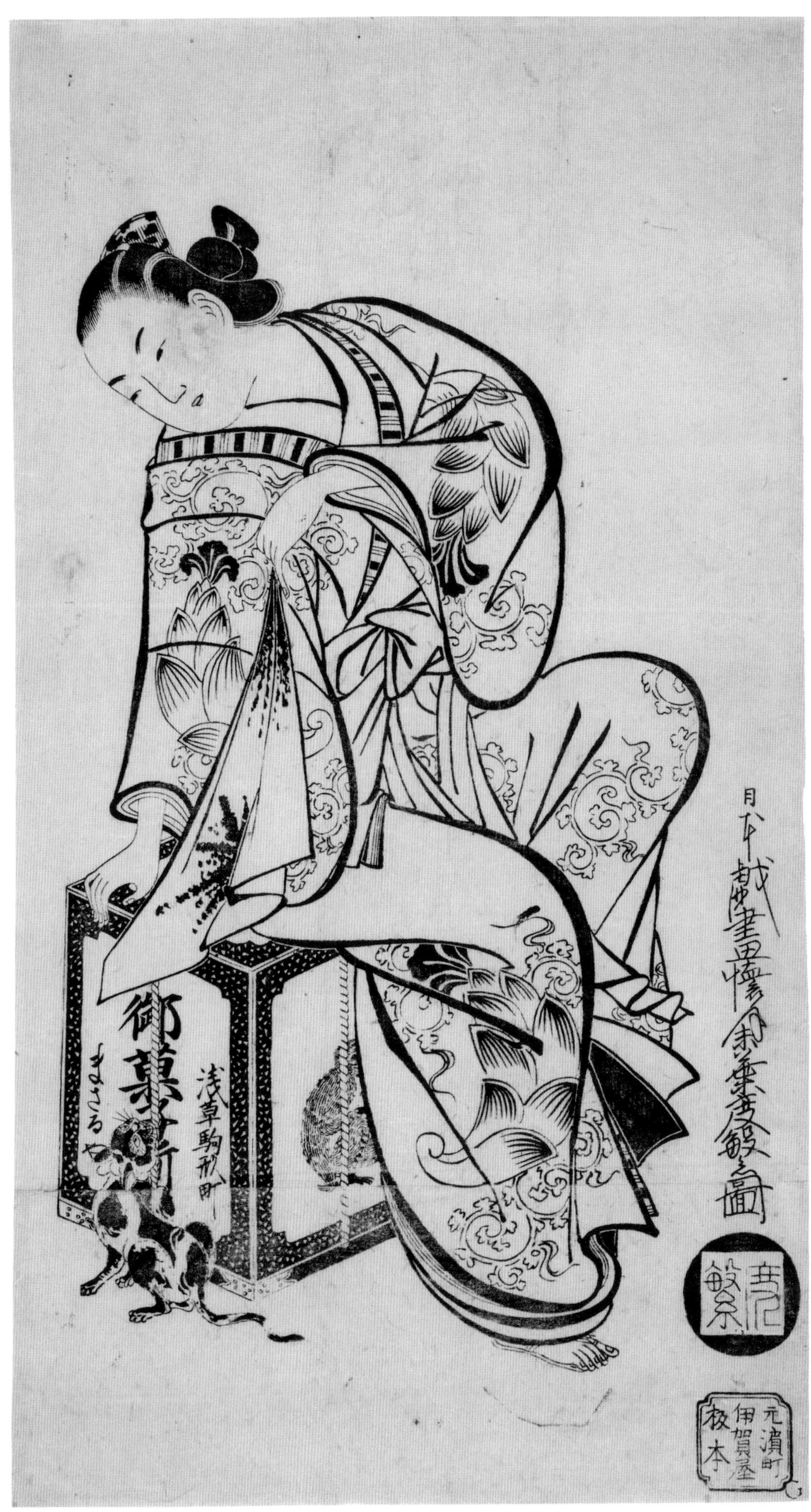

 | 5 Kaigetsudō Dohan, active c. 1704–1716, Courtesan playing with a cat

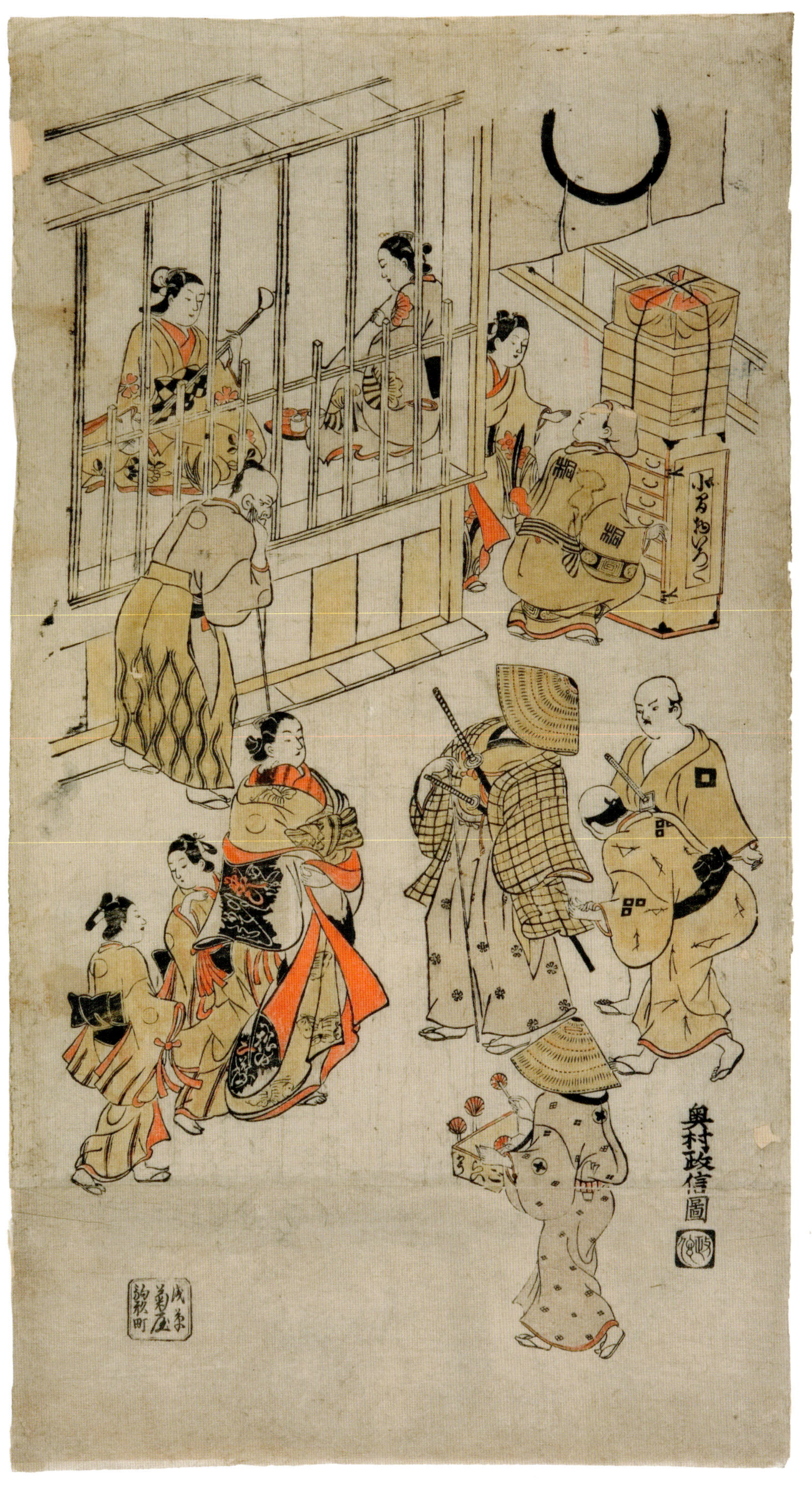

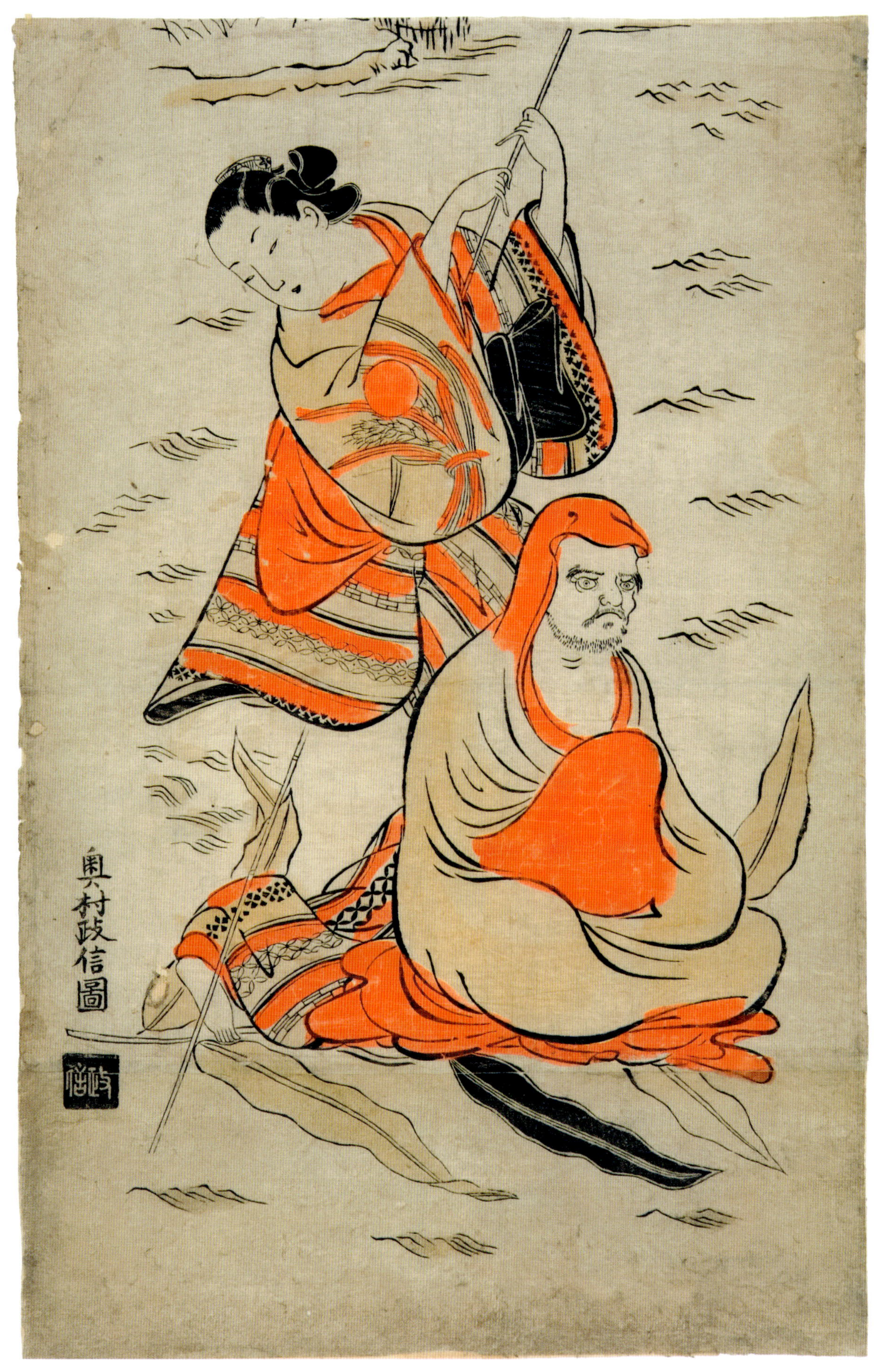

  7 Okumura Masanobu, 1686–1764, *Mitate* of Bodhidharma crossing the Yangzi River on a reed

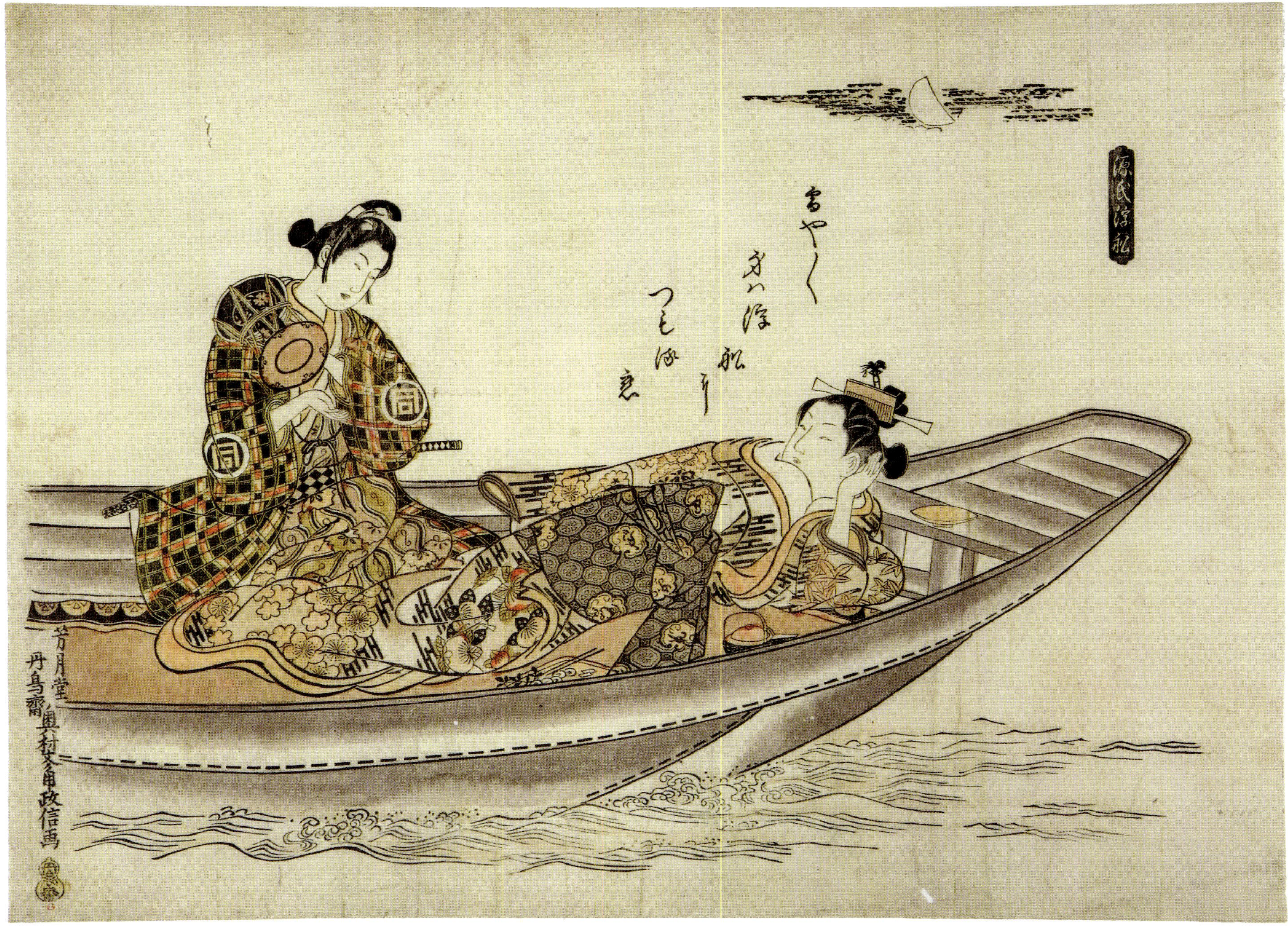

8 Okumura Masanobu, 1686–1764, "'Ukifune' [chapter] from *The Tale of Genji*"

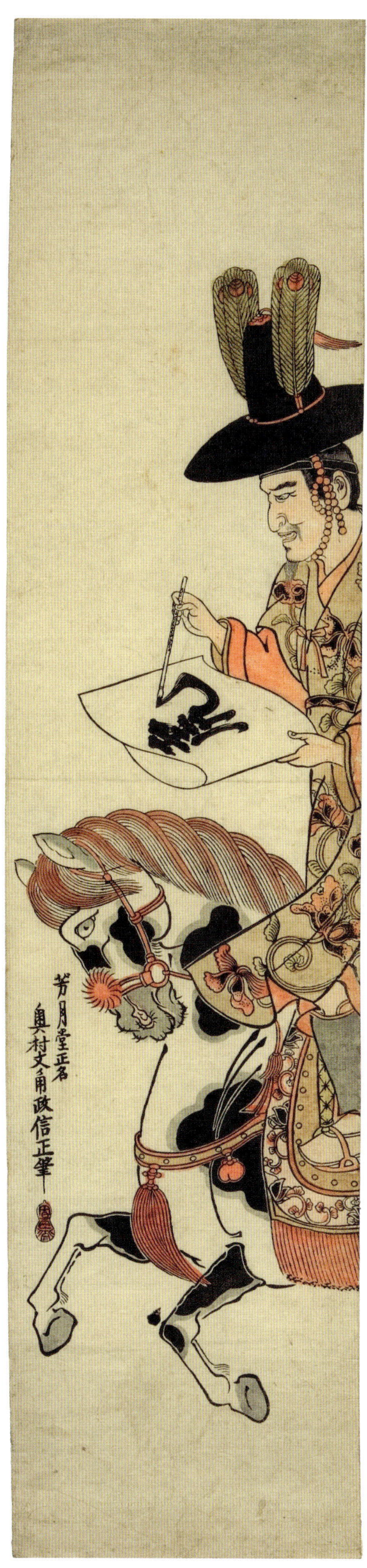

9 Okumura Masanobu, 1686–1764, Korean acrobatic rider writing the character "tiger"

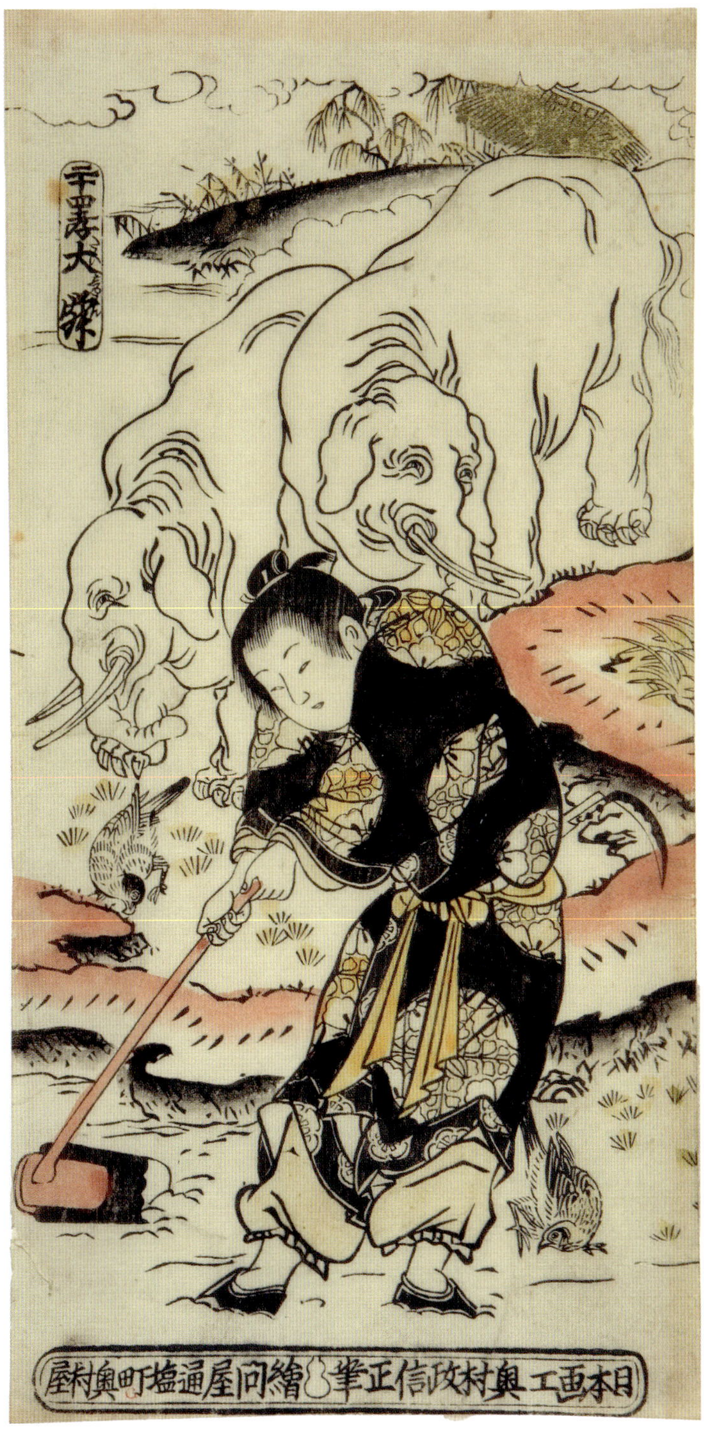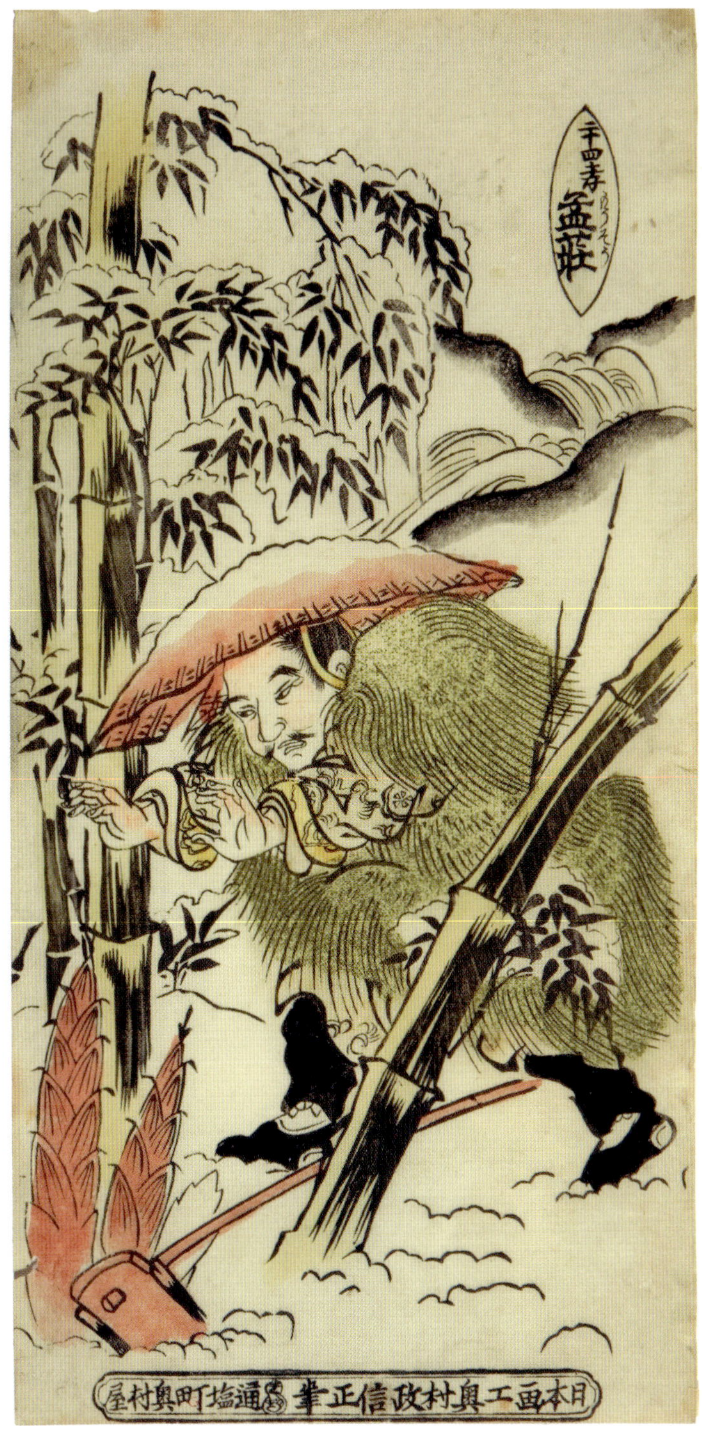

10 (LEFT)   Okumura Masanobu, 1686–1764, "Dashun," from the series *Twenty-four Paragons of Filial Piety*;
11 (RIGHT)   Okumura Masanobu, 1686–1764, "Meng Zong," from the series *Twenty-four Paragons of Filial Piety* | *41*

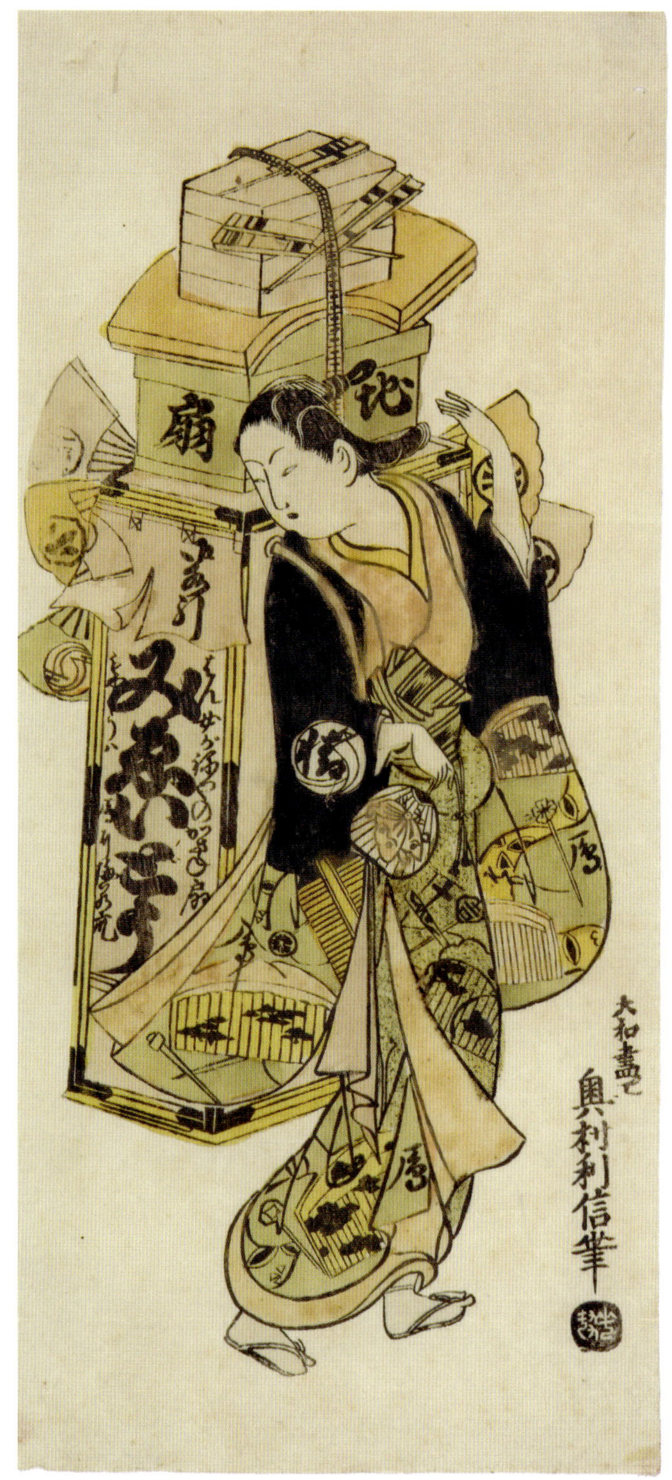
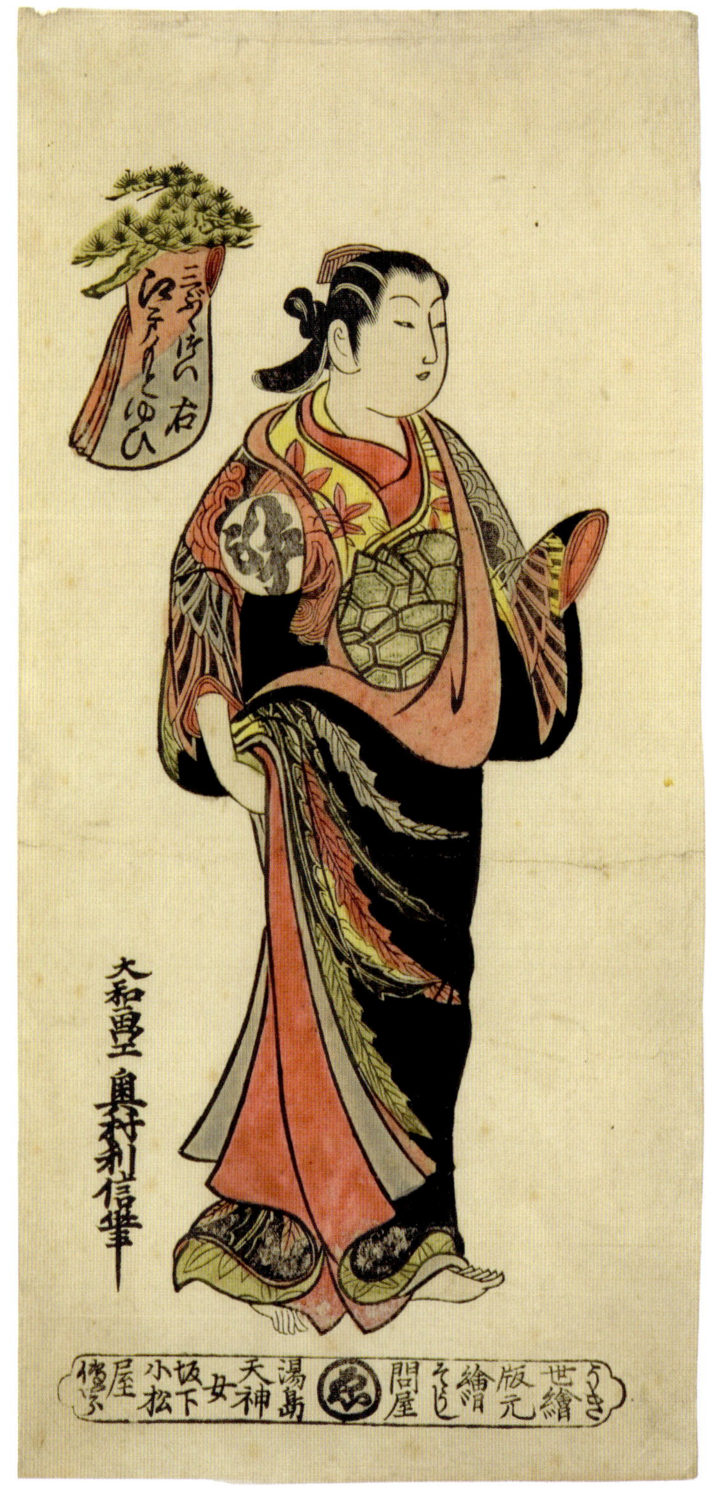

12 (LEFT)   Okumura Toshinobu, active c. 1718–1749, Fan vendor;

13 (RIGHT)   Okumura Toshinobu, active 1718–1749, "Right, Hair Tie from Edo," from *Triptych*

42   [Beauties of the three cities]

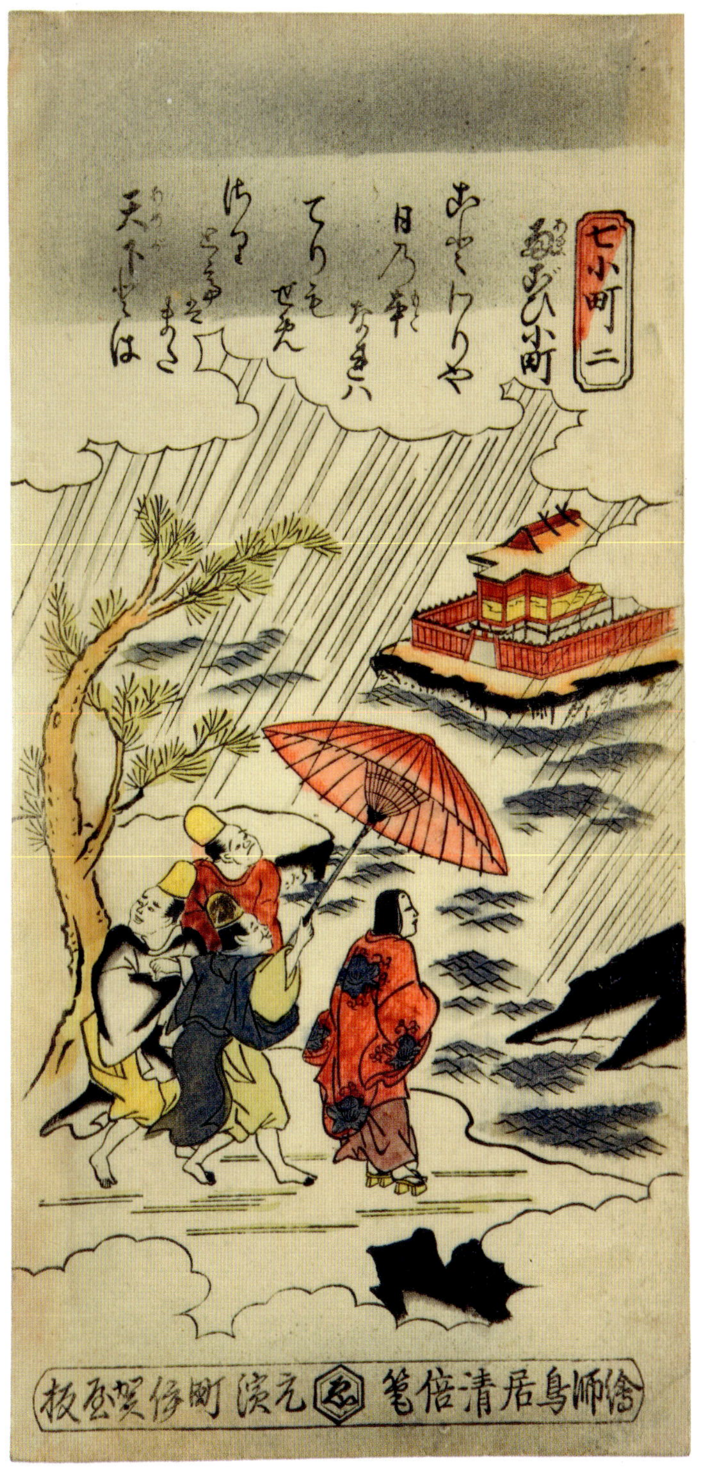
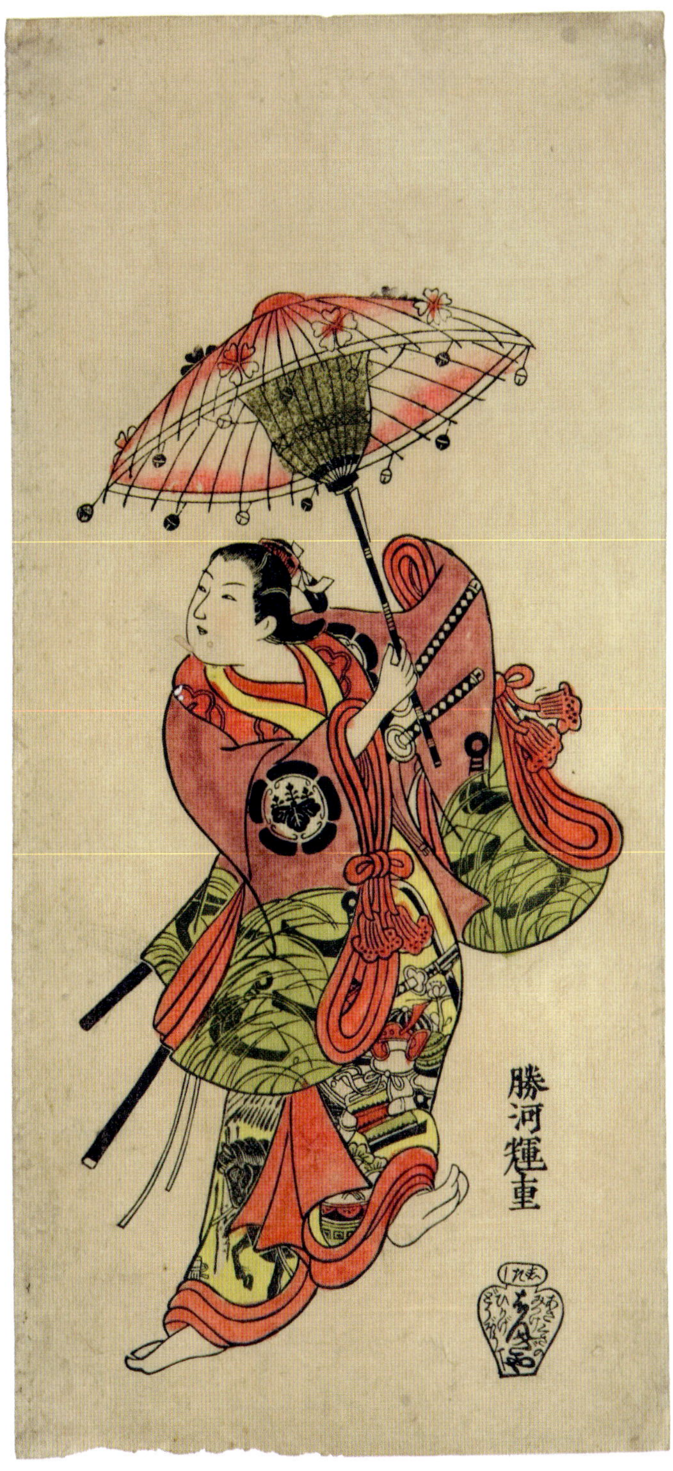

14 (LEFT)　Torii Kiyomasu II, 1706–1763, "No. 2, Komachi Praying for Rain," from the series *Seven Scenes from the Life of Ono Komachi*;

15 (RIGHT)　Katsukawa Terushige, active c. 1716–1736, The Actor Yoshizawa Ayame I dancing with a flower-decorated umbrella

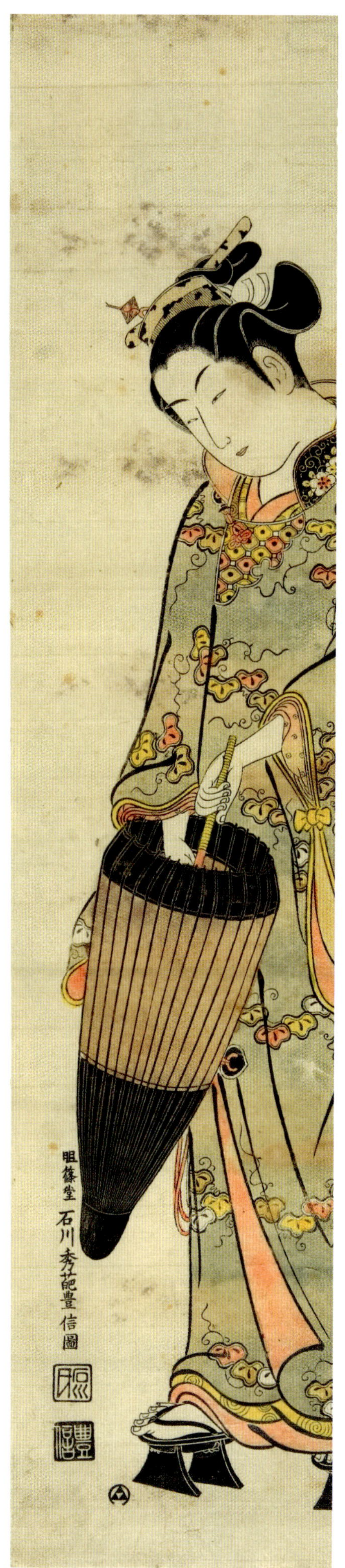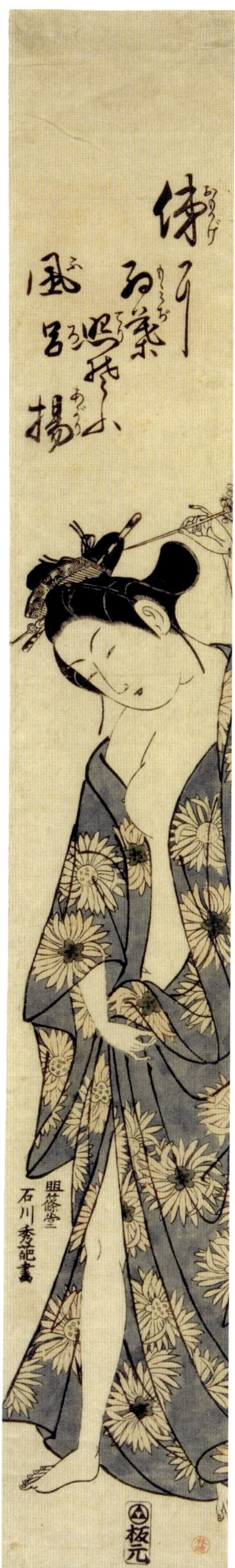

16 (LEFT)   Ishikawa Toyonobu, 1711–1785, Woman holding an umbrella;
17 (RIGHT)   Ishikawa Toyonobu, 1711–1785, Woman coming out of the bath

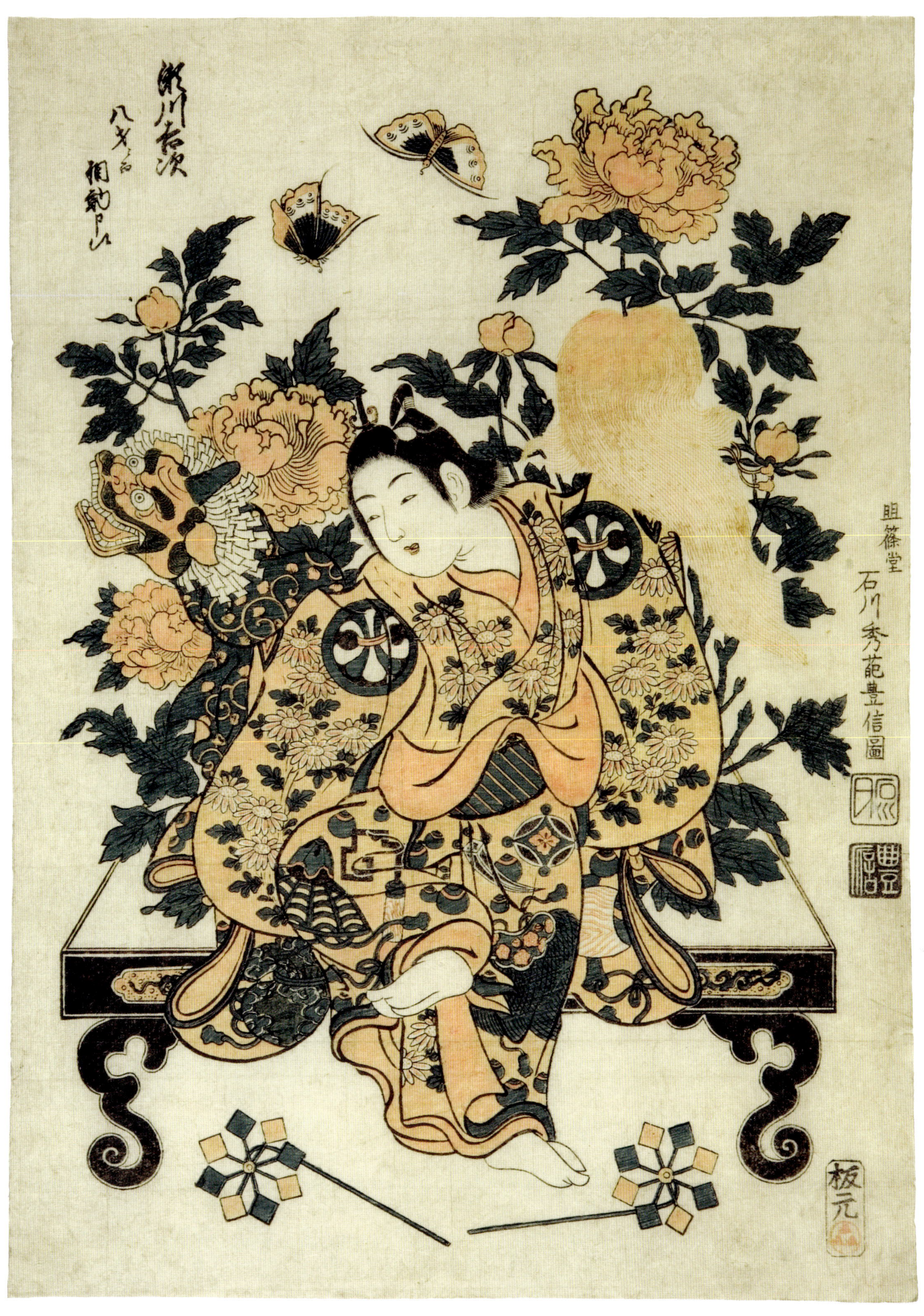

18   Ishikawa Toyonobu, 1711–1785, *The Actor Segawa Kichiji Performing at Age Eight*

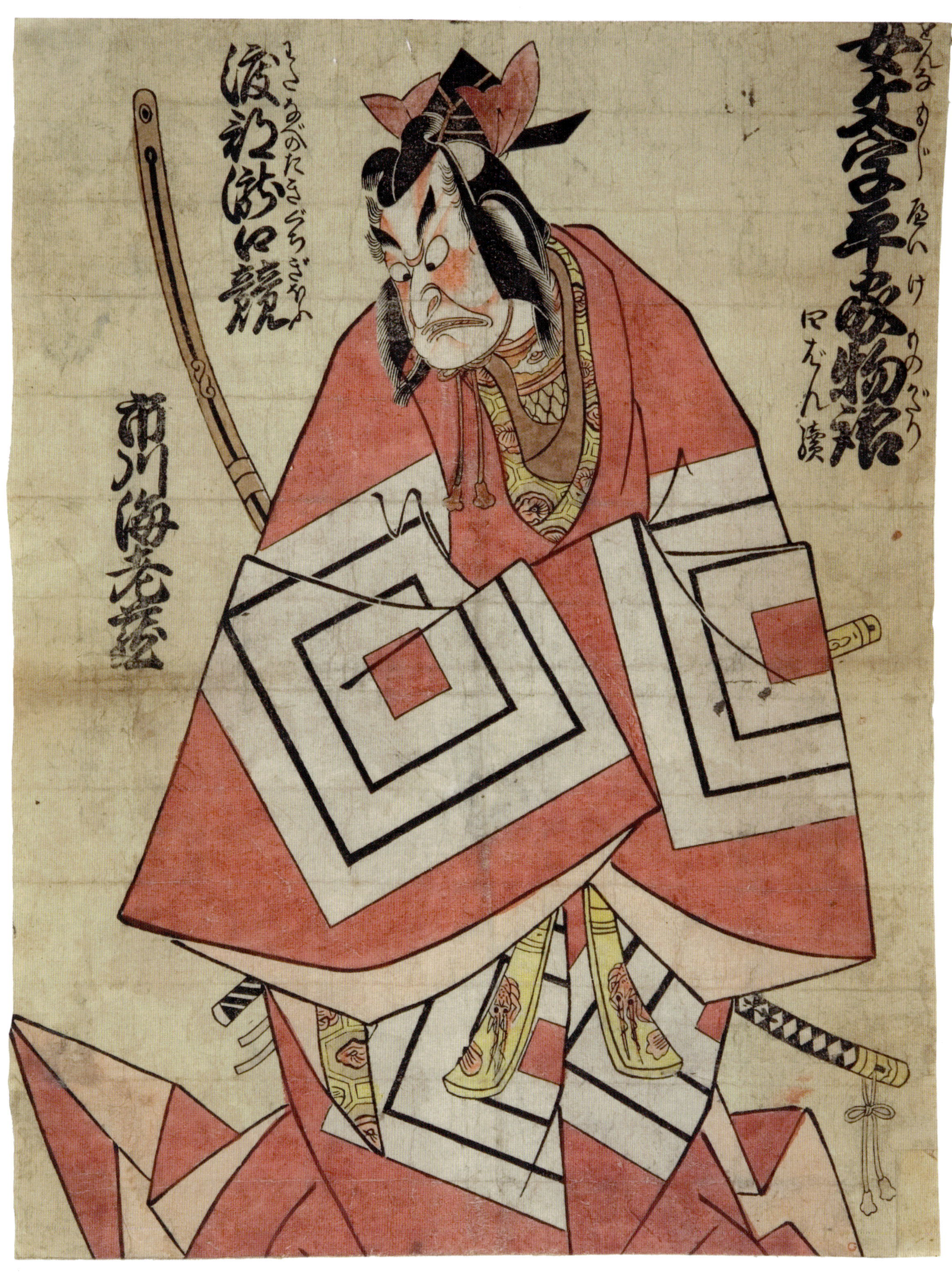

19 Torii Kiyoshige, active c. 1716–1764, "The Actor Ichikawa Ebizō II as Imperial Guard Watanabe Kisō in the Four-Act Play *Onna moji Heike monogatari*"

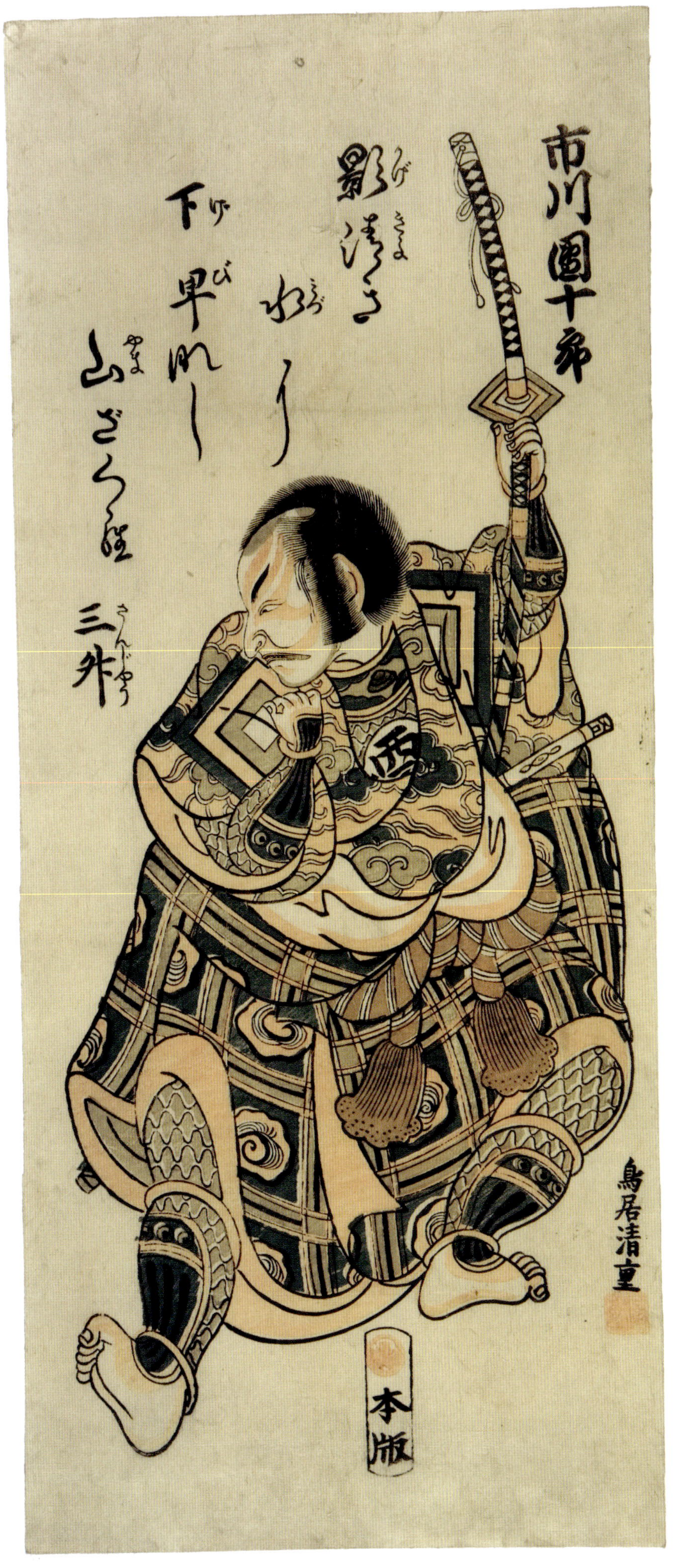

市川團十郎
影清きよ
下げ早びれ
山ざくら
三外さんがい
鳥居清重
本版

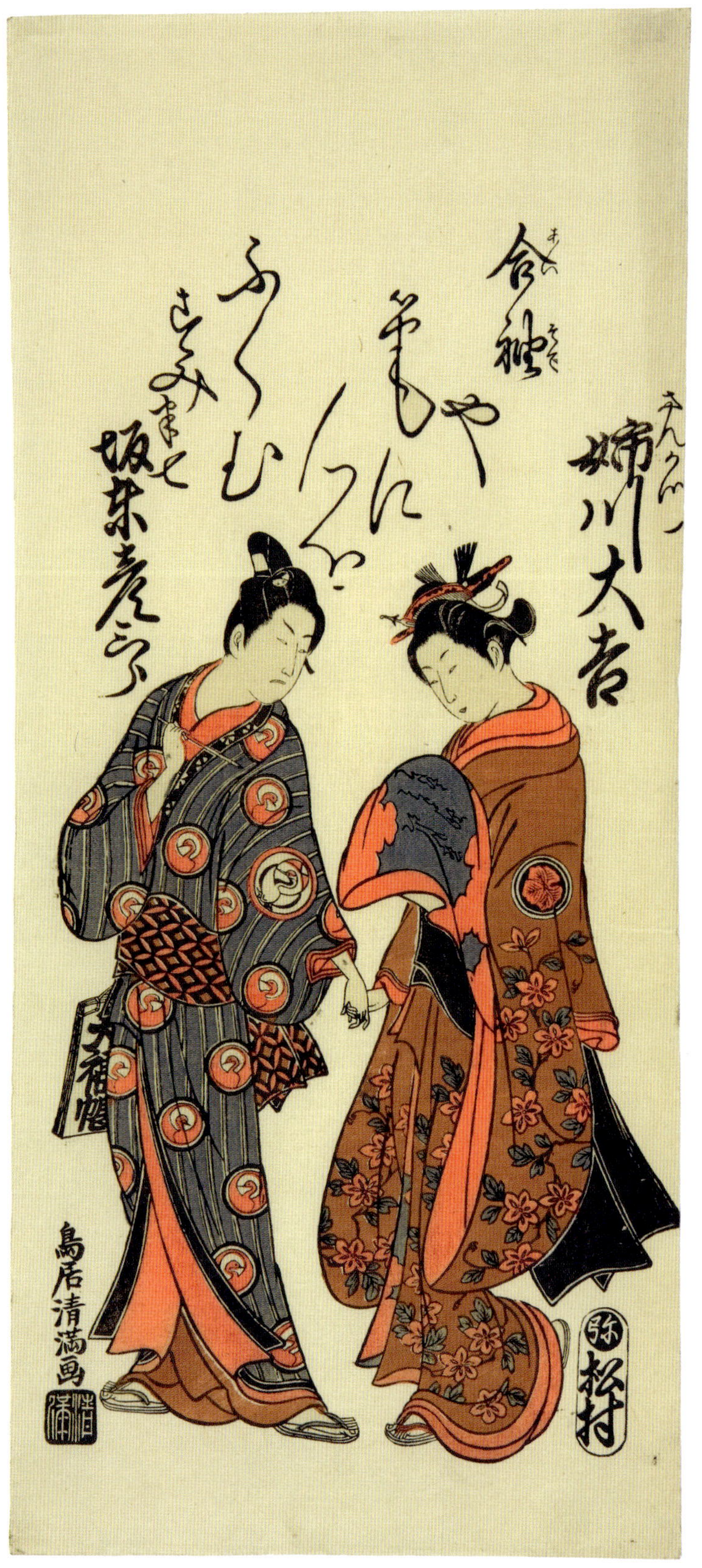

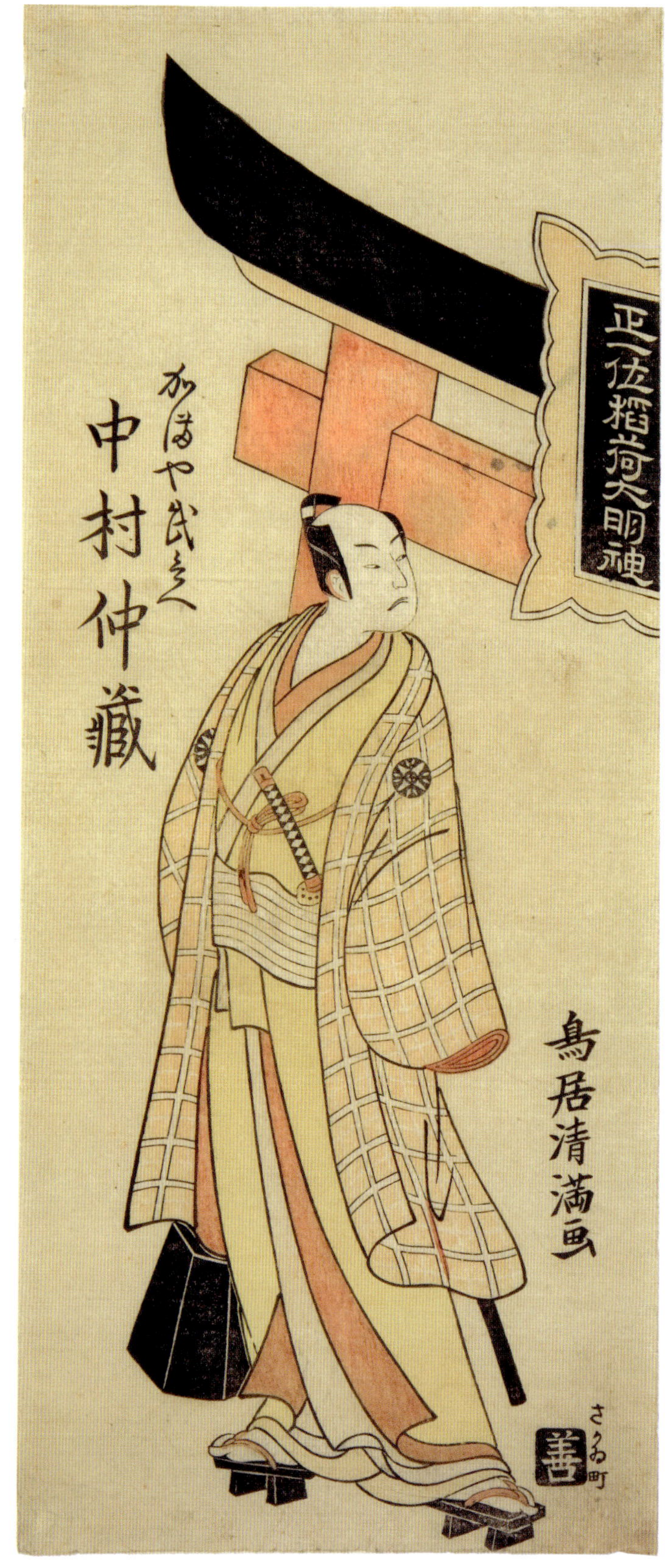

21 (LEFT) Torii Kiyomitsu I, 1735–1785, The Actors Anegawa Daikichi as Sankatsu and Bandō Hikosaburō II as Hanshichi;
22 (RIGHT) Torii Kiyomitsu I, 1735–1785, "The Actor Nakamura Nakazō as Kamaya Takebei"

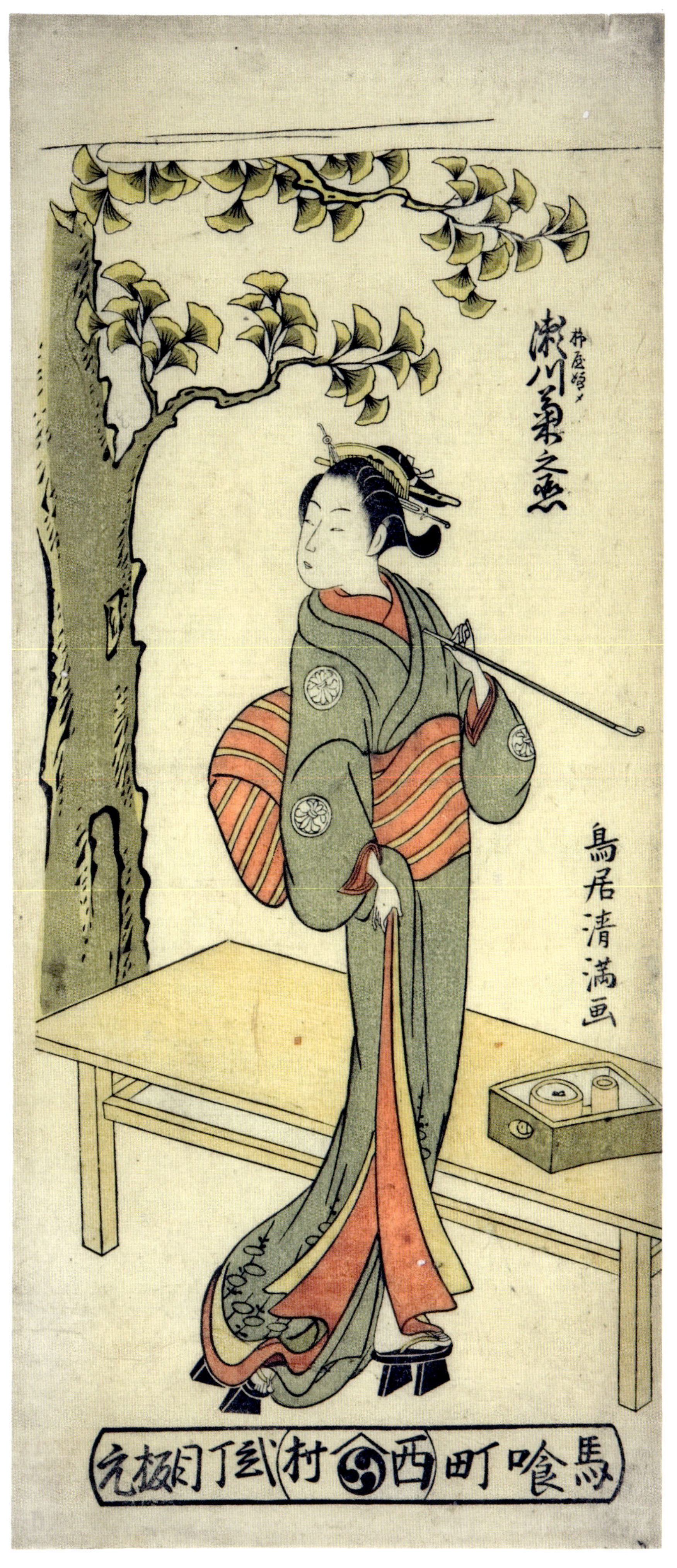

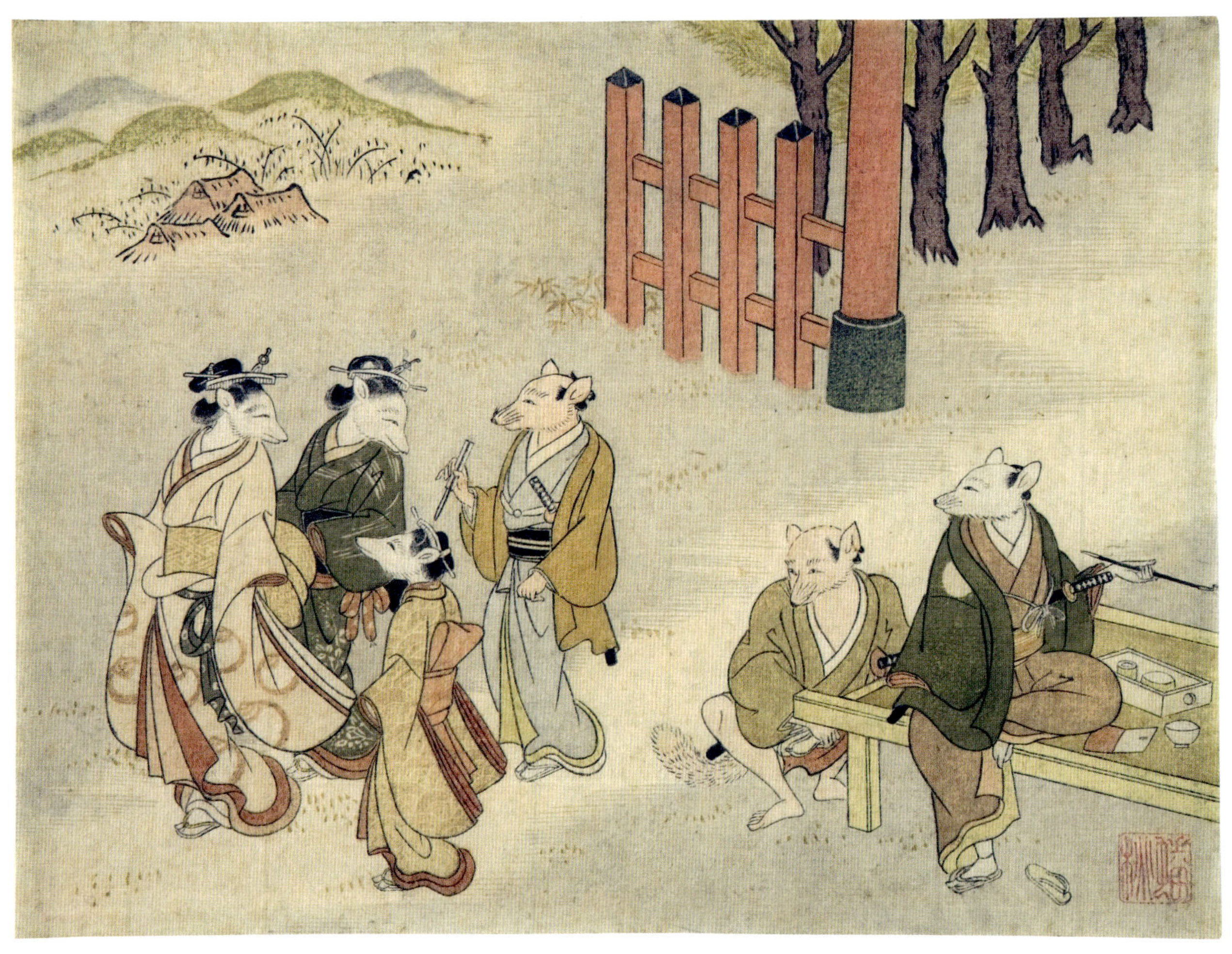

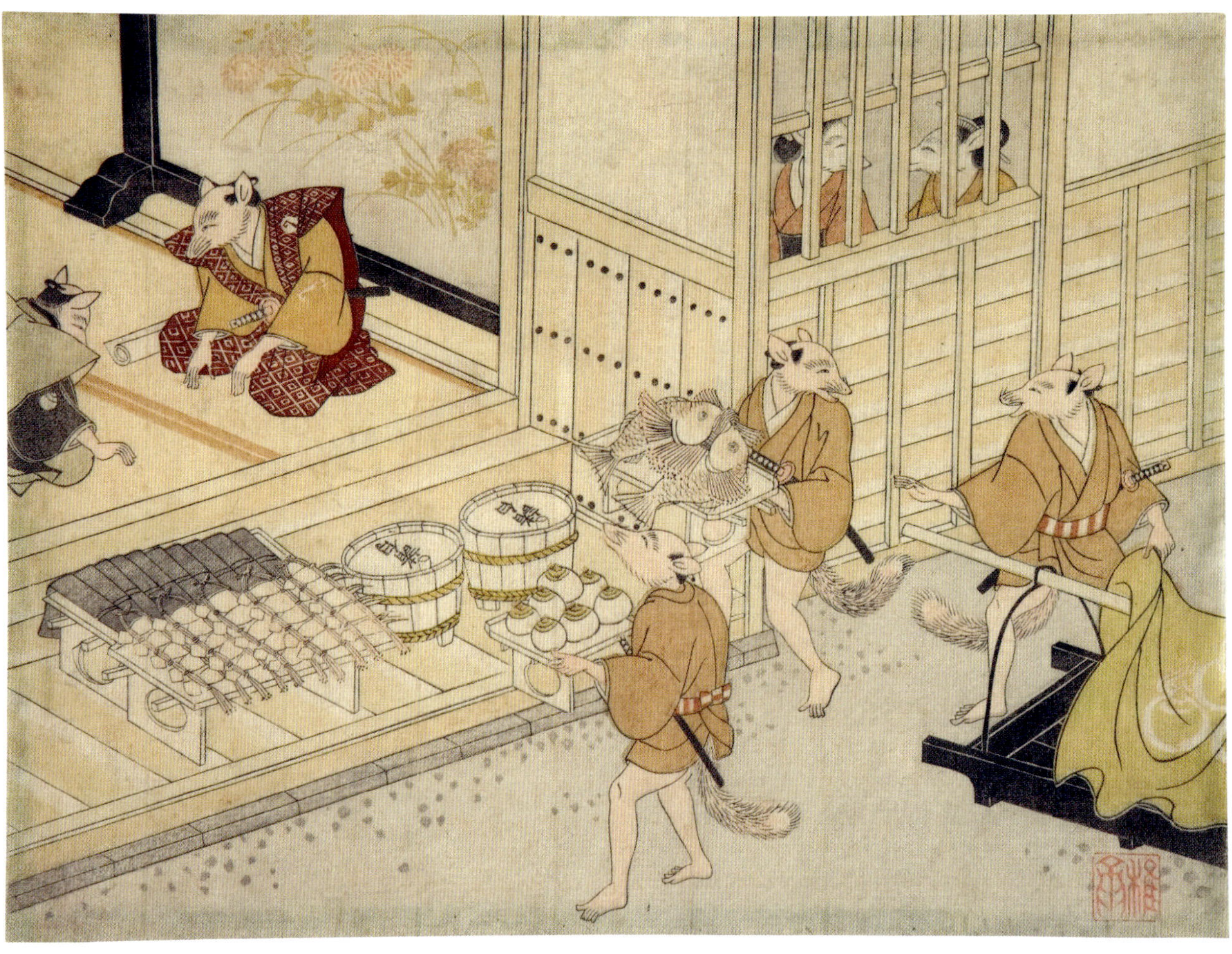

24 (TOP)   Tachibana Minkō, active 1764–1772, "The First Meeting," from the series *The Foxes' Wedding;*
25 (BOTTOM)   Tachibana Minkō, active 1764–1772, "Betrothal Gifts," from the series *The Foxes' Wedding*

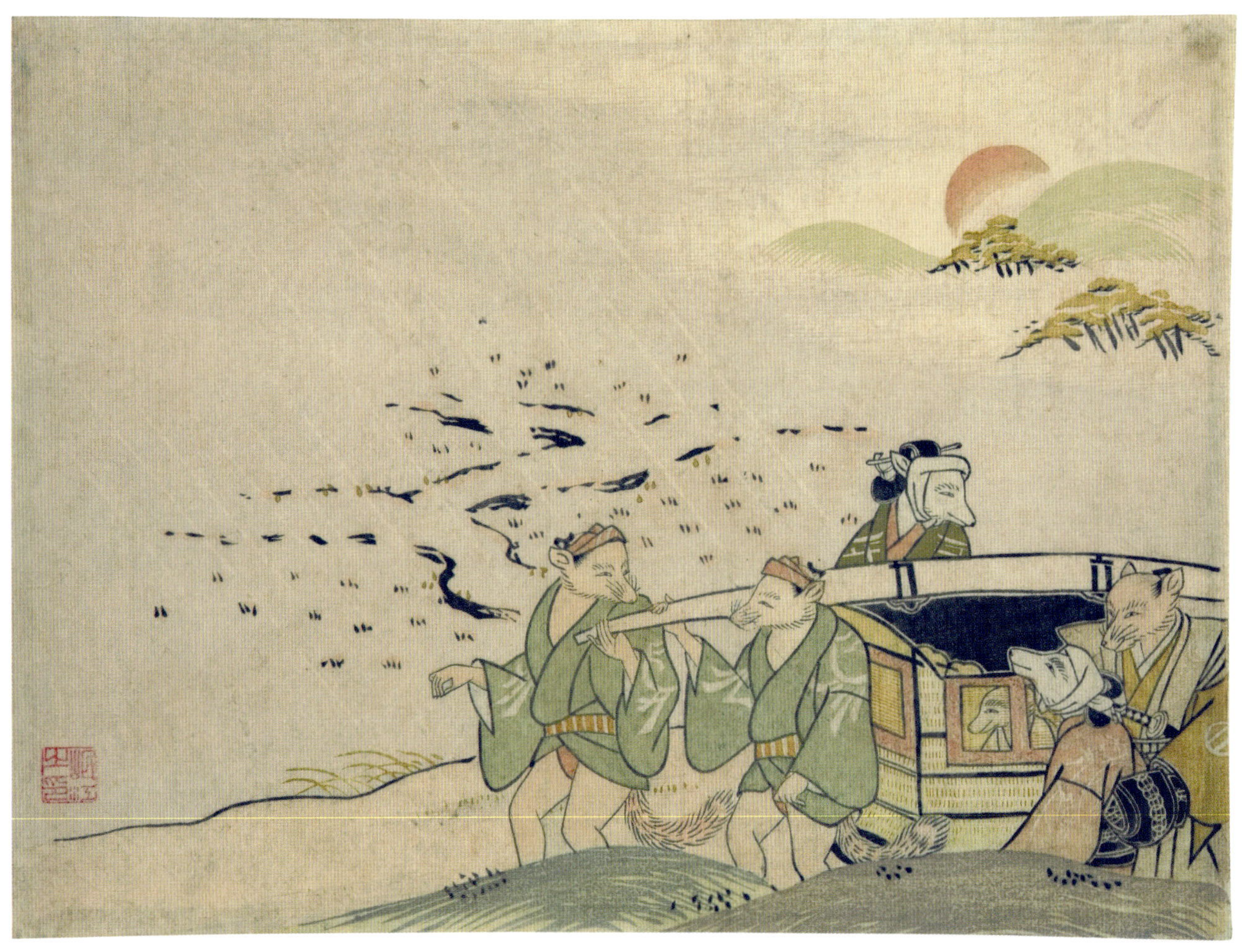

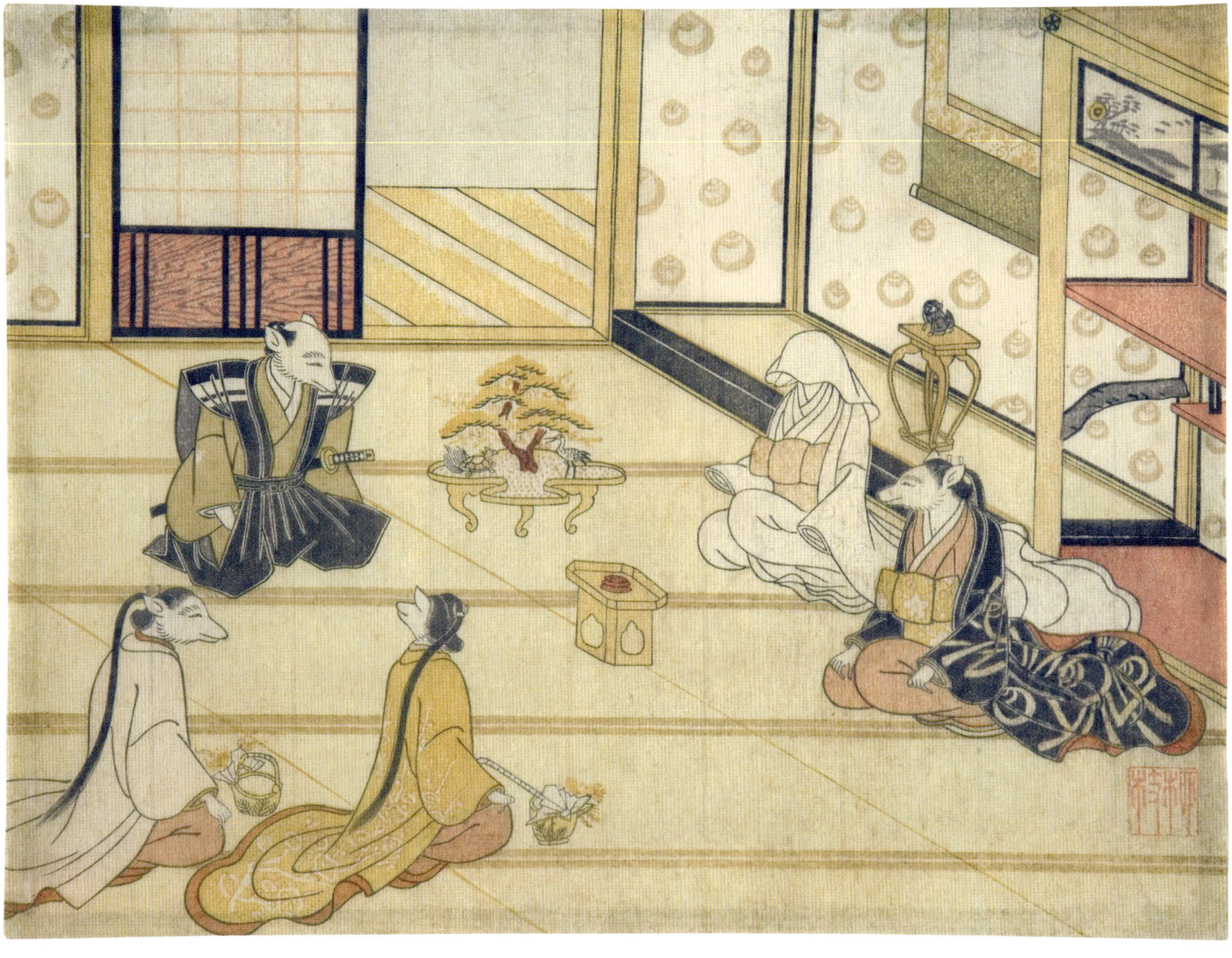

26 (TOP) Tachibana Minkō, active 1764–1772 , "Rain When the Sun Is Shining," from the series *The Foxes' Wedding*;
27 (BOTTOM) Tachibana Minkō, active 1764–1772, "Nuptial Sake Cup Ceremony," from the series *The Foxes' Wedding*

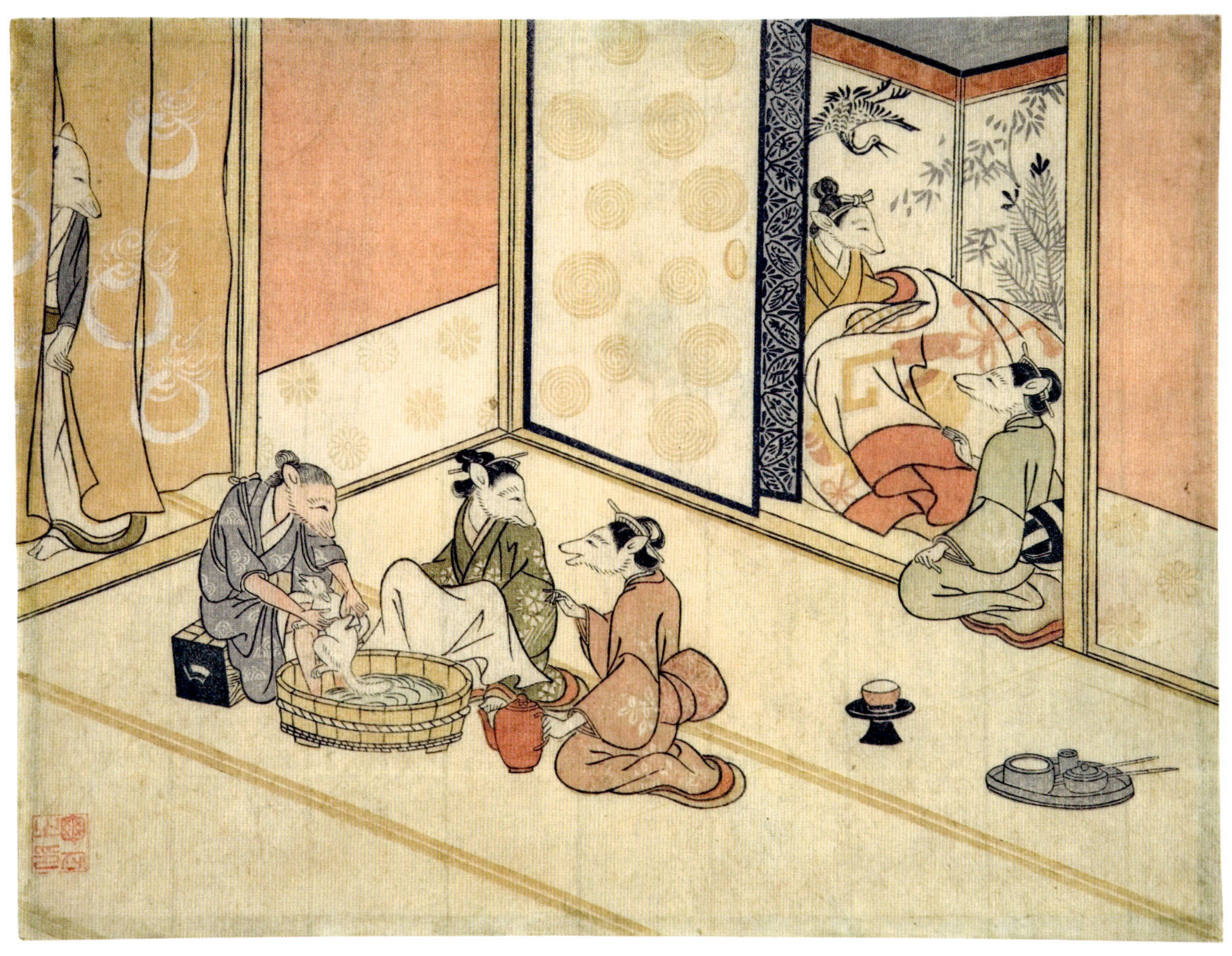

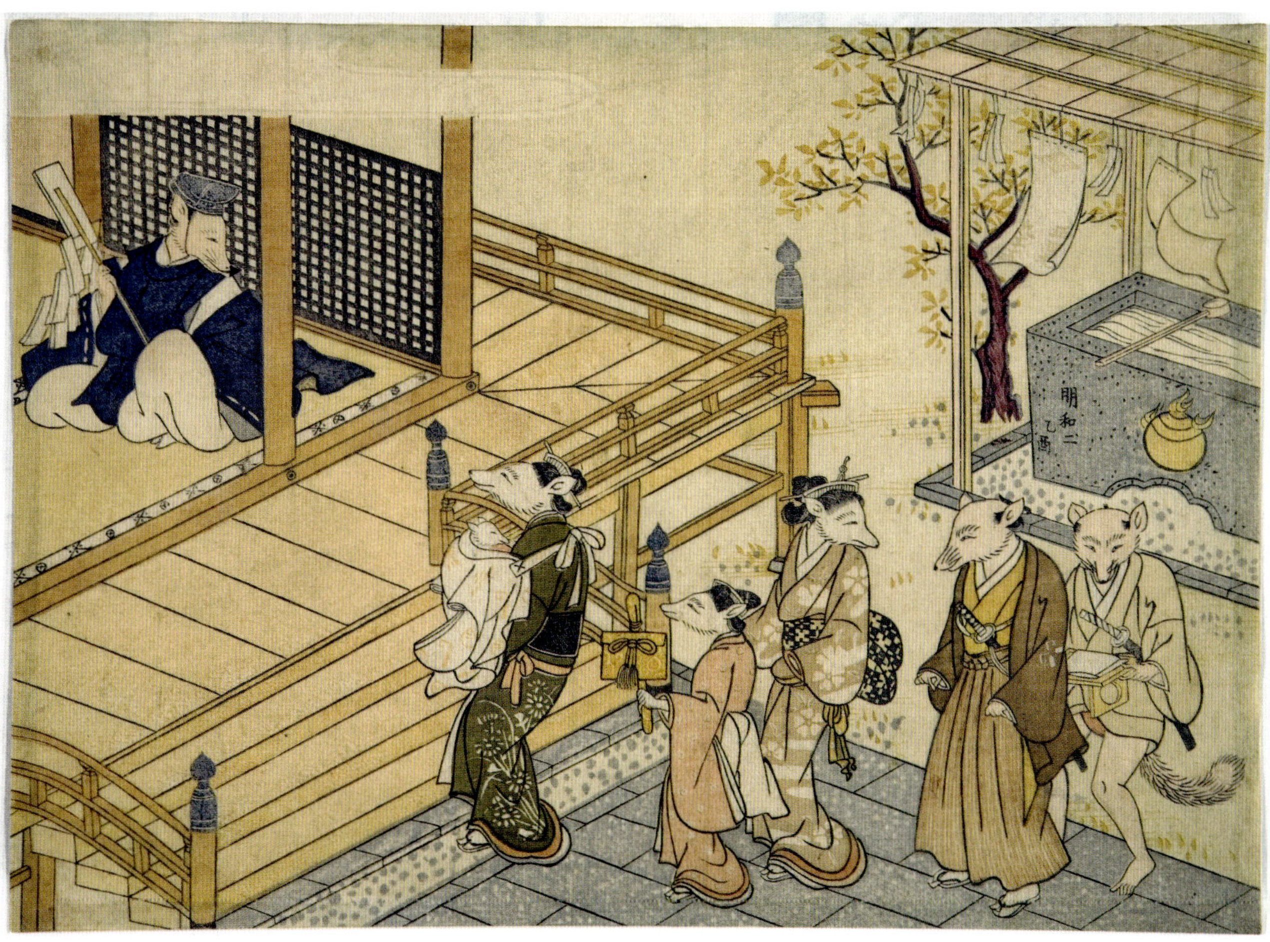

28 (TOP)   Tachibana Minkō, active 1764–1772, "First Bathing [of the Infant]," from the series *The Foxes' Wedding*;
29 (BOTTOM)   Tachibana Minkō, active 1764–1772, "Visit to the Shrine," from the series *The Foxes' Wedding*

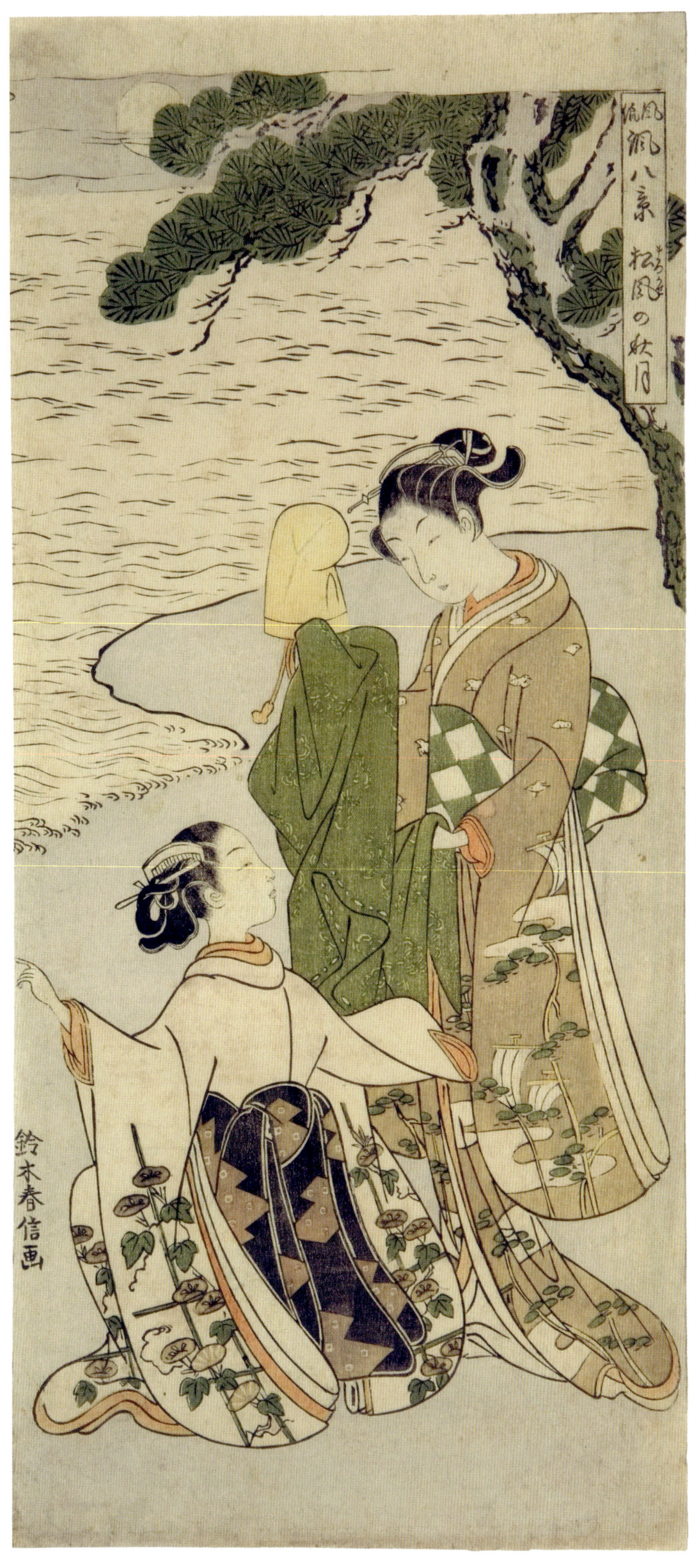

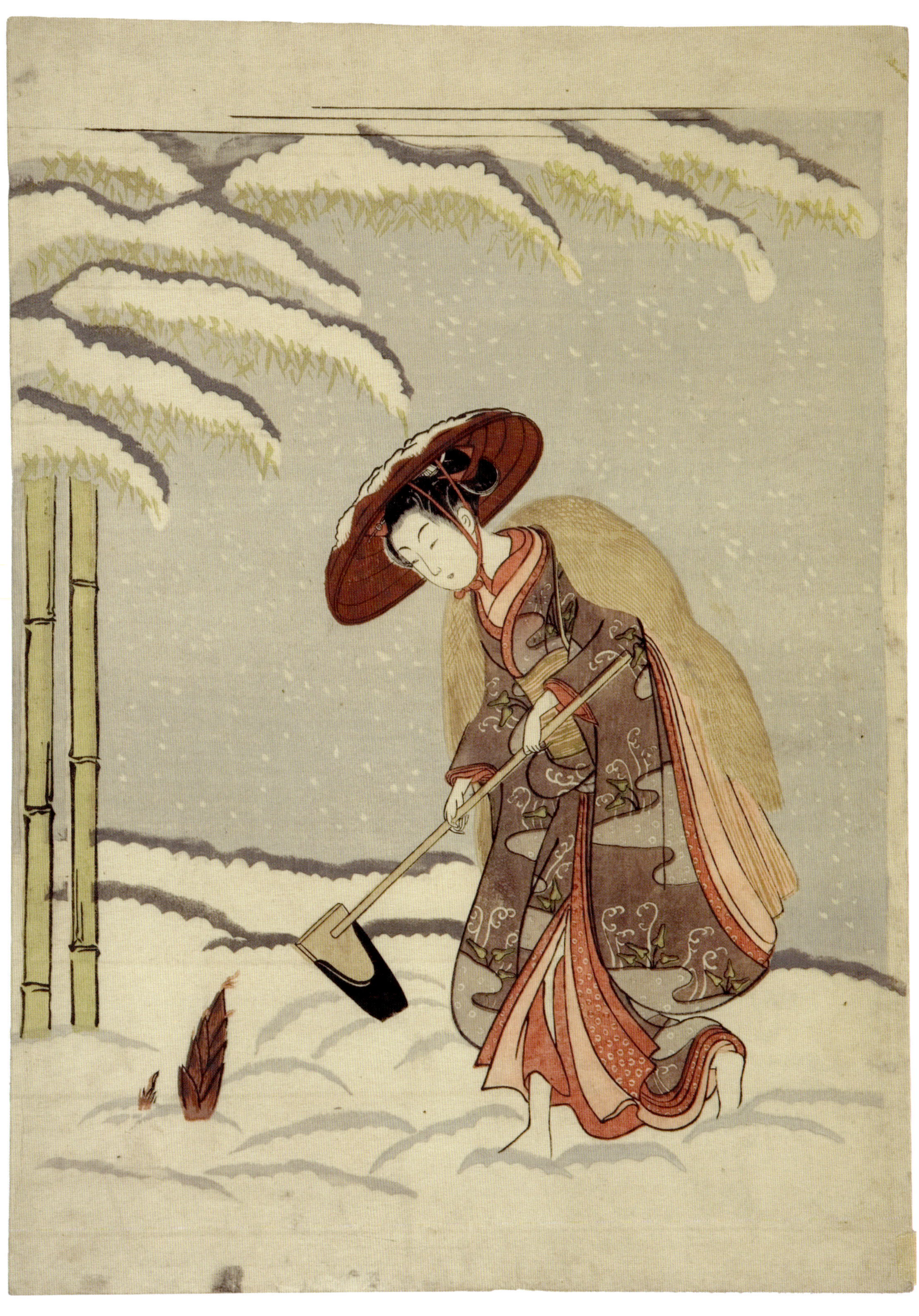

  31 Suzuki Harunobu, 1725?–1770, *Mitate* of Meng Zong, one of the Twenty-four Paragons of Filial Piety

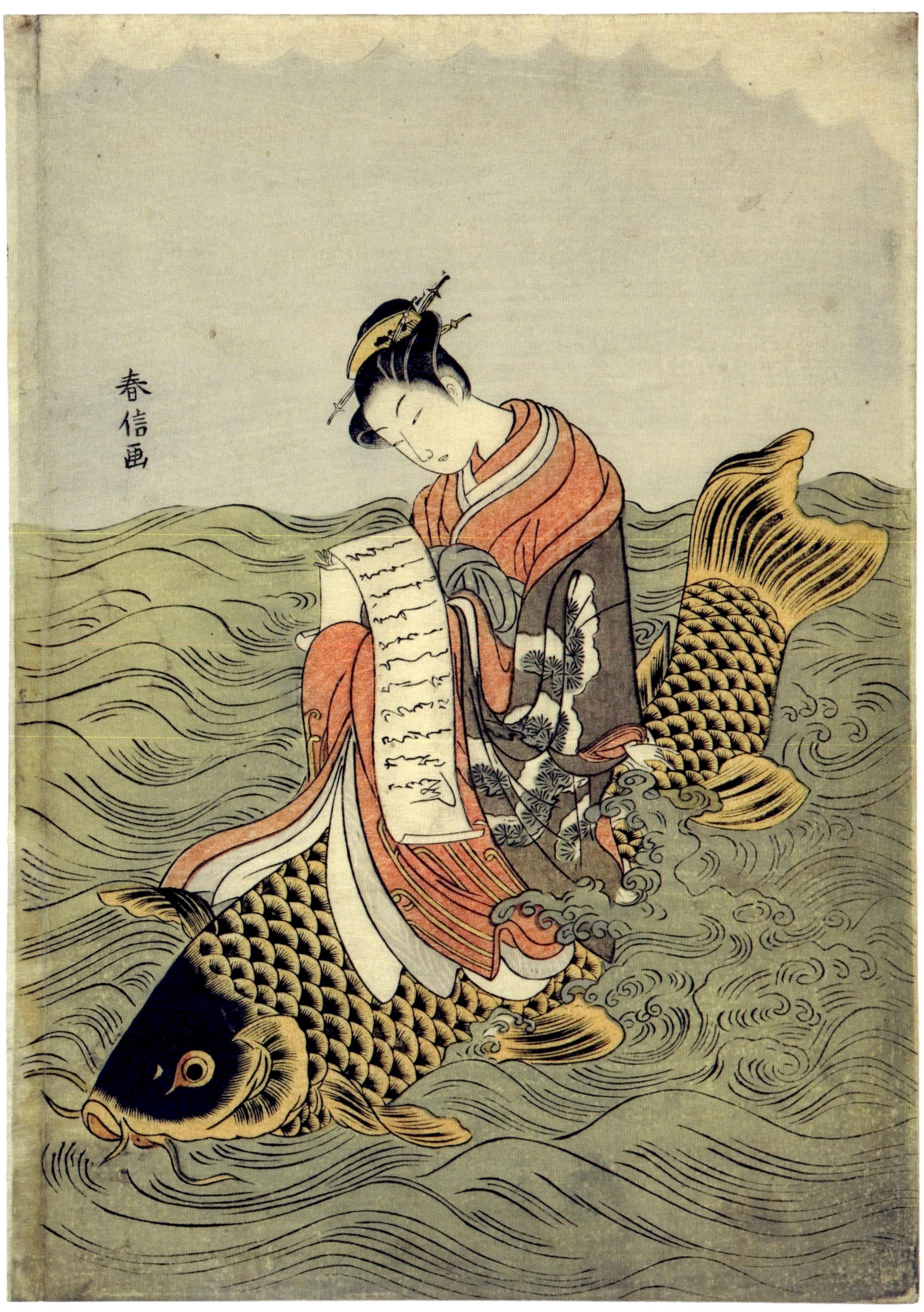

32　Suzuki Harunobu, 1725?–1770, *Mitate* of the Chinese immortal Qin Gao

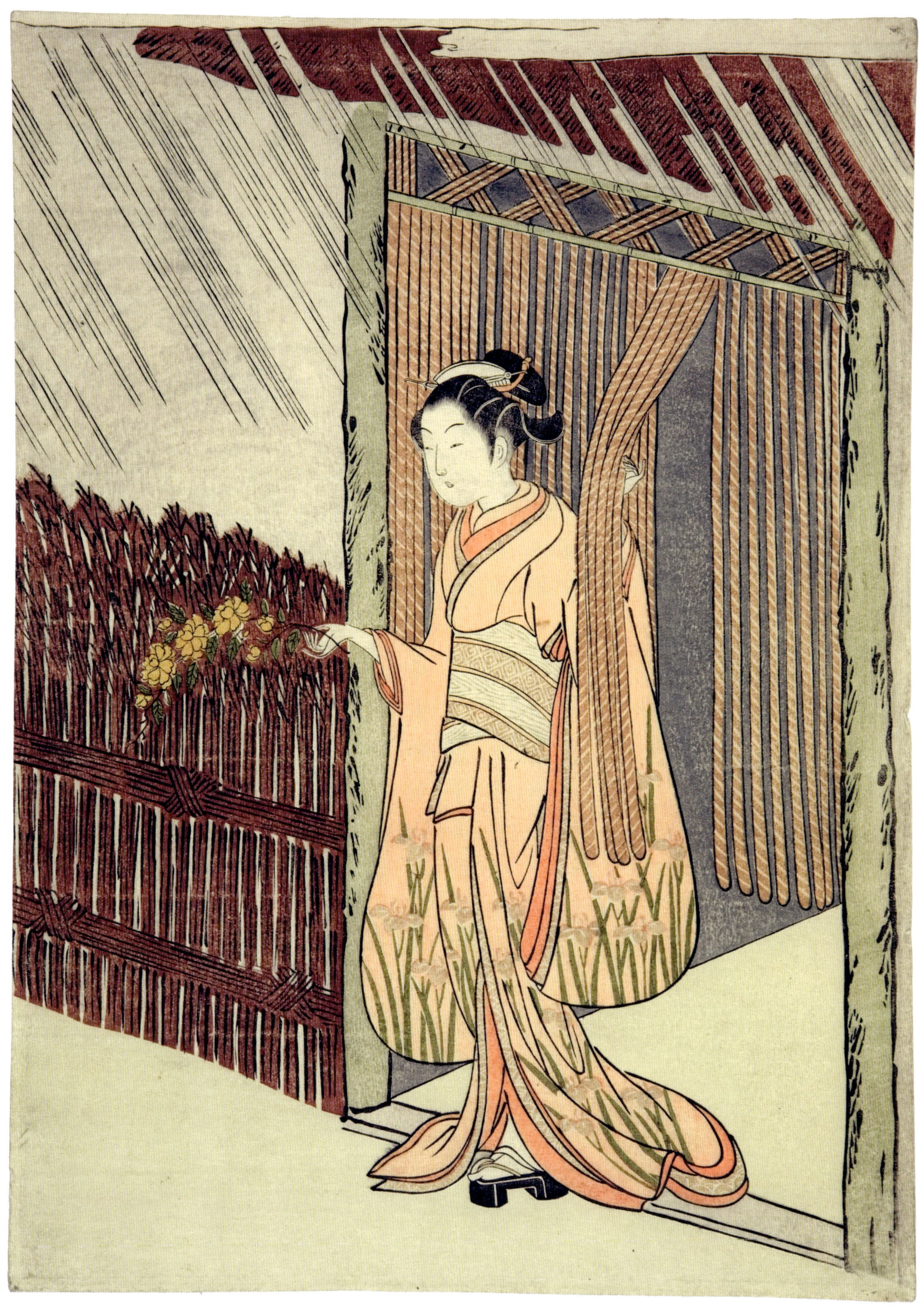

  33 Suzuki Harunobu, 1725?–1770, *Mitate* of the story of Ōta Dōkan

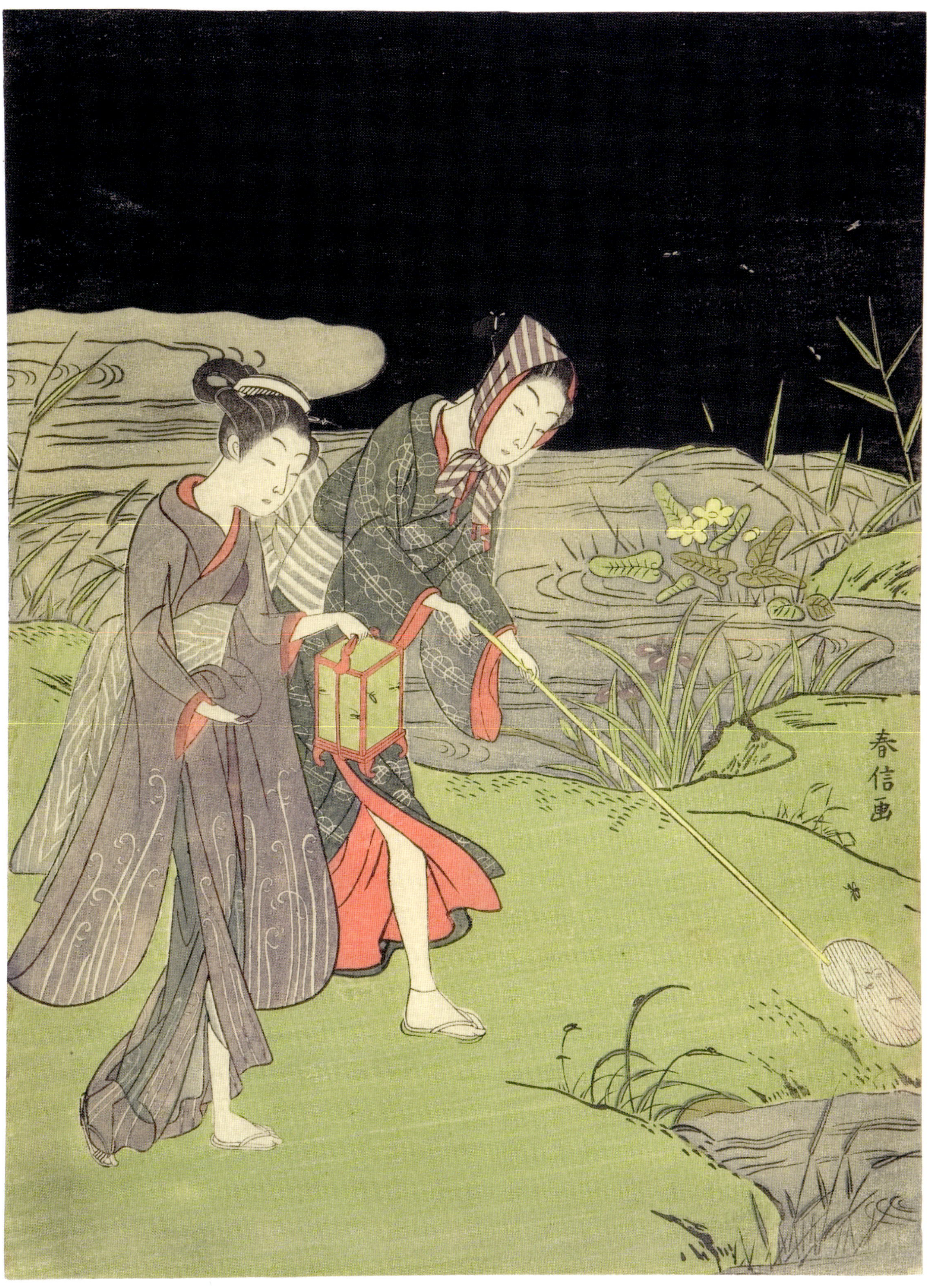

34   Suzuki Harunobu, 1725?–1770, Hunting for fireflies | *57*

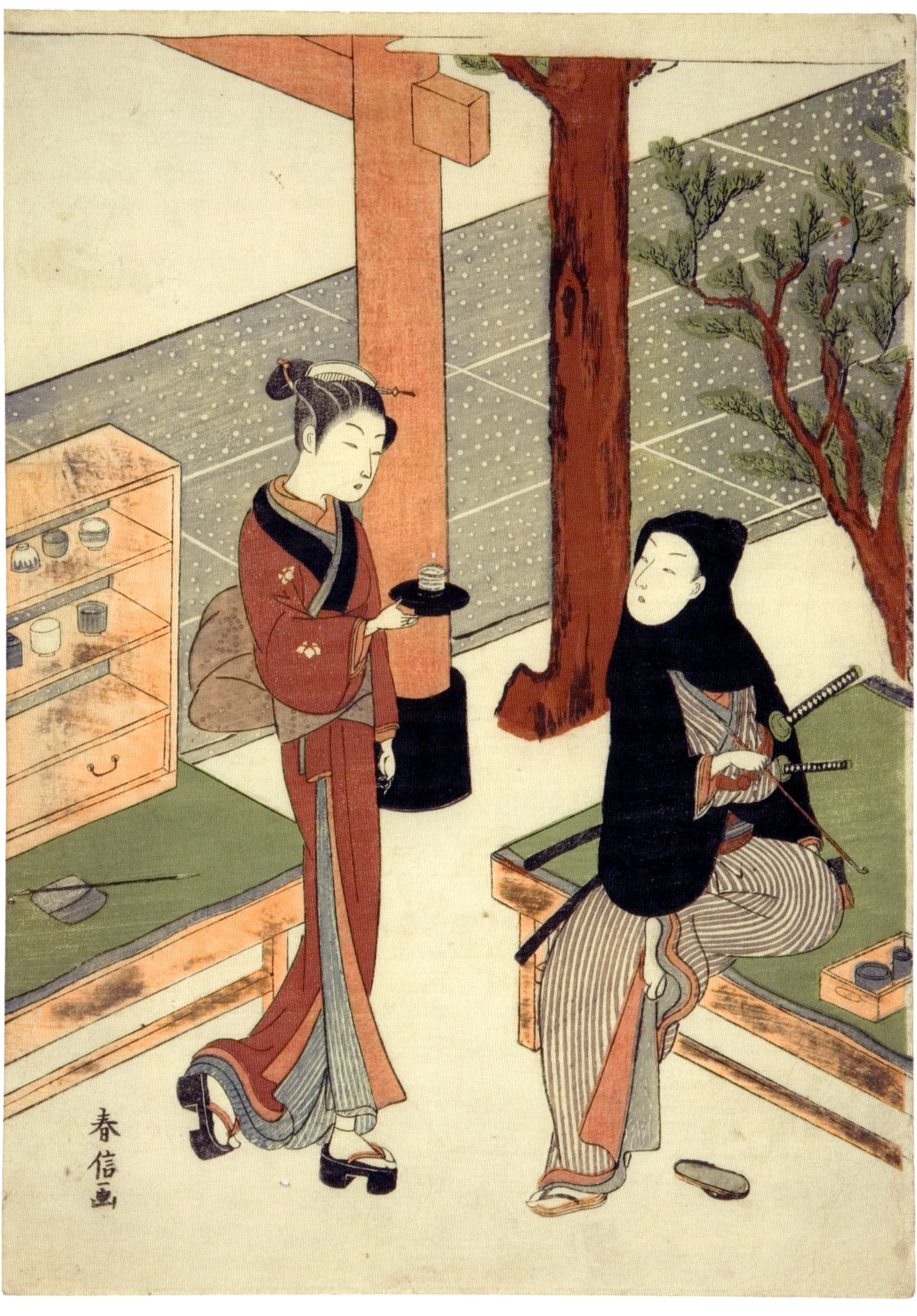

 | 35 Suzuki Harunobu, 1725?–1770, Osen of the Kagiya serving tea in front of Kasamori Shrine

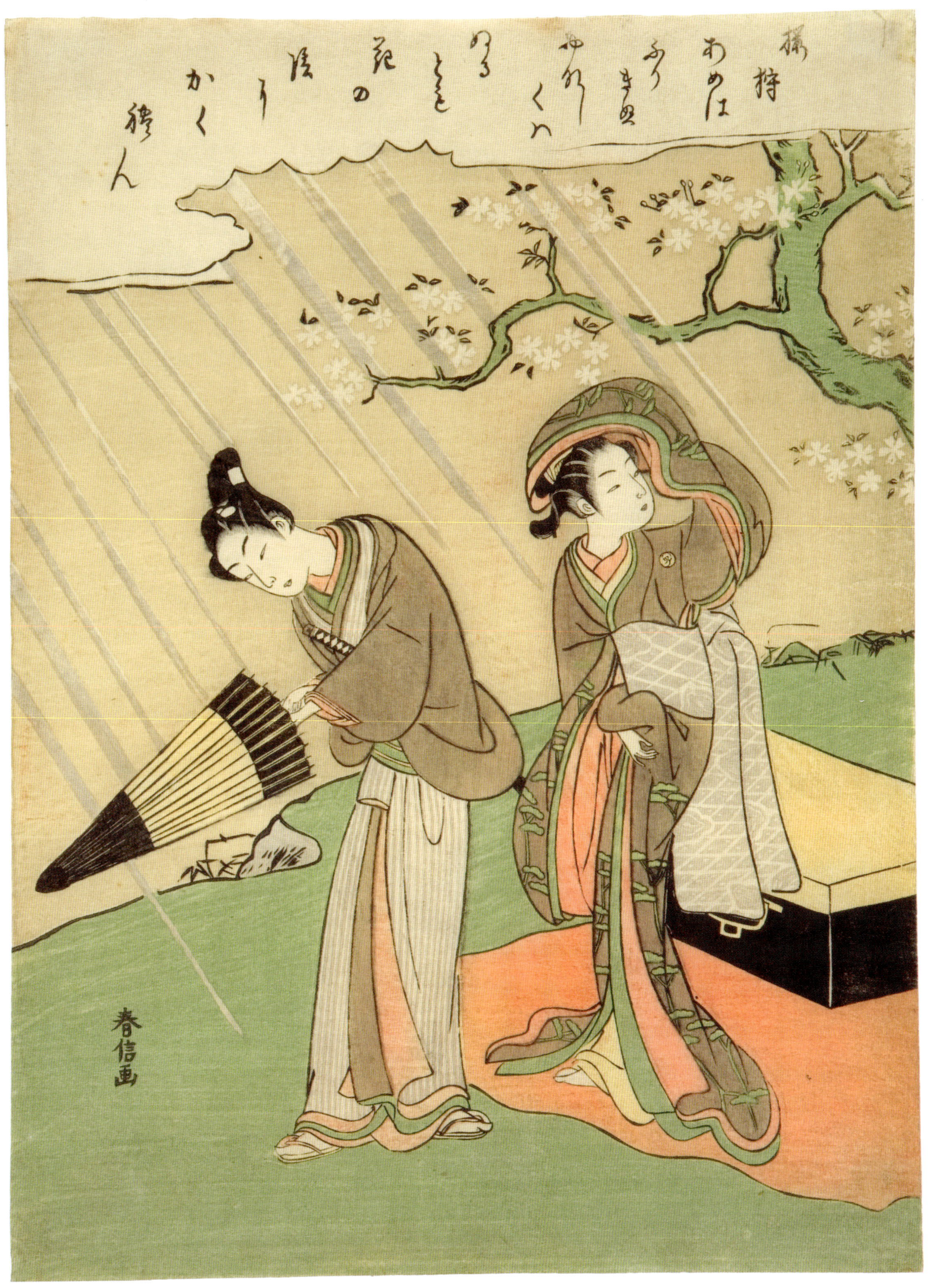

36   Suzuki Harunobu, 1725?–1770, Hunting cherry blossoms | *59*

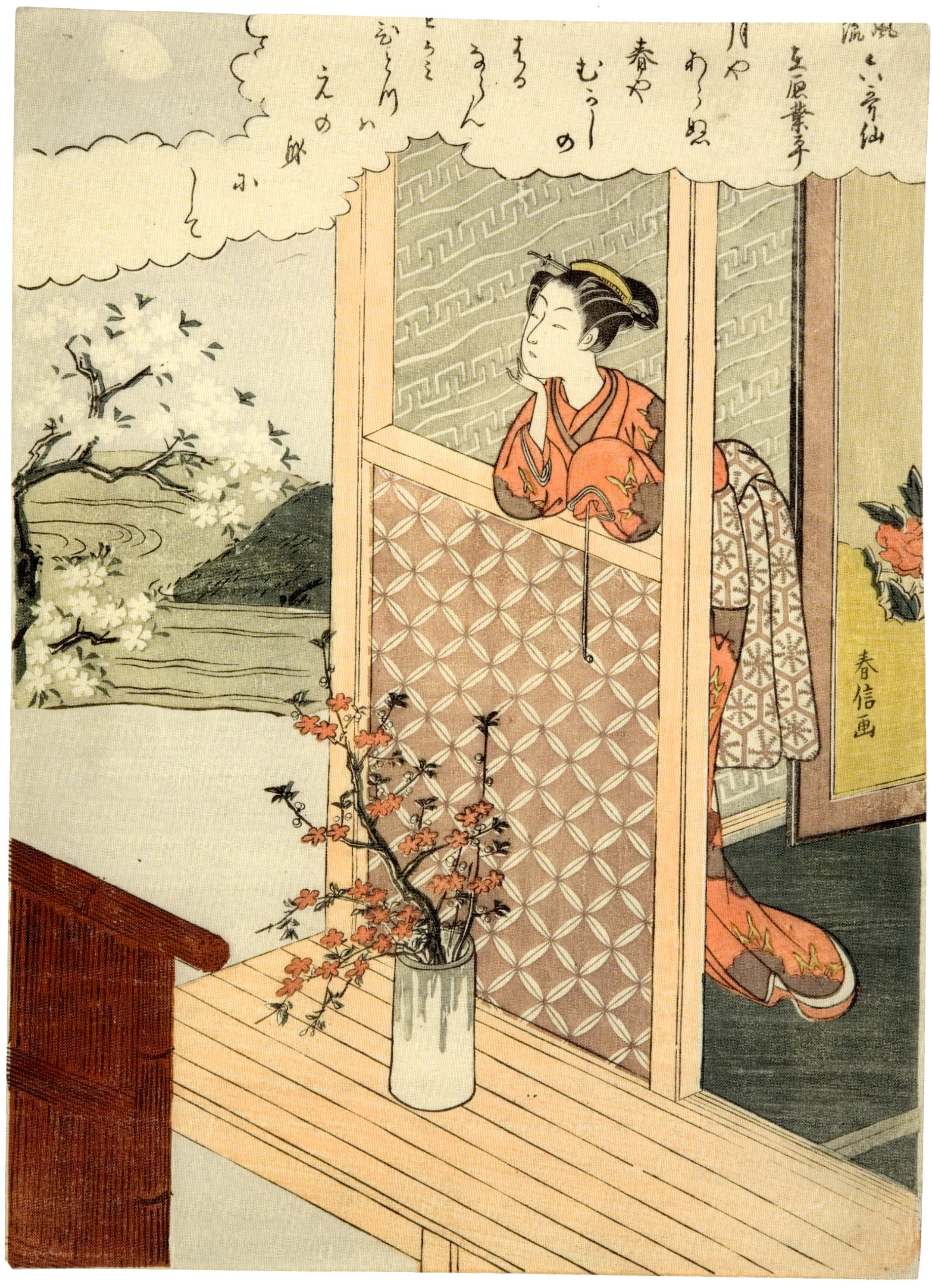

   37   Suzuki Harunobu, 1725?–1770, "Ariwara Narihira," from the series *Fashionable Six Poetic Immortals*

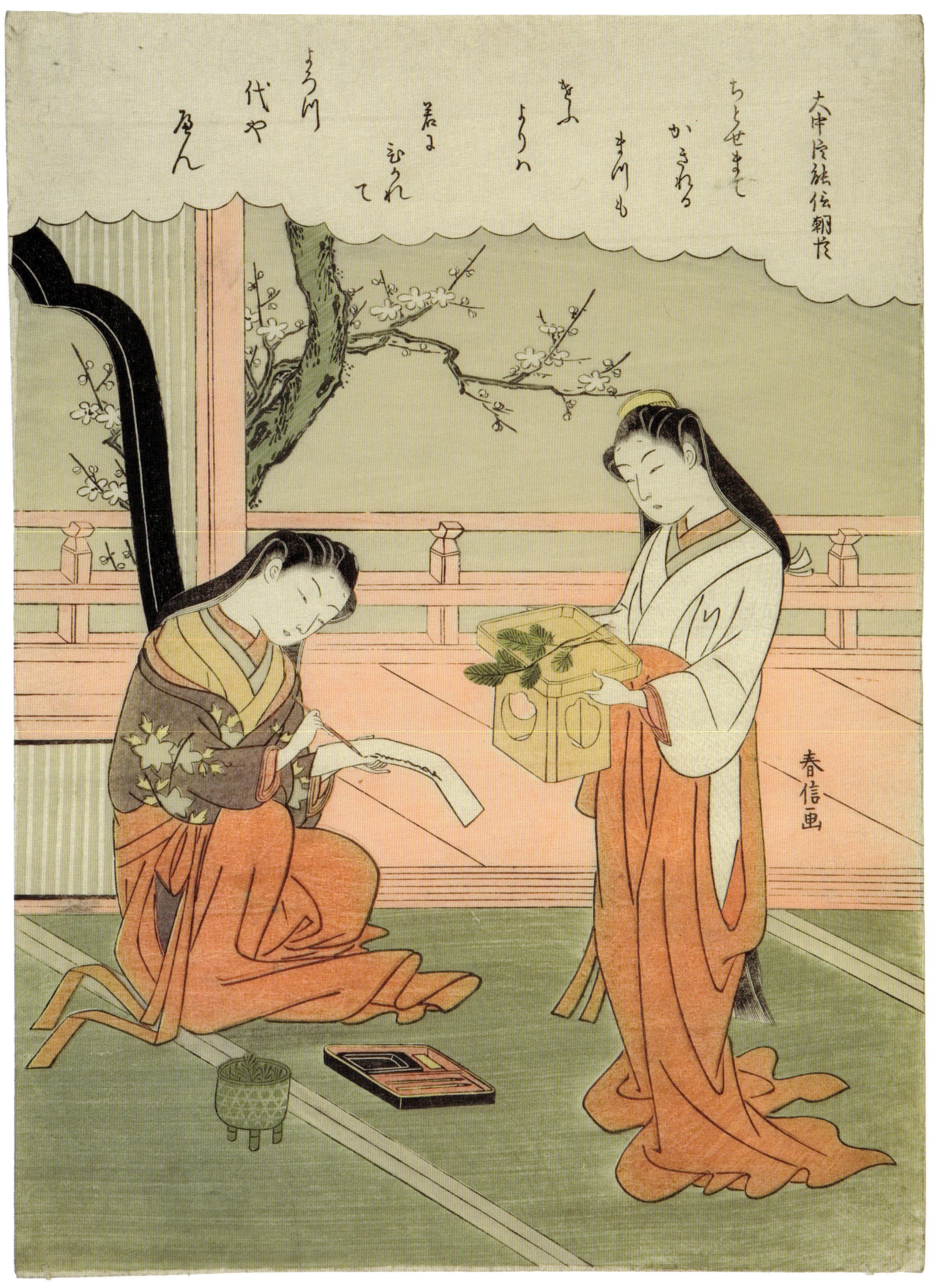

38   Suzuki Harunobu, 1725?–1770, Ōnakatomi Yoshinobu Ason, from an untitled series of Thirty-six Poetic Immortals

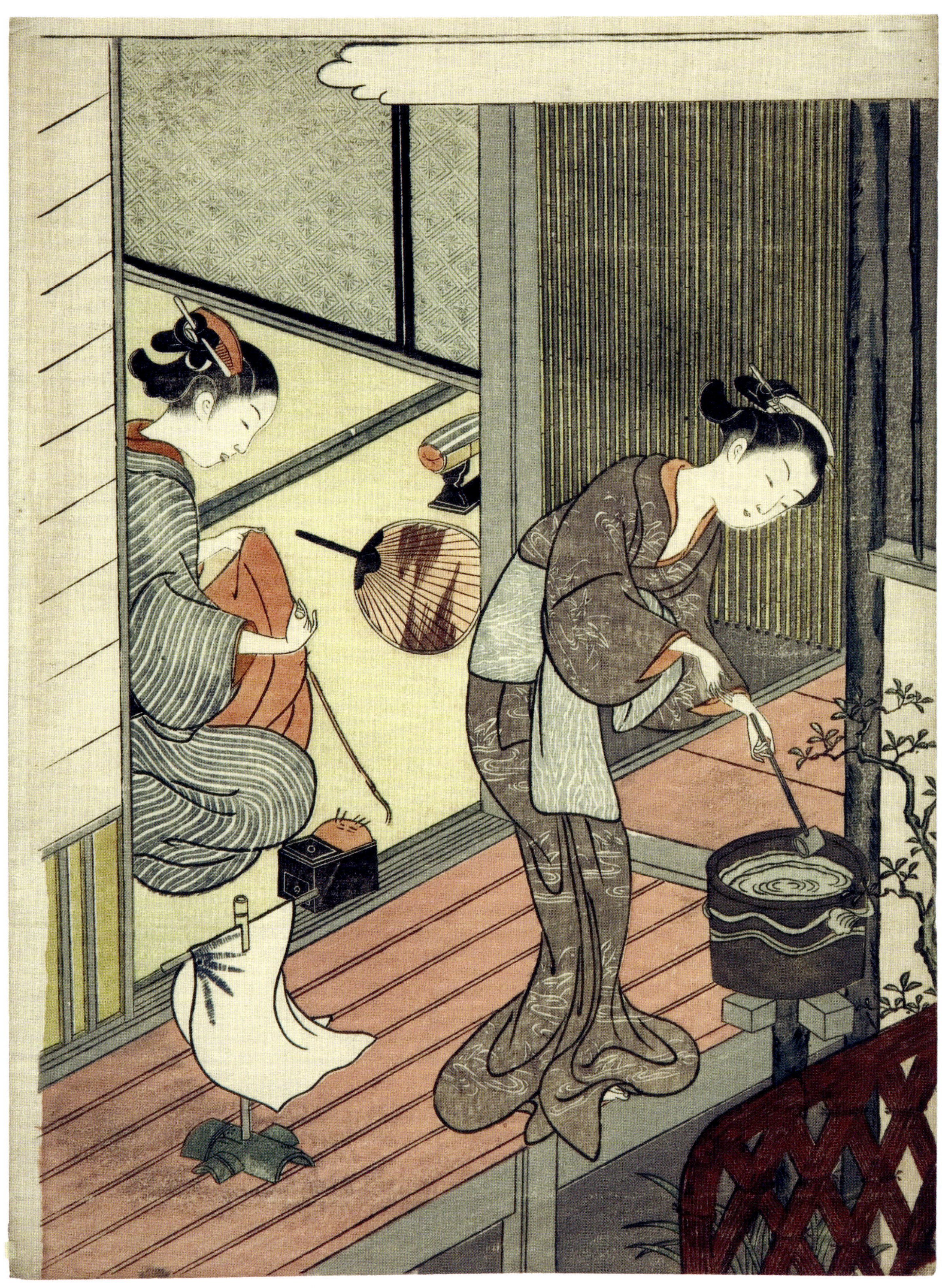

39 Suzuki Harunobu, 1725?–1770, "Returning Sails of the Towel Rack," from the series *Eight Parlor Views*

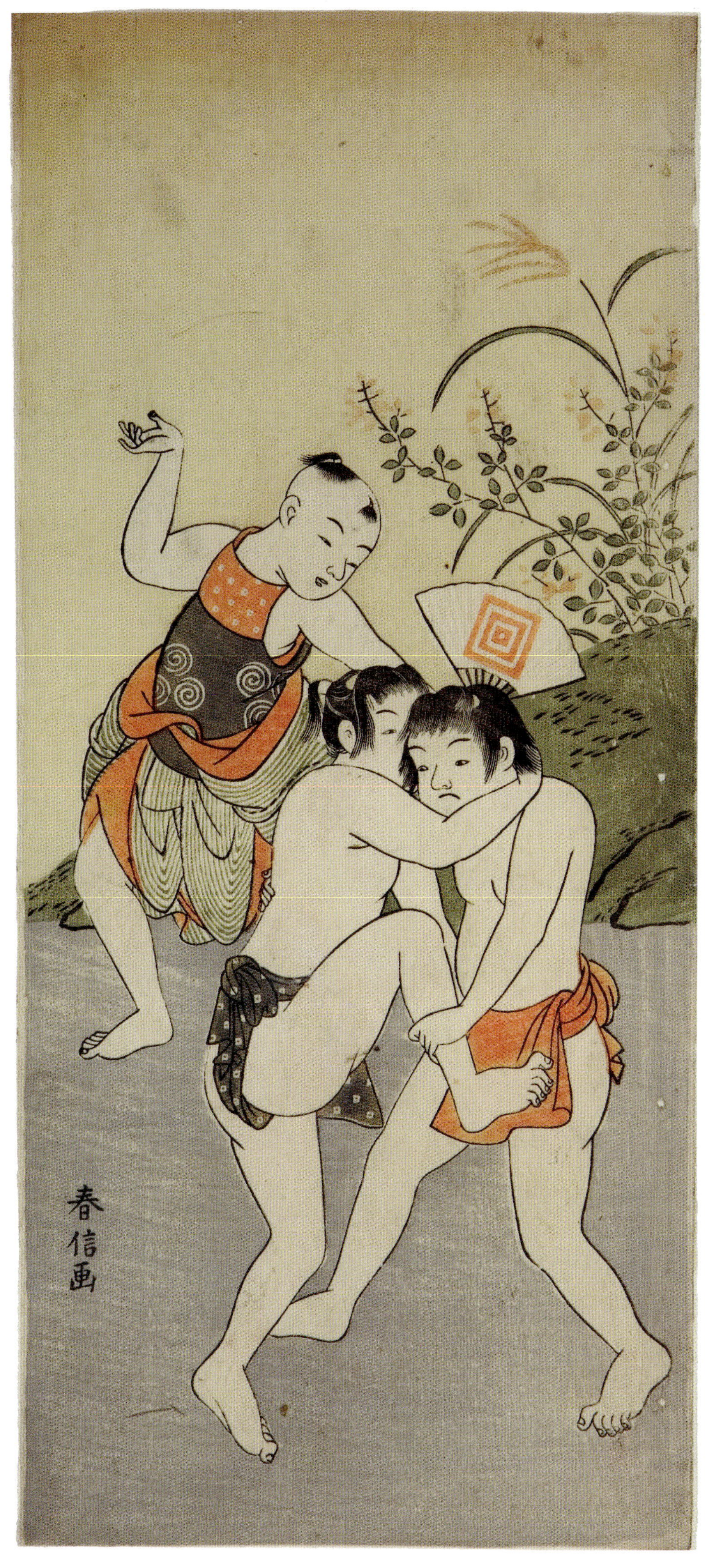

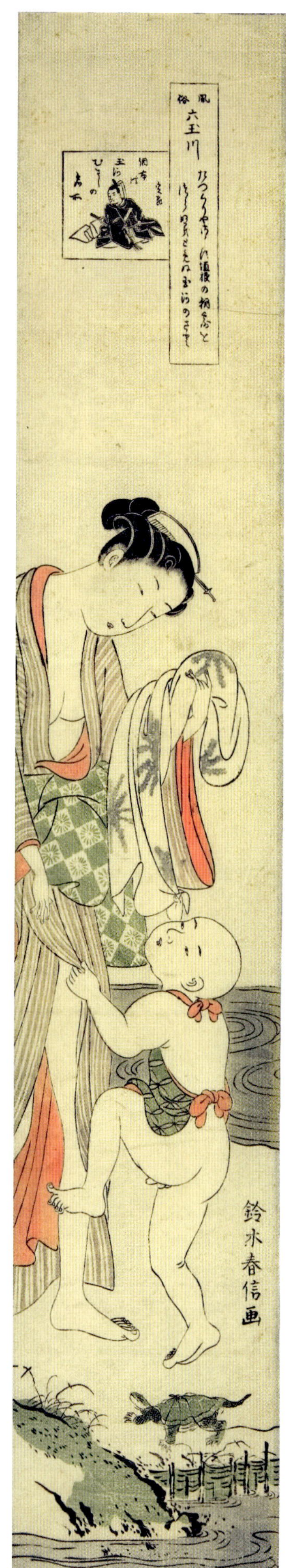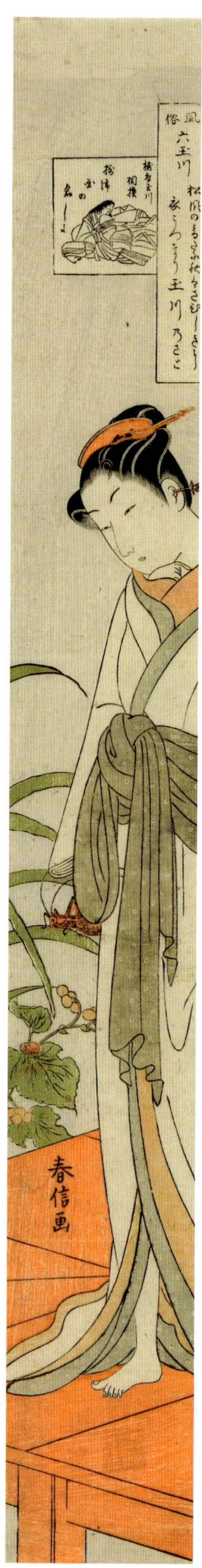

41 (LEFT)   Suzuki Harunobu, 1725?–1770, "Chōfu Jewel River, a Famous Place in Musashi Province," from the series *Six Jewel Rivers in Popular Customs*;

42 (RIGHT)   Suzuki Harunobu, 1725?–1770, "The Cloth-Fulling Jewel River, a Famous Place in Settsu Province," from the series *Six Jewel Rivers in Popular Customs*

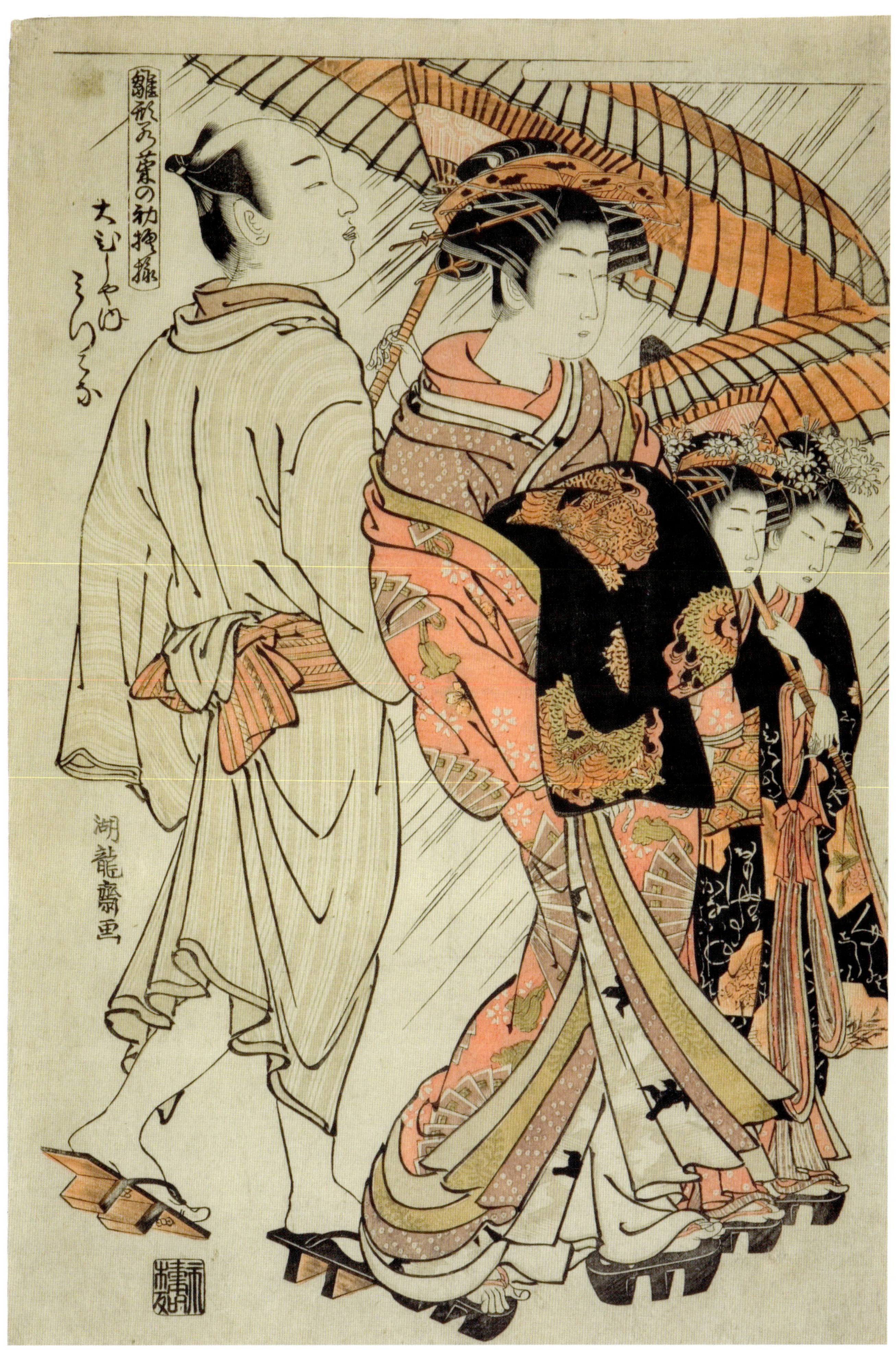

43   Isoda Koryūsai, active 1764–1788, "Mitsuhana of the Ōhishiya," from the series *Models for Fashion: New Year Designs as Fresh as Young Leaves*

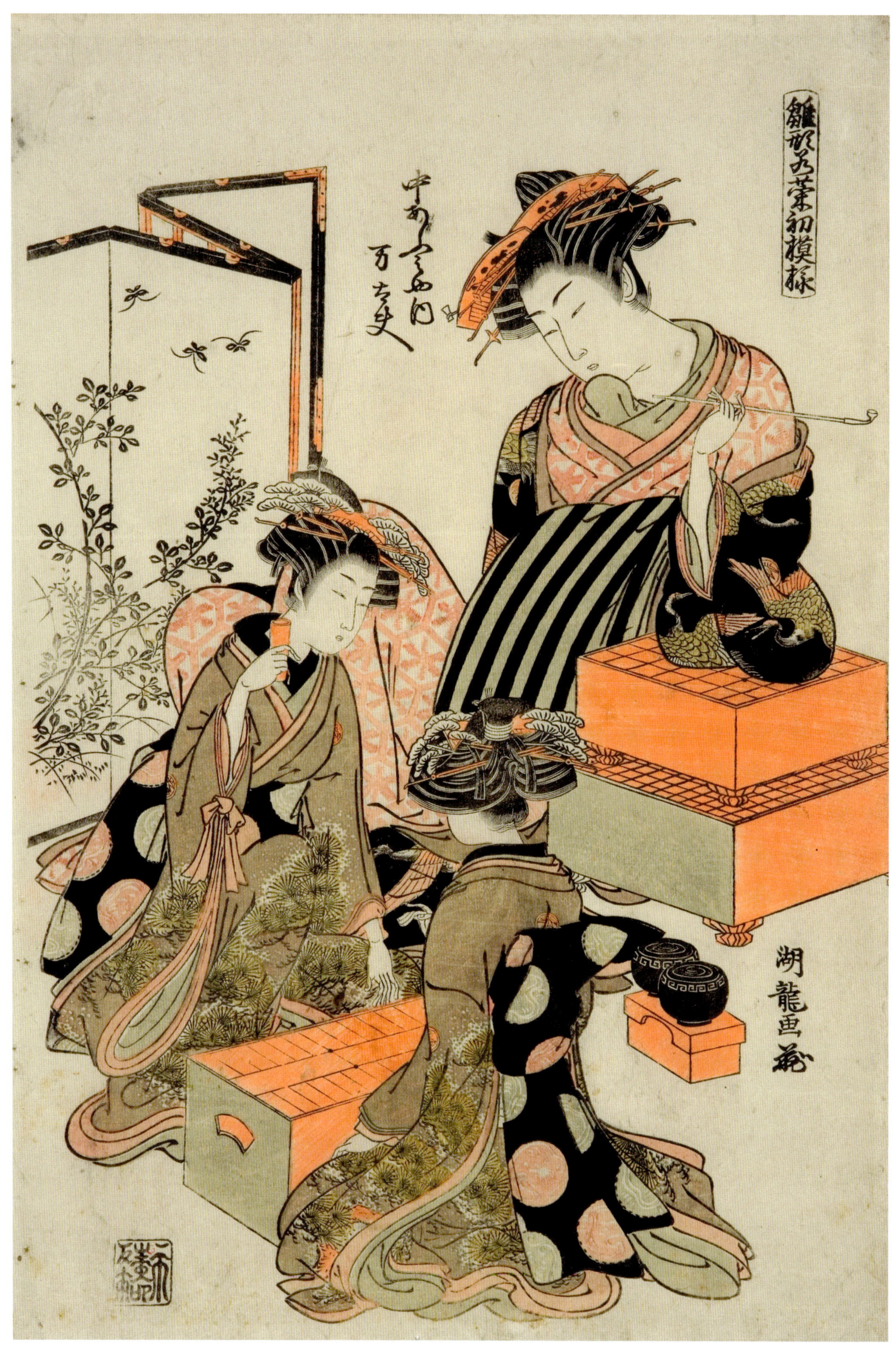

44   Isoda Koryūsai, active 1764–1788, "Mandayū of the Nakaōmiya," from the scrics *Models for Fashion: New Year Designs as Fresh as Young Leaves*

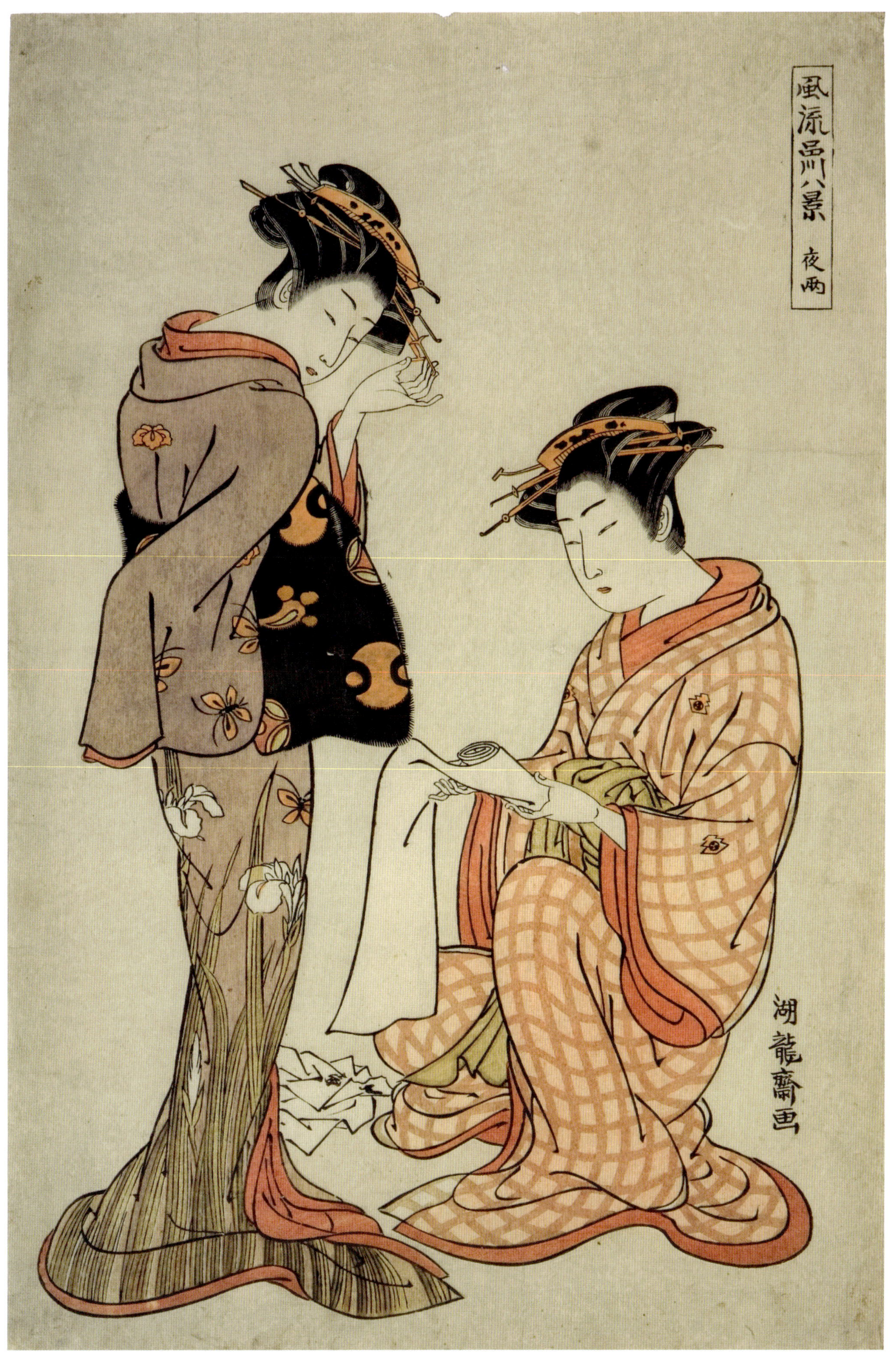

45　Isoda Koryūsai, active 1764–1788, "Night Rain," from the series *Fashionable Eight Views of Shinagawa*

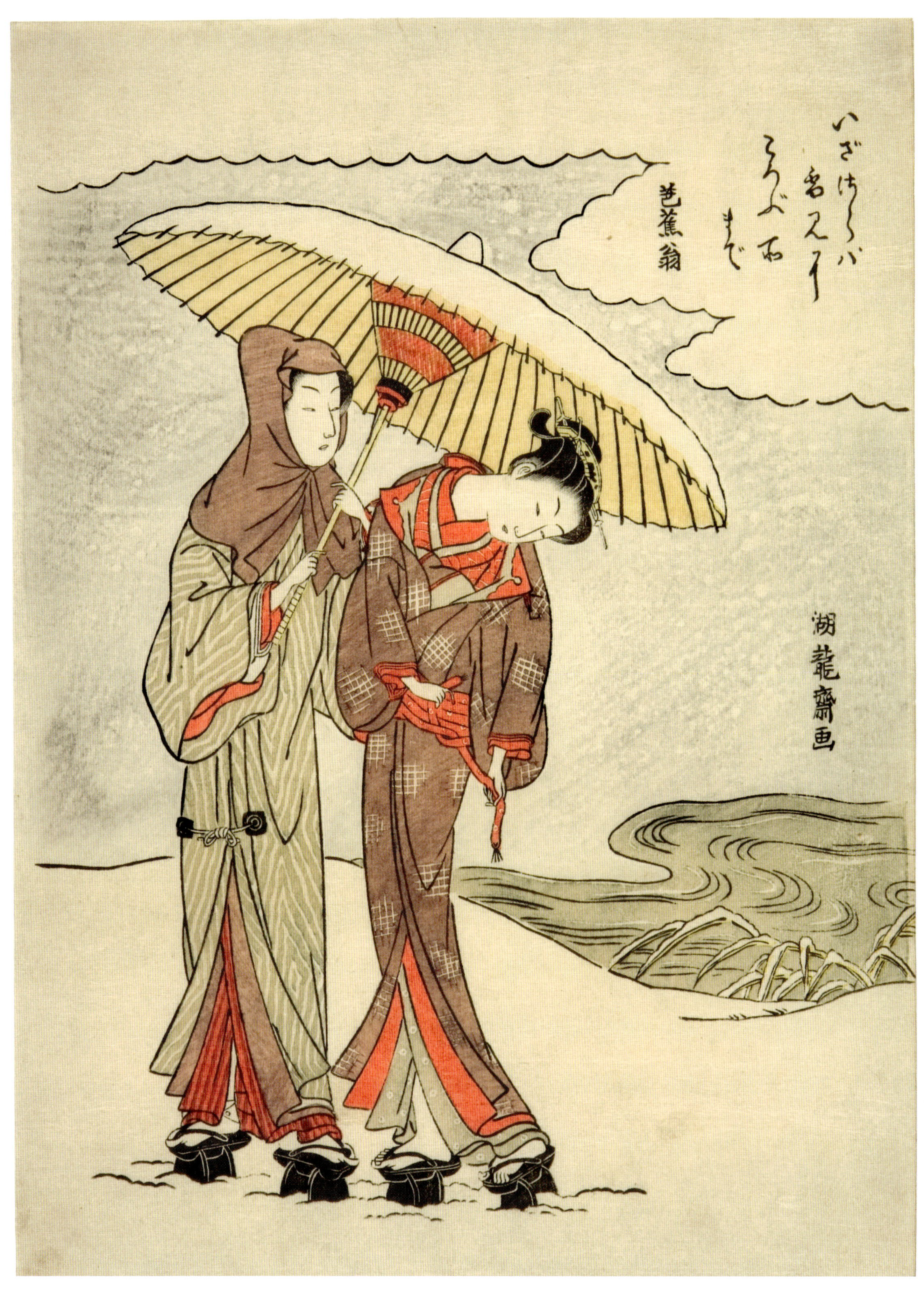

46   Isoda Koryūsai, active 1764–1788, Lovers sharing an umbrella, with poem by Bashō, from an untitled
      series with haiku poems

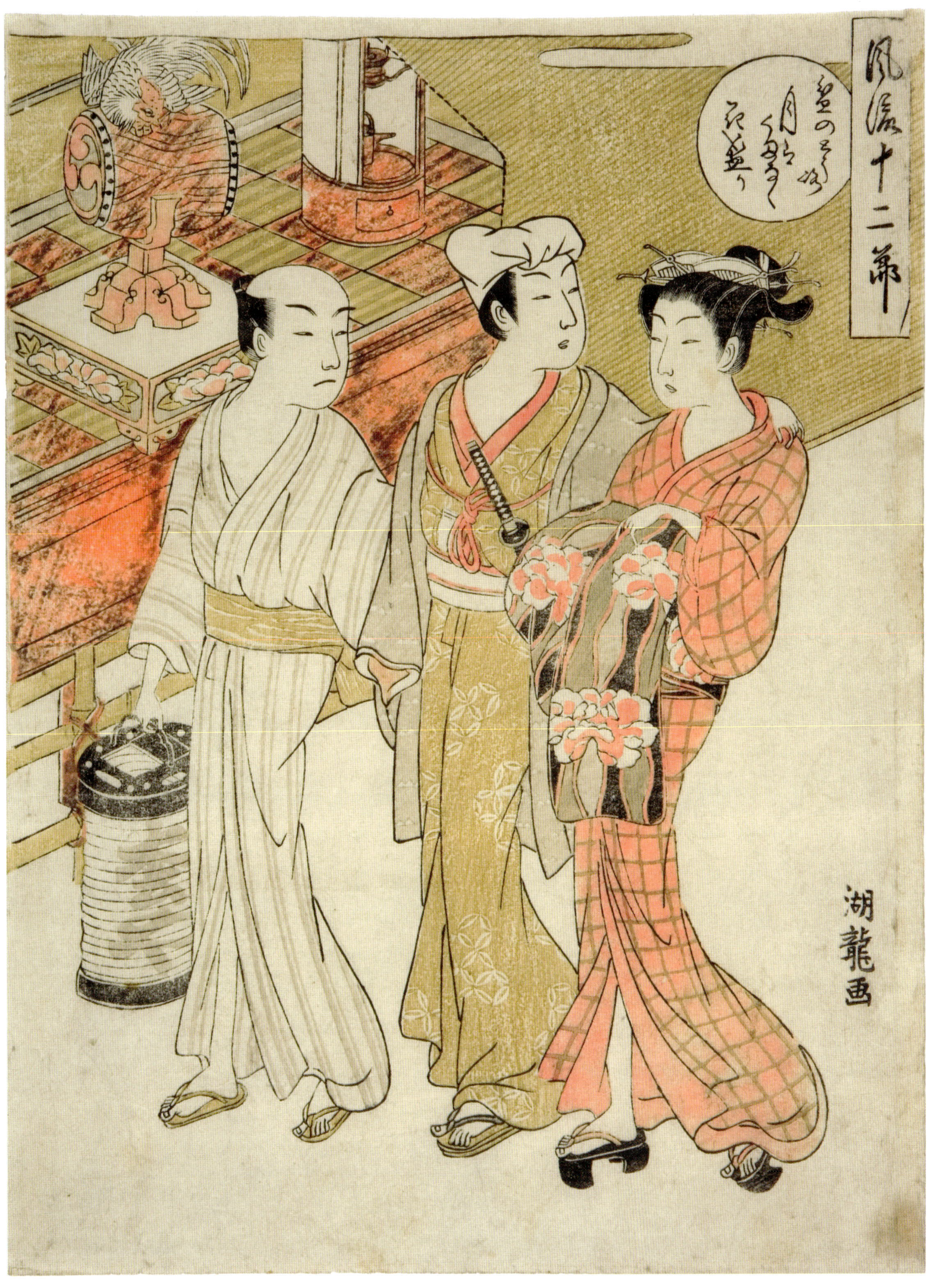

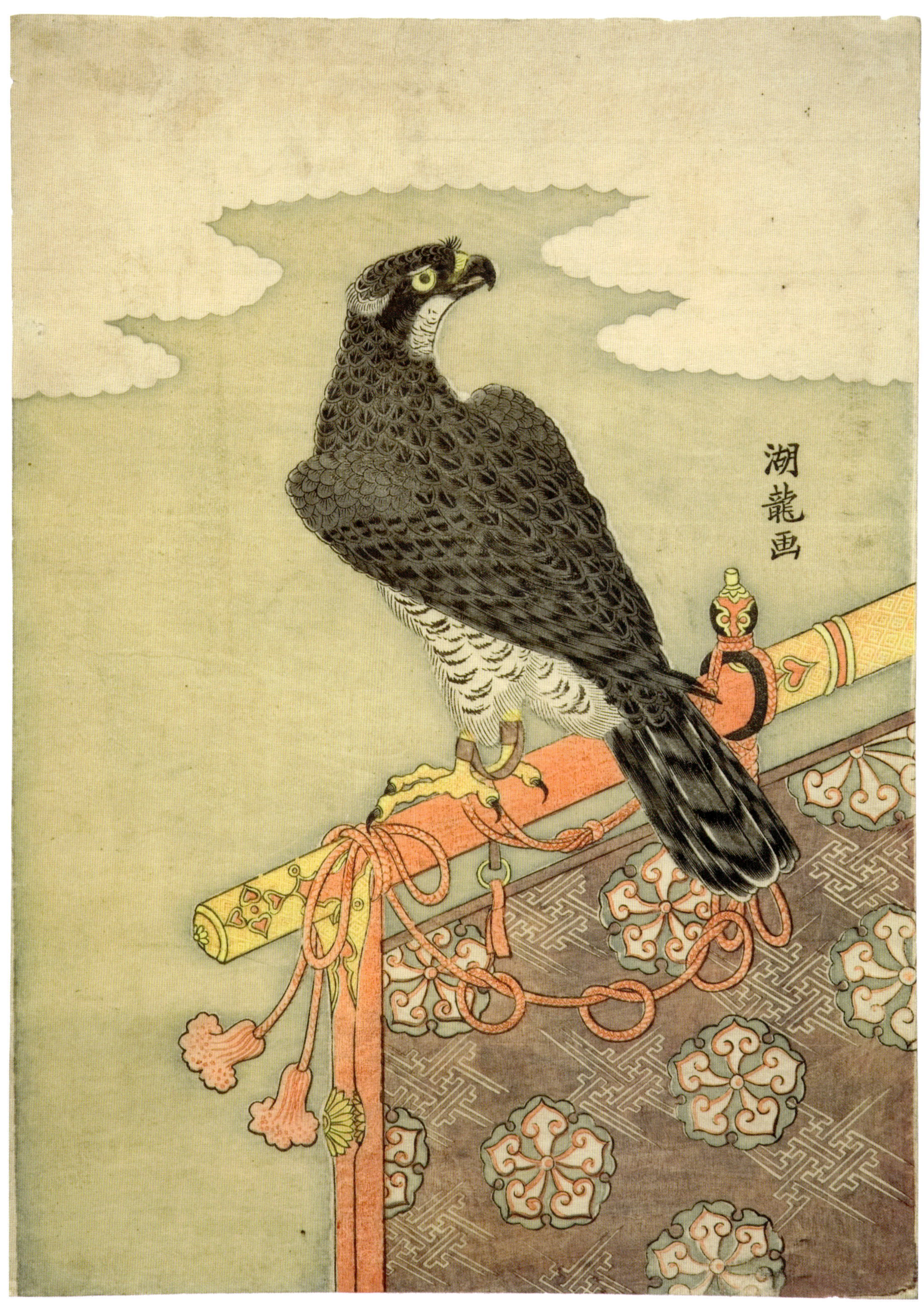

   48   Isoda Koryūsai, active 1764–1788, Falcon on its perch

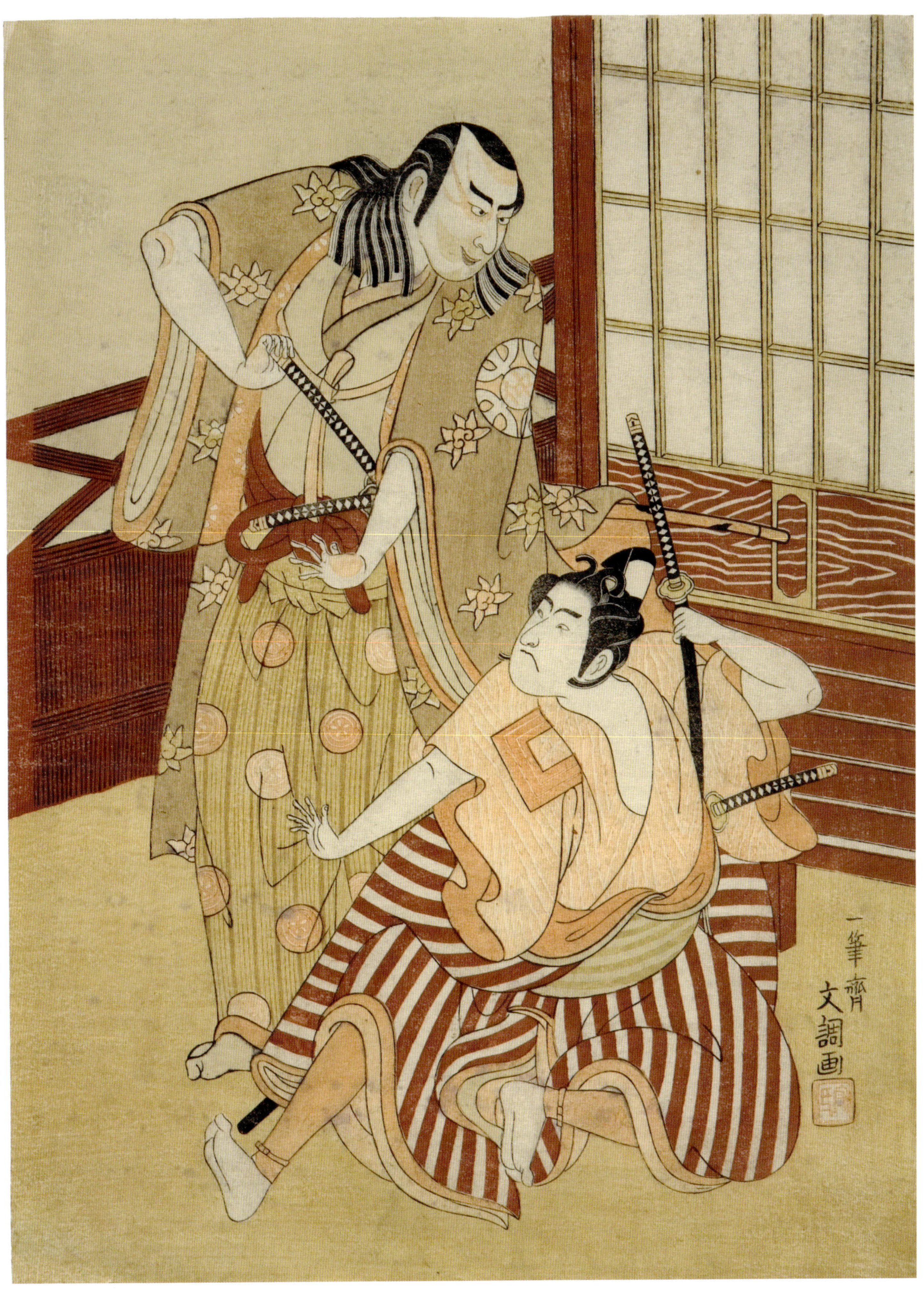

49   Ippitsusai Bunchō, active 1765–1792, The actors Ichikawa Benzō I as Tsunewakamaru and
Nakamura Nakazō I as the ghost of Noritsune

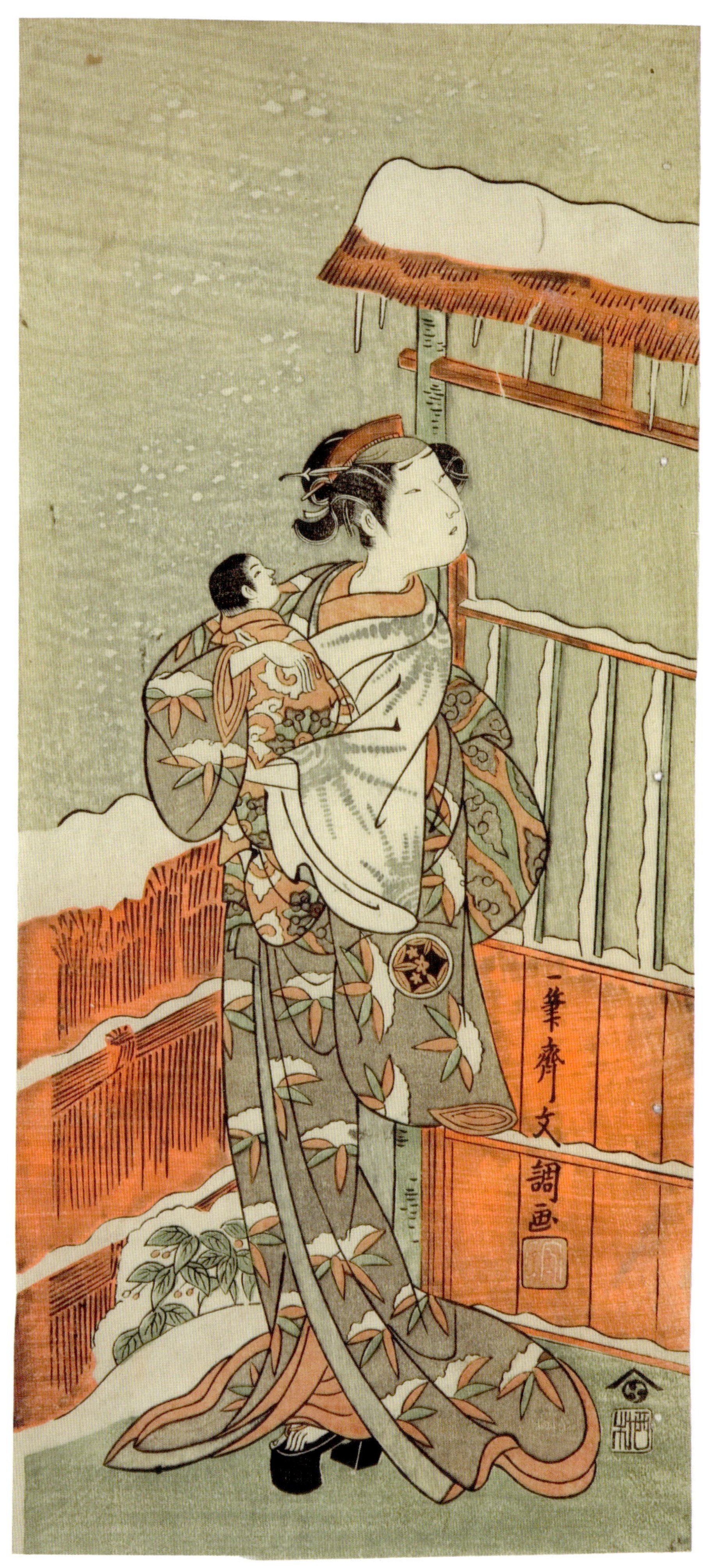

   50   Ippitsusai Bunchō, active 1765–1792, The actor Yamashita Kinsaku II as the wife of Itō Kurō

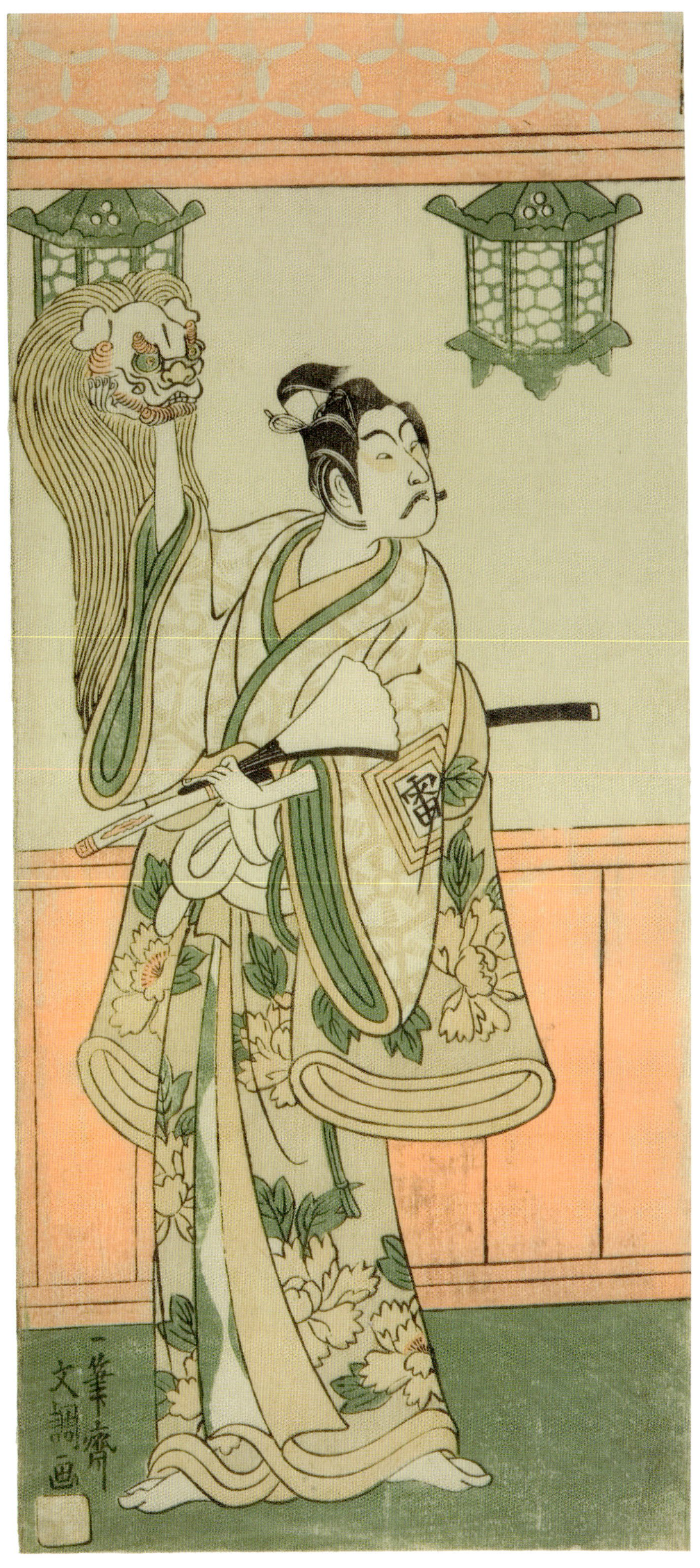

51 Ippitsusai Bunchō, active 1765–1792, The actor Ichikawa Raizō II performing the Shakkyō Lion Dance

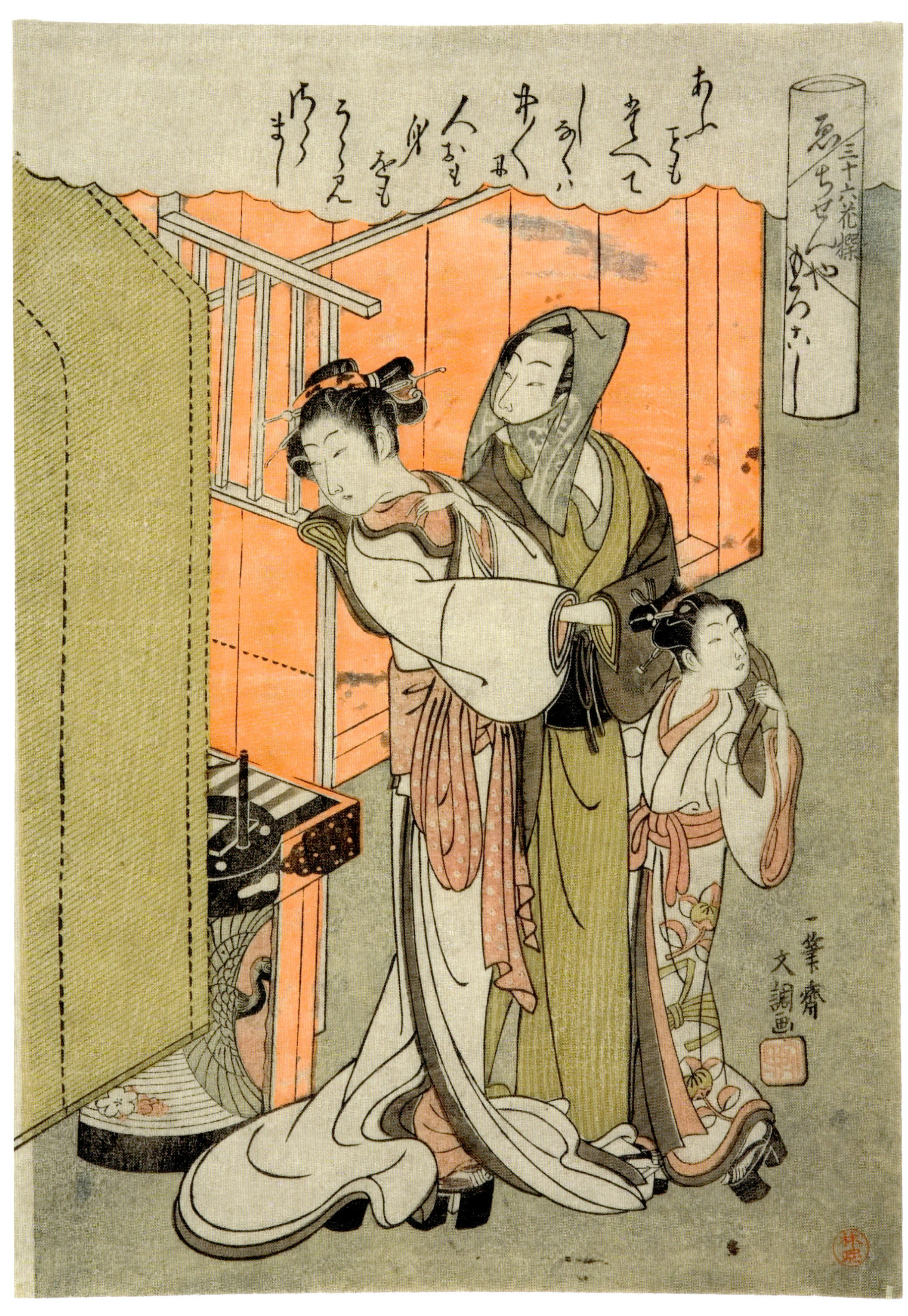

52   Ippitsusai Bunchō, active 1765–1792, "Morokoshi of the Echizenya," from the series *The Thirty-six Poetic Immortals as Selected Flowers*

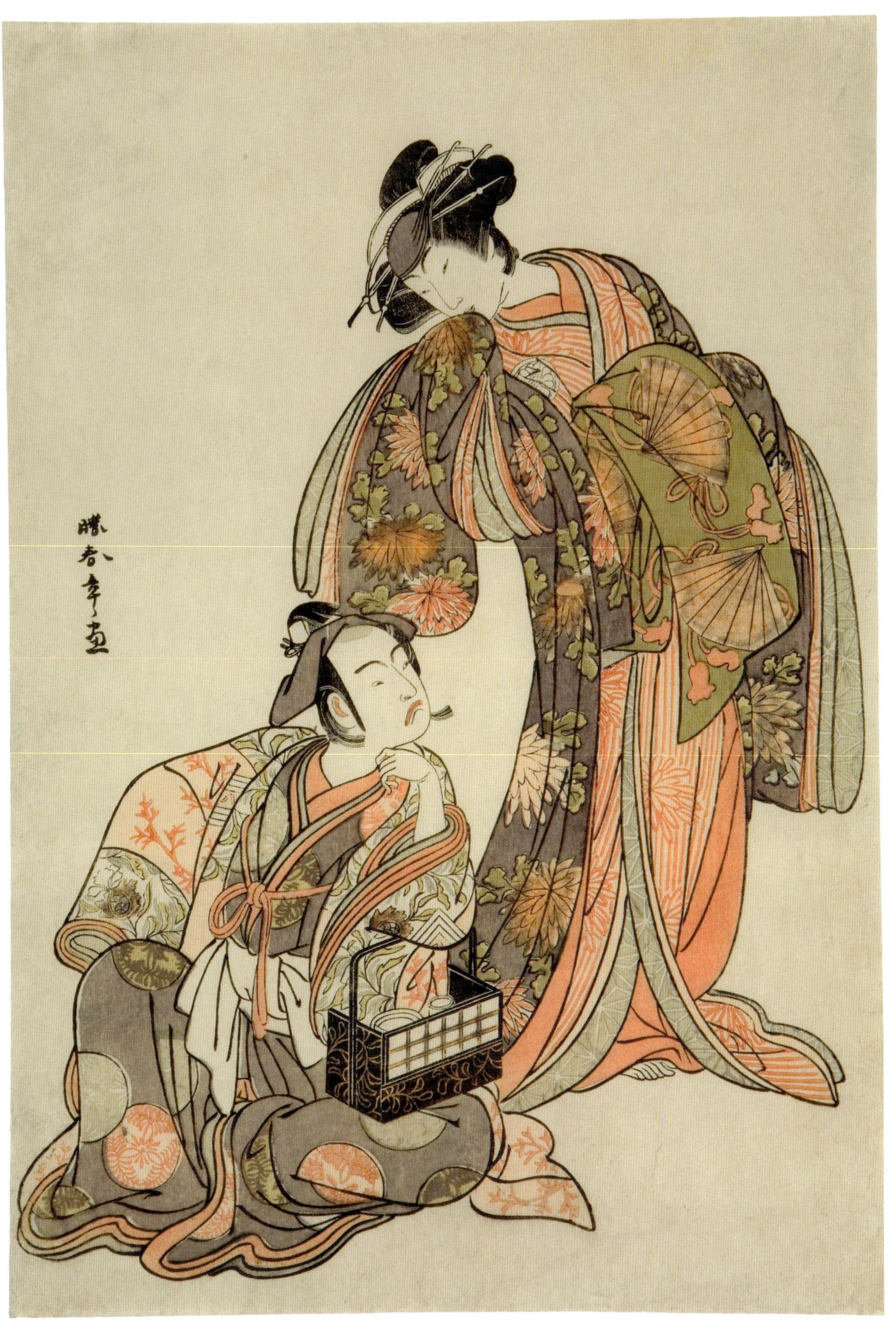

53 Katsukawa Shunshō, 1726–1792, The actors Segawa Kikunojō III as the courtesan
Takamura and Ichikawa Yaozō II as Shii Shōshō

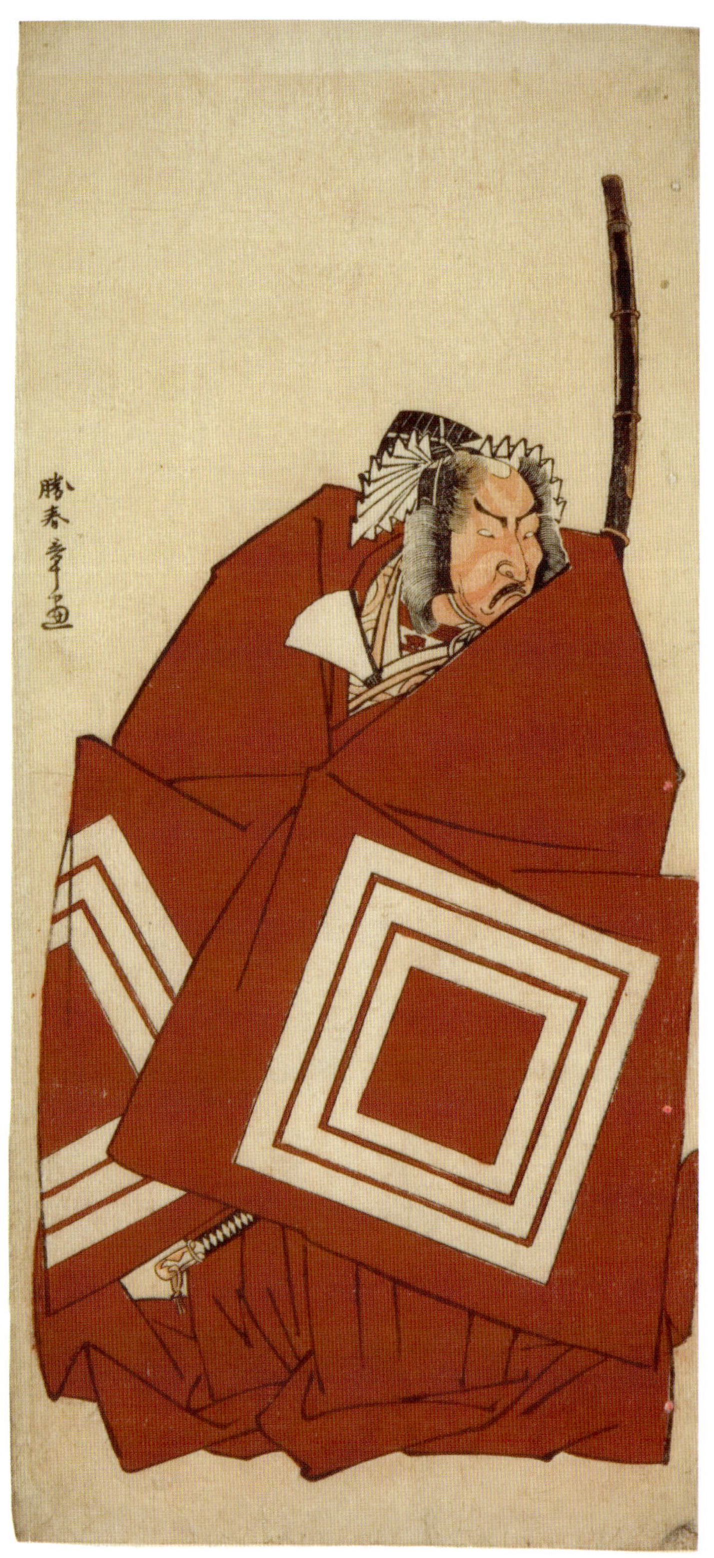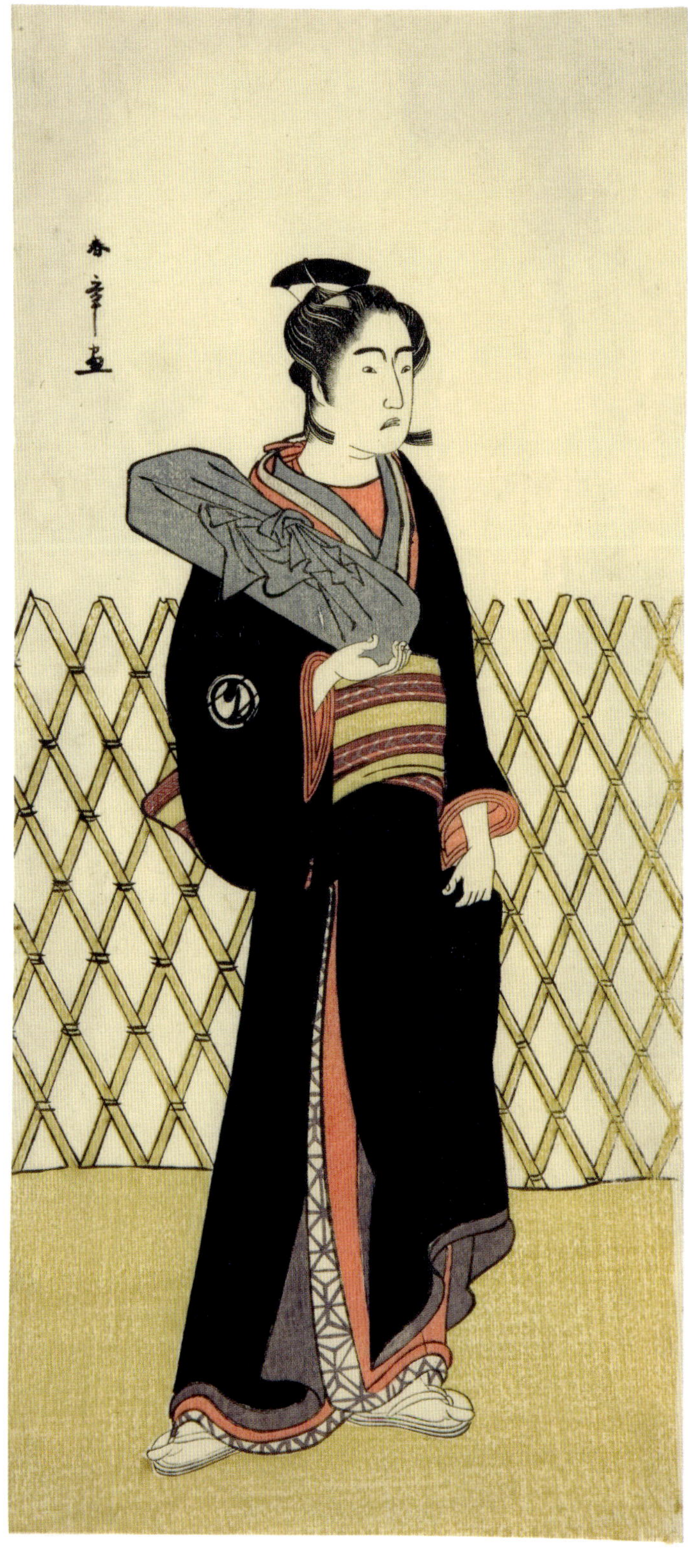

54 (LEFT)   Katsukawa Shunshō, 1726–1792, The actor Ichikawa Danzō IV in a Shibaraku role;
55 (RIGHT)   Katsukawa Shunshō, 1726–1792, The actor Sawamura Sōjūrō III as the hairdresser Jirōkichi

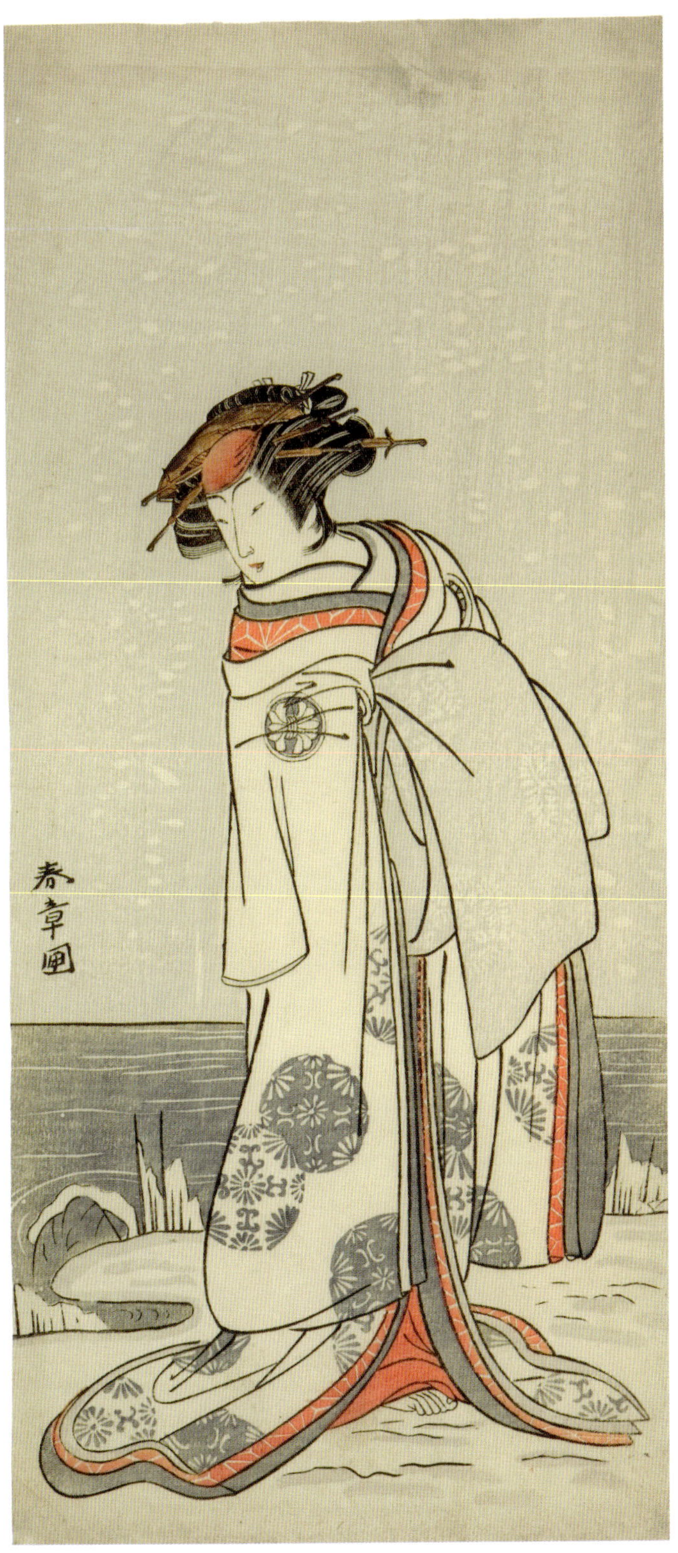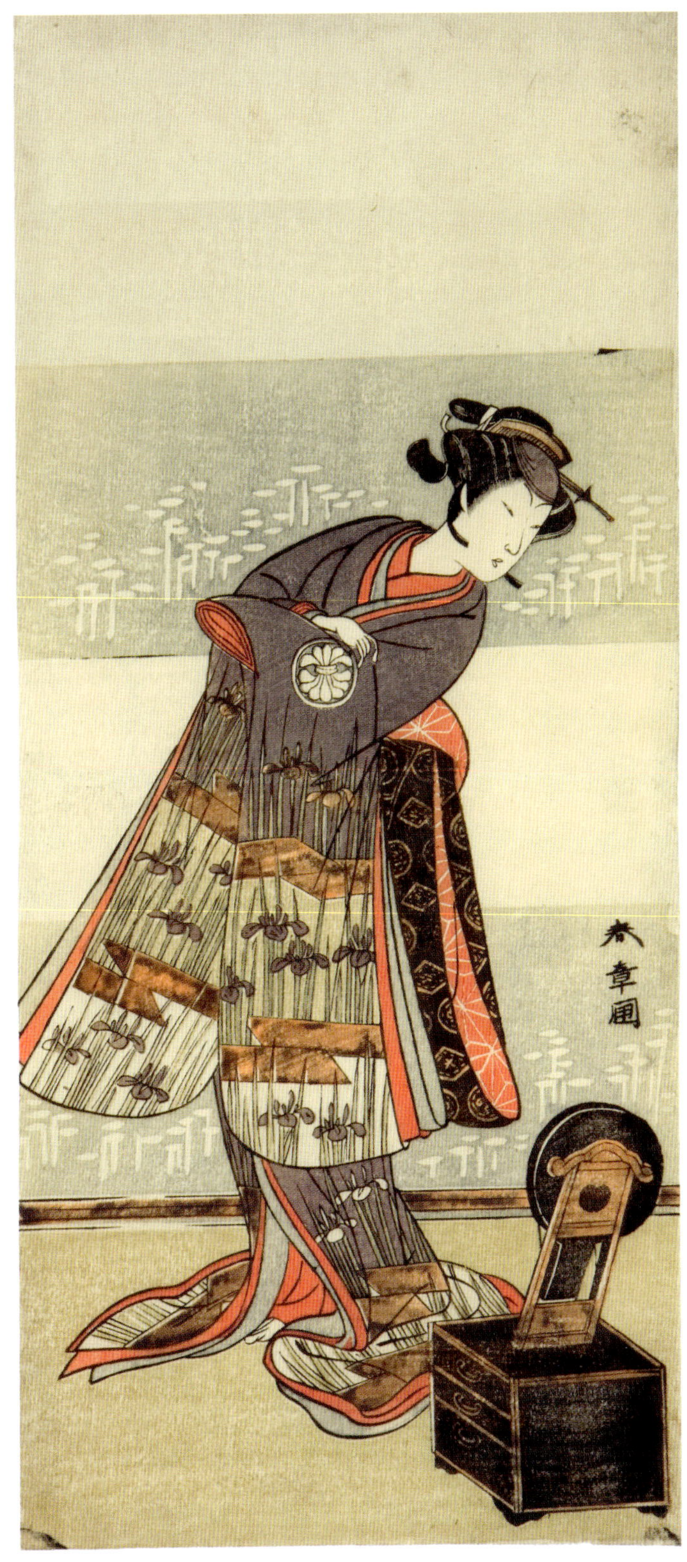

56 (LEFT)   Katsukawa Shunshō, 1726–1792, The actor Segawa Kikunojō III as the Heron Maiden;
57 (RIGHT)   Katsukawa Shunshō, 1726–1792, The actor Segawa Kikunojō III in a female role, looking in a mirror

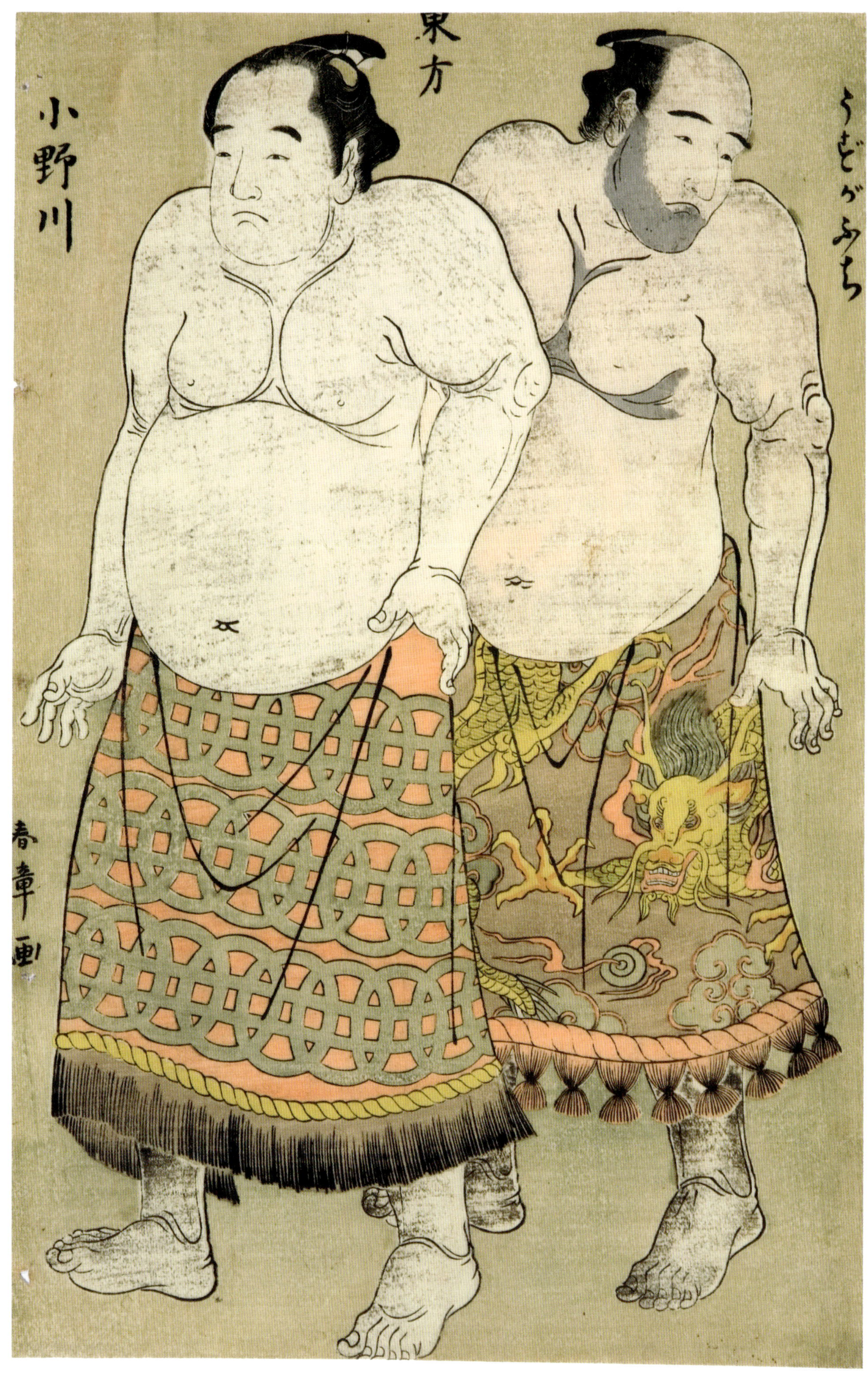

    58   Katsukawa Shunshō, 1726–1792, [Sumo Wrestlers of the] Eastern Section, Uzugafuchi and Onogawa

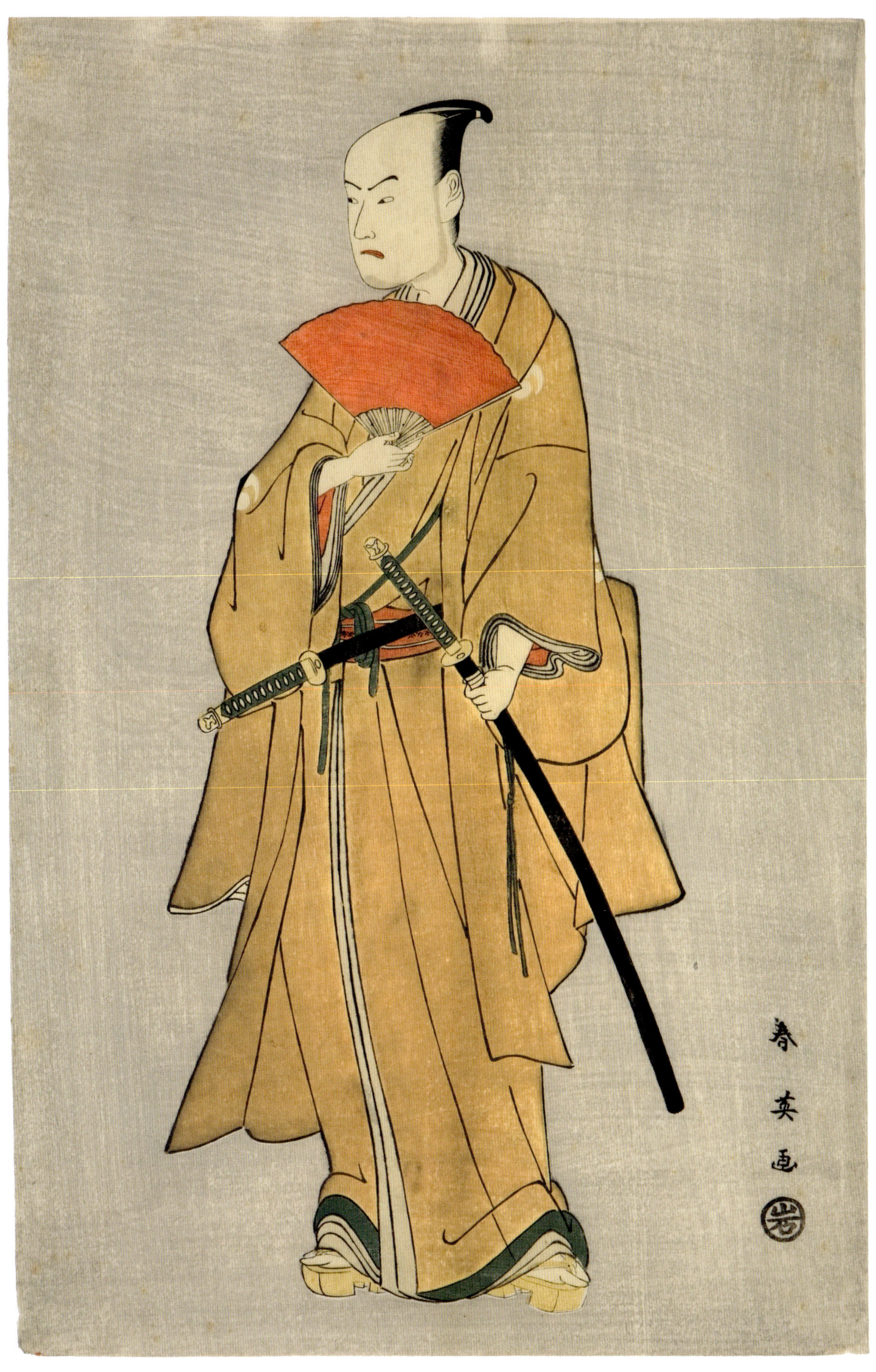

59 Katsukawa Shun'ei, 1762–1819, The actor Bandō Hikosaburō III as Ōboshi Yuranosuke

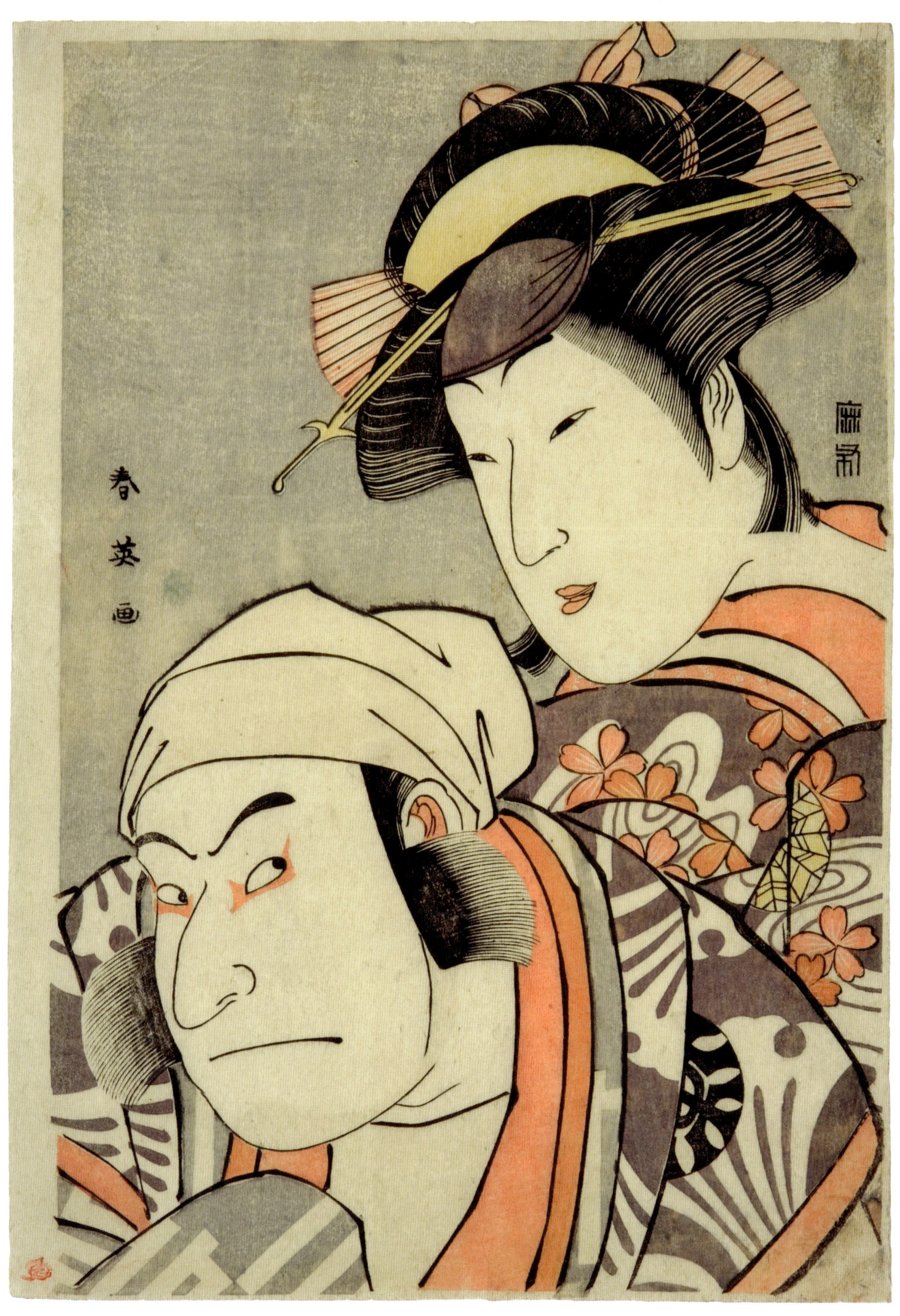

60   Katsukawa Shun'ei, 1762–1819, The actors Nakamura Nakazō II as Aramaki Mimishirō and Nakamura
Noshio II as Konohana, daughter of Ki Tsurayuki

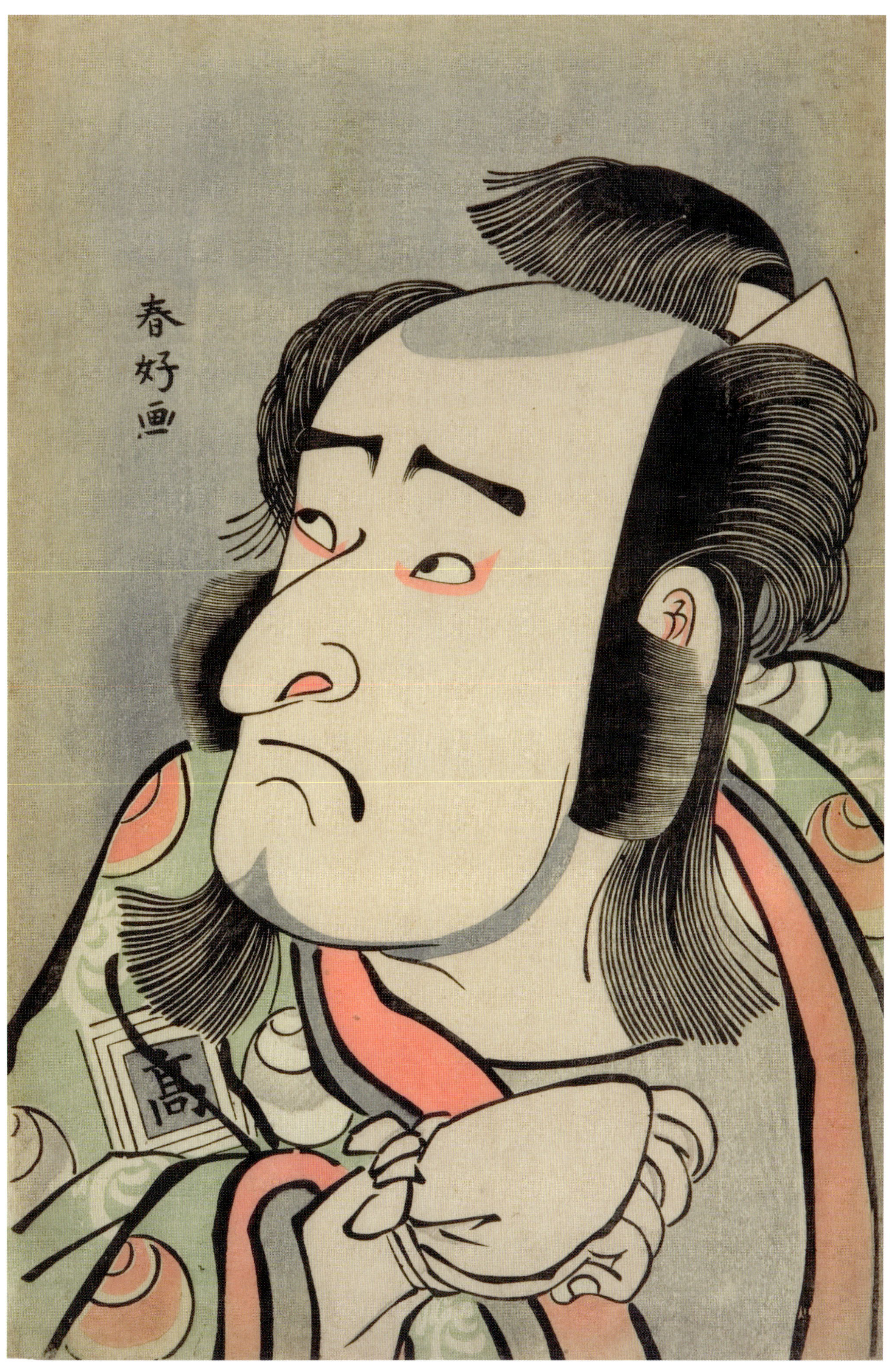

61　Katsukawa Shunkō, 1743–1812, The actor Ichikawa Komazō III as Ashigaru Sanpei

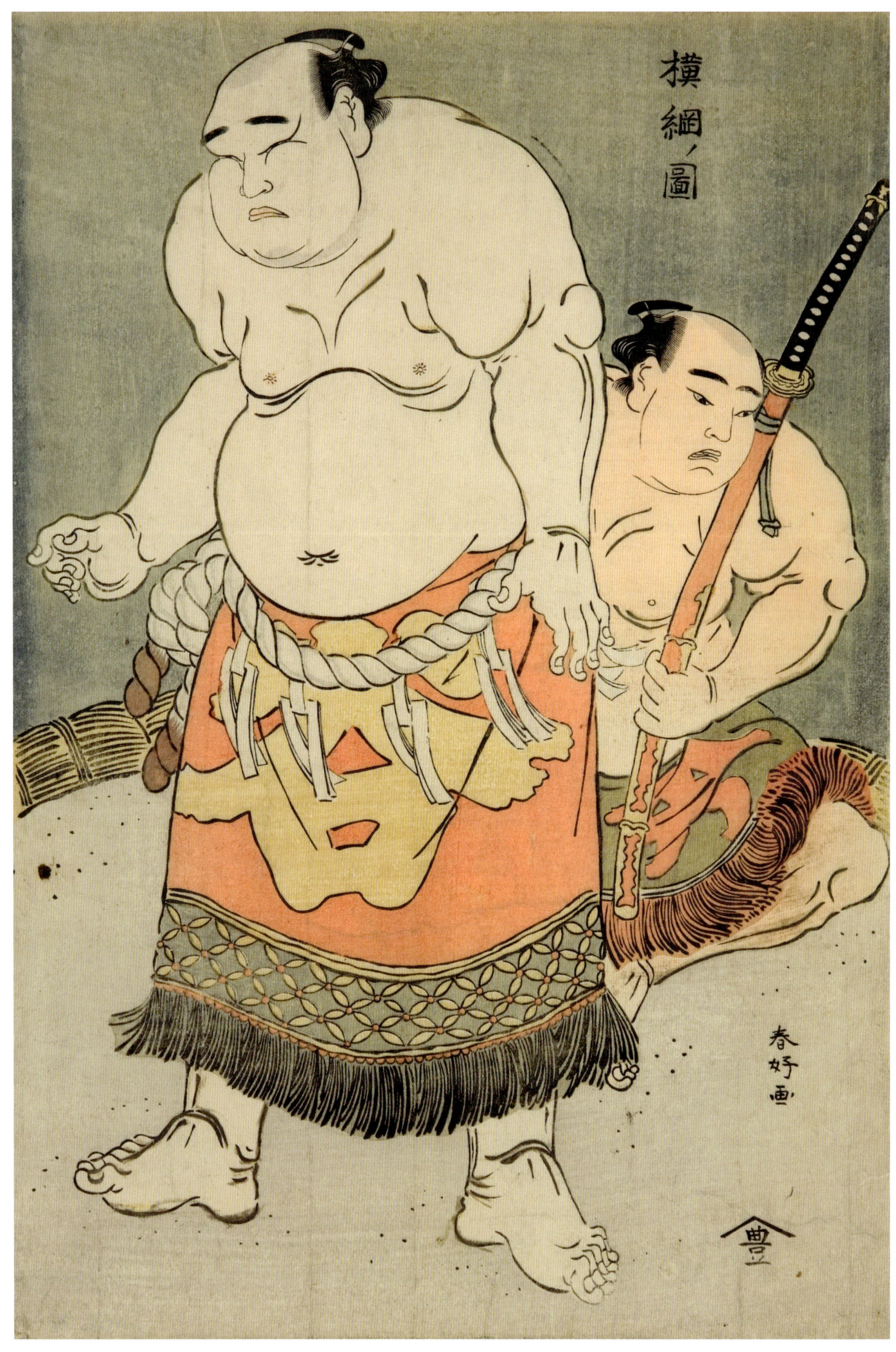

   62   Katsukawa Shunkō, 1743–1812, The Sumo Wrestler Tanikaze, from the series *Yokozuna*

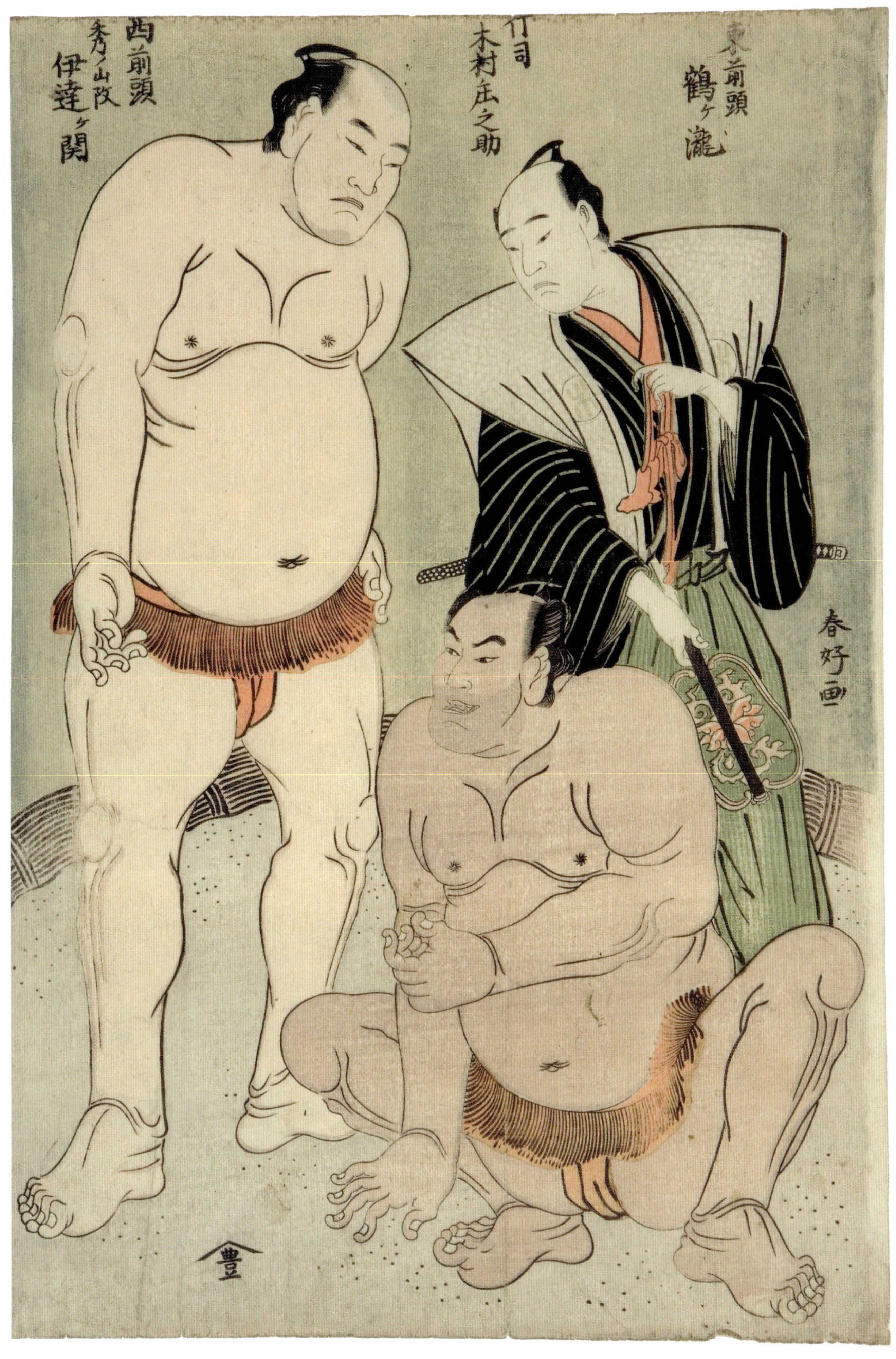

63   Katsukawa Shunkō, 1743–1812, "The Sumo Wrestler Tsurugataki, Maegashira of the Eastern Section, the Referee Kimura Shōnosuke, and the Sumo Wrestler Hidenoyama, Renamed Dategaseki, Maegashira of the Western Section"

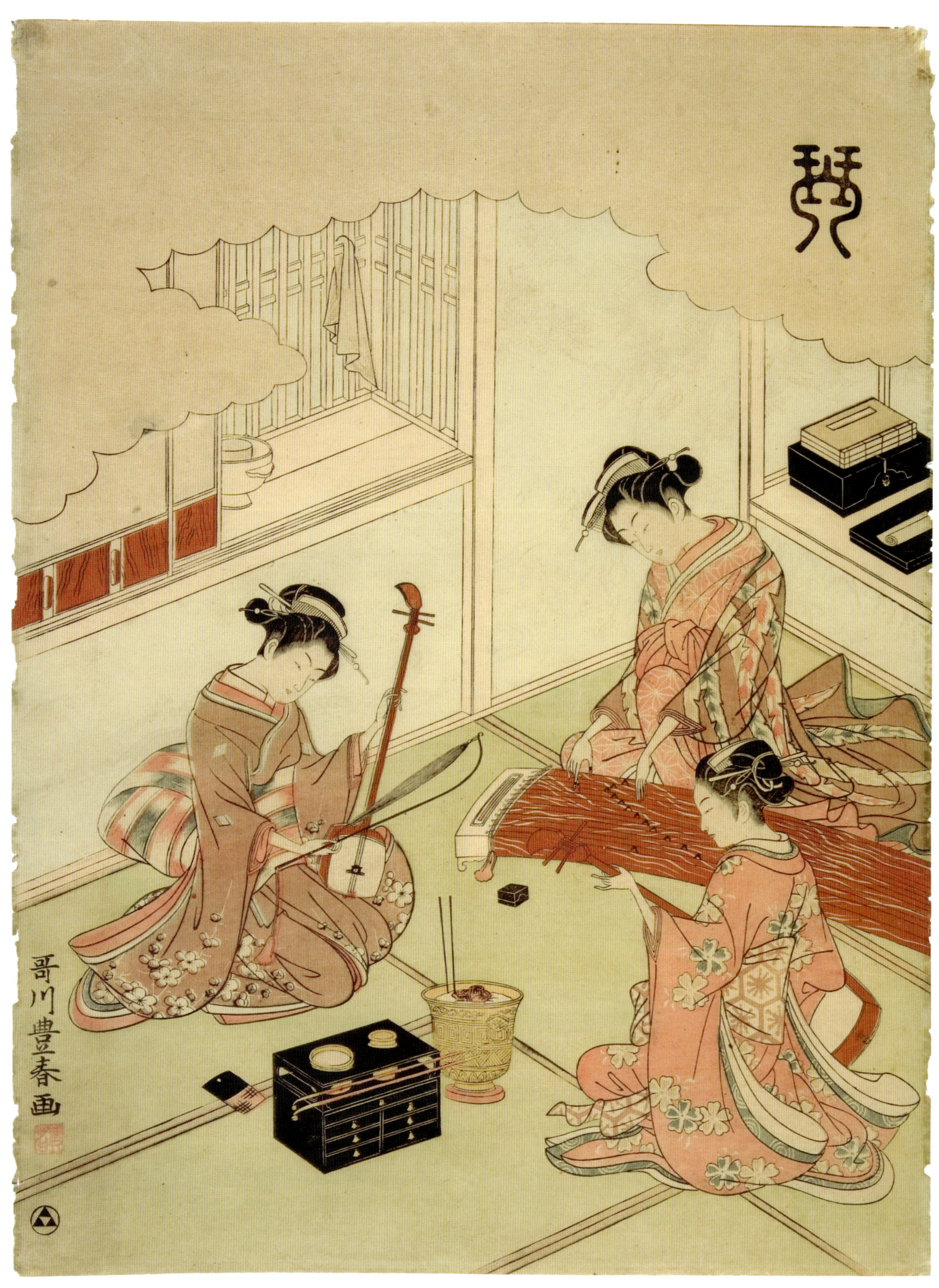

   64   Utagawa Toyoharu, 1735–1814, "Music" (*Kin*), from an untitled series of the Four Accomplishments

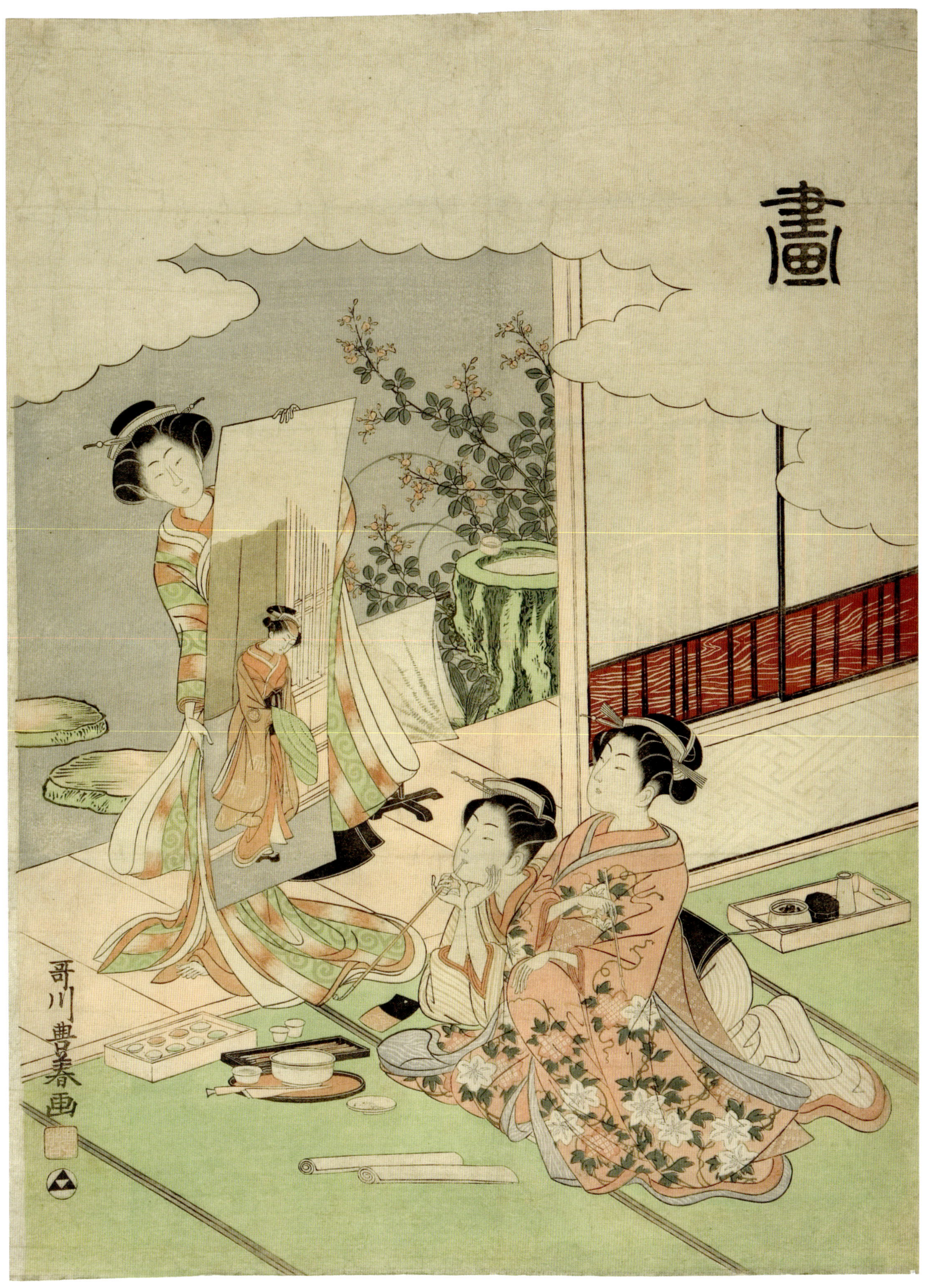

65　Utagawa Toyoharu, 1735–1814, "Painting "(*Ga*), from an untitled series of the Four Accomplishments　|　*85*

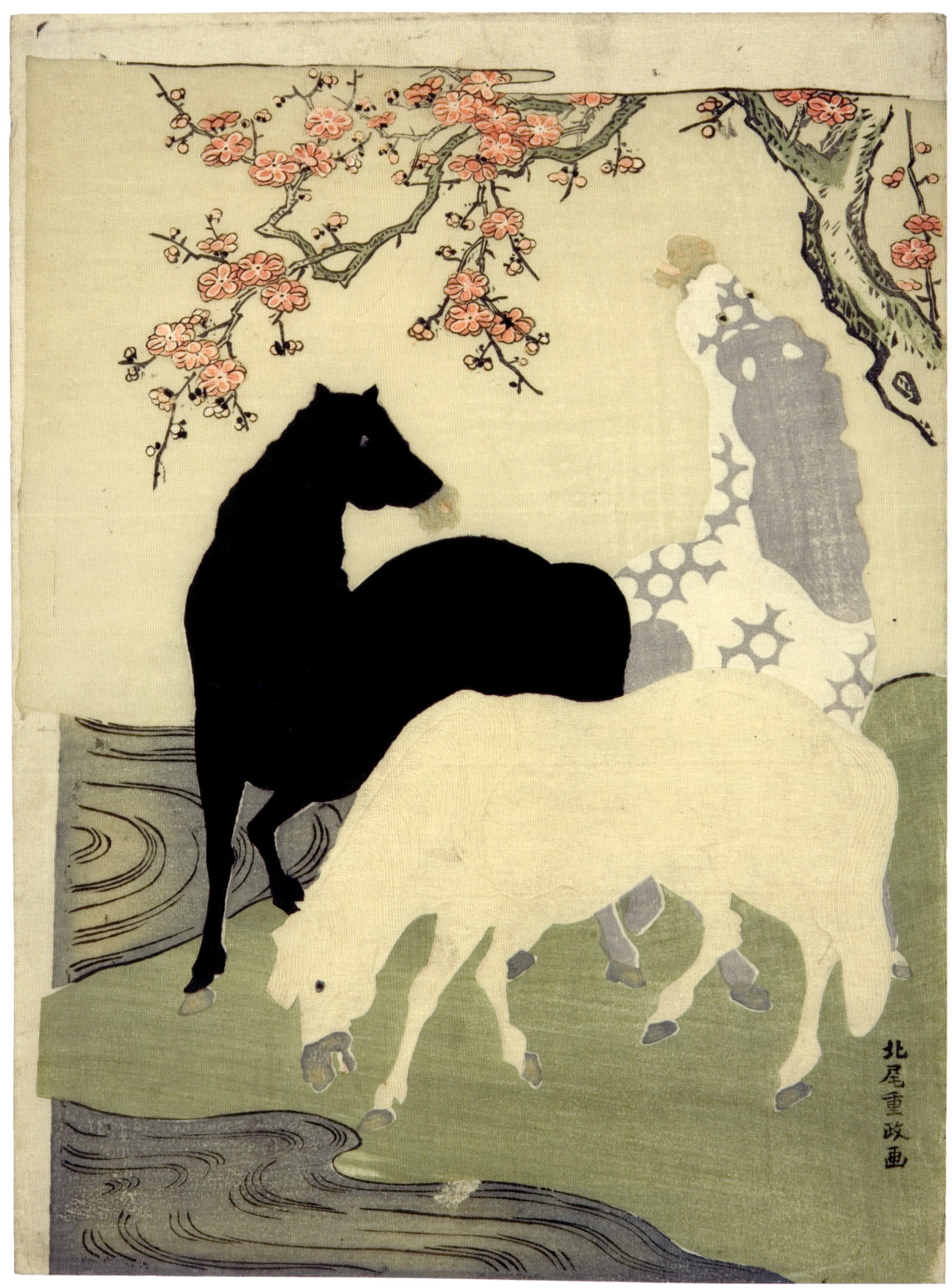

   66   Kitao Shigemasa, 1739–1820, Horses beneath a flowering plum tree

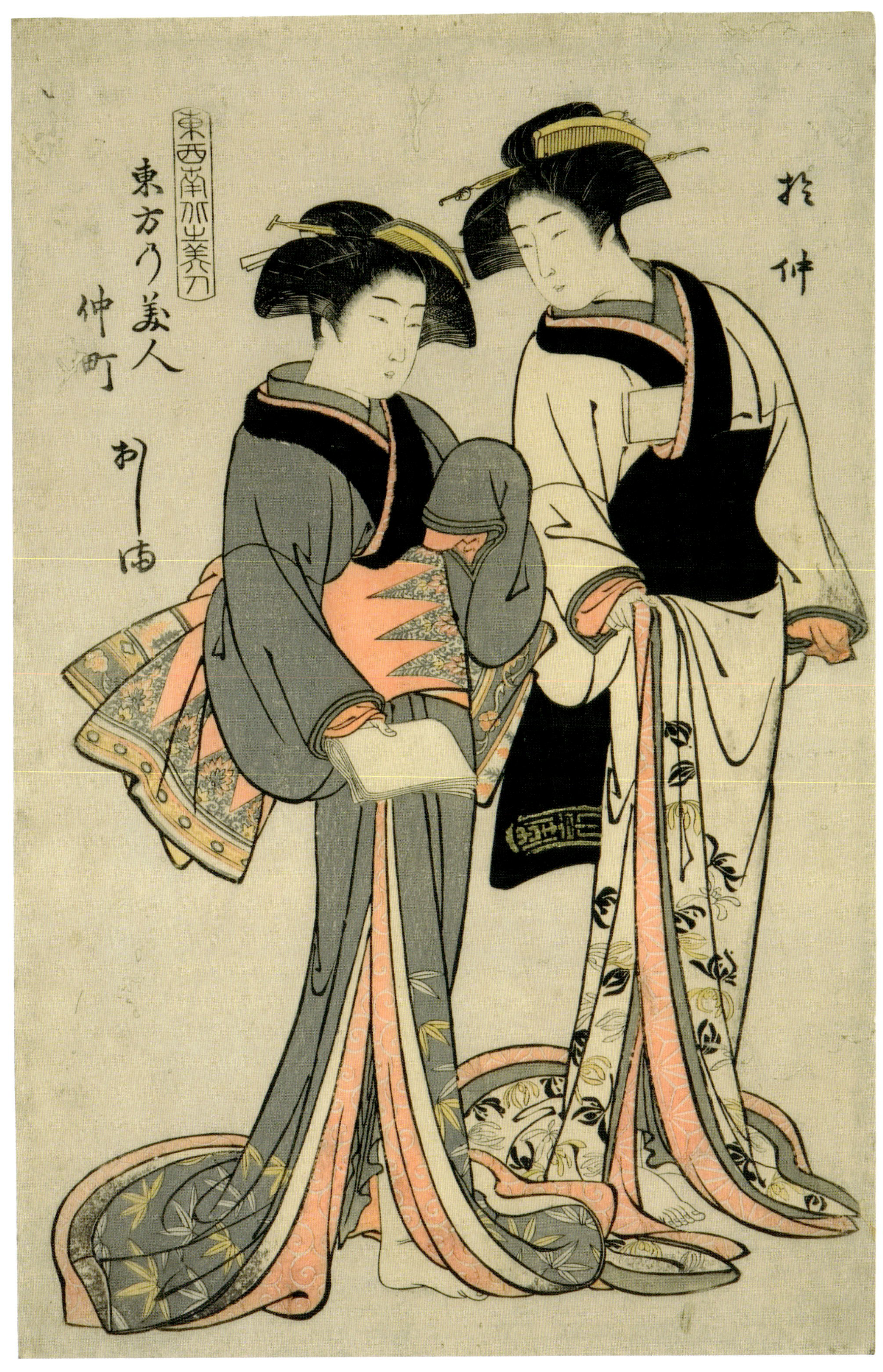

67   Kitao Shigemasa, 1739–1820, "Beauties of the Eastern Quarter: Onaka and Oshima of the Nakamachi,"
from the series *Beauties of the East, West, South, and North* | *87*

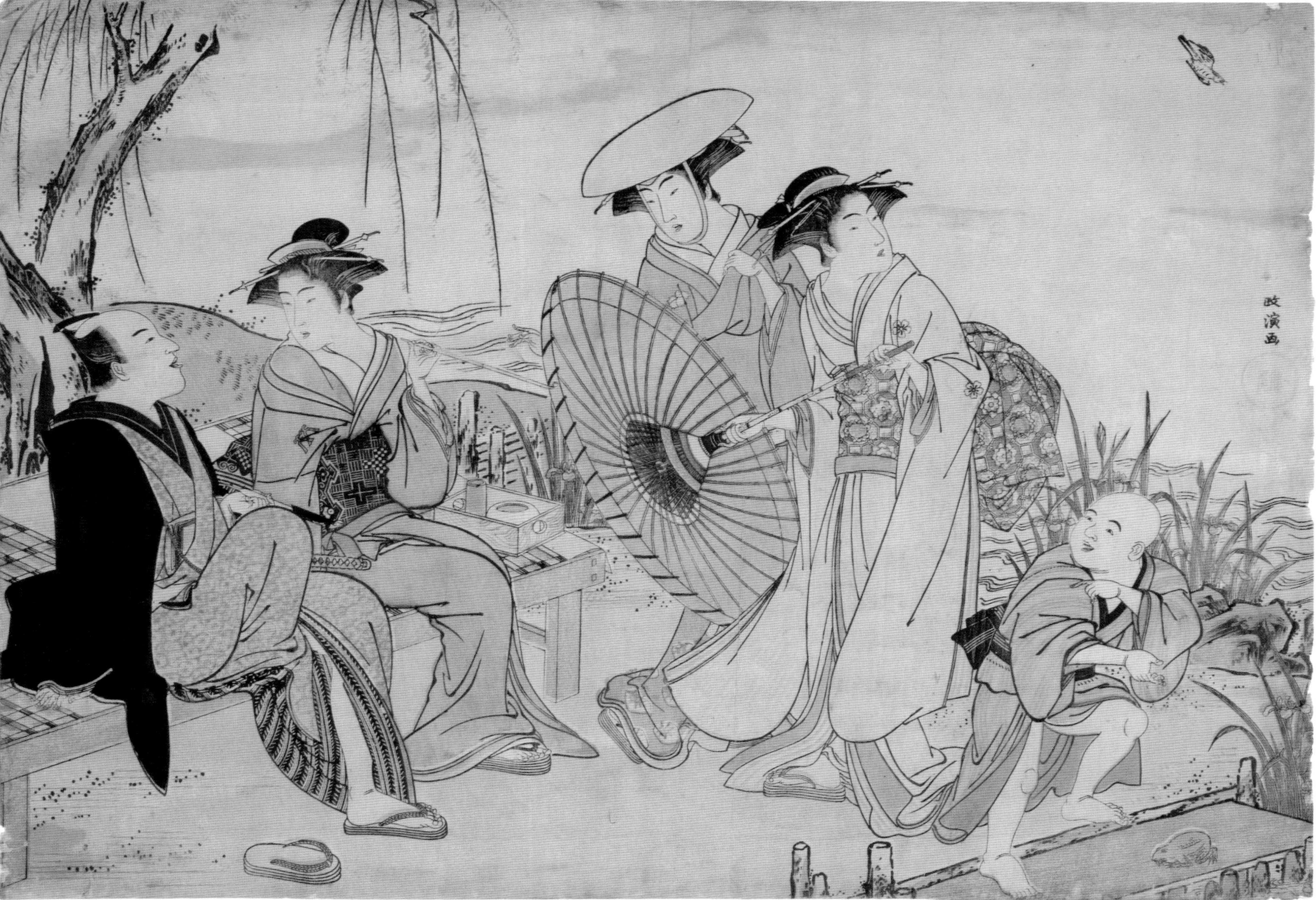

68   Kitao Masanobu, 1761–1816, Listening to the first cuckoo on a late spring outing

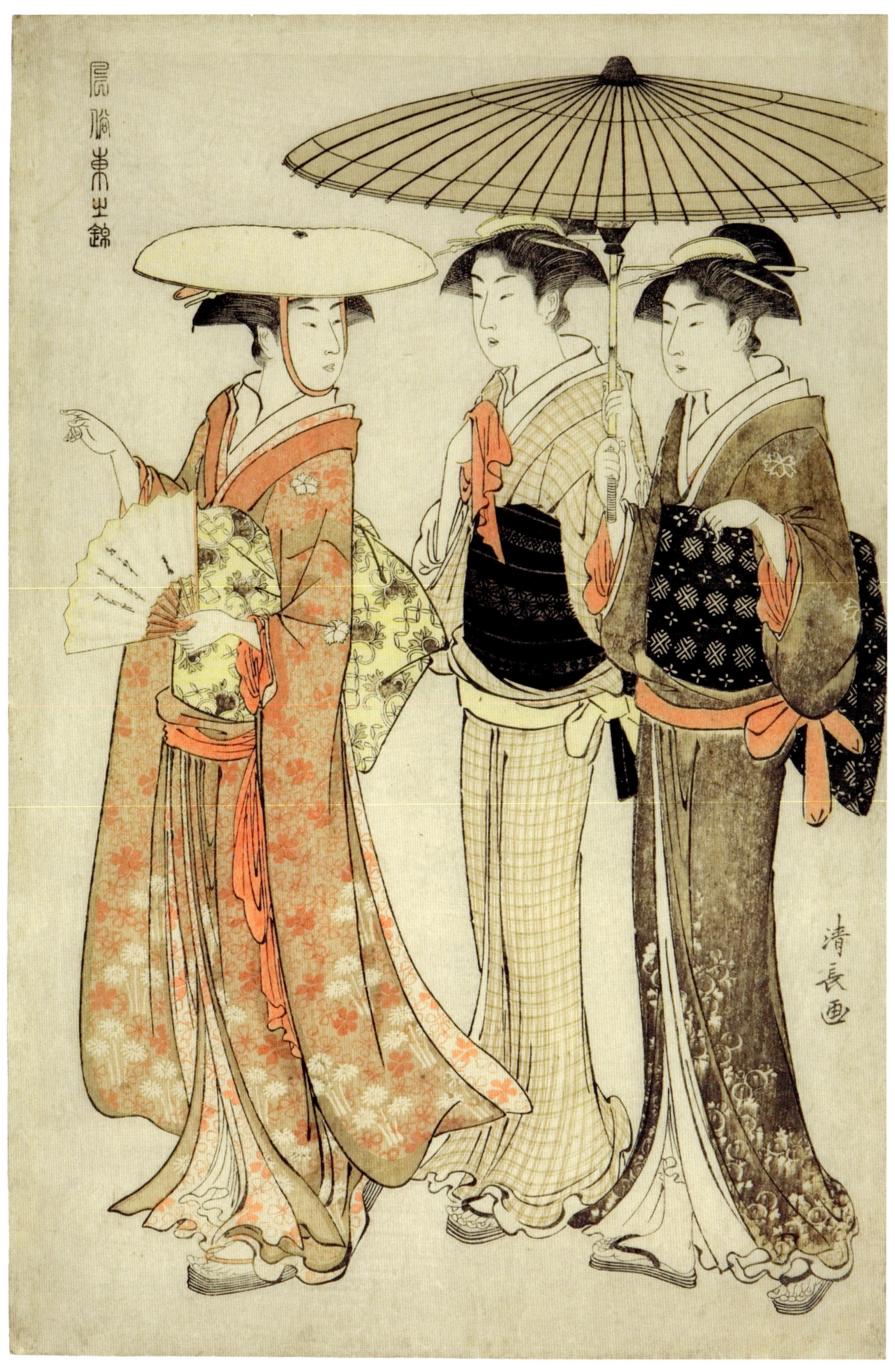

69   Torii Kiyonaga, 1752–1815, Woman on an outing with two female attendants, from the series *Current Manners in Eastern Brocade*

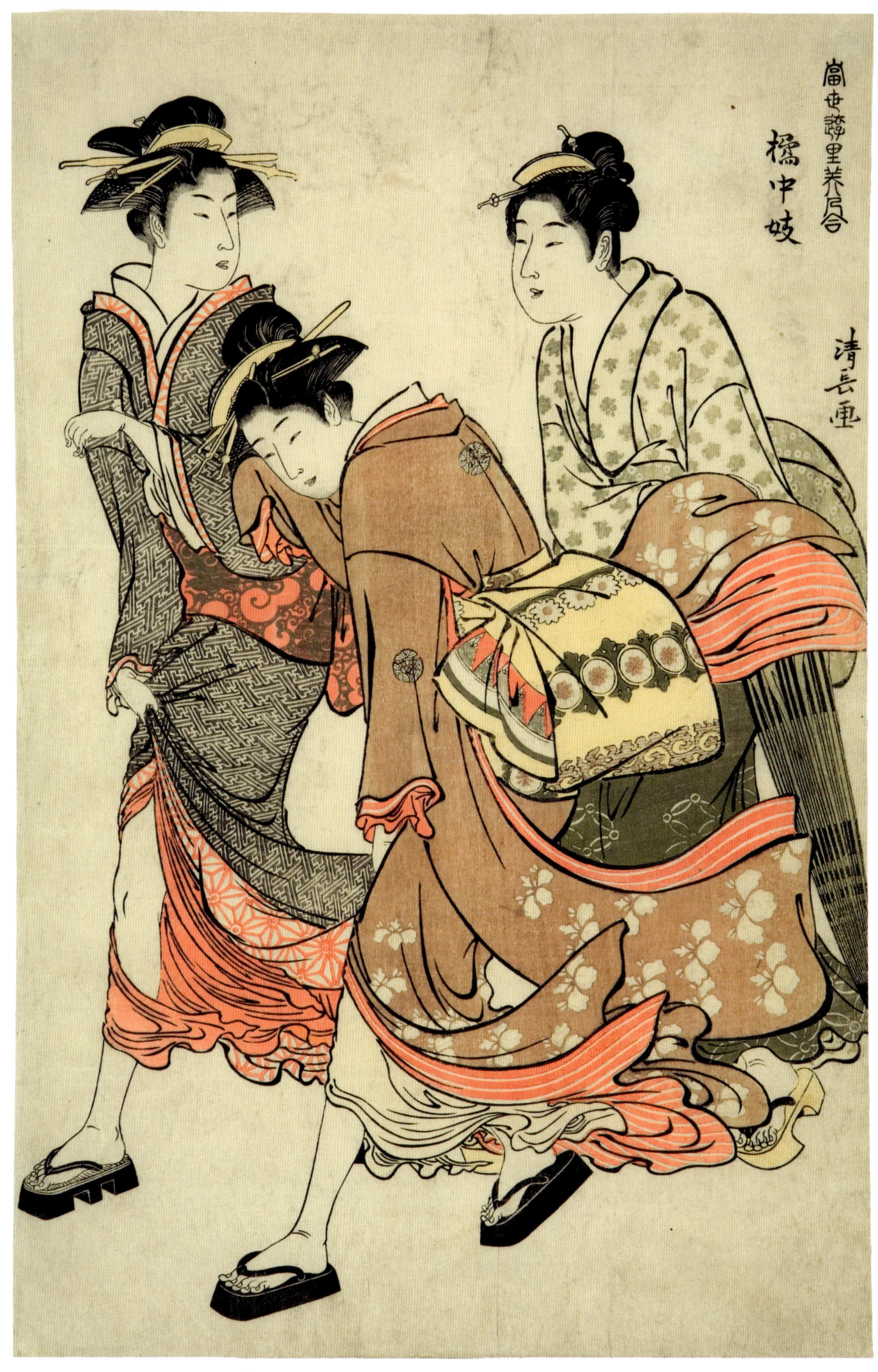

   70   Torii Kiyonaga, 1752–1815, "Geisha from Tachibana-chō," from the series *Contest of Modern Beauties of the Pleasure Quarters*

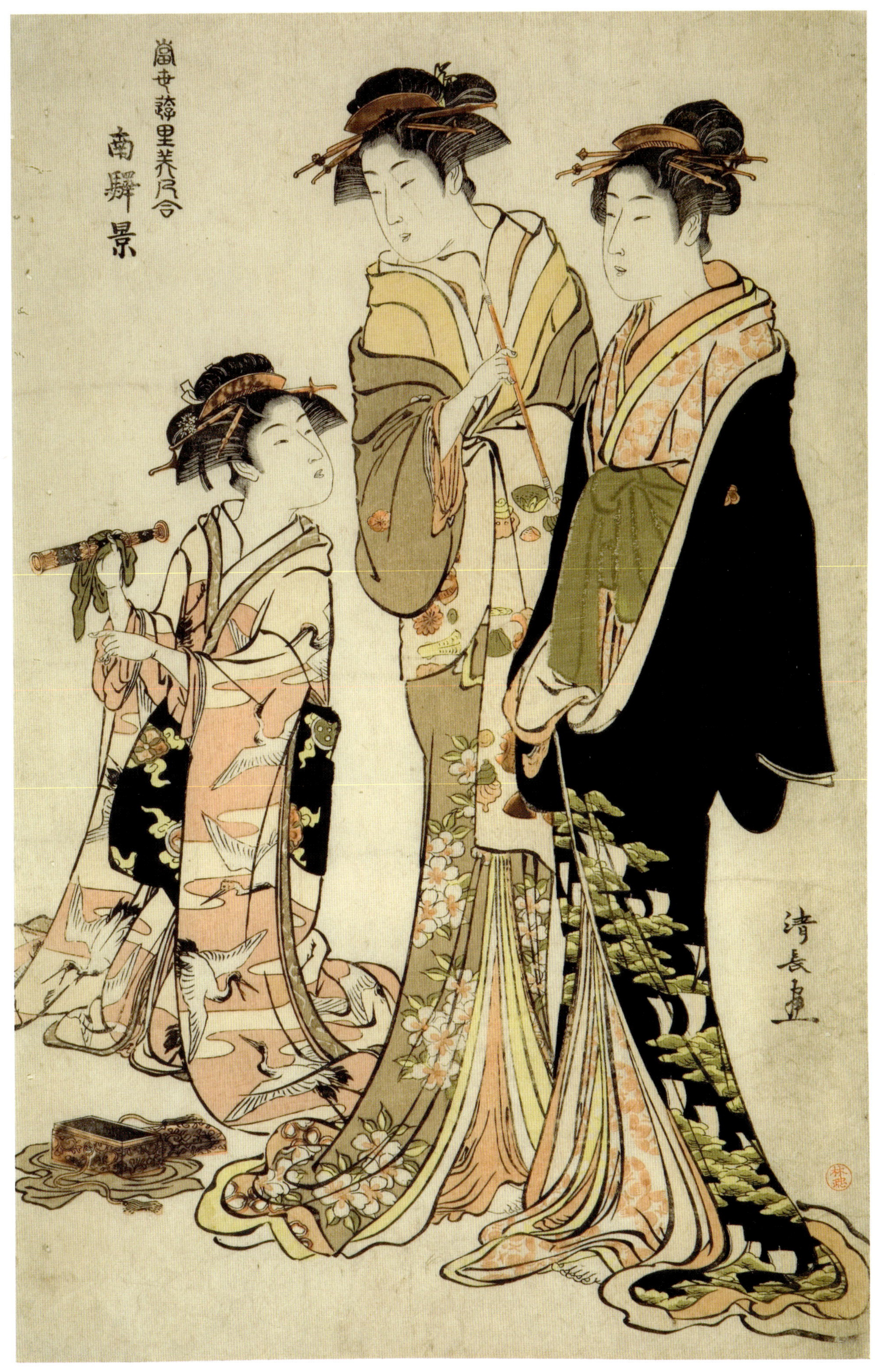

71   Torii Kiyonaga, 1752–1815, "Courtesans of the South Station," from the series *Contest of Modern Beauties of the Pleasure Quarters*

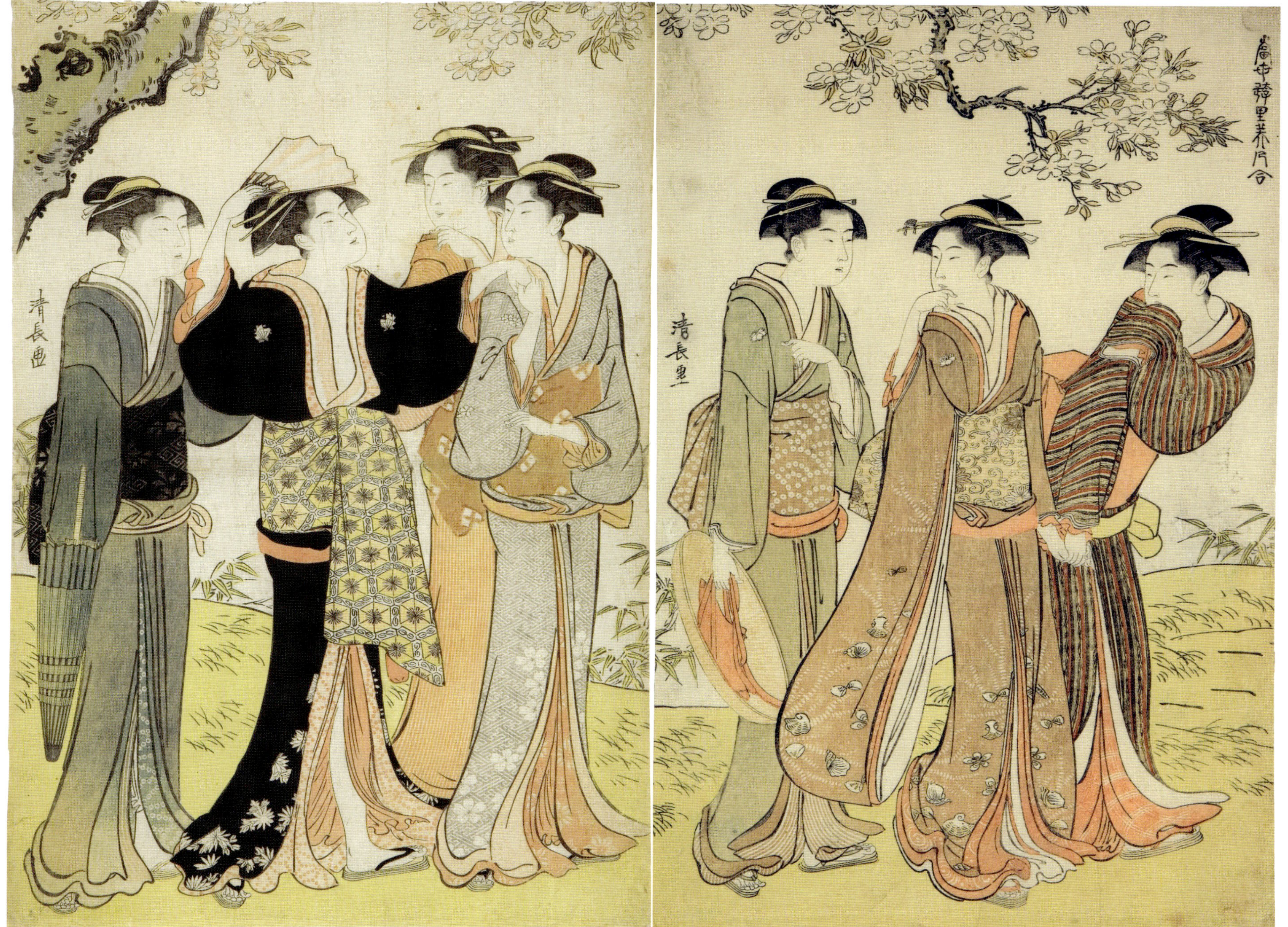

72   Torii Kiyonaga, 1752–1815, A drunken beauty beneath cherry blossoms, from the series *Contest of Modern Beauties of the Pleasure Quarters*

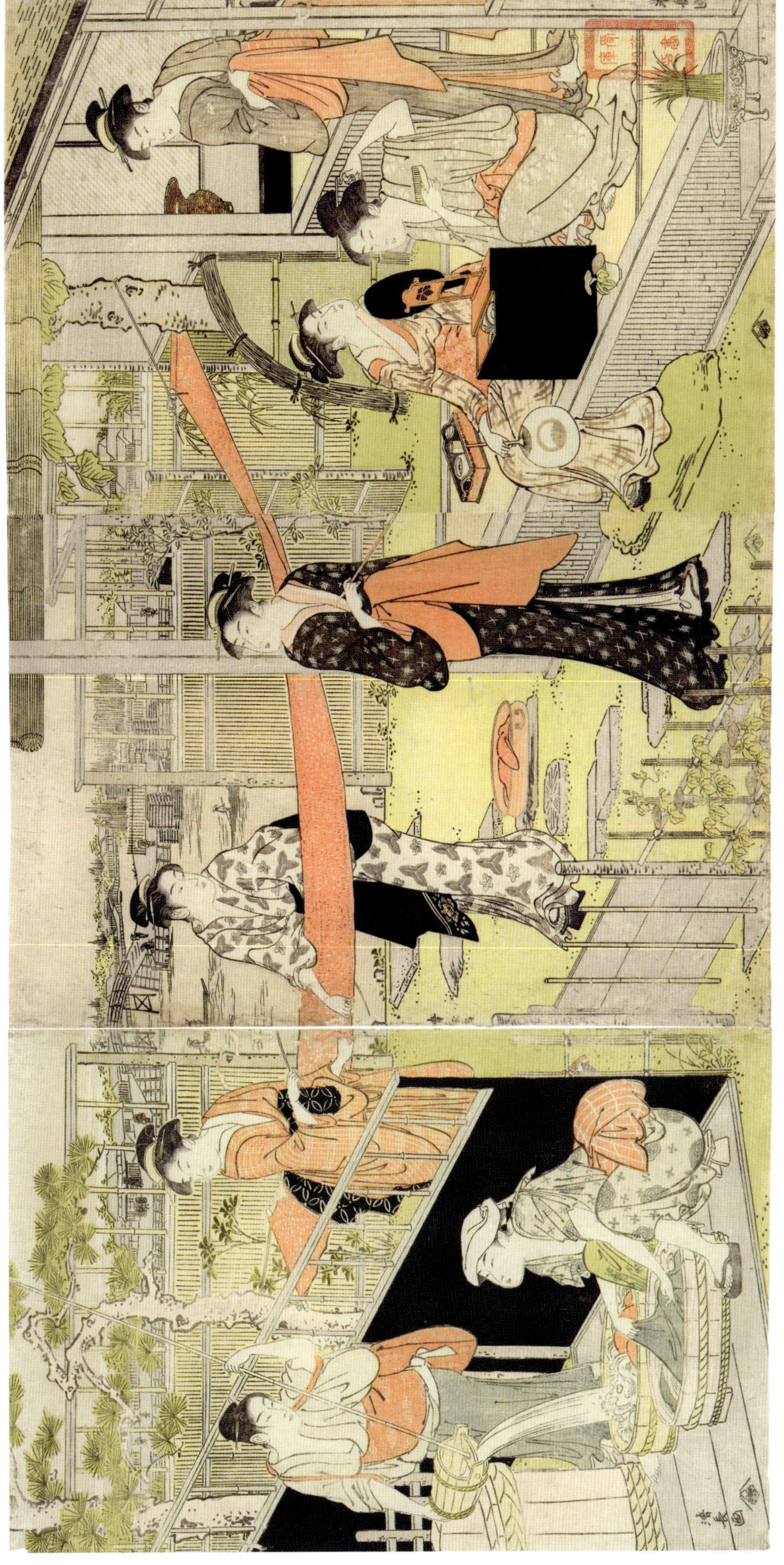

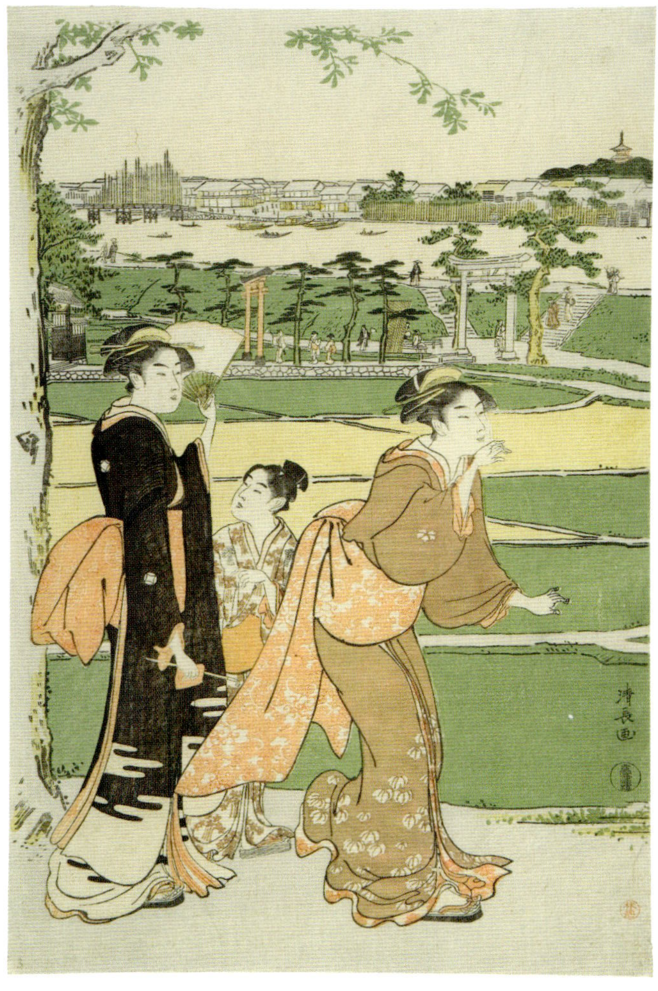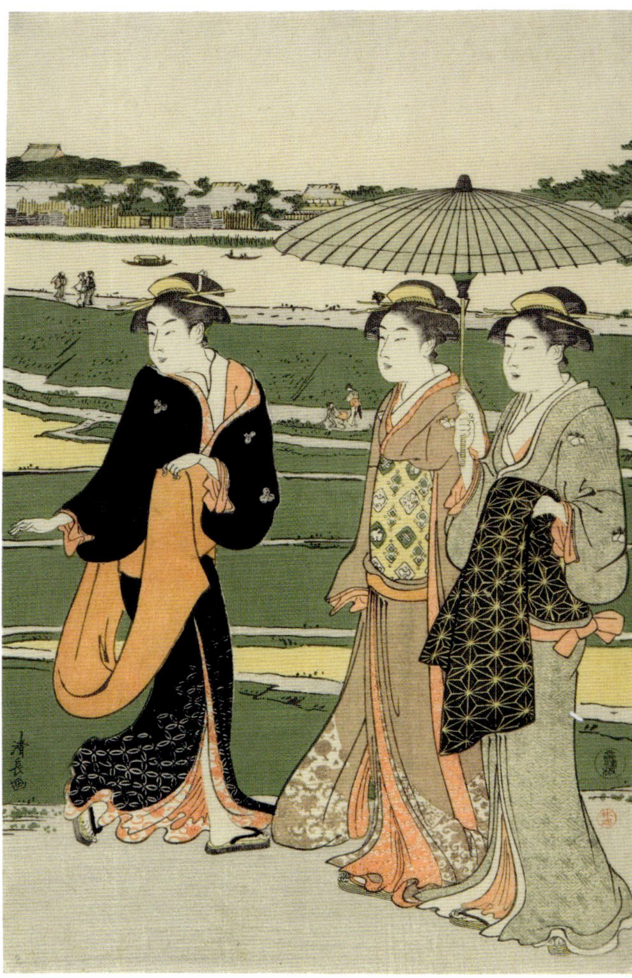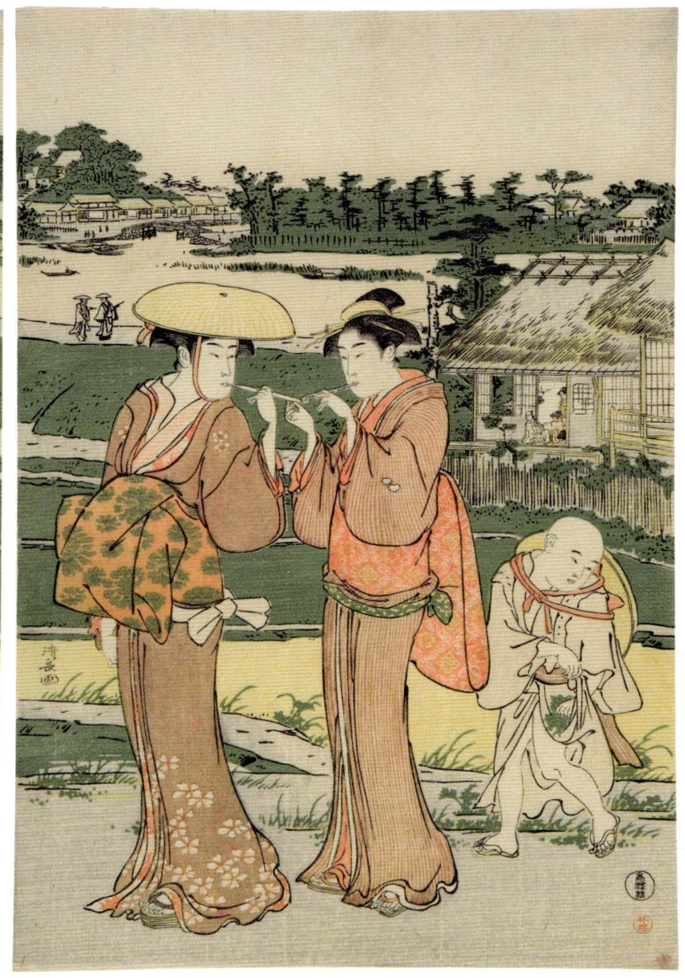

74   Torii Kiyonaga, 1752–1815, A spring excursion to Mimeguri Shrine at Mukōjima

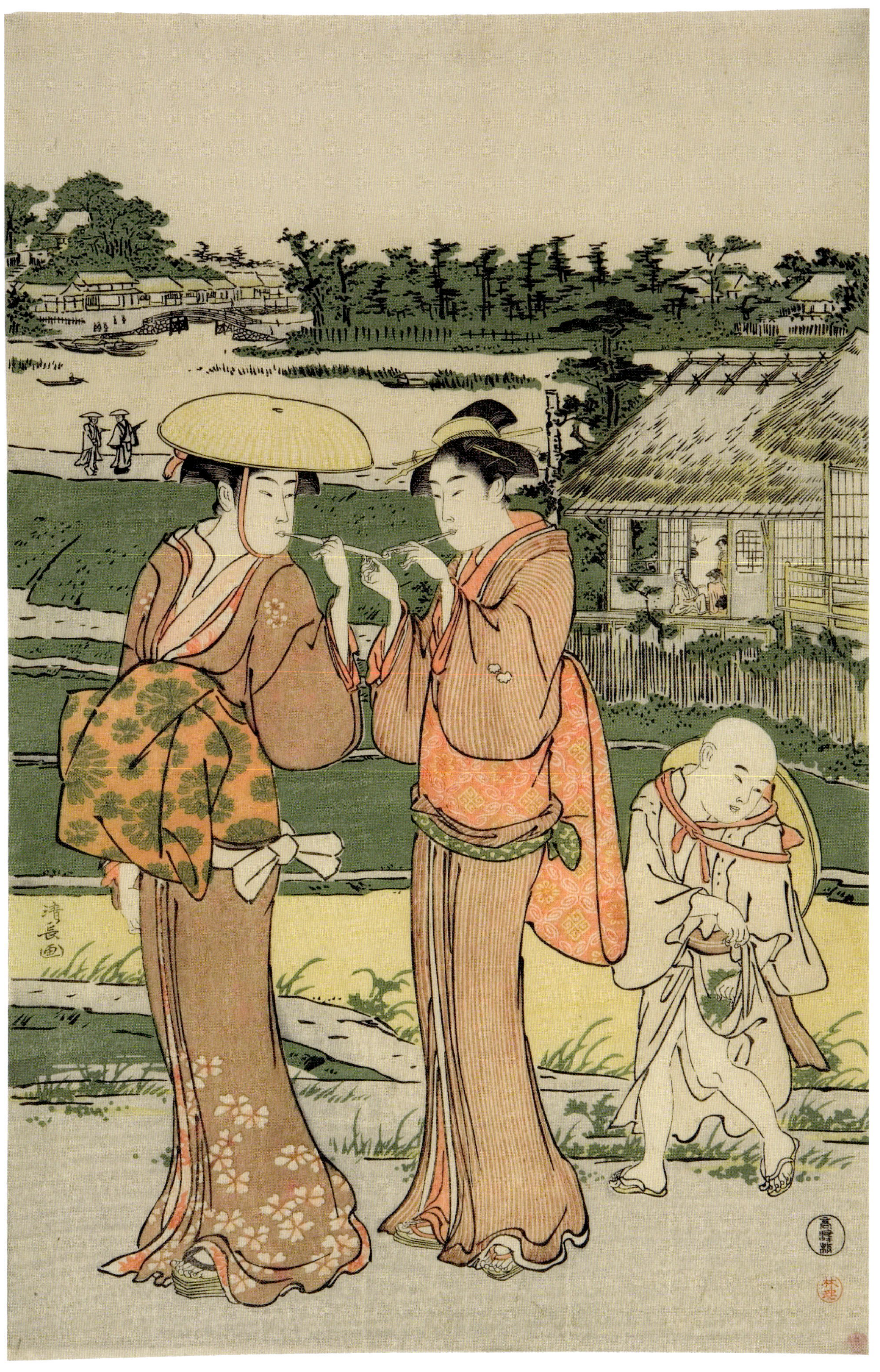

75   Torii Kiyonaga, 1752–1815, A spring excursion to Mimeguri Shrine at Mukōjima (detail, right sheet)

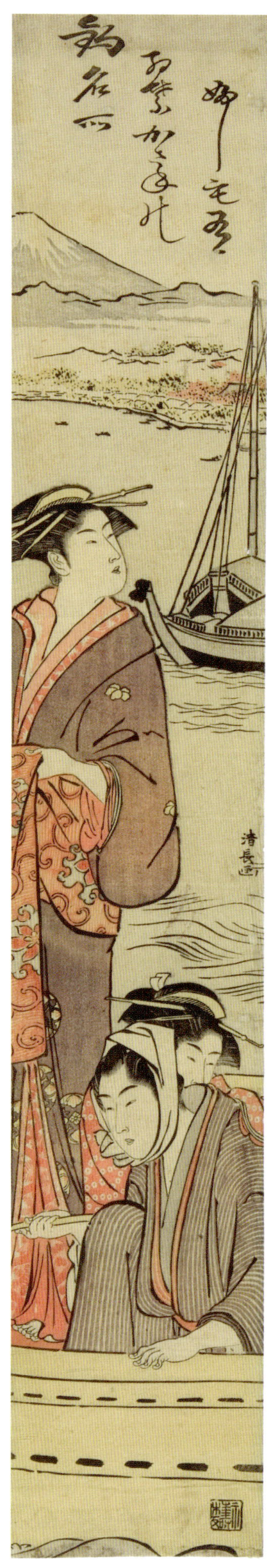

76 Torii Kiyonaga, 1752–1815, A fishing party

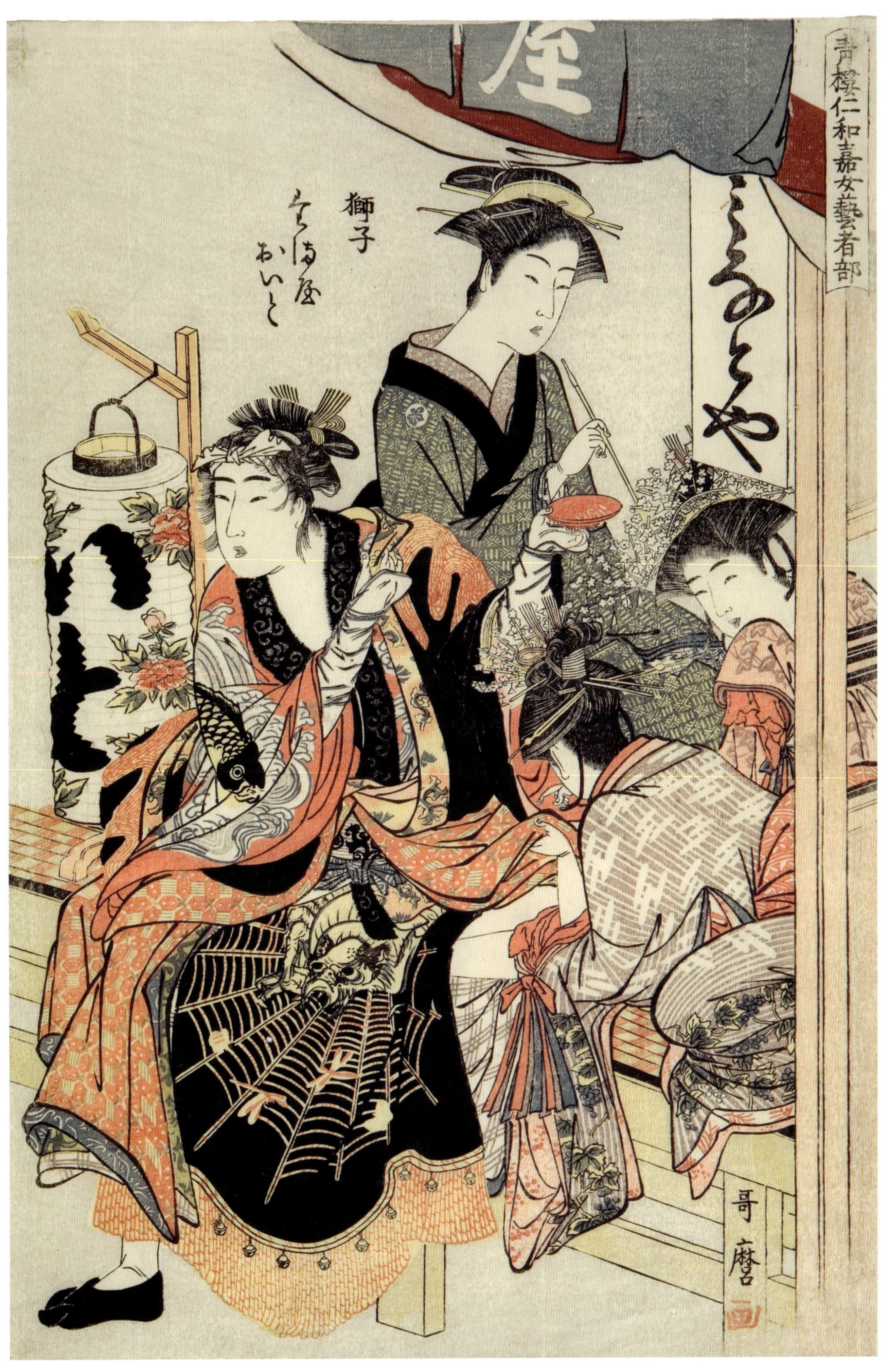

77   Kitagawa Utamaro, 1754–1806, "Lion Dance: Oito of the Tamaya," from the series *The Female Geisha Section of the Niwaka Festival in the Yoshiwara*

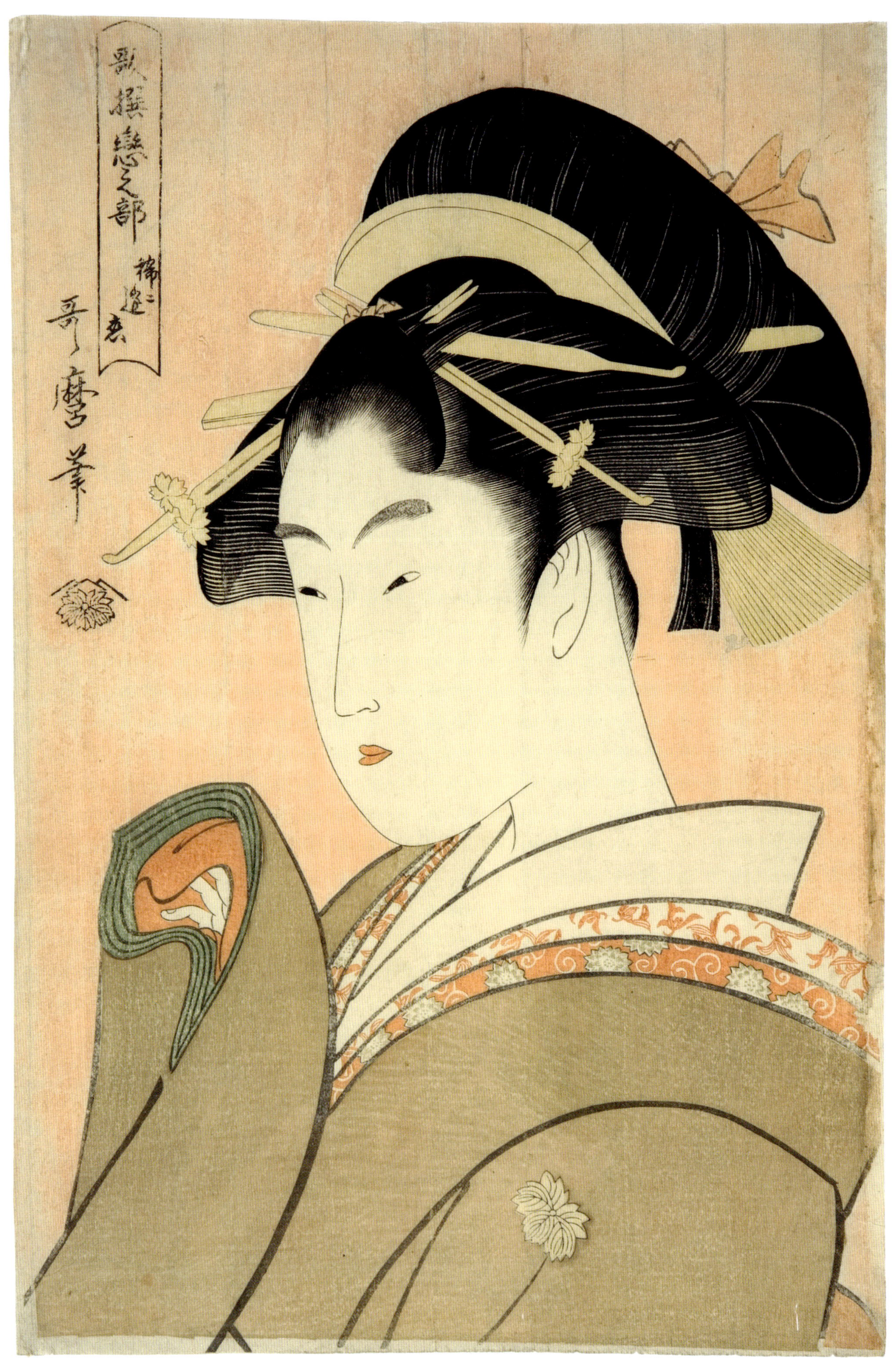

 | 78 Kitagawa Utamaro, 1754–1806, "Love That Rarely Meets," from the series *Anthology of Poems: The Love Section*

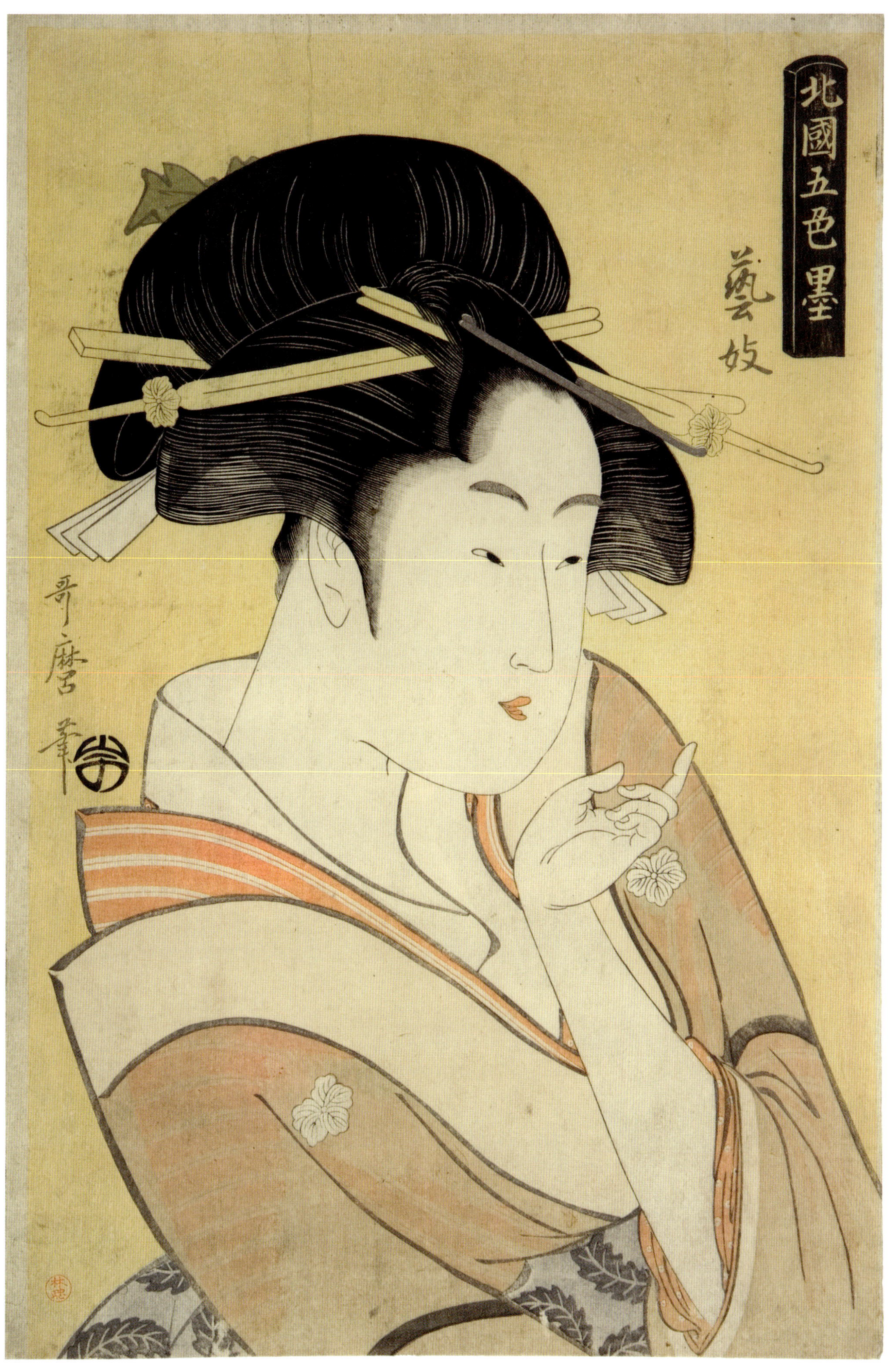

79   Kitagawa Utamaro, 1754–1806, "Geisha," from the series *Five Shades of Ink in the Northern Quarter* | *99*

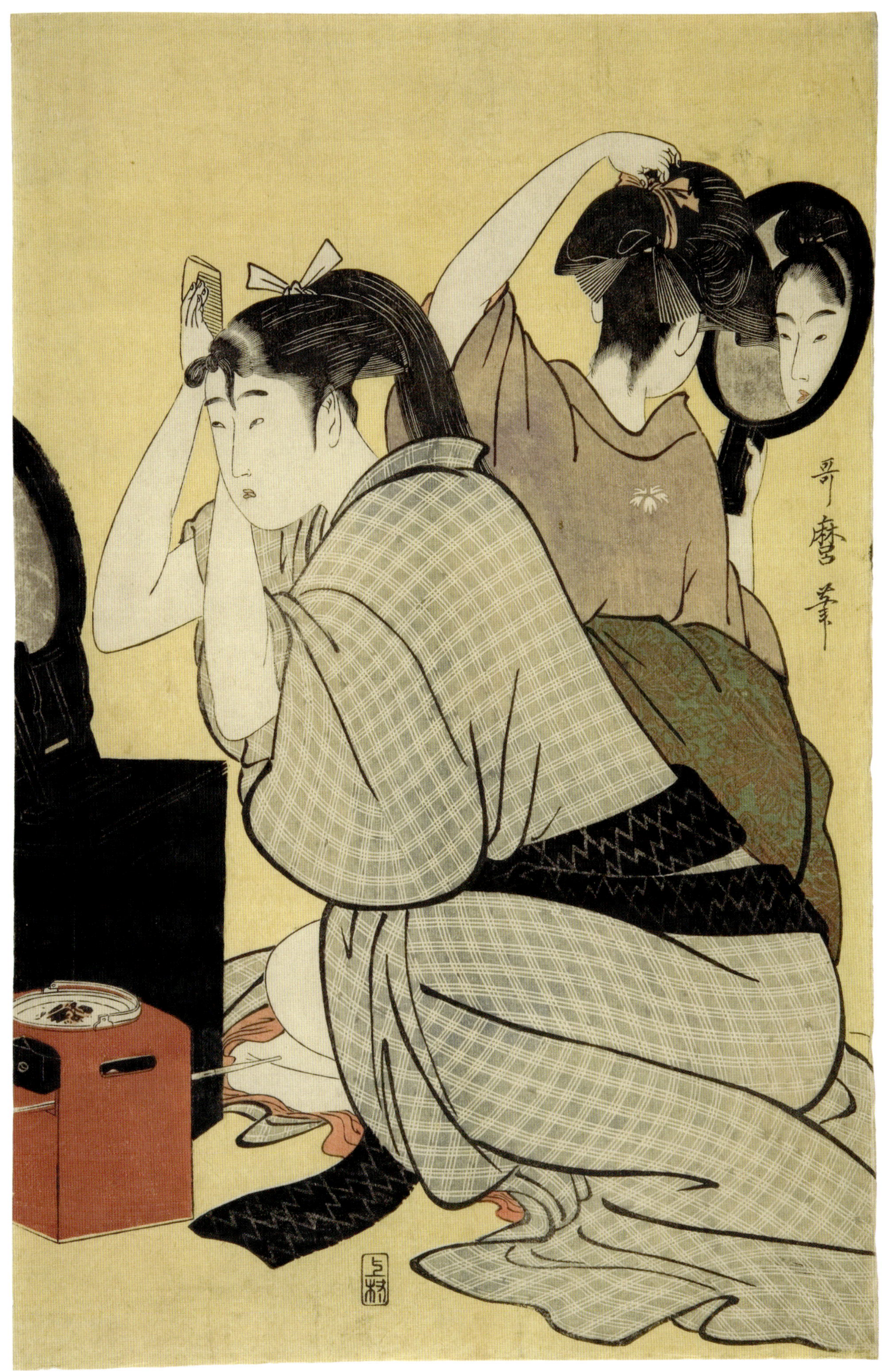

 | 80   Kitagawa Utamaro, 1754–1806, Dressing the hair

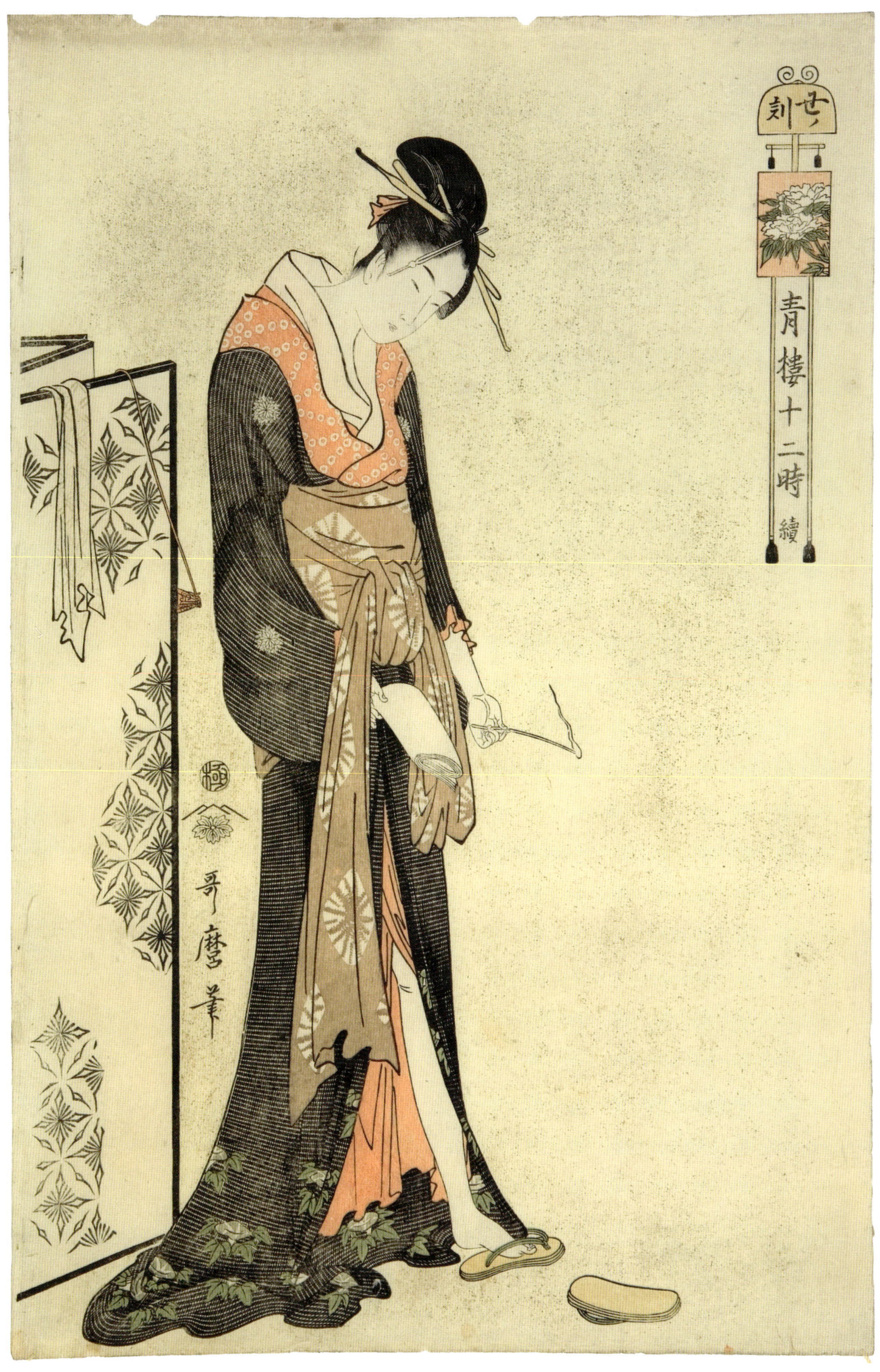

81   Kitagawa Utamaro, 1754–1806, "Hour of the Ox," from the series *The Twelve Hours of the Yoshiwara*

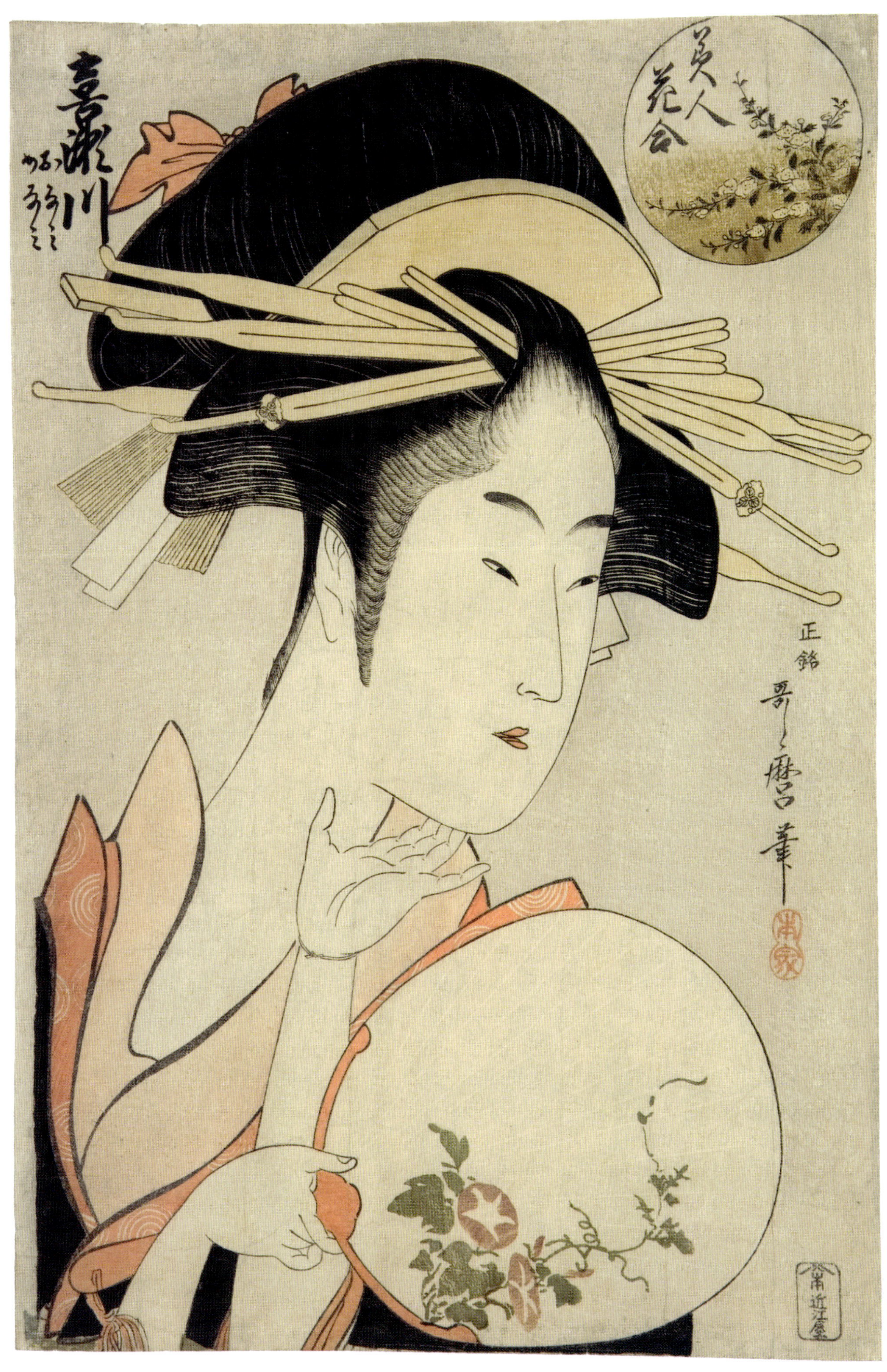

82   Kitagawa Utamaro, 1754–1806, "Kisegawa" (*kamuro* Onami and Menami), from the series *Beauties Compared to Flowers*

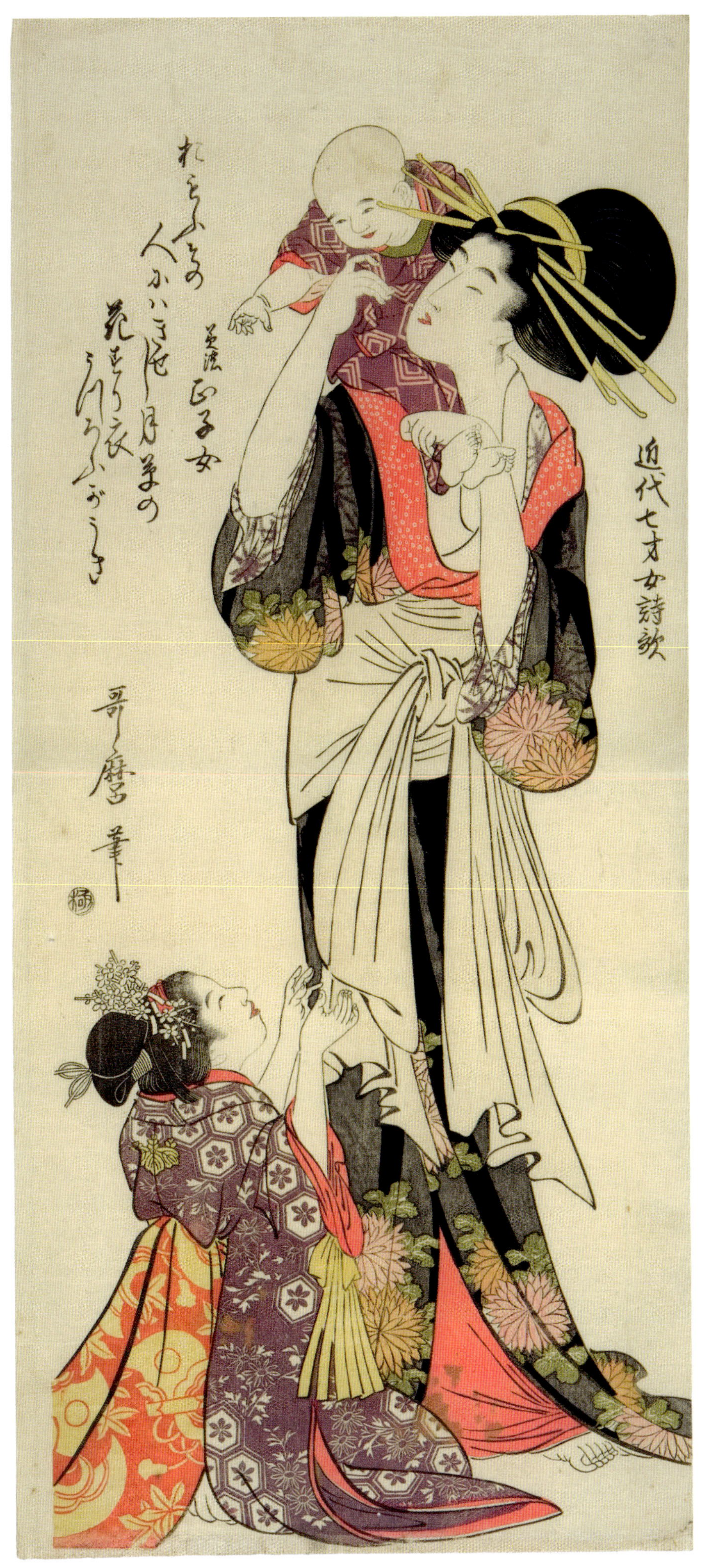

83   Kitagawa Utamaro, 1754–1806, "Masako of Mino [Prefecture]," from the series *Chinese and Japanese Poems by Seven Talented Women of the Present Day*

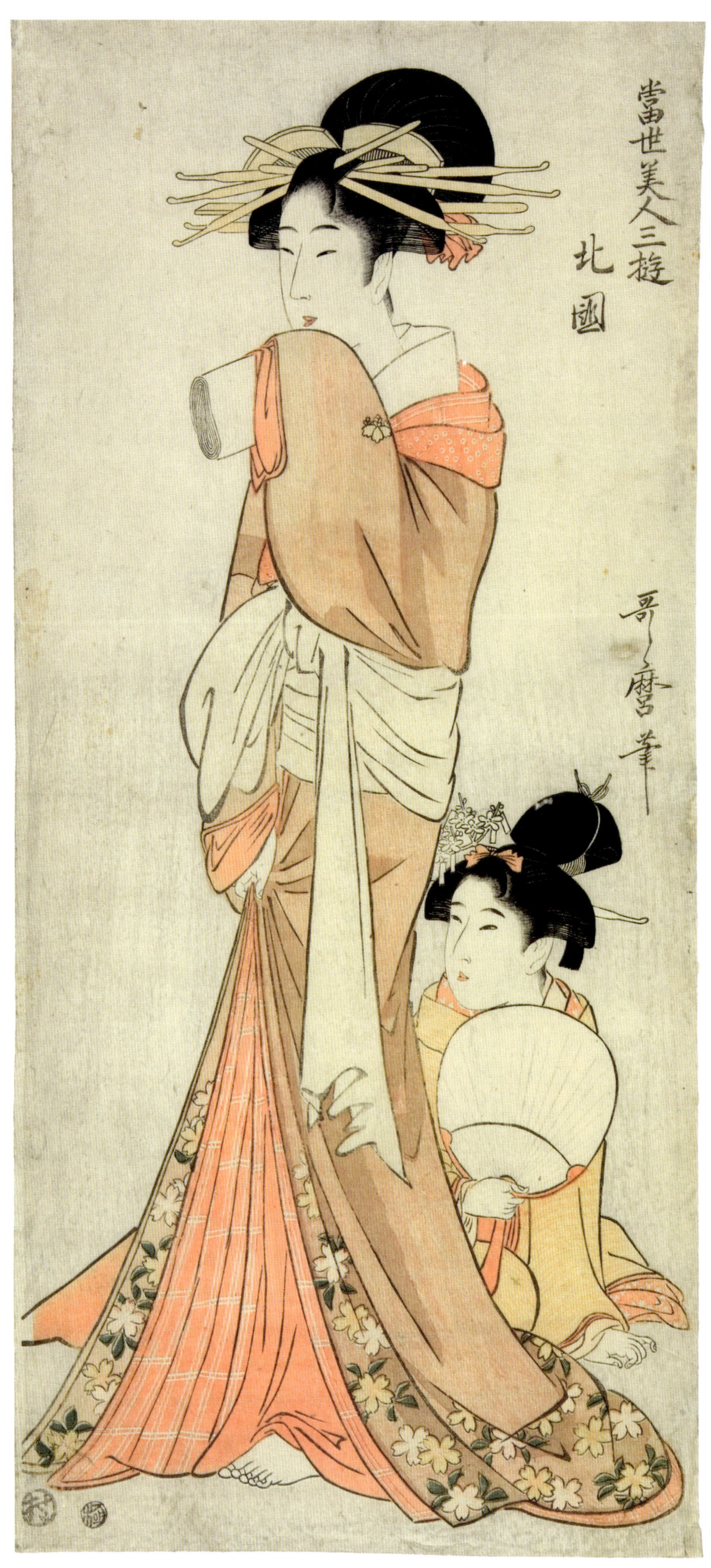

  84 Kitagawa Utamaro, 1754–1806, "Northern Quarter," from the series *Three Amusements of Modern Beauties*

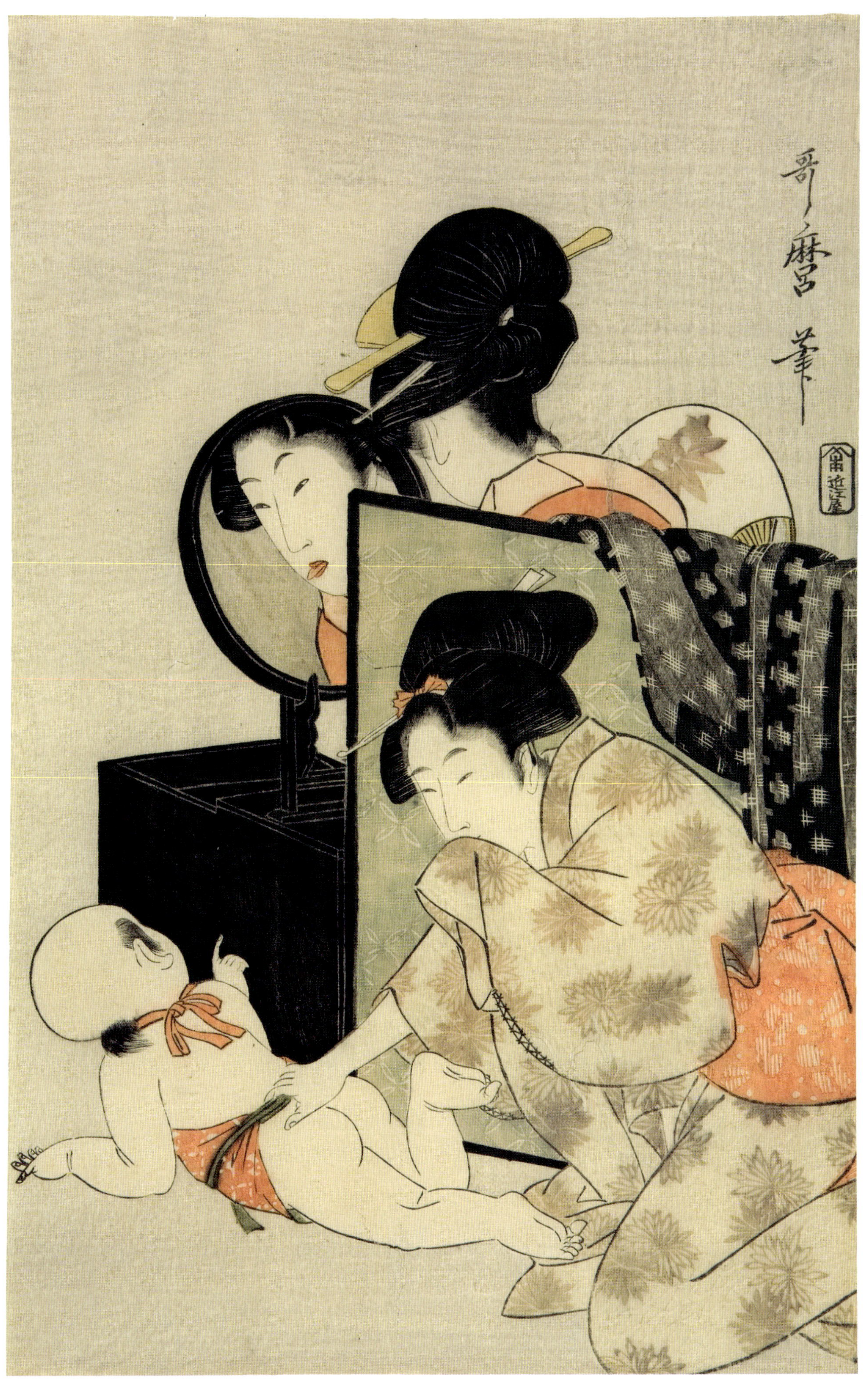

85   Kitagawa Utamaro, 1754–1806, Mother peeping at her baby | *105*

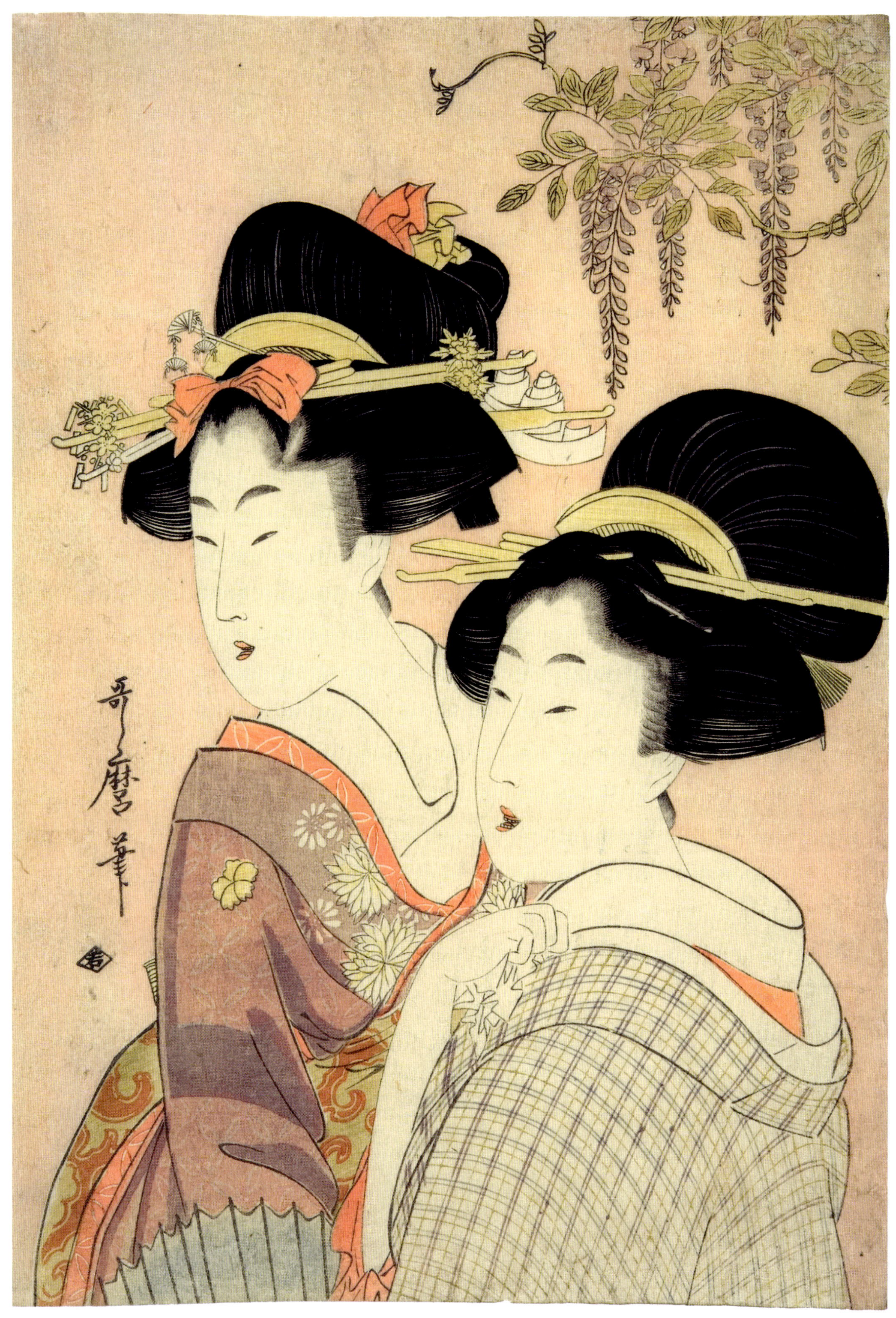

   86   Kitagawa Utamaro, 1754–1806, Two women under wisteria flowers

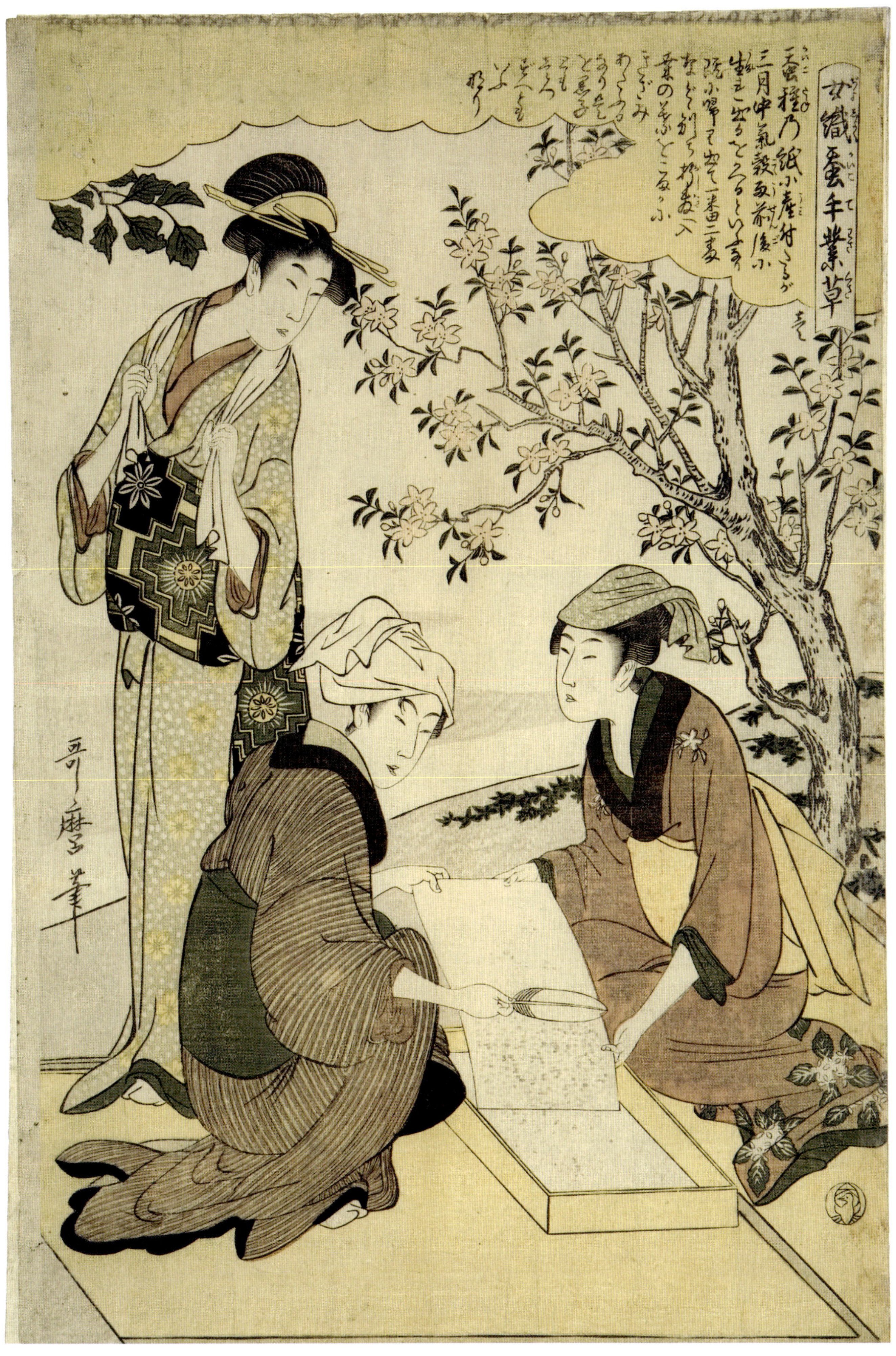

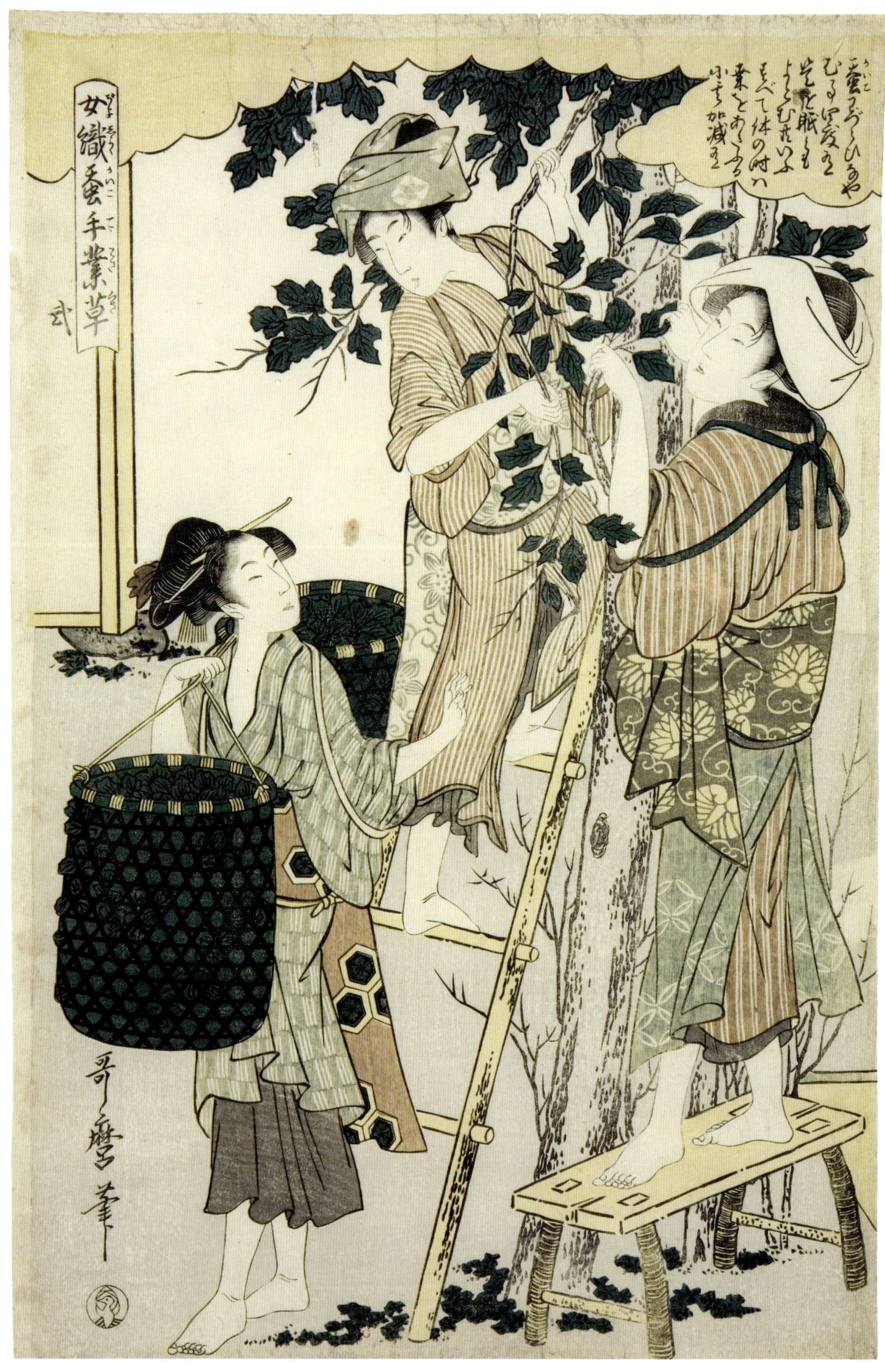

   88   Kitagawa Utamaro, 1754–1806, "Number Two," from the series *Women Engaged in the Sericulture Industry*

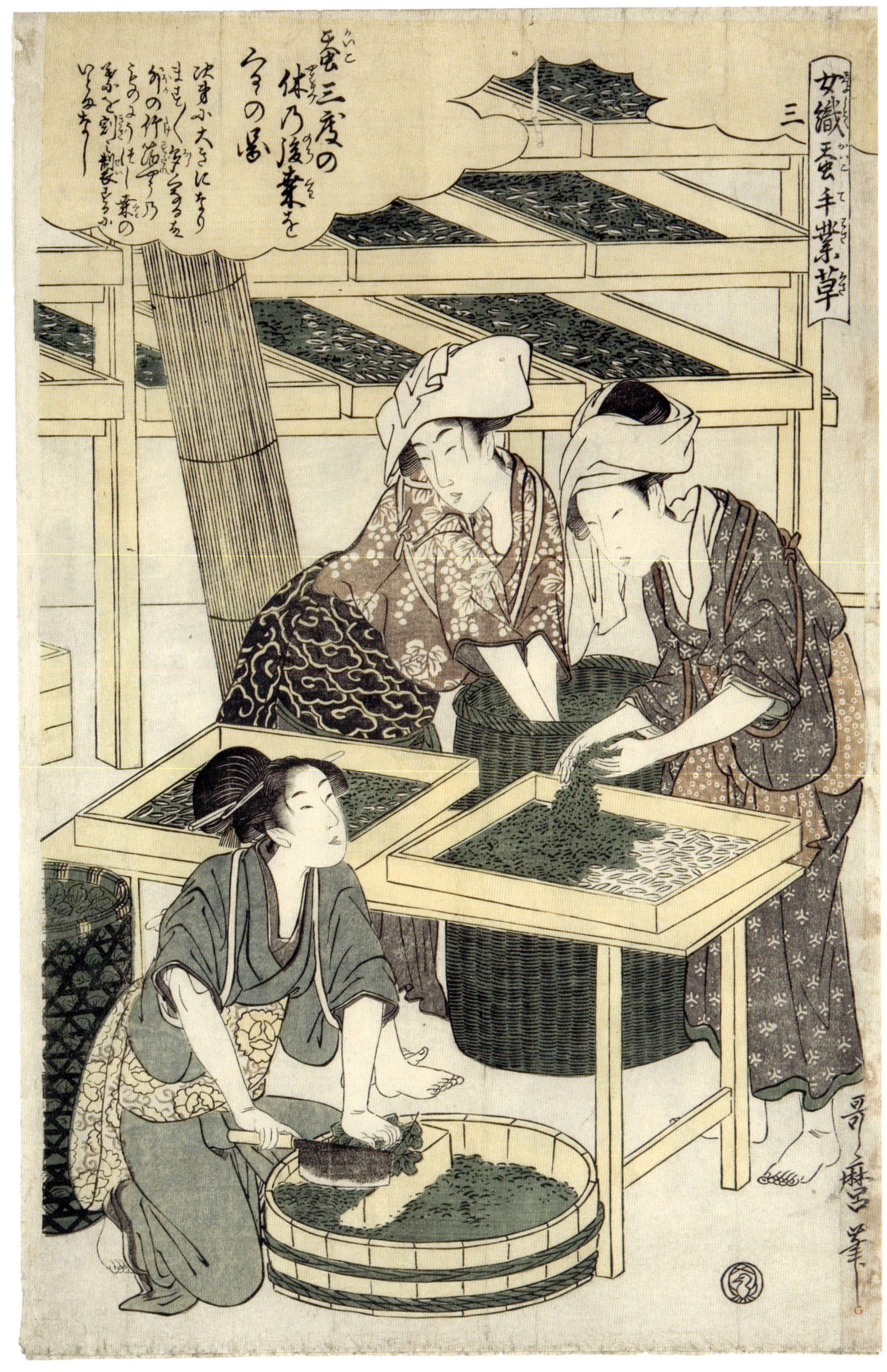

89   Kitagawa Utamaro, 1754–1806, "Number Three," from the series *Women Engaged in the Sericulture Industry*

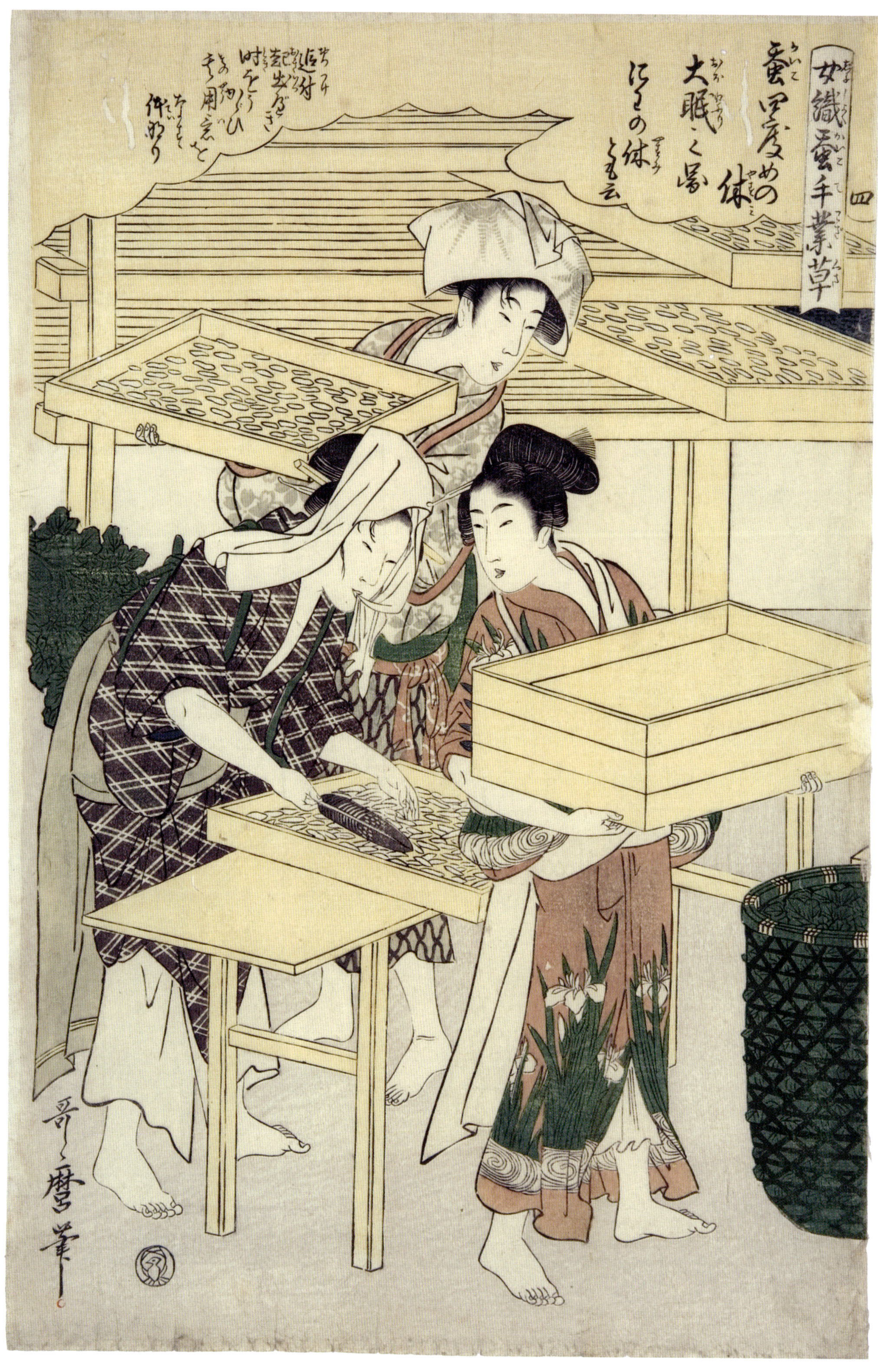

90 Kitagawa Utamaro, 1754–1806, "Number Four," from the series *Women Engaged in the Sericulture Industry*

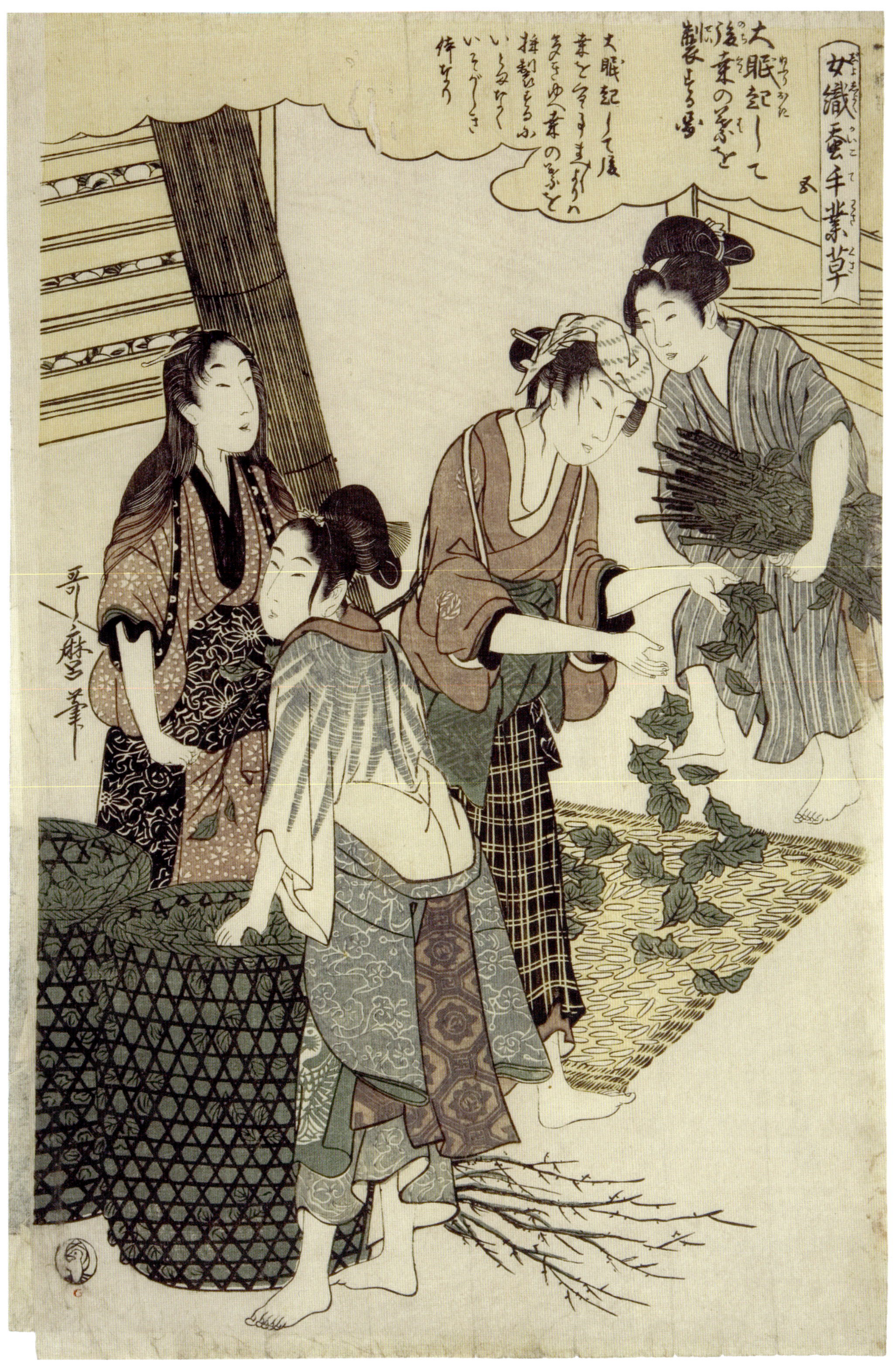

女織蚕手業草
五
大眠起して後桑の葉を製よする場
大眠記して後
桑と今まゝより
多きゆへ桑の葉を
揉割とるふ
いよなく
いそぐべき
侍なり

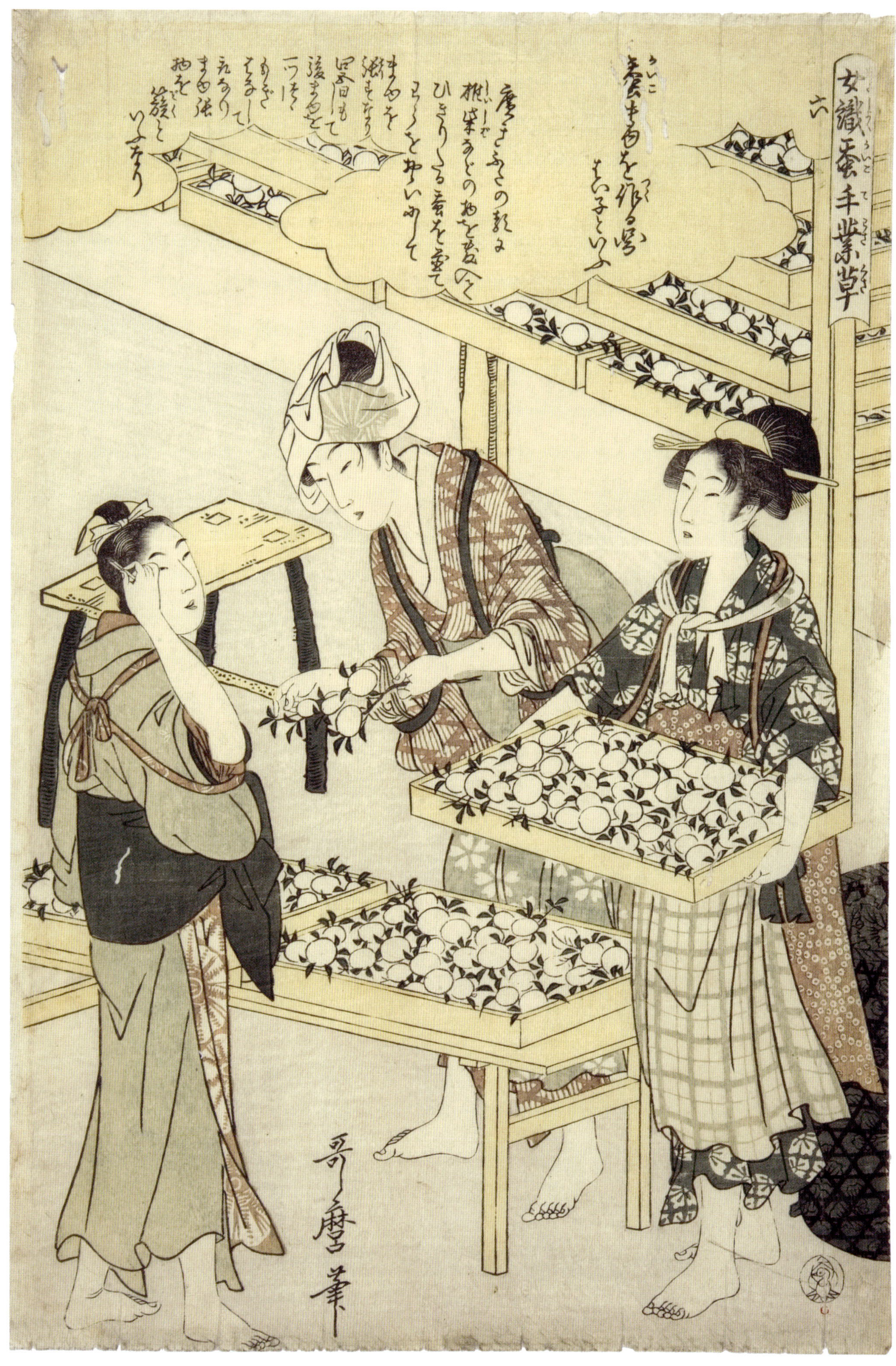

女織蚕手業草
六
こいに
まゆを白くつくる家
その子といふ
まゆをとふとの教え
桑をして
桑をみどりのおとを忘れ
ひとりくる音をあて
ろくと申れうて
まゆを
漆をなして
宮田も
後まろを
宮田も
一つよく
ろくぎ
とくして
えろり
まろ後
おゑゝゝ
地をよく
籏といふ
いふをとり

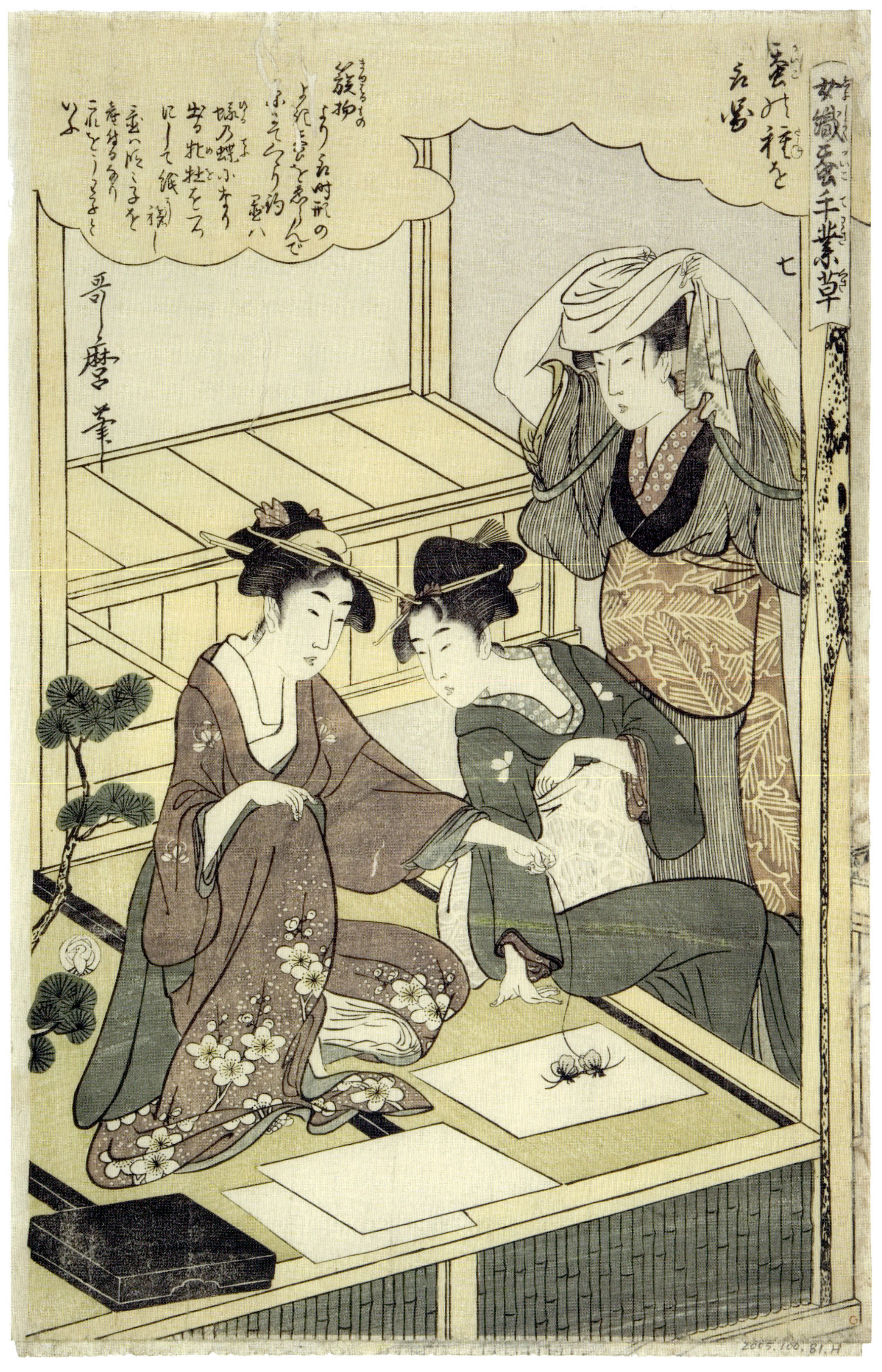

93 Kitagawa Utamaro, 1754–1806, "Number Seven," from the series *Women Engaged in the Sericulture Industry*

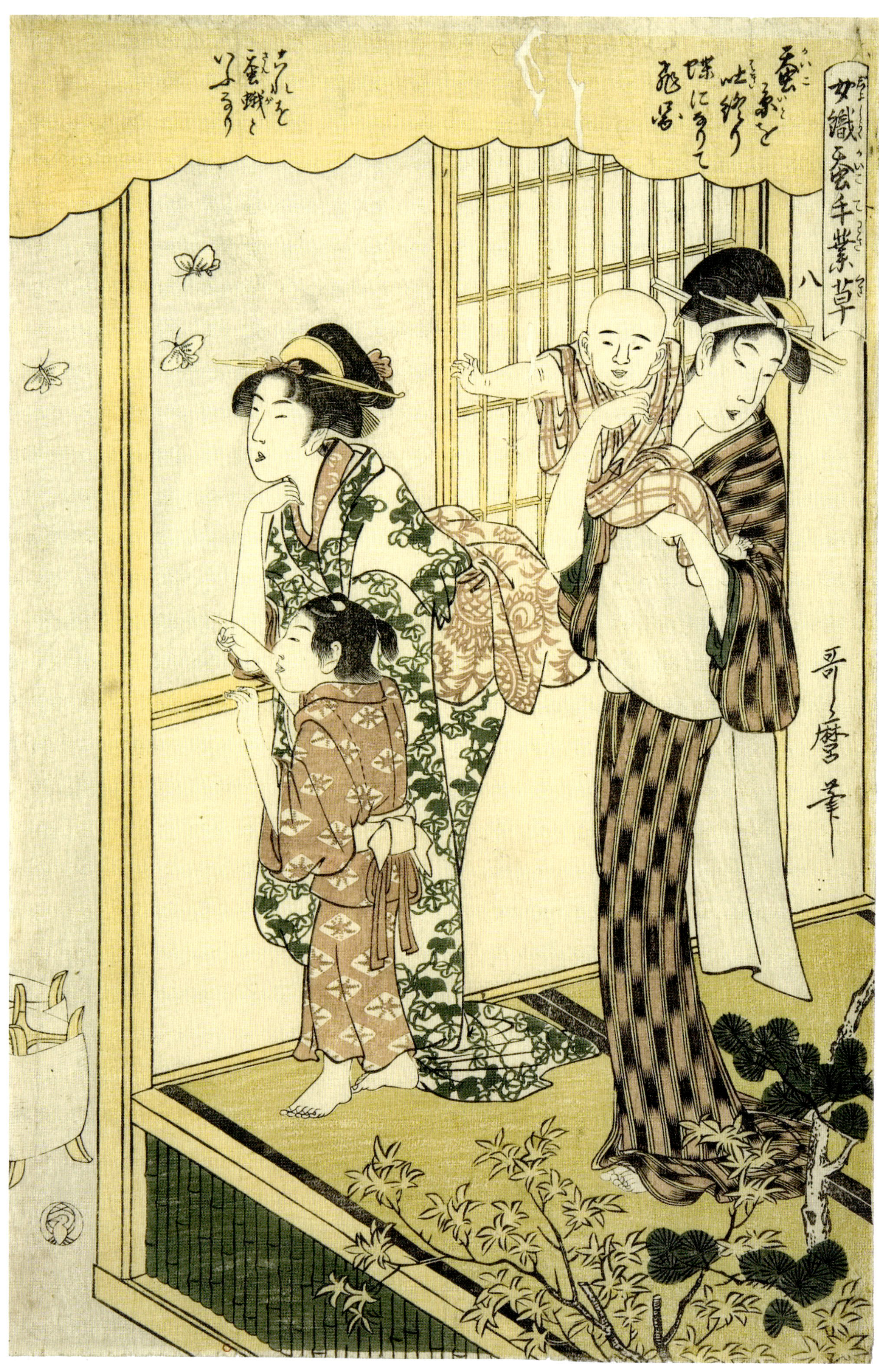

   94   Kitagawa Utamaro, 1754–1806, "Number Eight," from the series *Women Engaged in the Sericulture Industry*

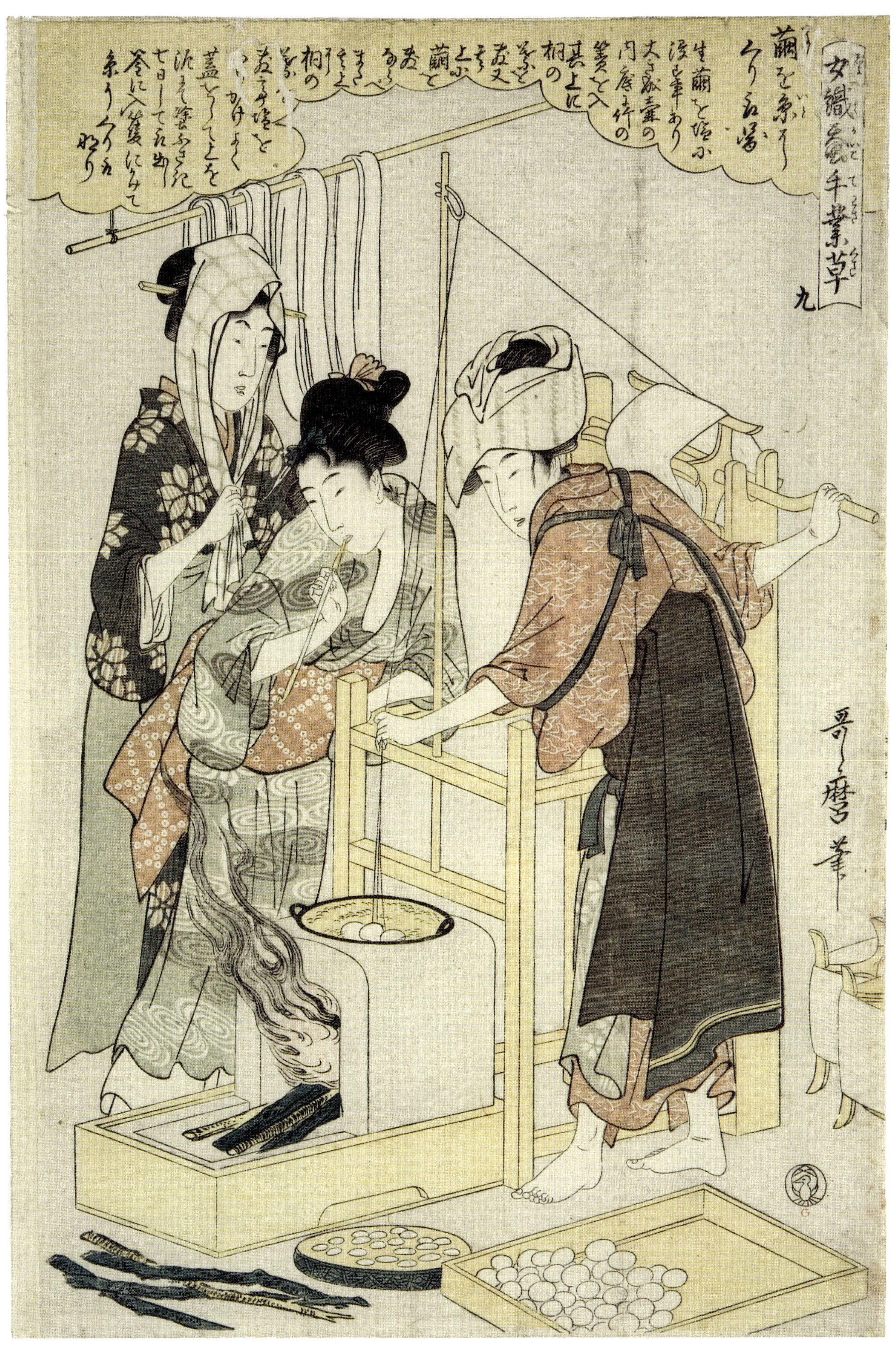

95   Kitagawa Utamaro, 1754–1806, "Number Nine," from the series *Women Engaged in the Sericulture Industry* | 115

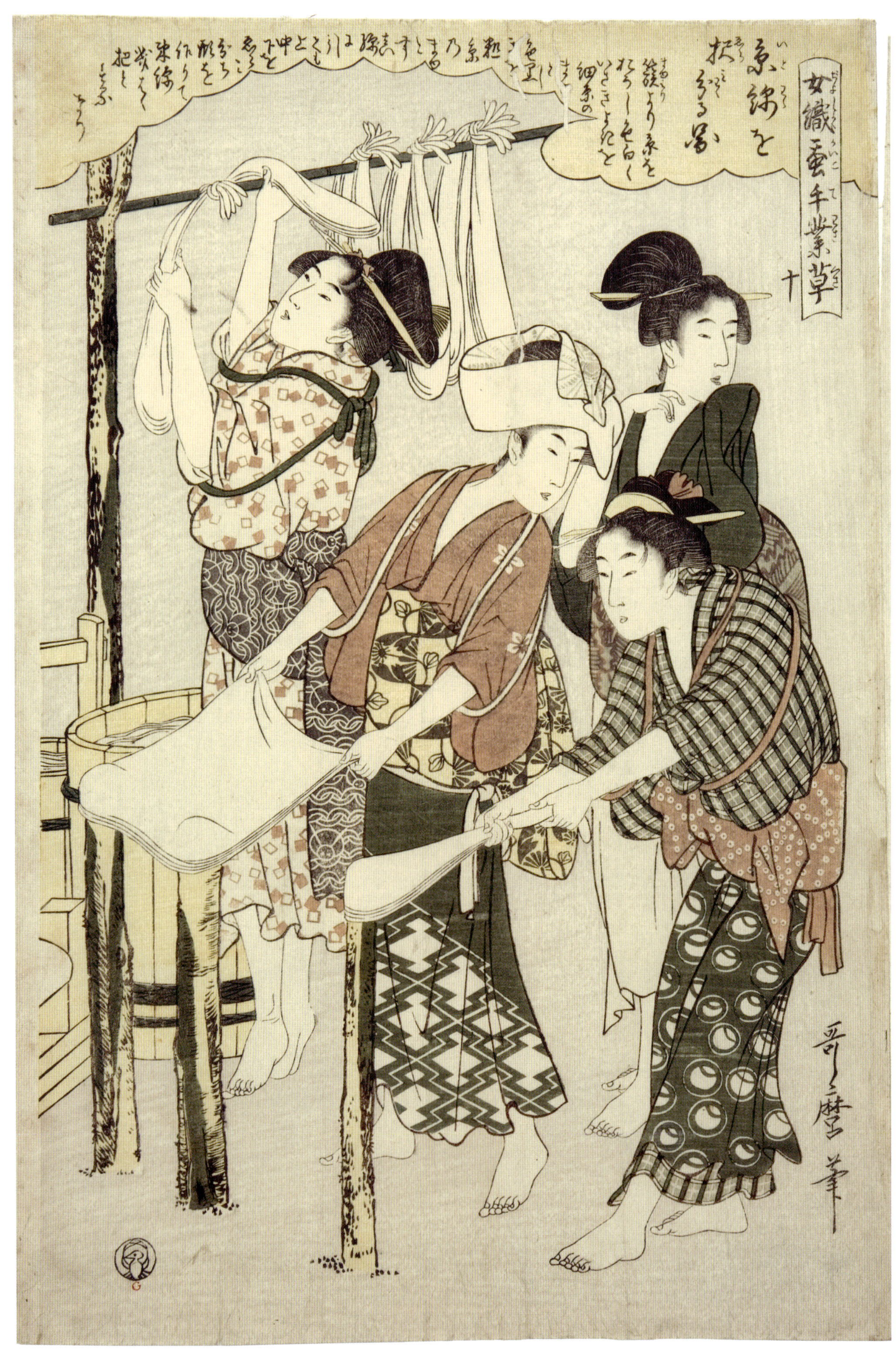

    96   Kitagawa Utamaro, 1754–1806, "Number Ten," from the series *Women Engaged in the Sericulture Industry*

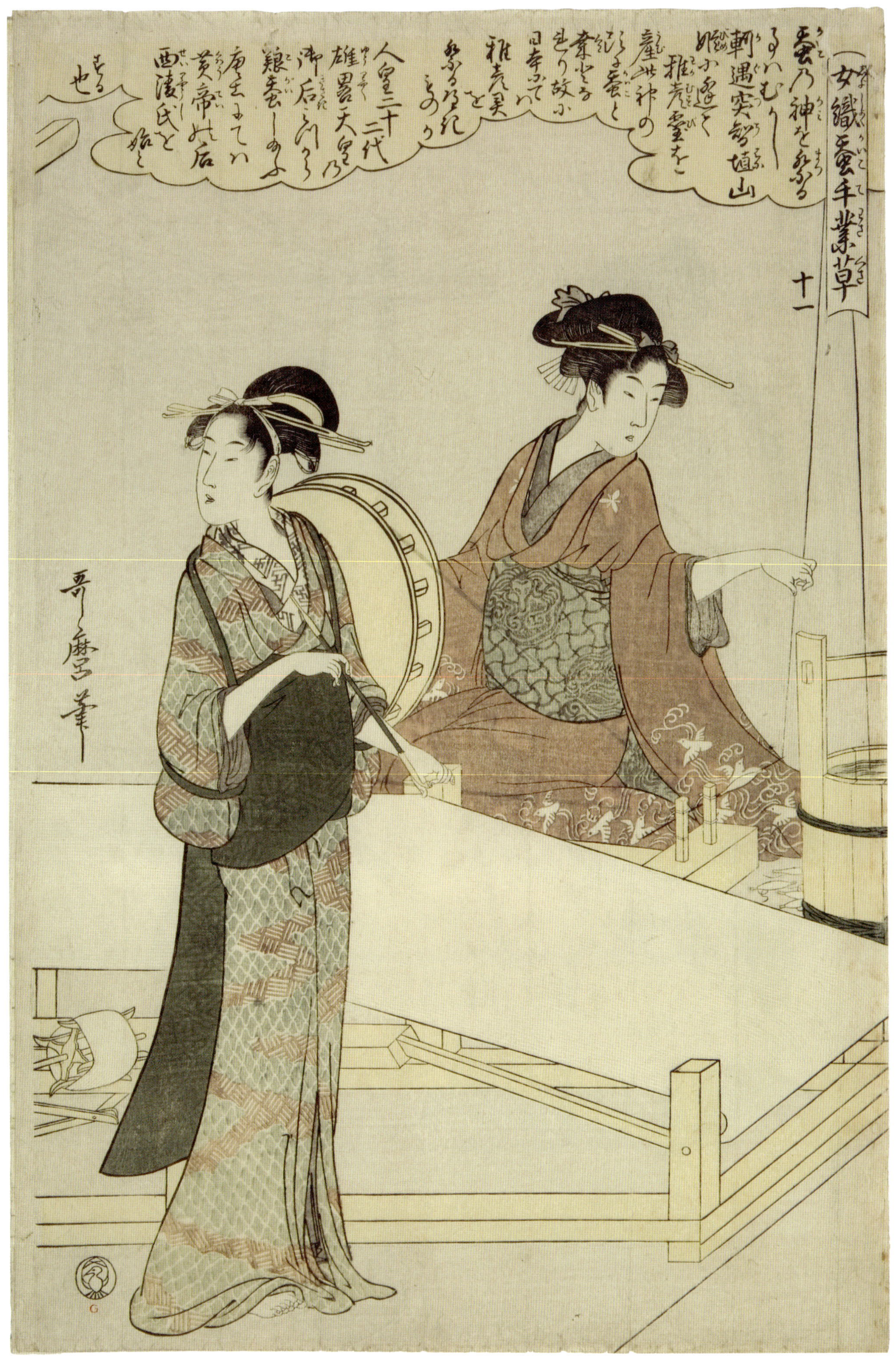

97 Kitagawa Utamaro, 1754–1806, "Number Eleven," from the series *Women Engaged in the Sericulture Industry*

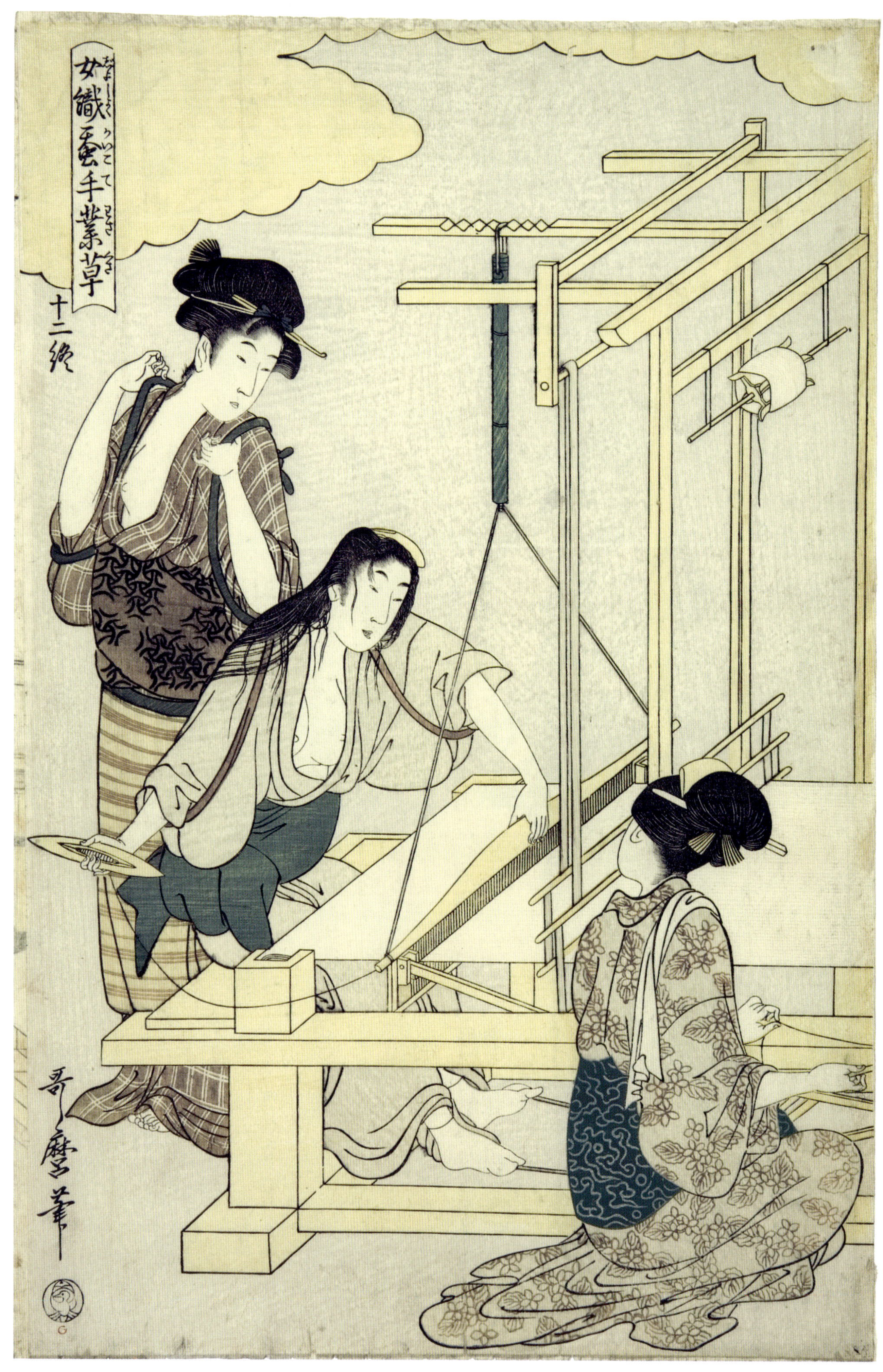

98 Kitagawa Utamaro, 1754–1806, "Number Twelve, The End," from the series *Women Engaged in the Sericulture Industry*

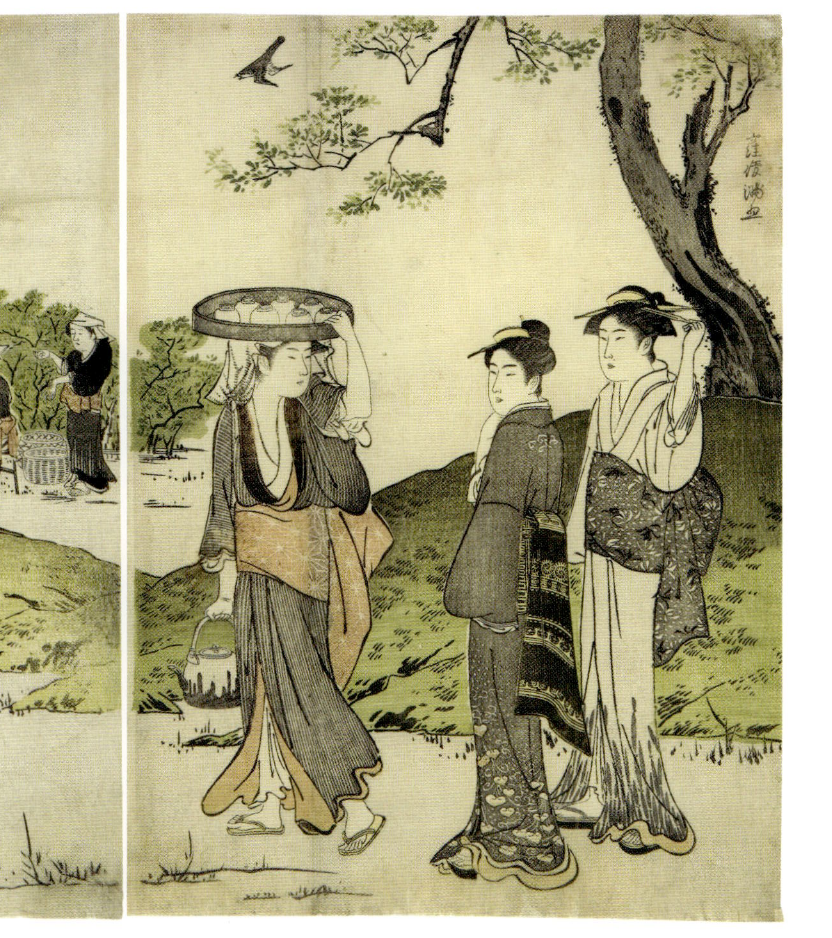
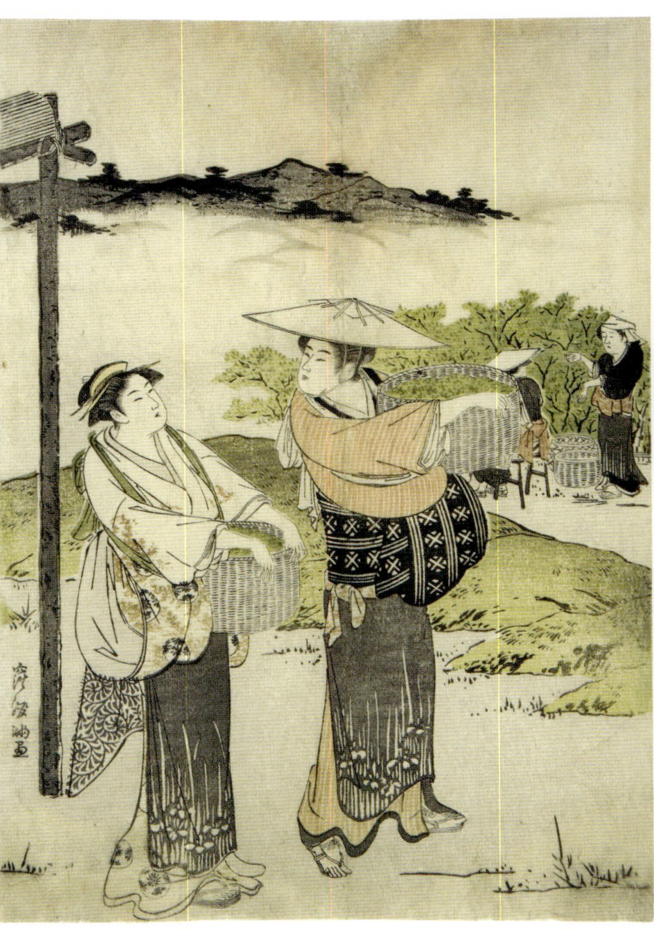
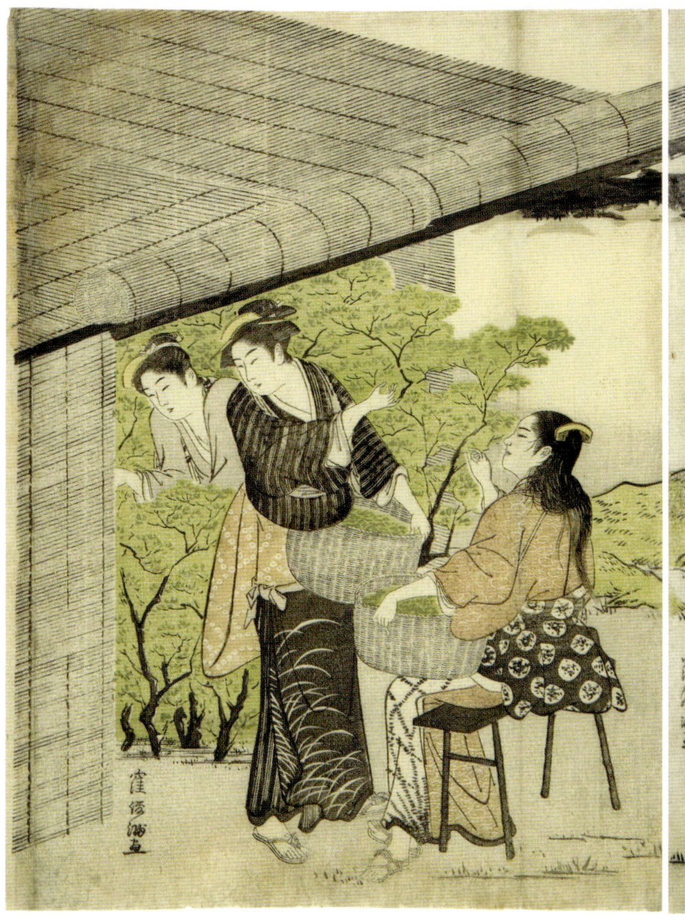

99   Kubo Shunman, 1757–1820, Picking tea in Uji

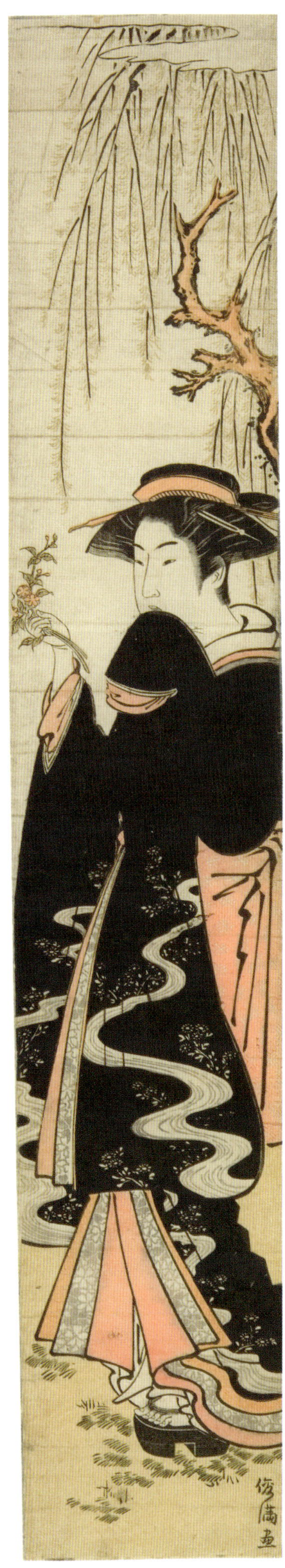

    100   Kubo Shunman, 1757–1820, Young woman under a willow tree

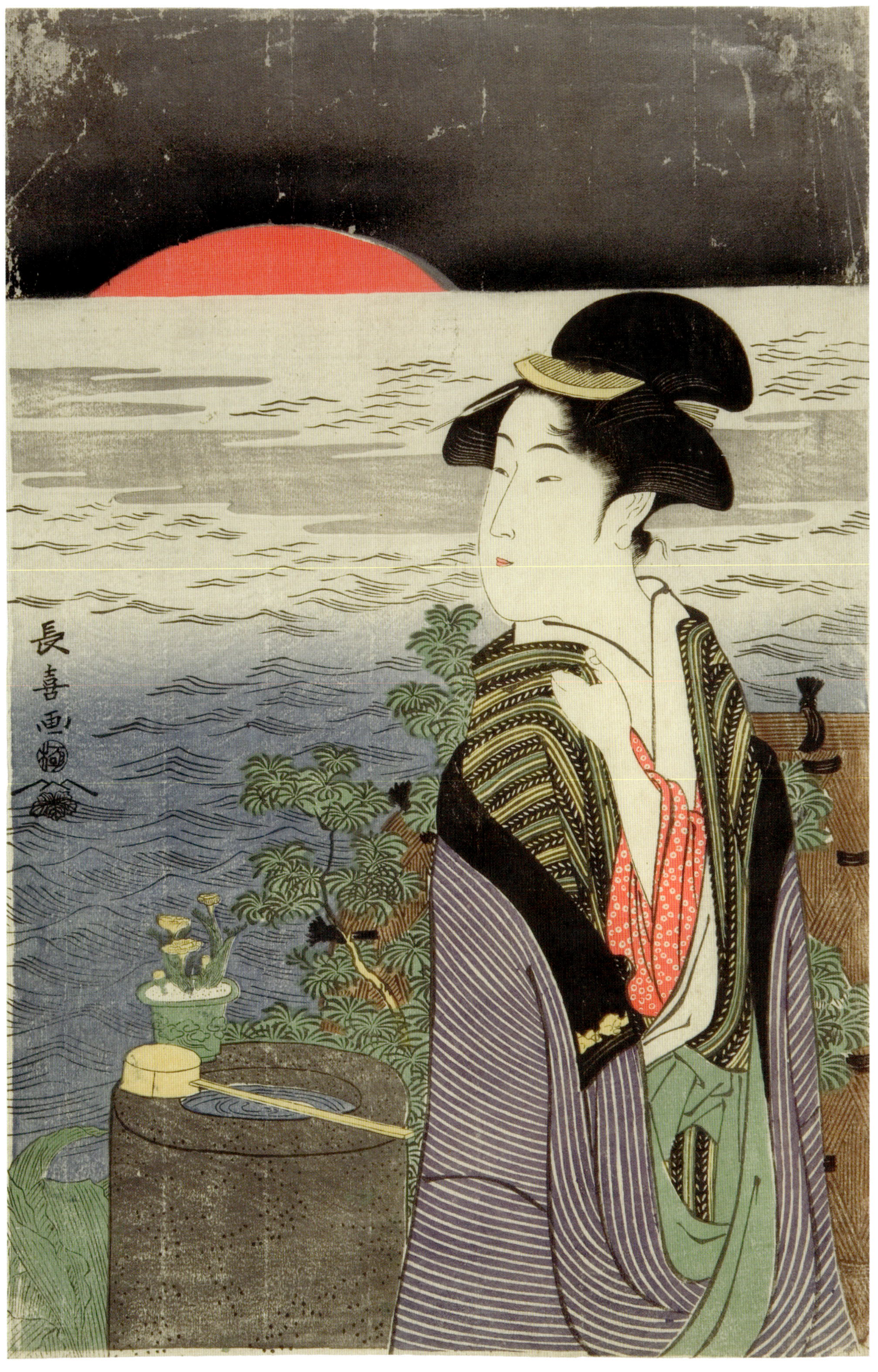

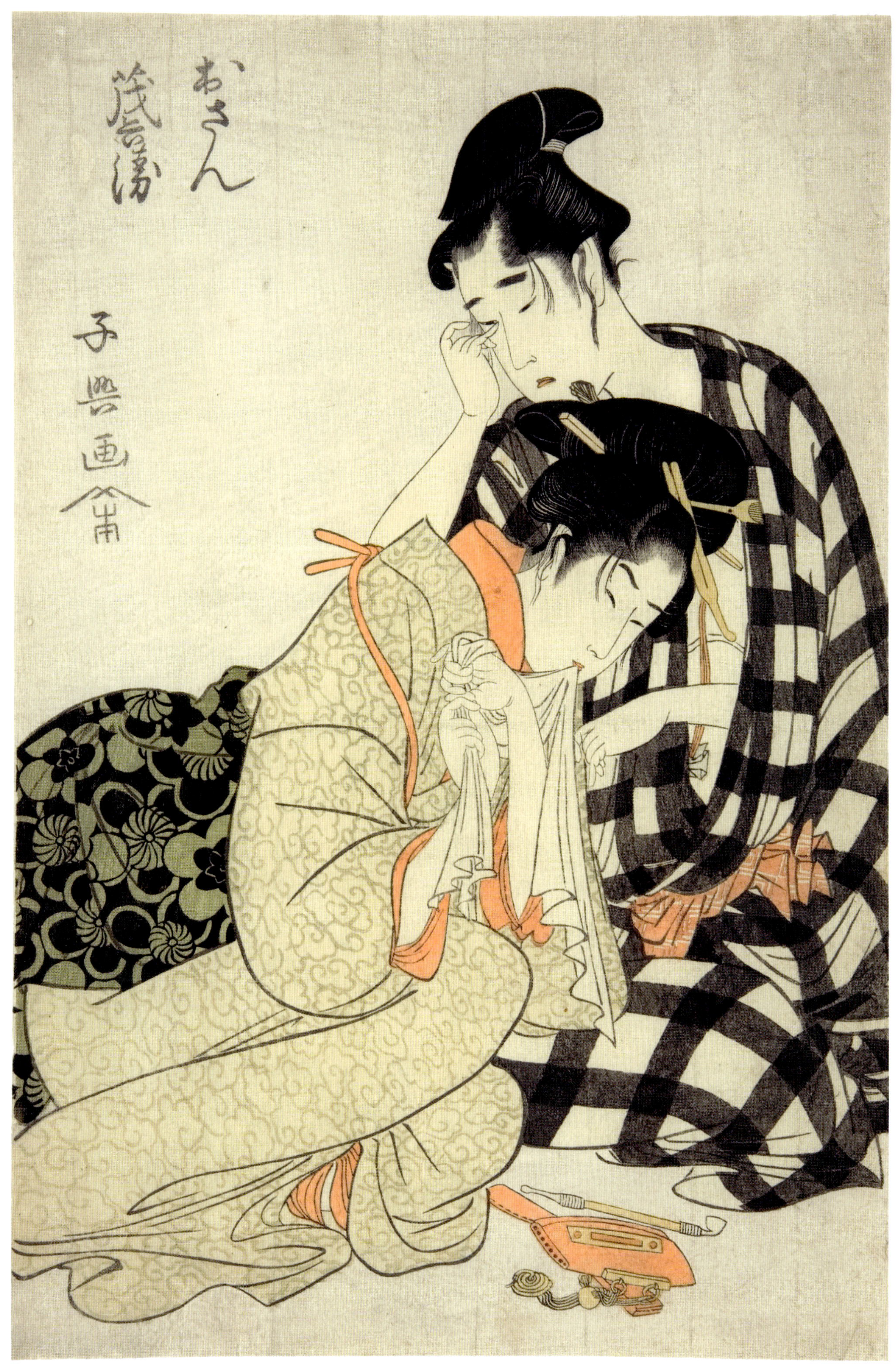

    102   Eishōsai Chōki, 1775–1825, "[The tragic lovers] Osan and Mohei"

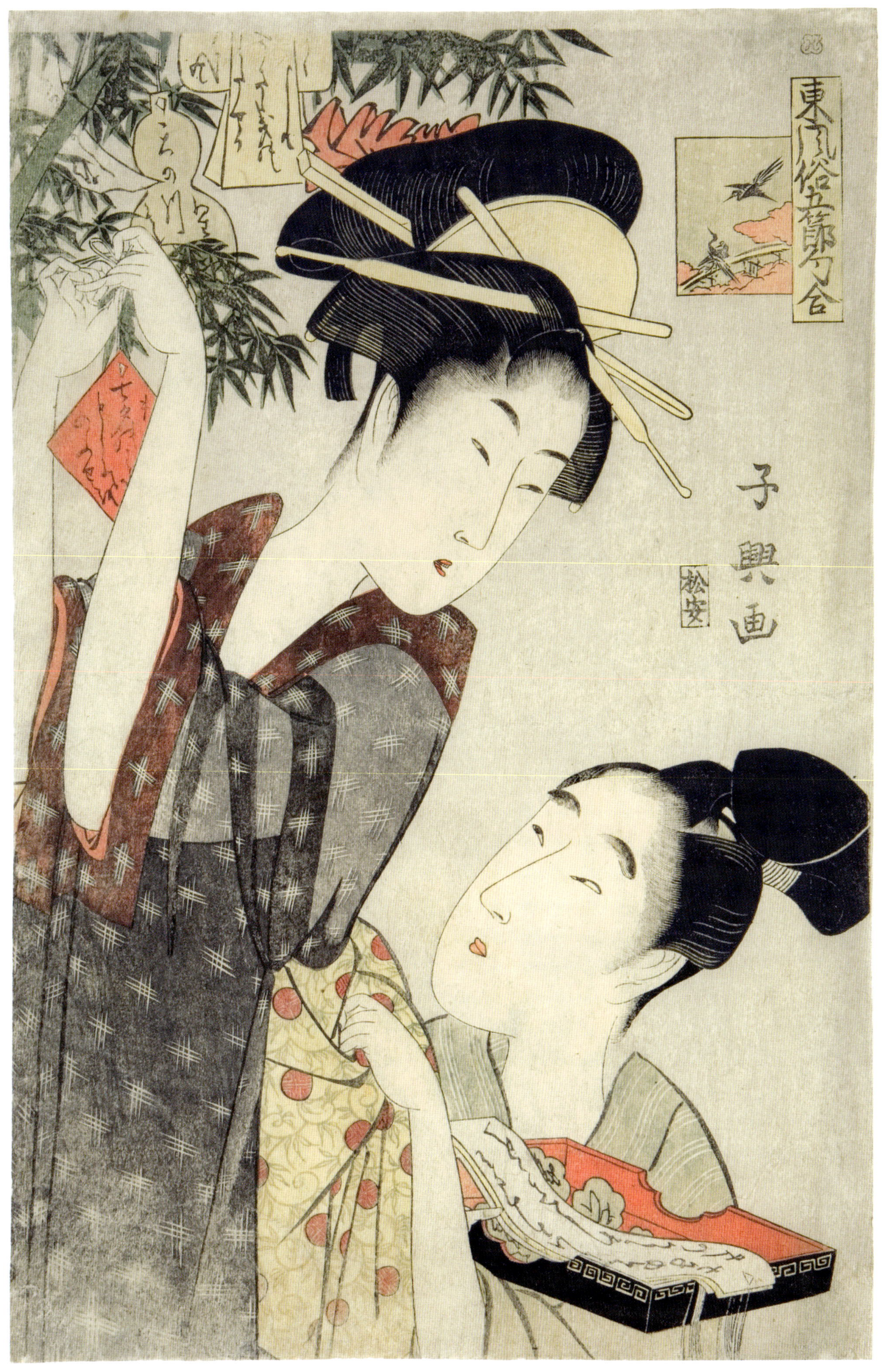

103   Eishōsai Chōki, 1775–1825, Tanabata Festival, from the series *Comparison of the Customs of the Five Festivals in Eastern Japan*

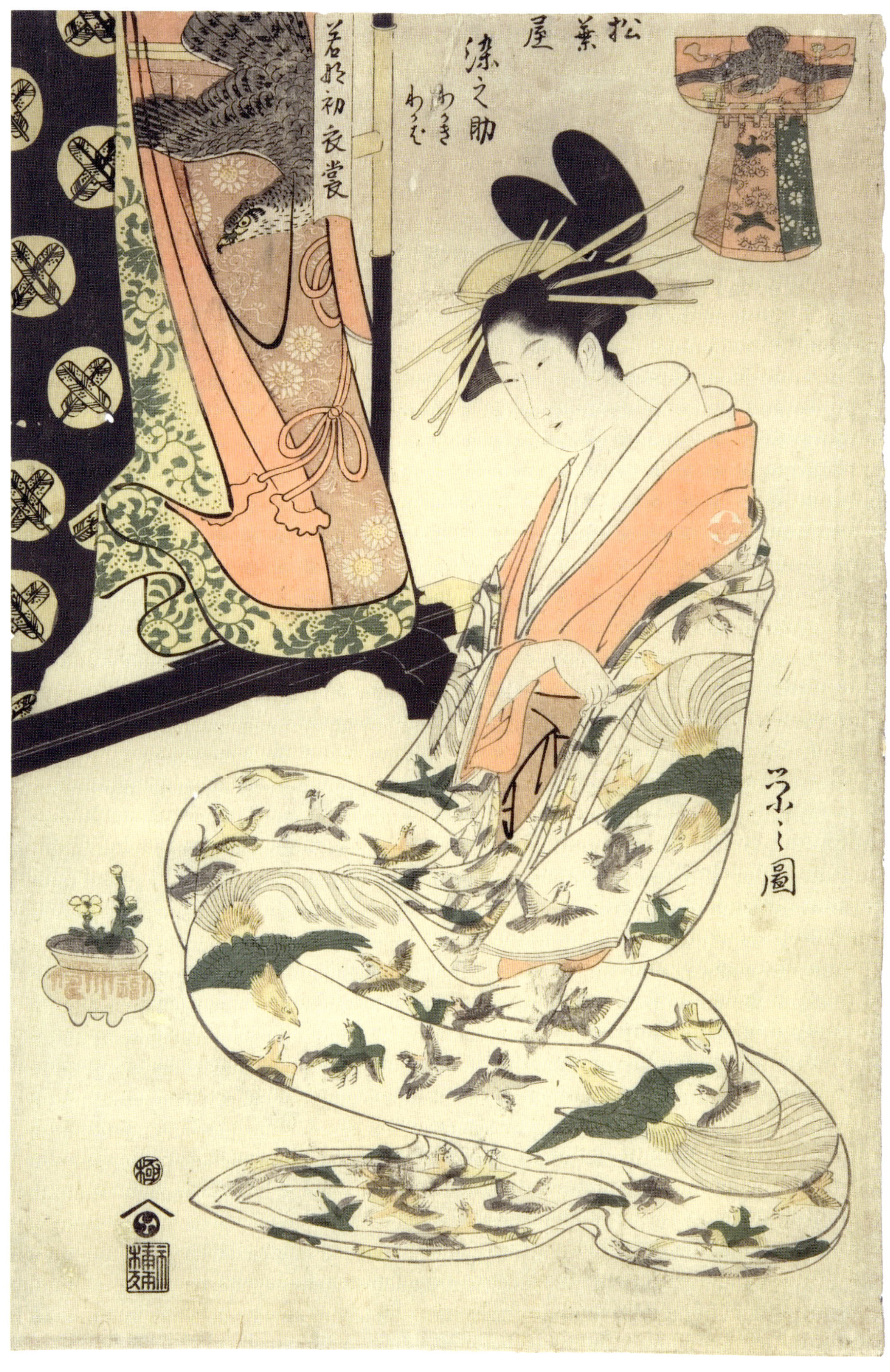

104 Chōbunsai Eishi, 1756–1829, "Somenosuke of the Matsubaya [*kamuro*] Wakaki and Wakaba," from the series *New Year Fashions as Fresh as Young Leaves*

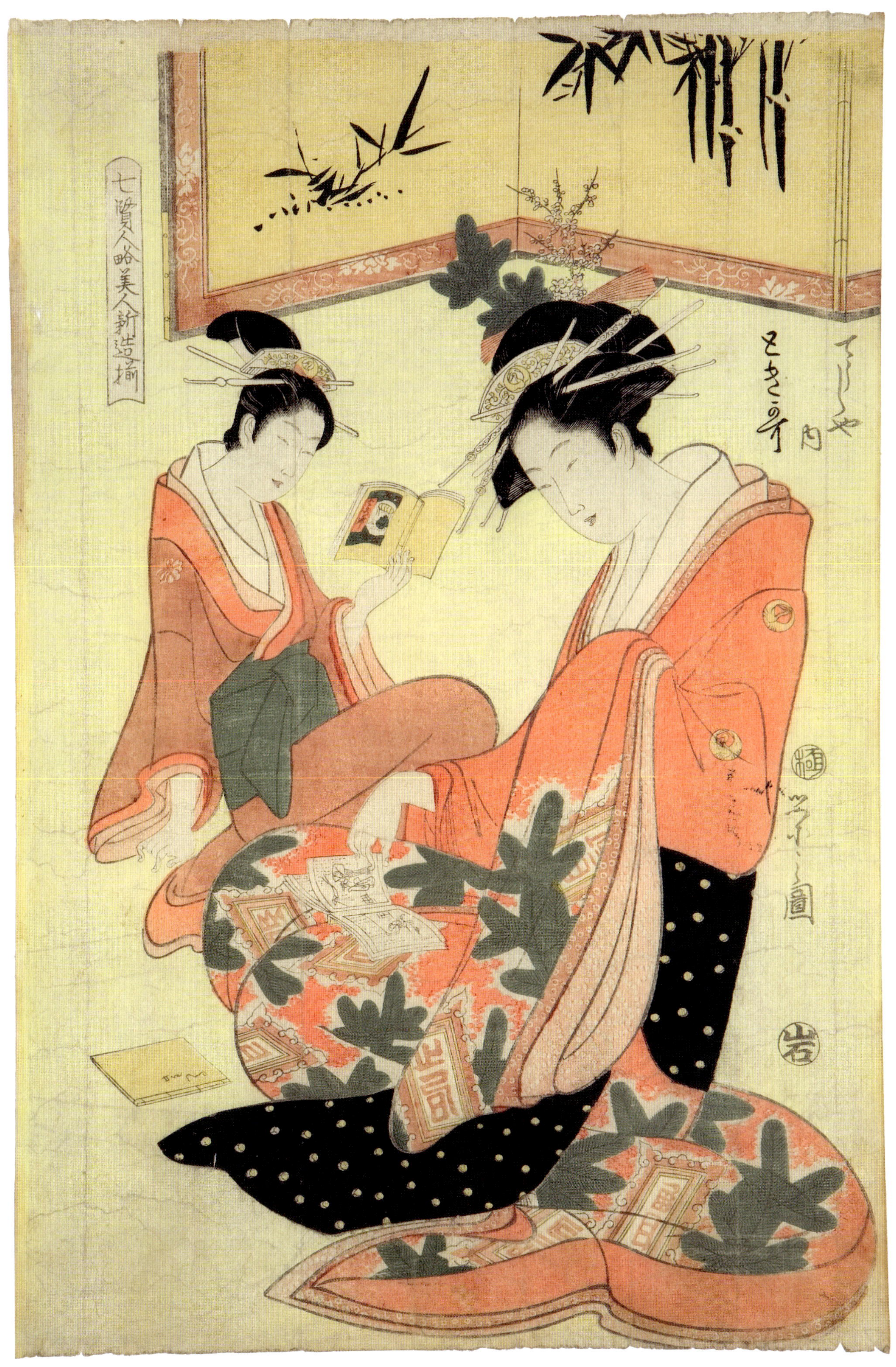

105   Chōbunsai Eishi, 1756–1829, "Tokiuta of the Chōjiya," from the series *An Array of Beautiful Apprenctice Courtesans as the Seven Sages of the Bamboo Grove*

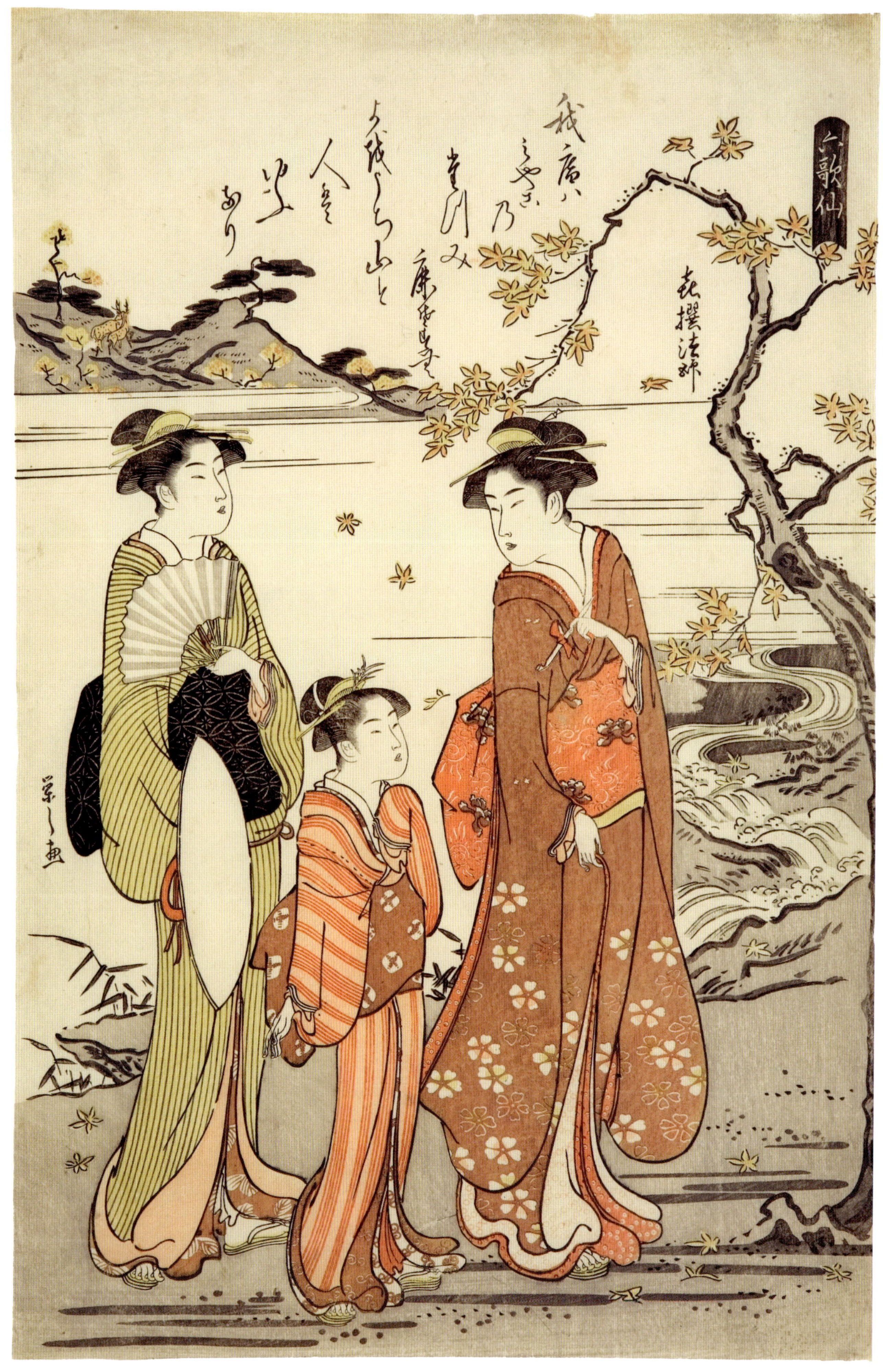

106   Chōbunsai Eishi, 1756–1829, "Monk Kisen," from the series *Six Poetic Immortals*

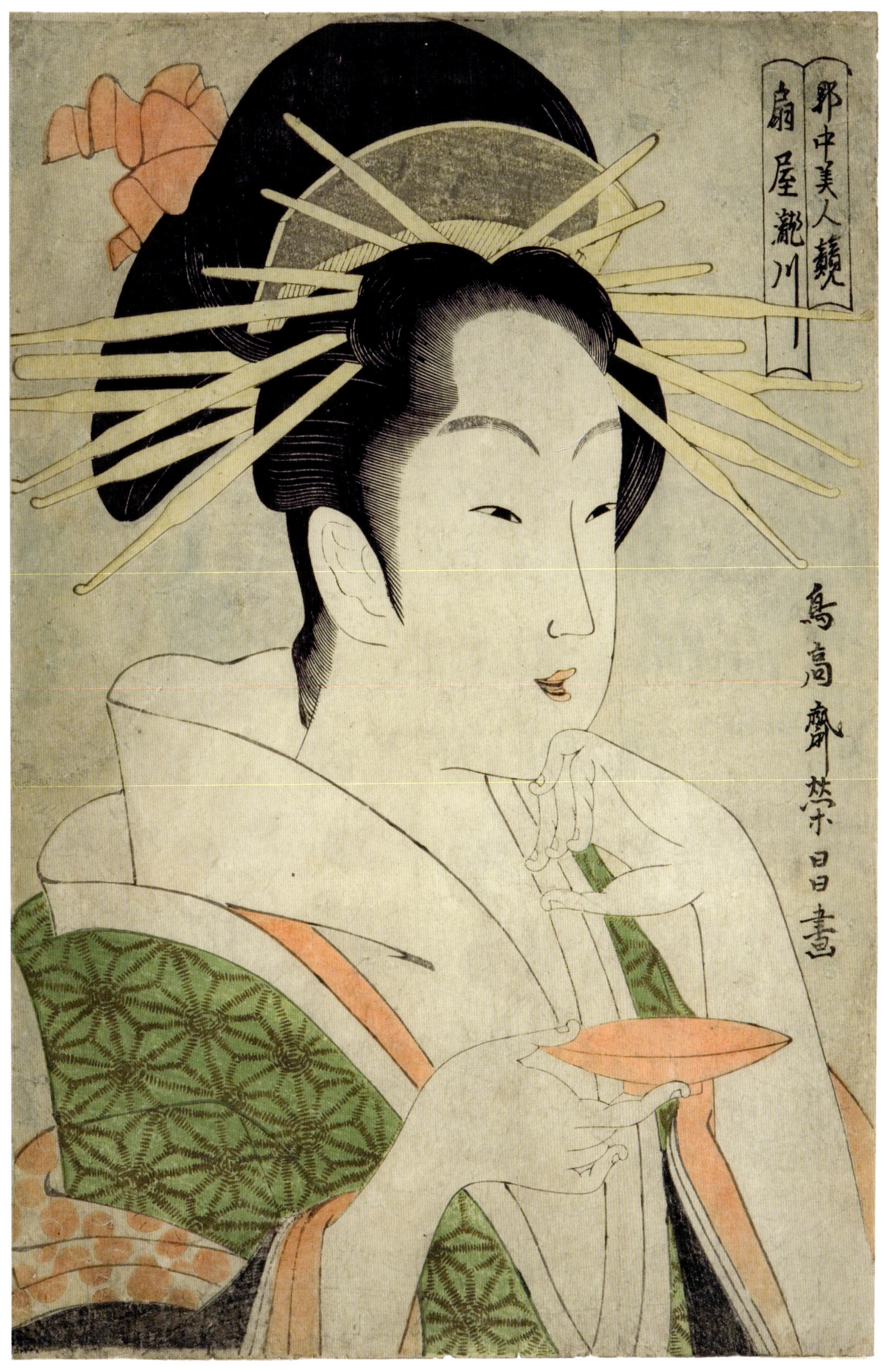

107 Chōkōsai Eishō, active 1780–1800, "Takigawa of the Ōgiya," from the series *Contest of Beauties in the Pleasure Quarters*

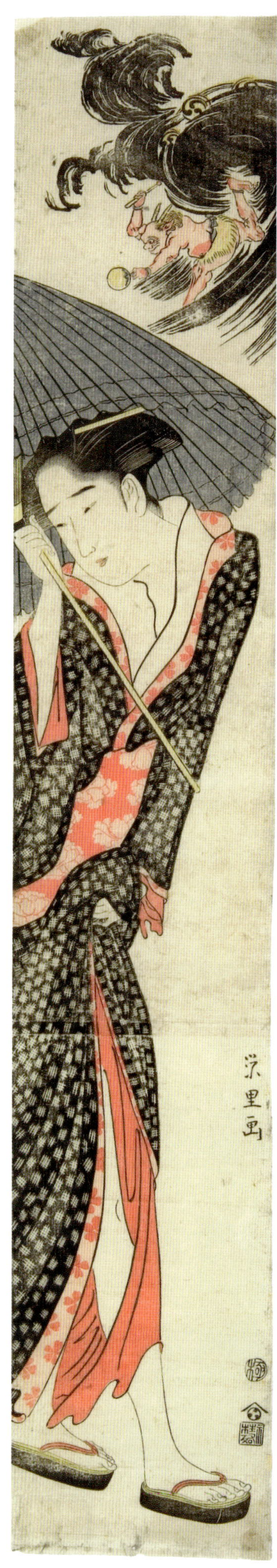

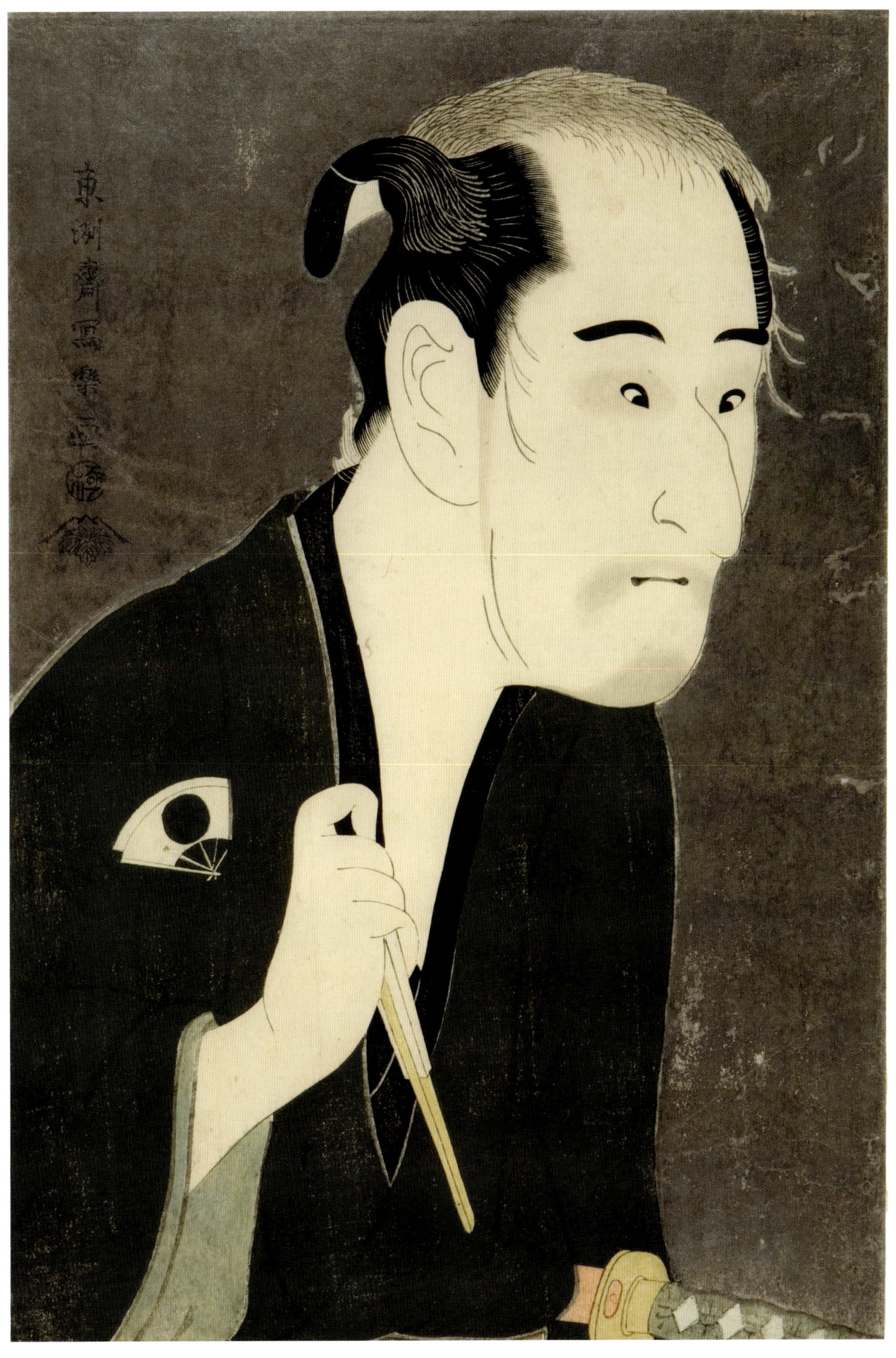

109   Tōshūsai Sharaku, active 1794–1795, *The Actor Onoe Matsusuke I as Matsushita Mikinoshin* | *129*

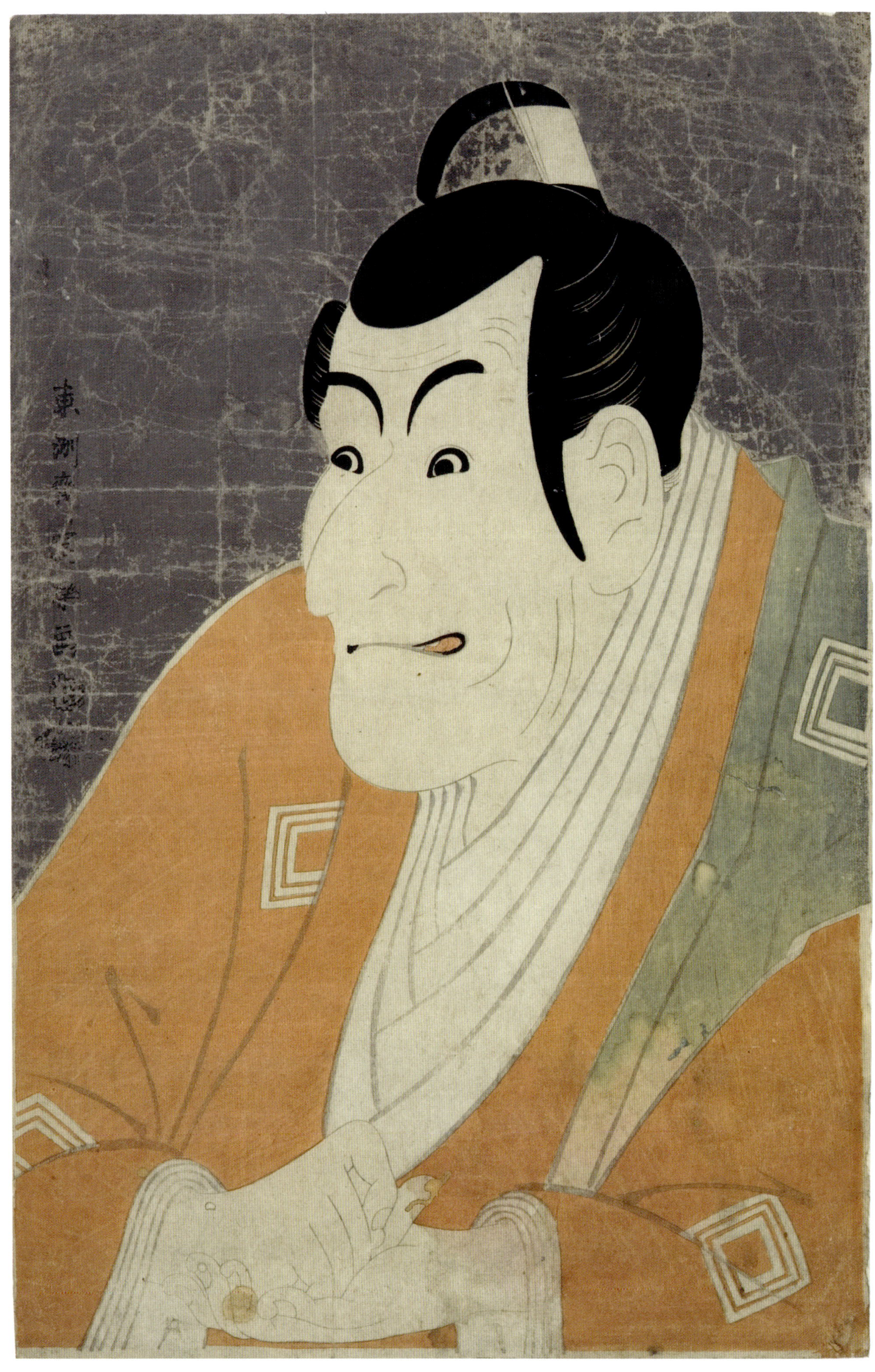

 | 110 Tōshūsai Sharaku, active 1794–1795, *The Actor Ichikawa Ebizō IV as Takemura Sadanoshin*

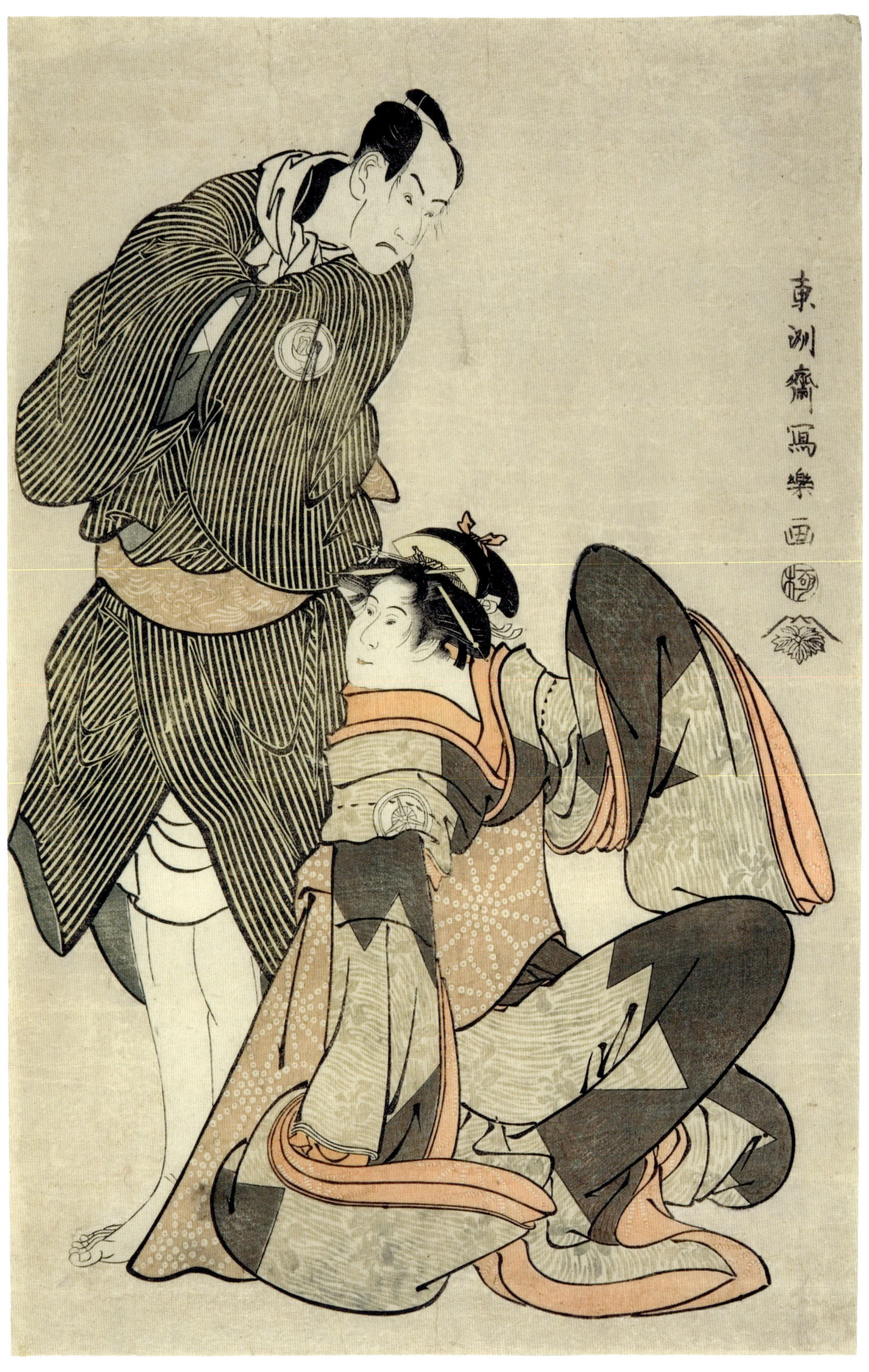

111   Tōshūsai Sharaku, active 1794–1795, The actors Iwai Hanshirō IV as Shinanoya Ohan and Bandō Hikosaburō III as Obiya Chōemon

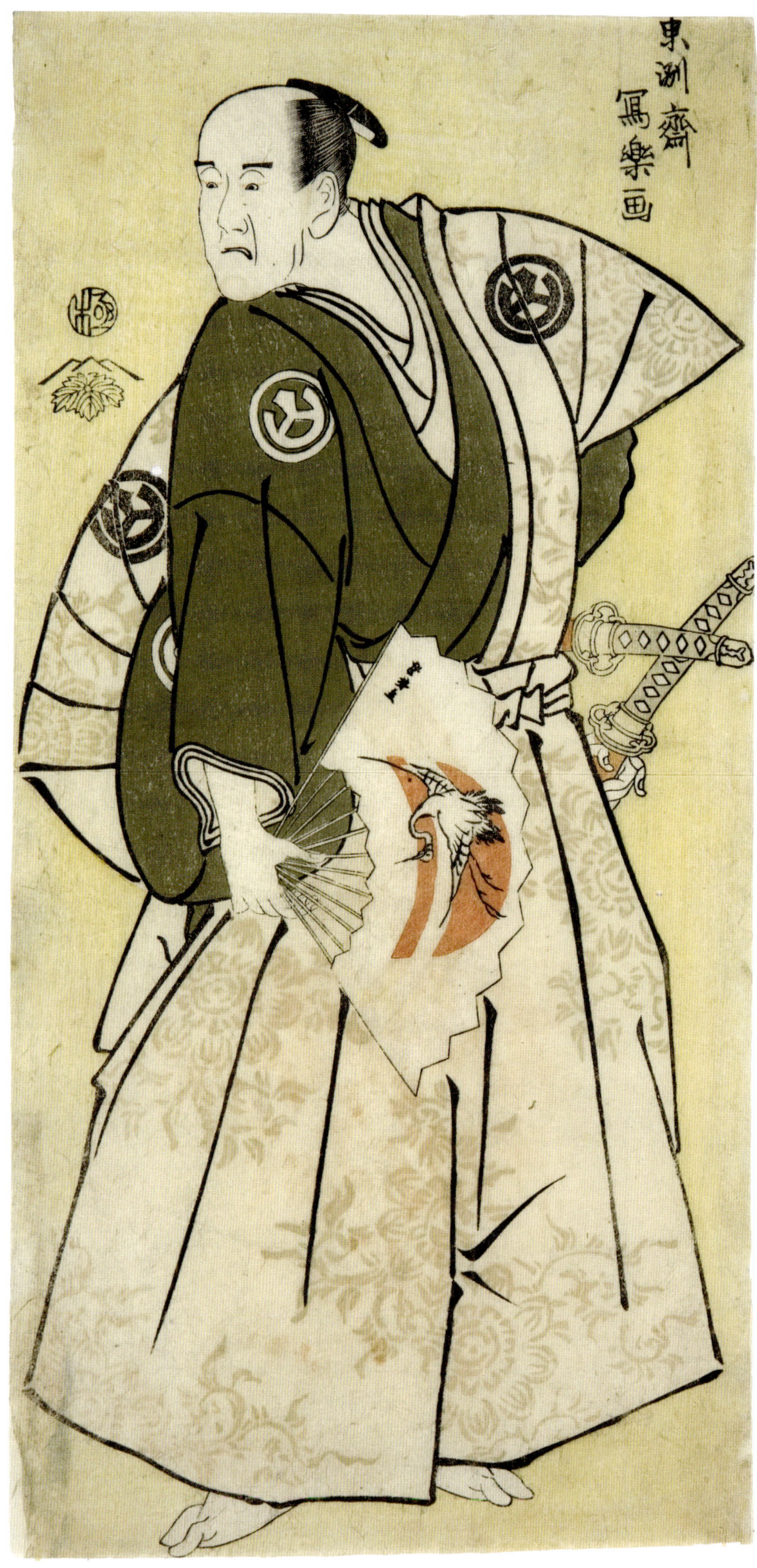

 | 112 Tōshūsai Sharaku, active 1794–1795, The actor Yamashina Shirōjūrō as Nagoya Sanzaemon

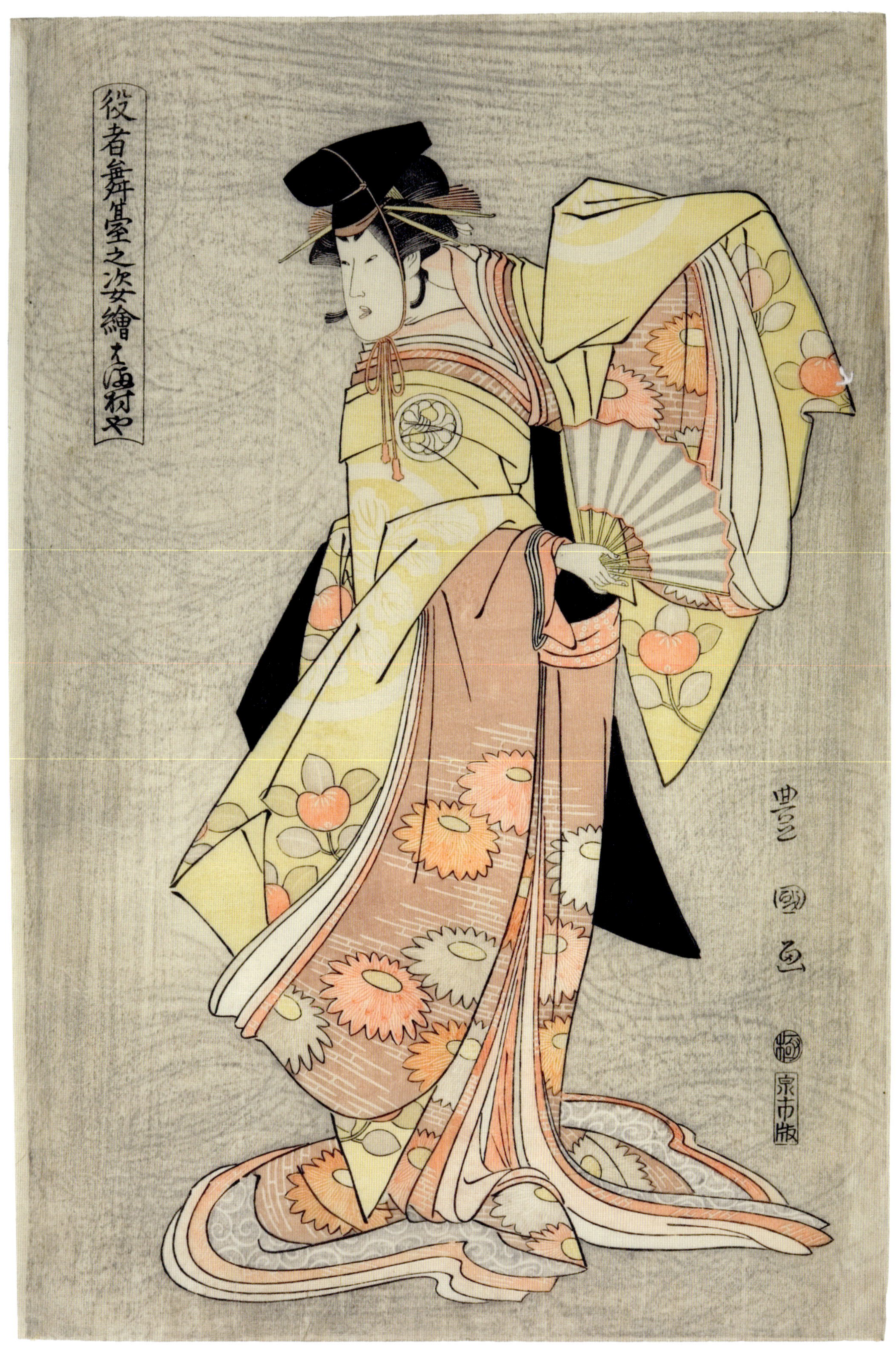

113   Utagawa Toyokuni, 1769–1825, "Hamamuraya" (The actor Segawa Kikunojō III as Yamato Manzai,
actually Shirabyōshi Hisakata of Miyako Kujō), from the series *Portraits of Actors on Stage*

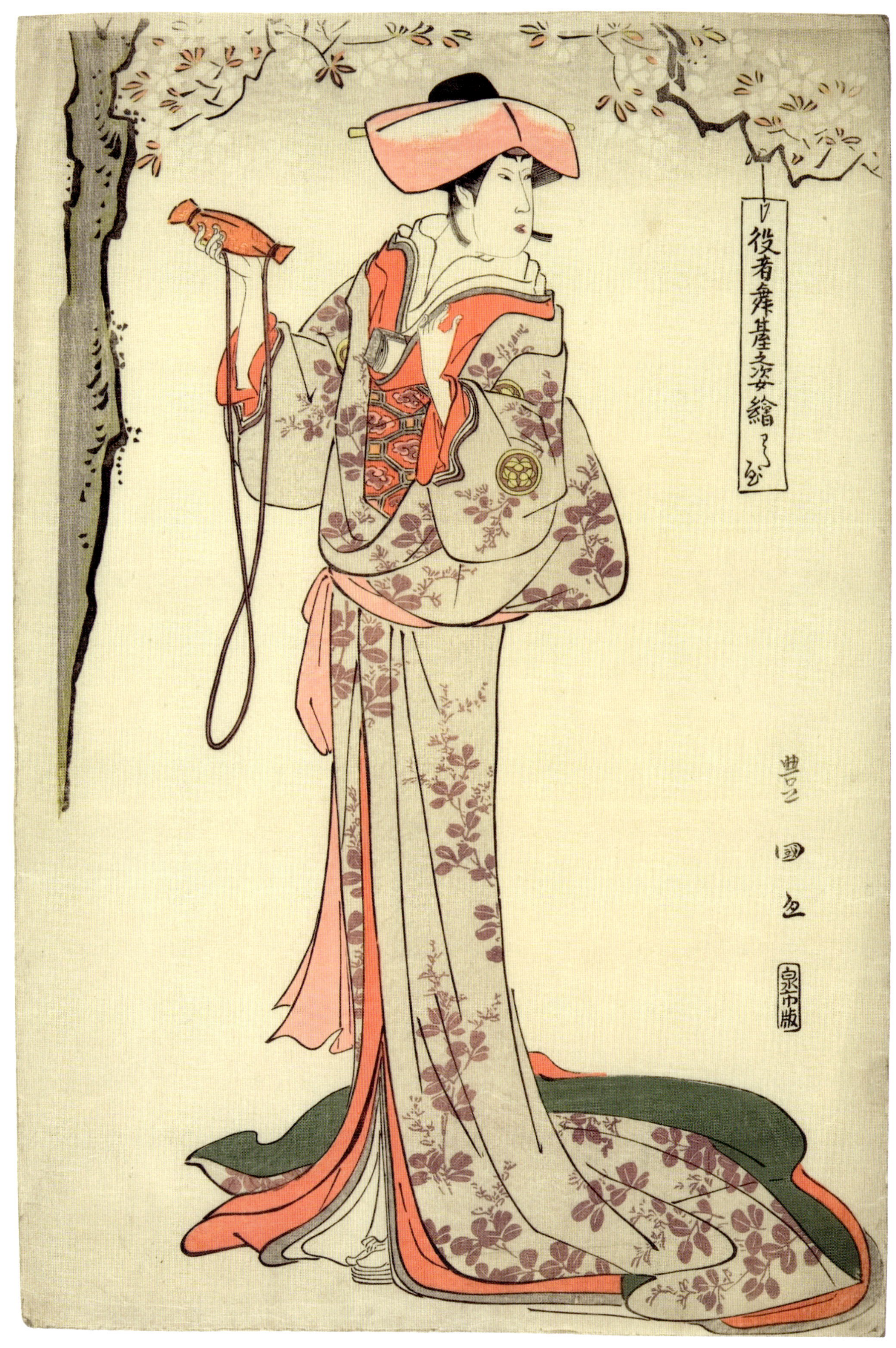

114　Utagawa Toyokuni, 1769–1825, "Wataya" (The actor Osagawa Tsuneyo II as Chūrō Onoe), from the series *Portraits of Actors on Stage*

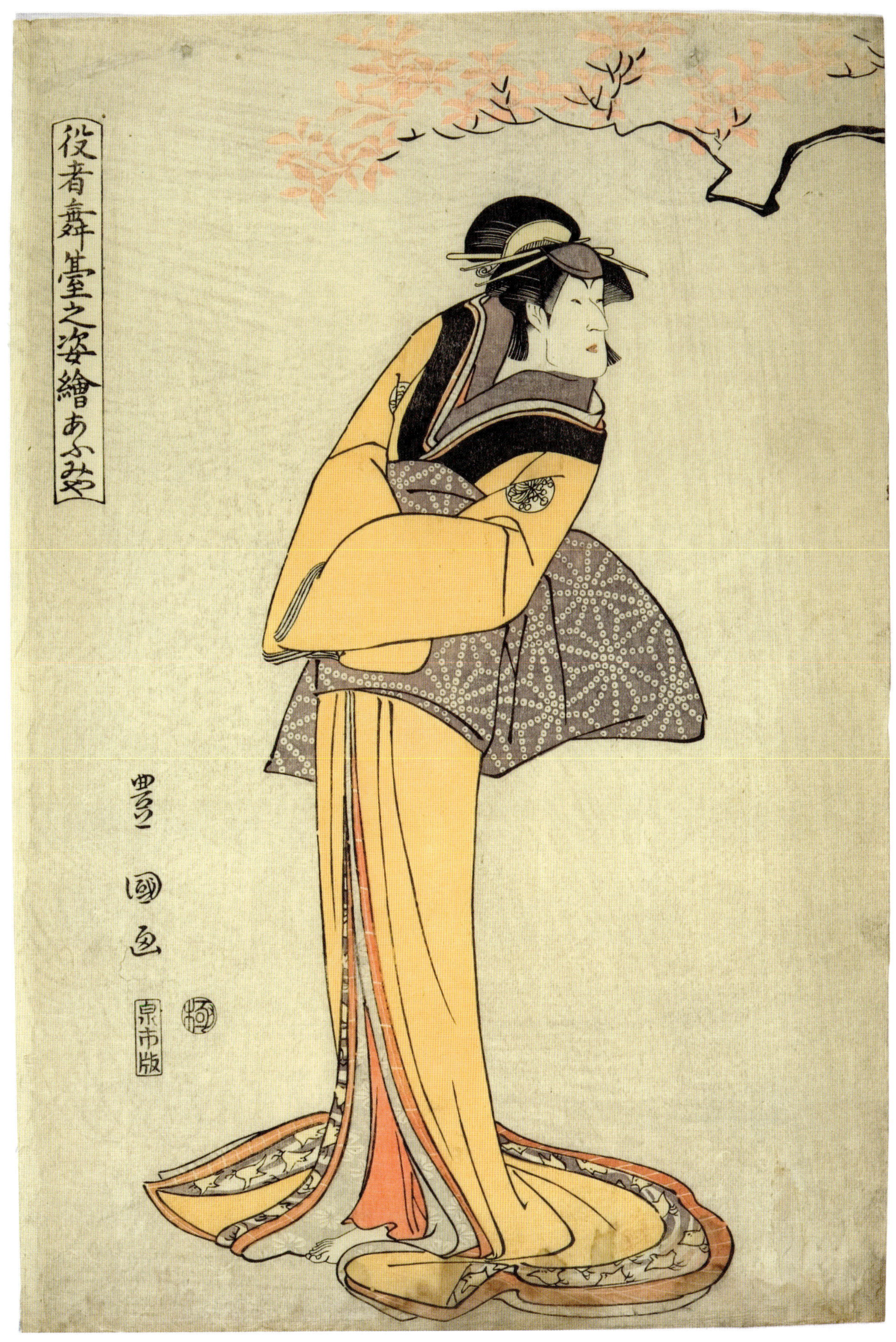

115　Utagawa Toyokuni, 1769–1825, "Ōmiya" [The actor Nakayama Tomisaburō I as Ohide, wife of Sazanami Tatsugorō, actually Teriha, younger sister of Abe Munetō and Abe Sadatō], from the series *Portraits of Actors on Stage*

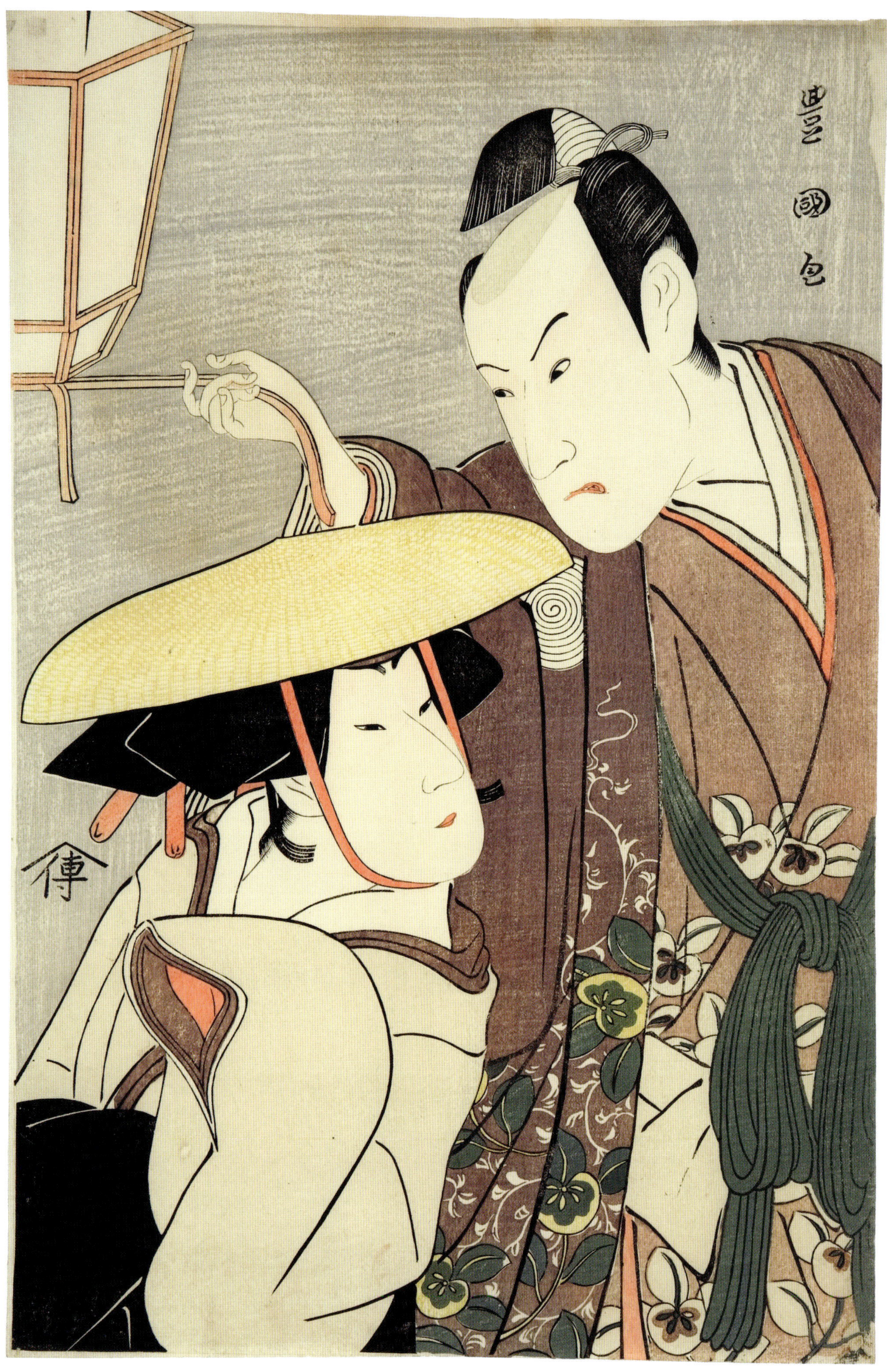

116   Utagawa Toyokuni, 1769–1825, The actors Bandō Hikosaburō III as Fujitarō and Nakamura Noshio II as Imayō Utabikuni

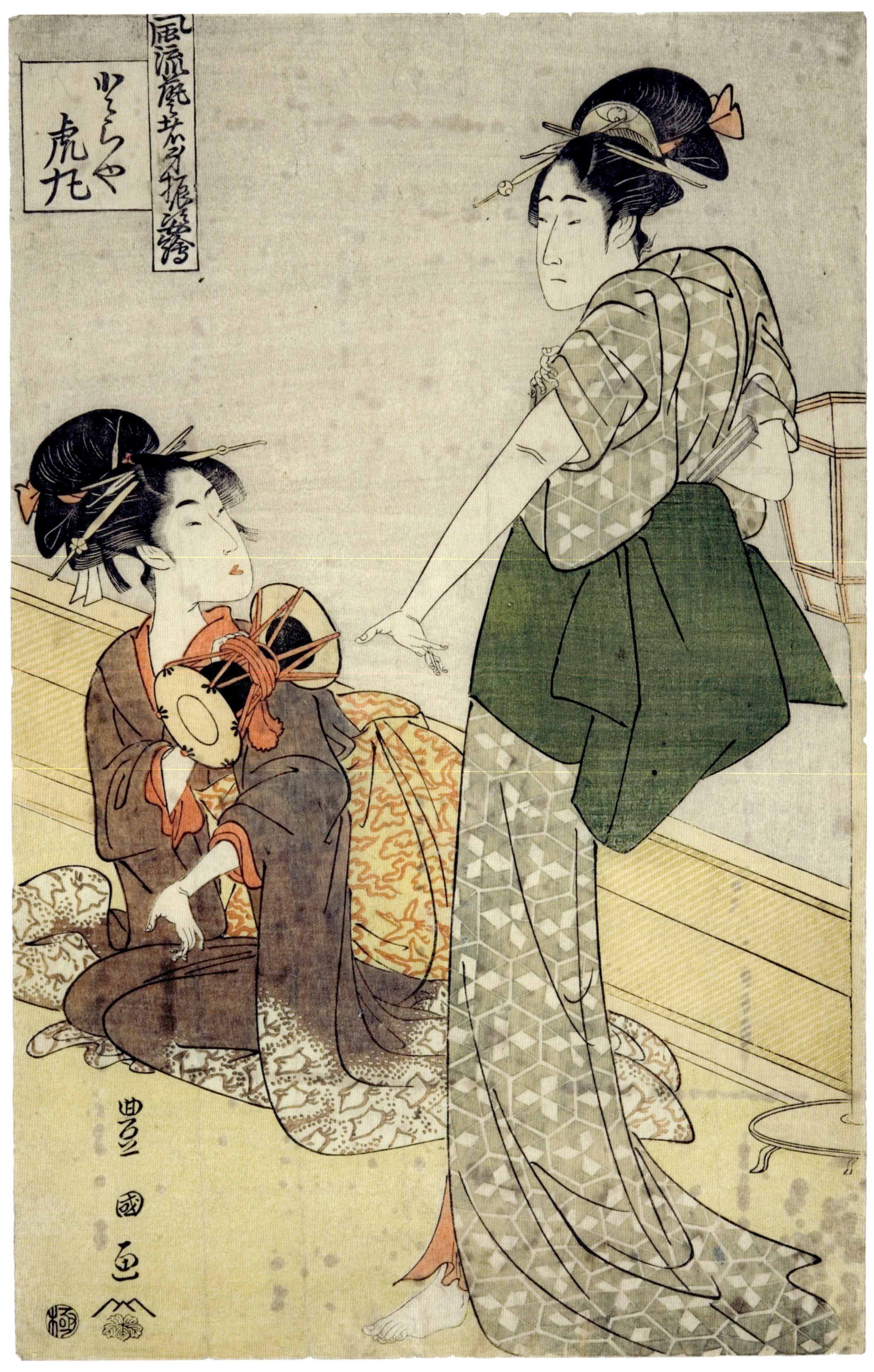

117　Utagawa Toyokuni, 1769–1825, "Toramaru of the Toraya," from the series *Portraits of Fashionable Geisha Imitating Actors*

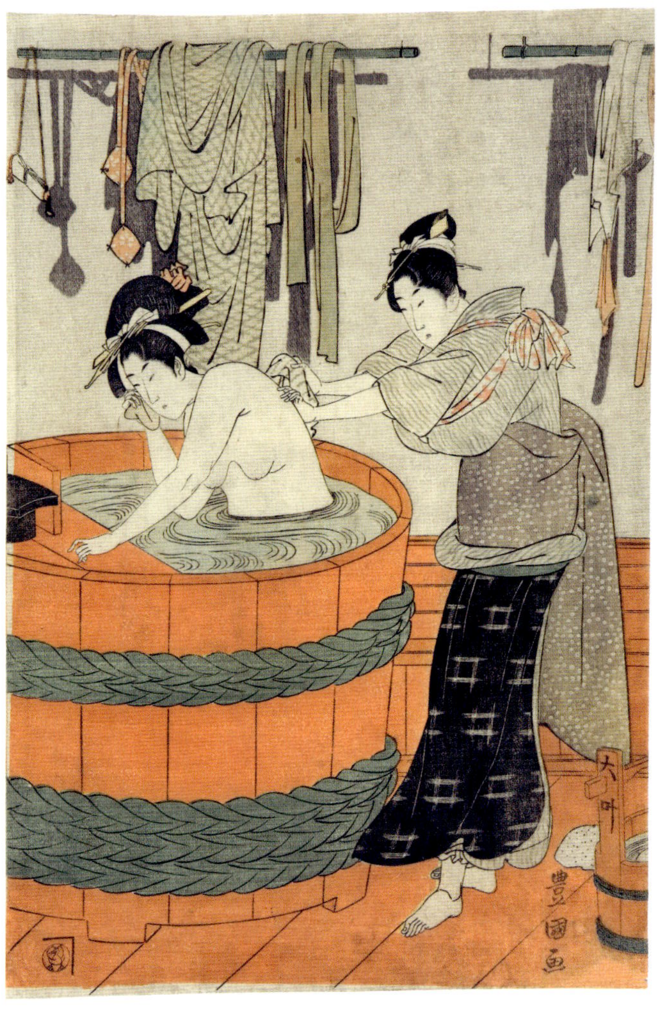

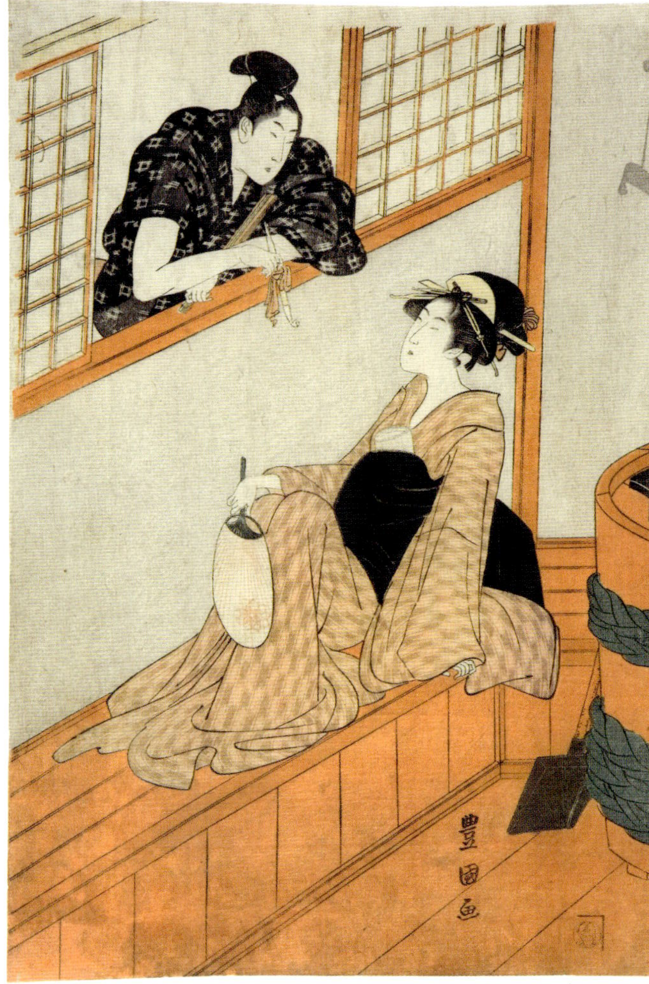

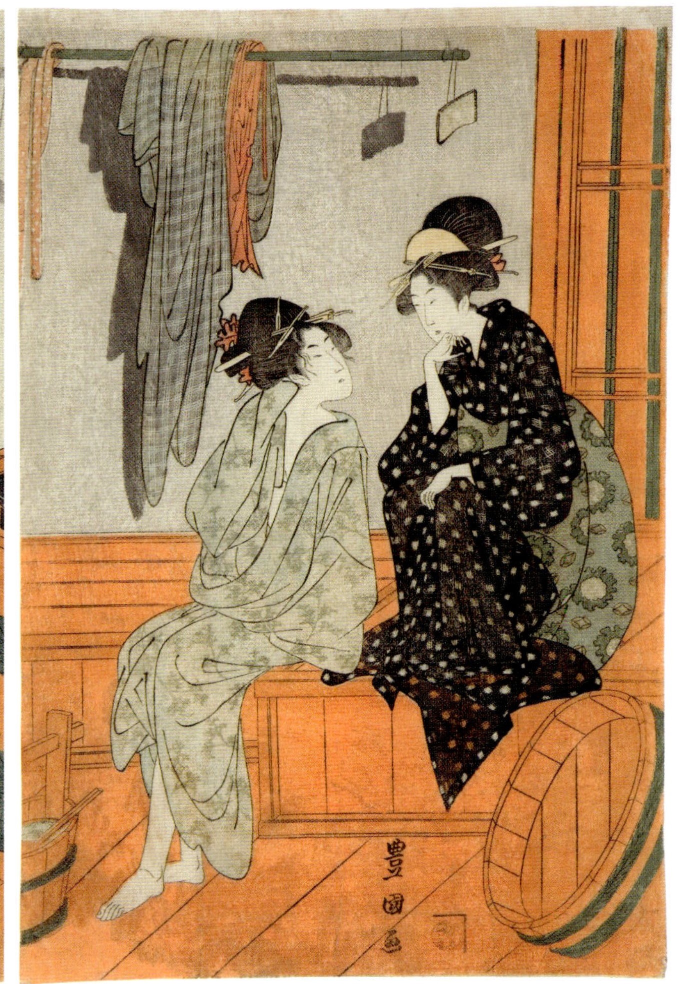

118   Utagawa Toyokuni, 1769–1825, The bathhouse

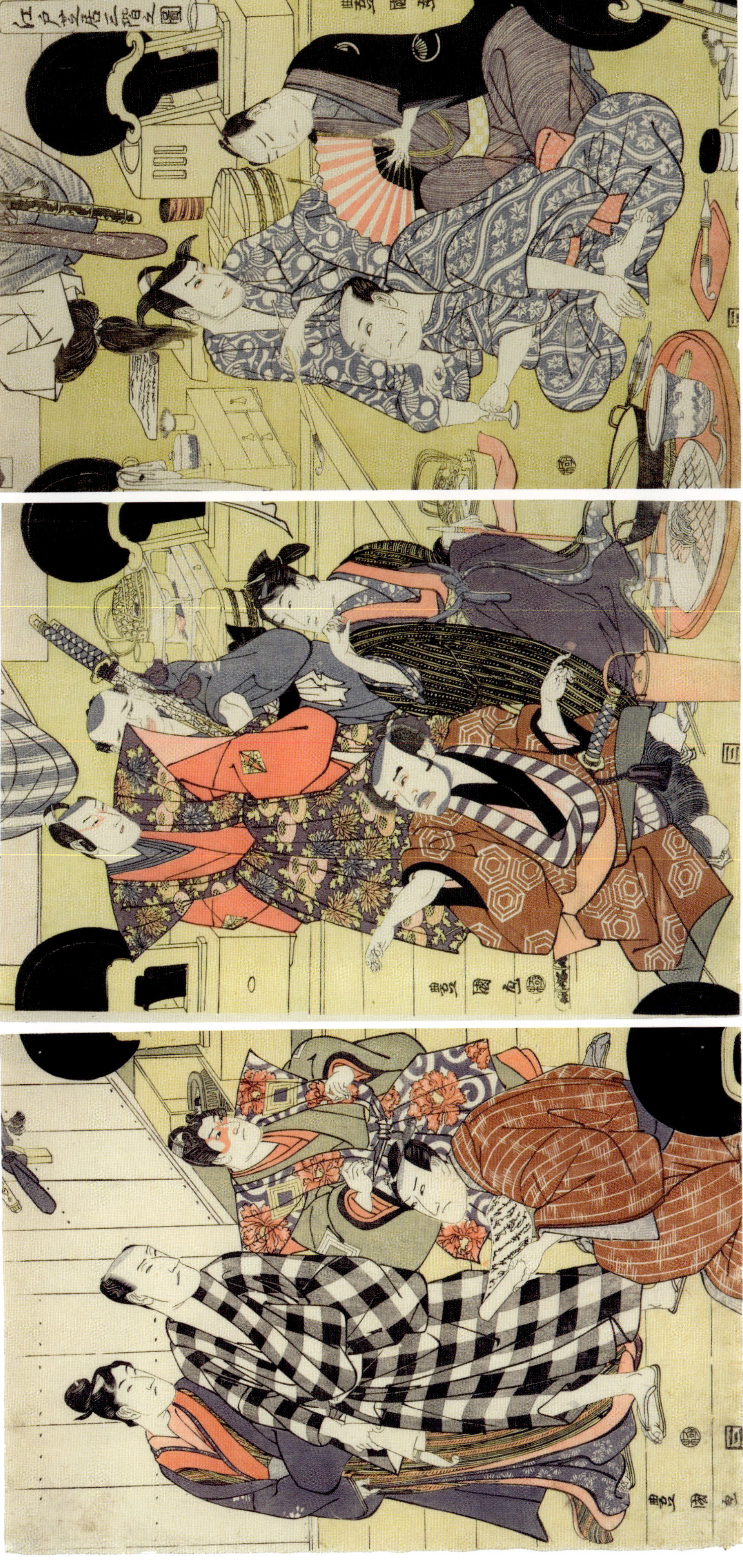

119   Utagawa Toyokuni, 1769–1825, "The Third Floor of a Theater in Edo"

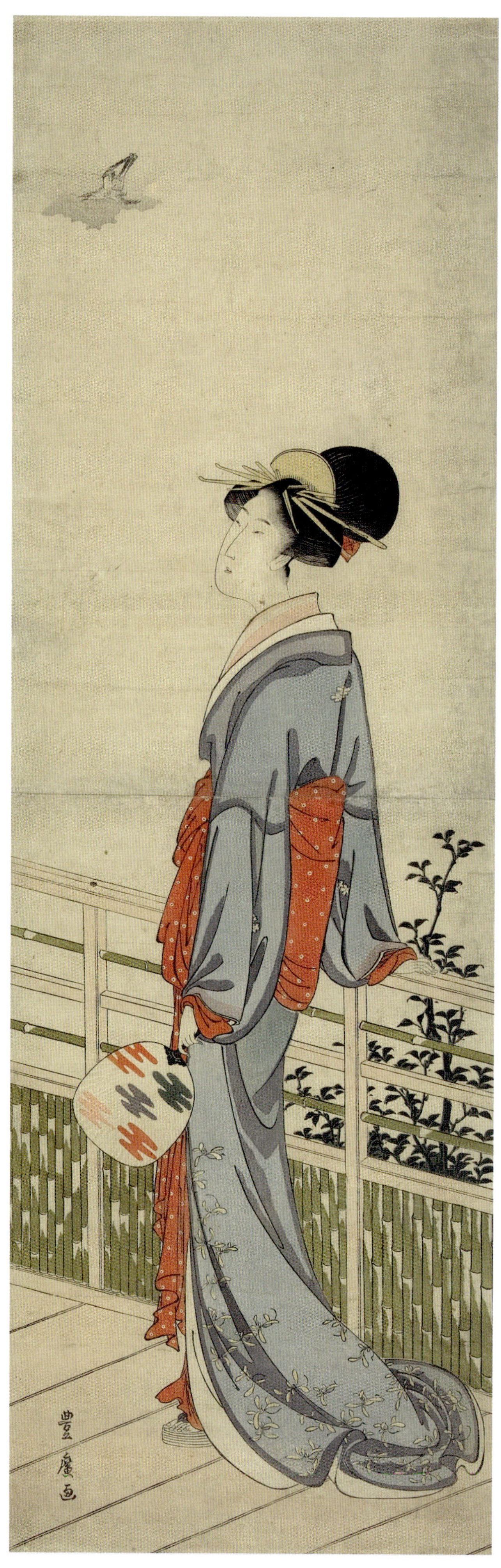

120 Utagawa Toyohiro, 1773–1828, Woman listening to a cuckoo

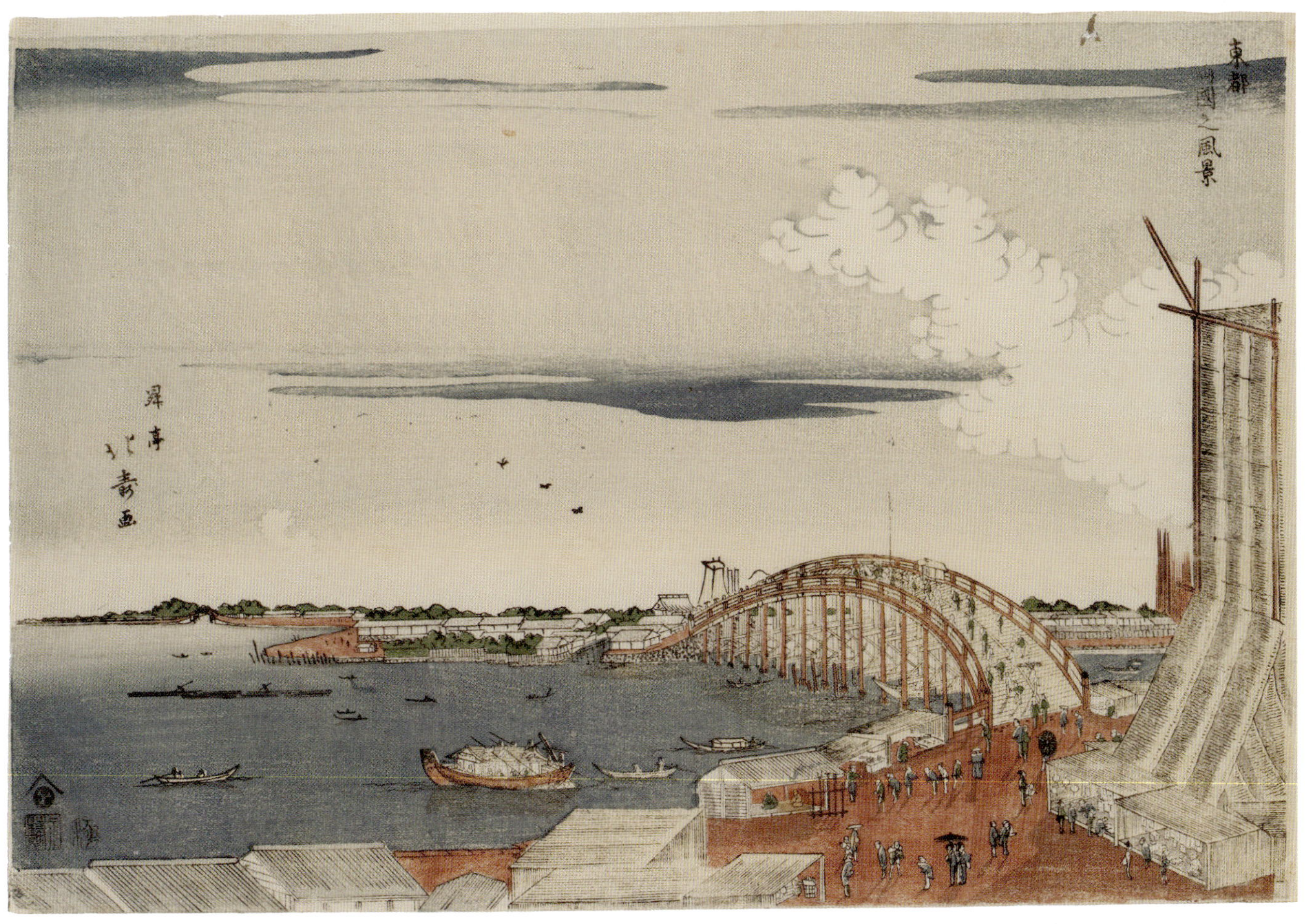

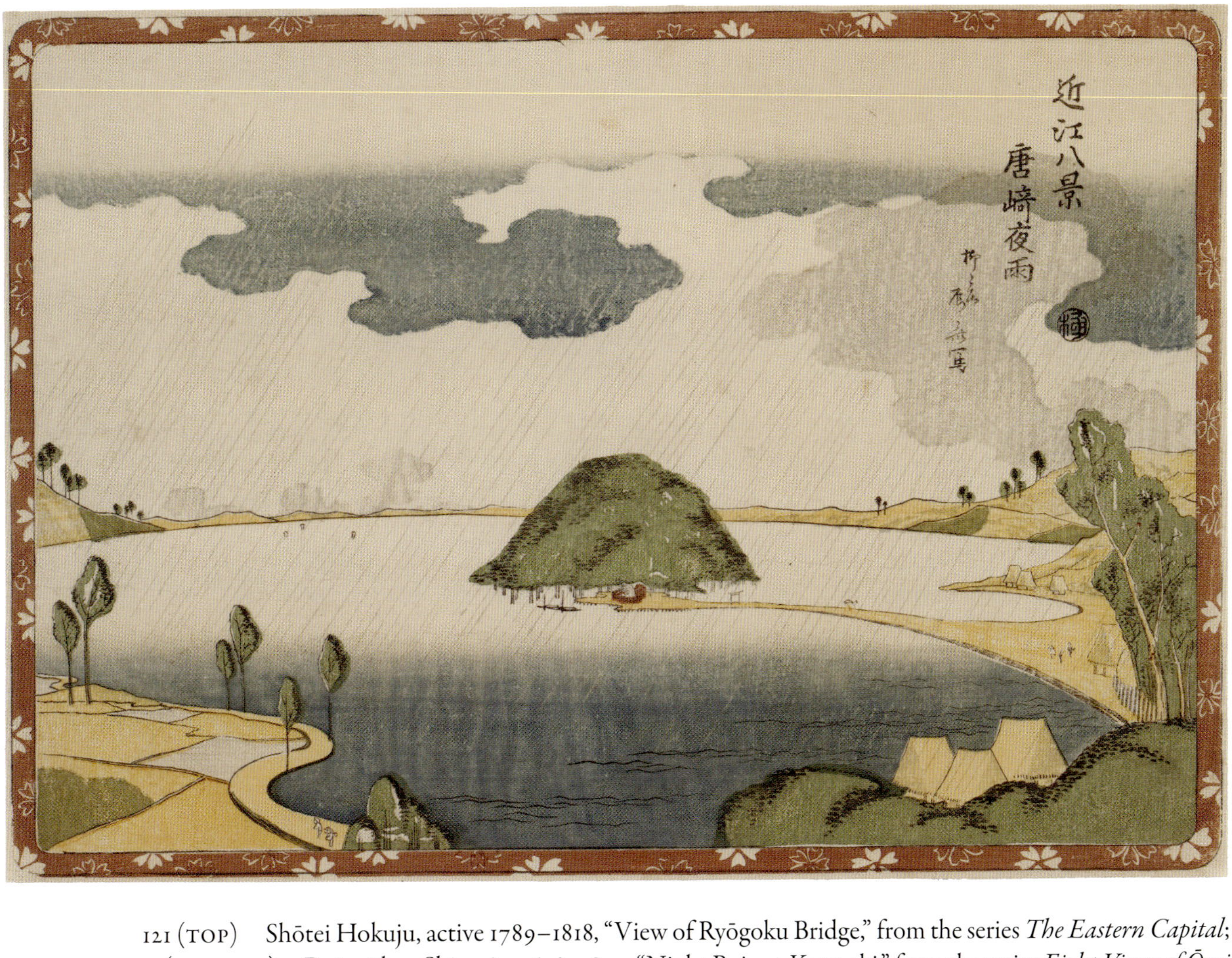

121 (TOP)   Shōtei Hokuju, active 1789–1818, "View of Ryōgoku Bridge," from the series *The Eastern Capital*;
122 (BOTTOM)   Ryūryūkyo Shinsai, 1764?–1820, "Night Rain at Karazaki," from the series *Eight Views of Ōmi*

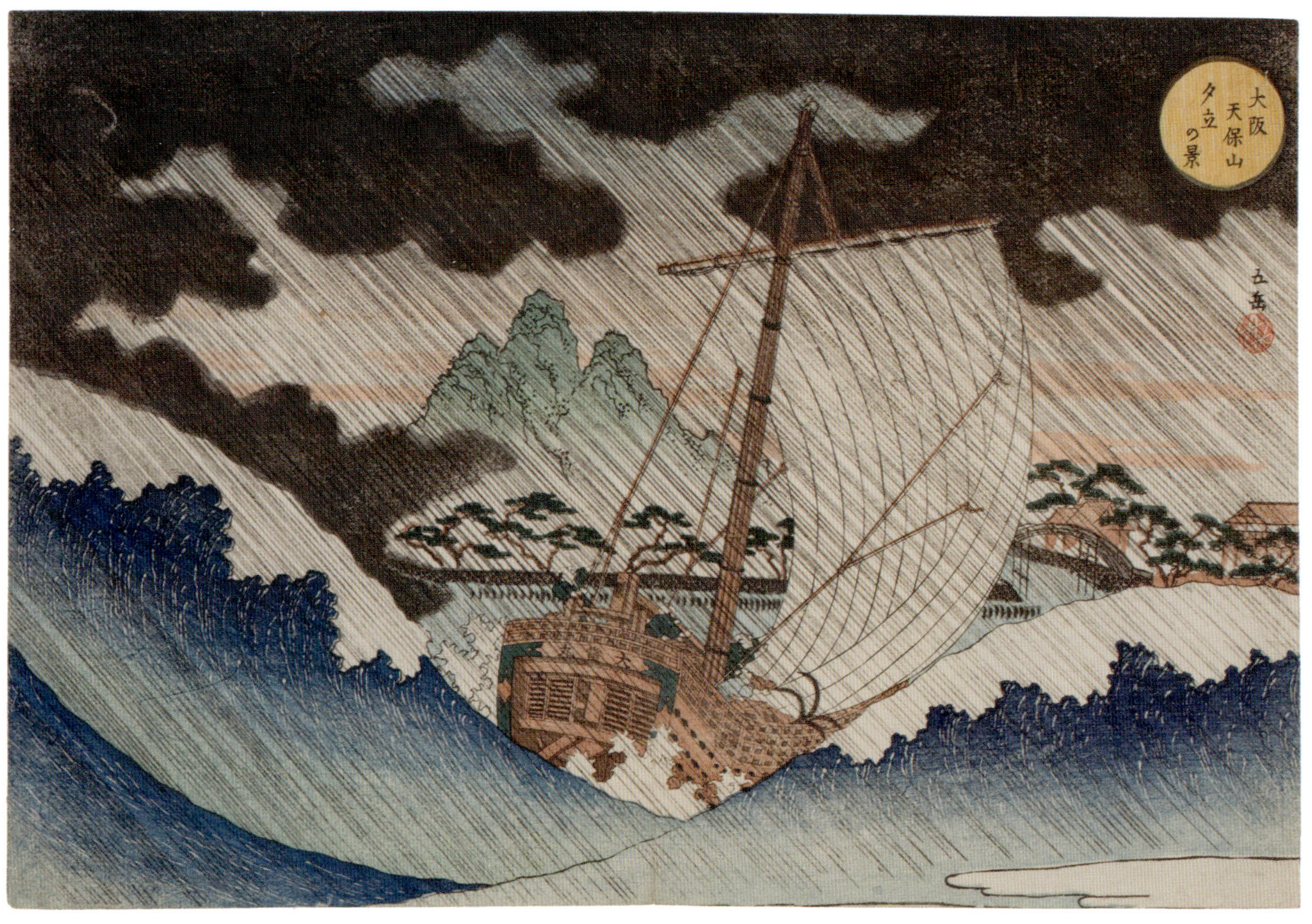

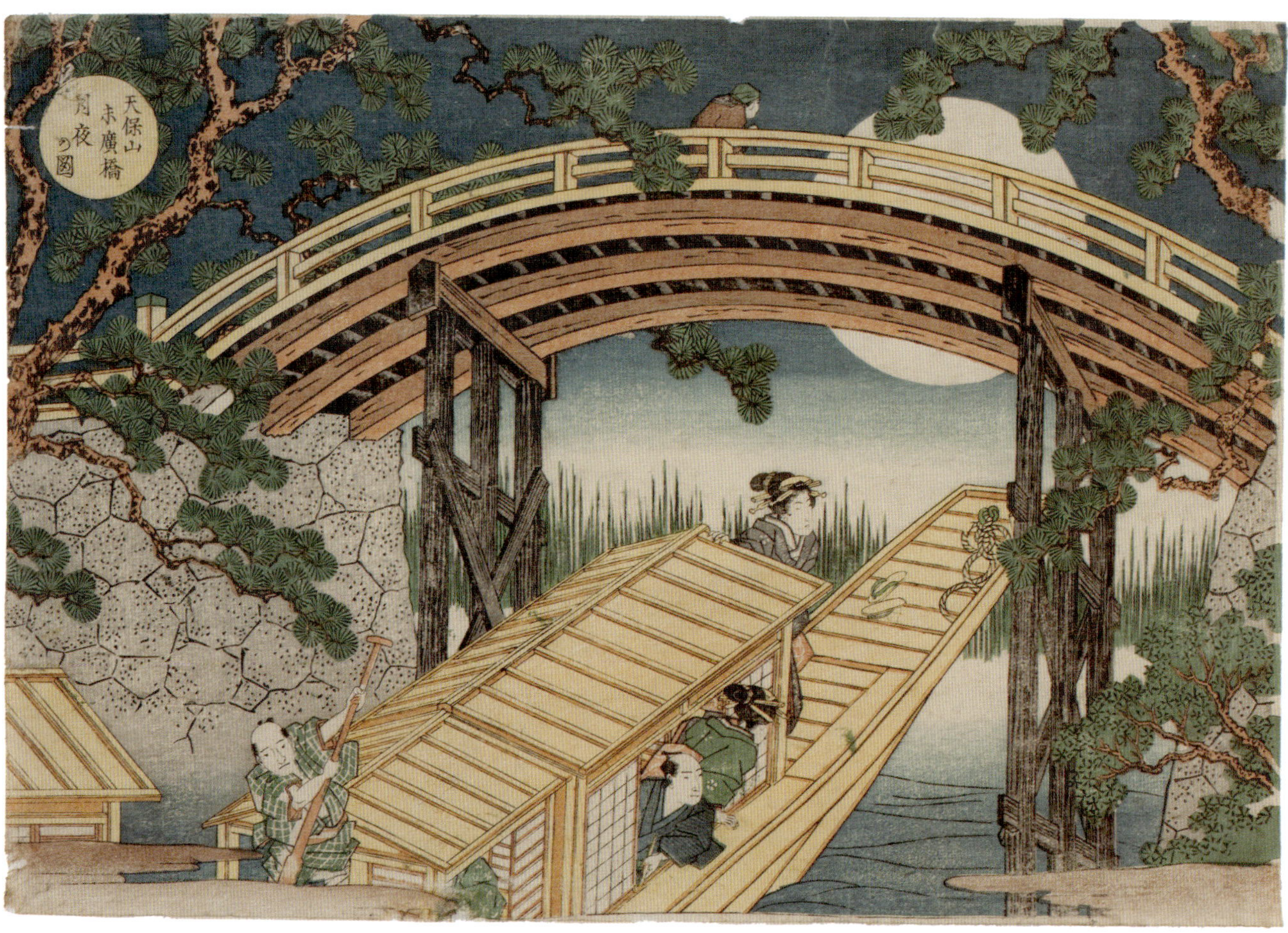

123 (TOP)   Yashima Gakutei, 1786?–1868, "View of an Afternoon Downpour at Mt. Tenpō in Osaka," from the series
Famous Places in Osaka: Scenic Views of Mt. Tenpō;
124 (BOTTOM)   Yashima Gakutei, 1786?–1868, "Moonlit night at the Suehiro Bridge at Mt. Tenpō," from the series
Famous Places in Osaka: Scenic Views of Mt. Tenpō

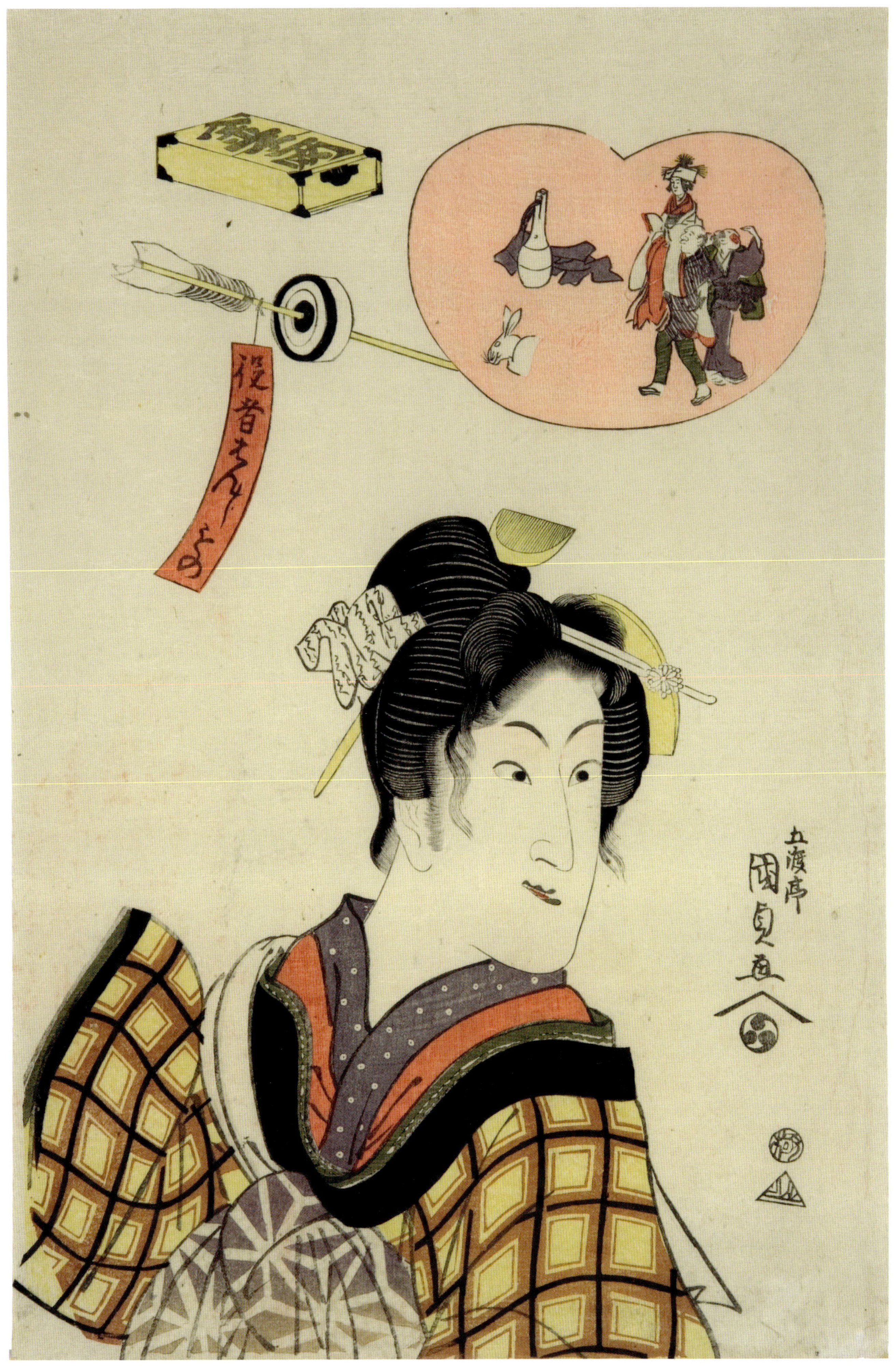

125 Utagawa Kunisada, 1786–1865, Iwai Hanshirō V, from the series *Actor Rebuses*

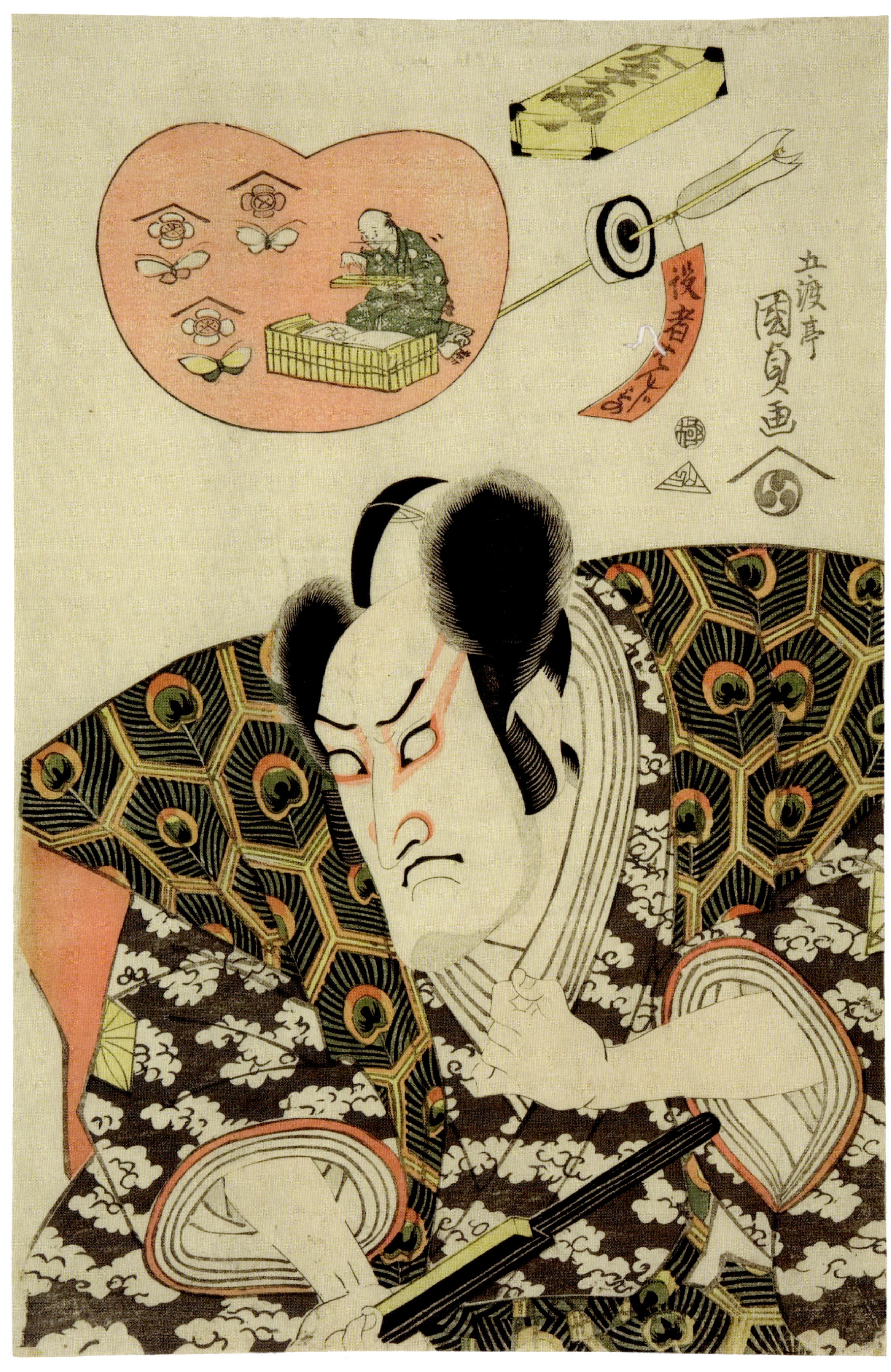

    126   Utagawa Kunisada, 1786–1865, Bandō Mitsugorō III, from the series *Actor Rebuses*

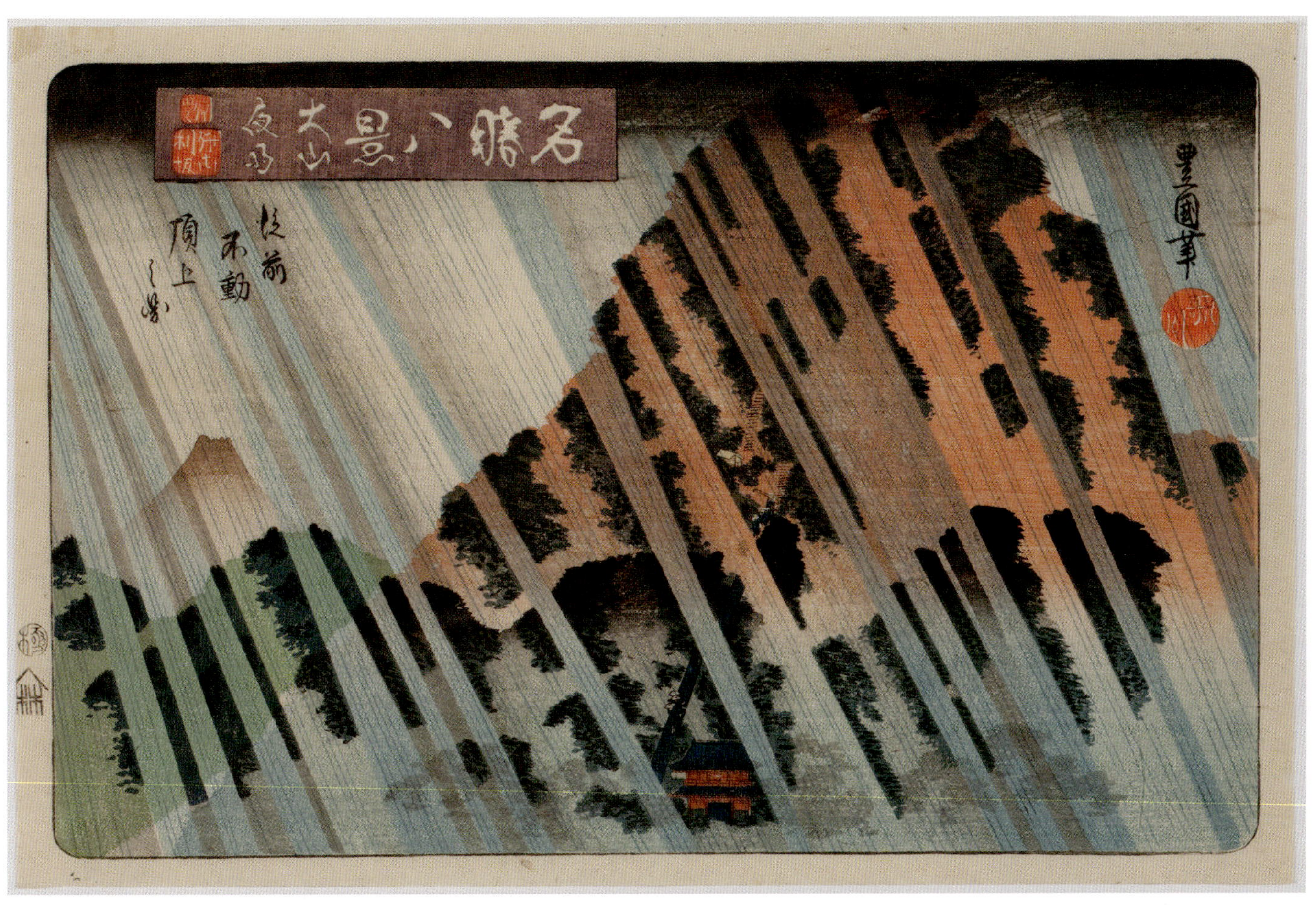

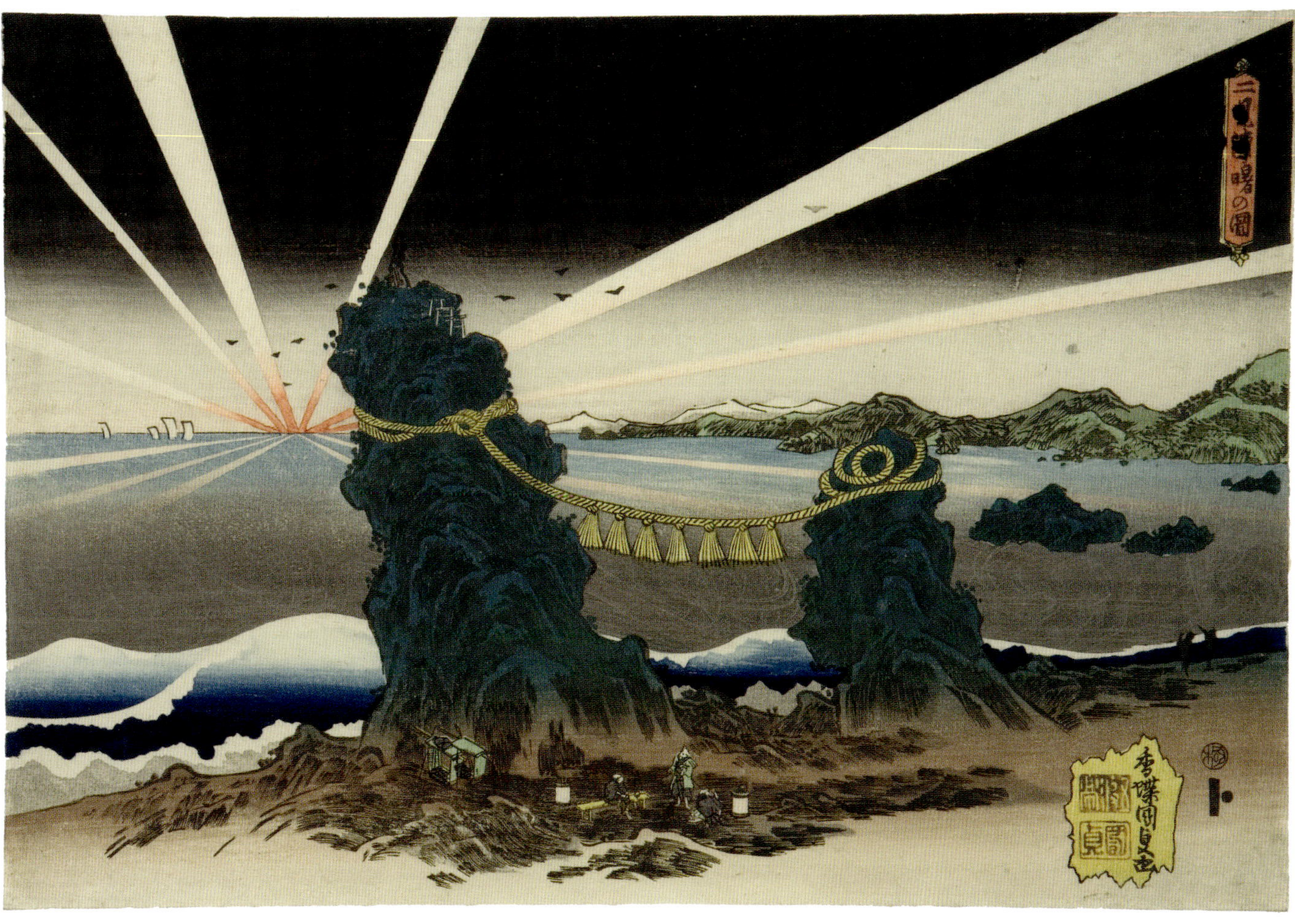

127 (TOP)   Utagawa Toyoshige (Toyokuni II), 1777–1835, "Night Rain over Ōyama: View of the Summit of the Former Fudō Temple," from the series *Eight Views of Scenic Places*;
128 (BOTTOM)   Utagawa Kunisada, 1786–1865, "Dawn at Futamigaura," from an untitled series of landscapes

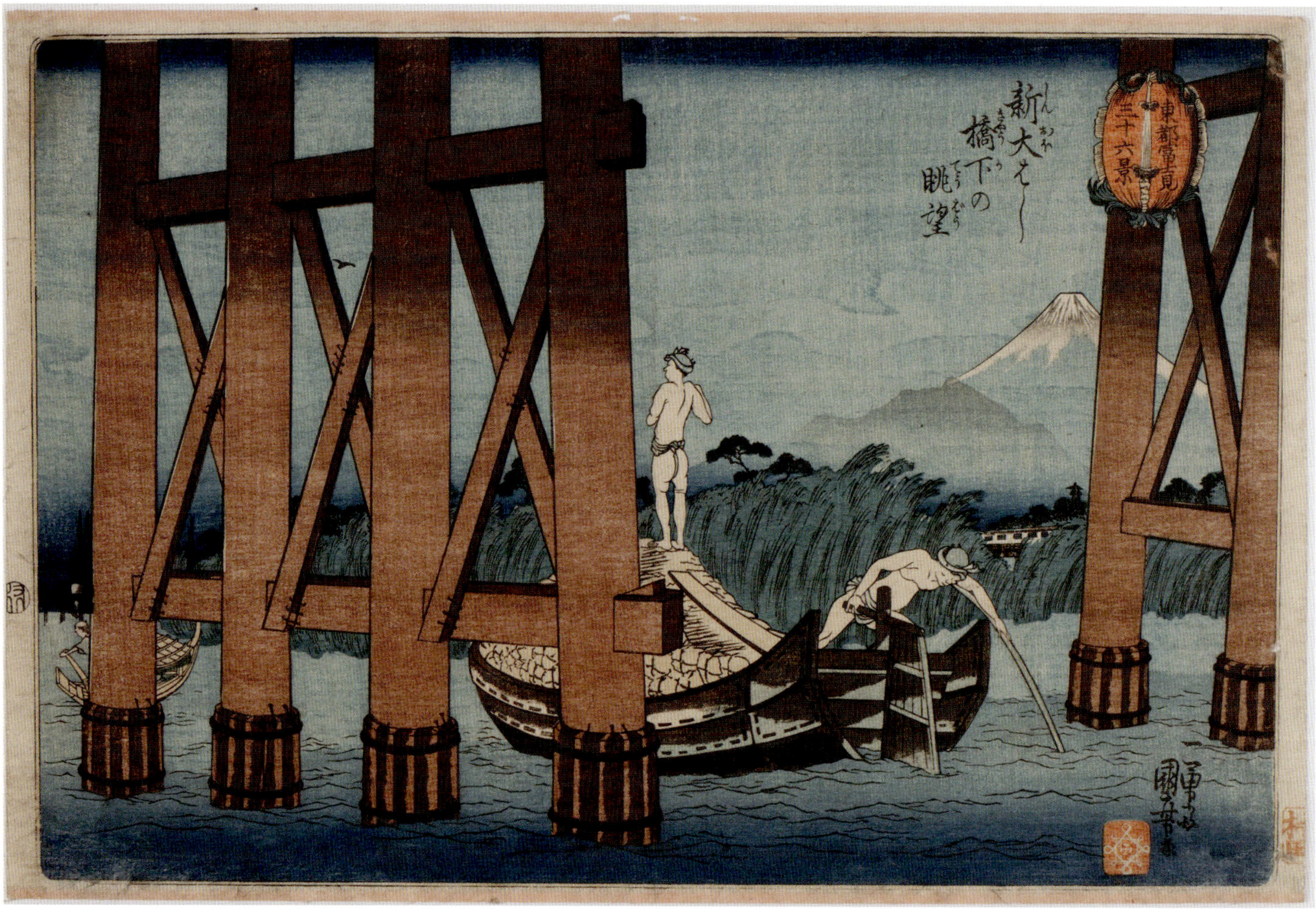

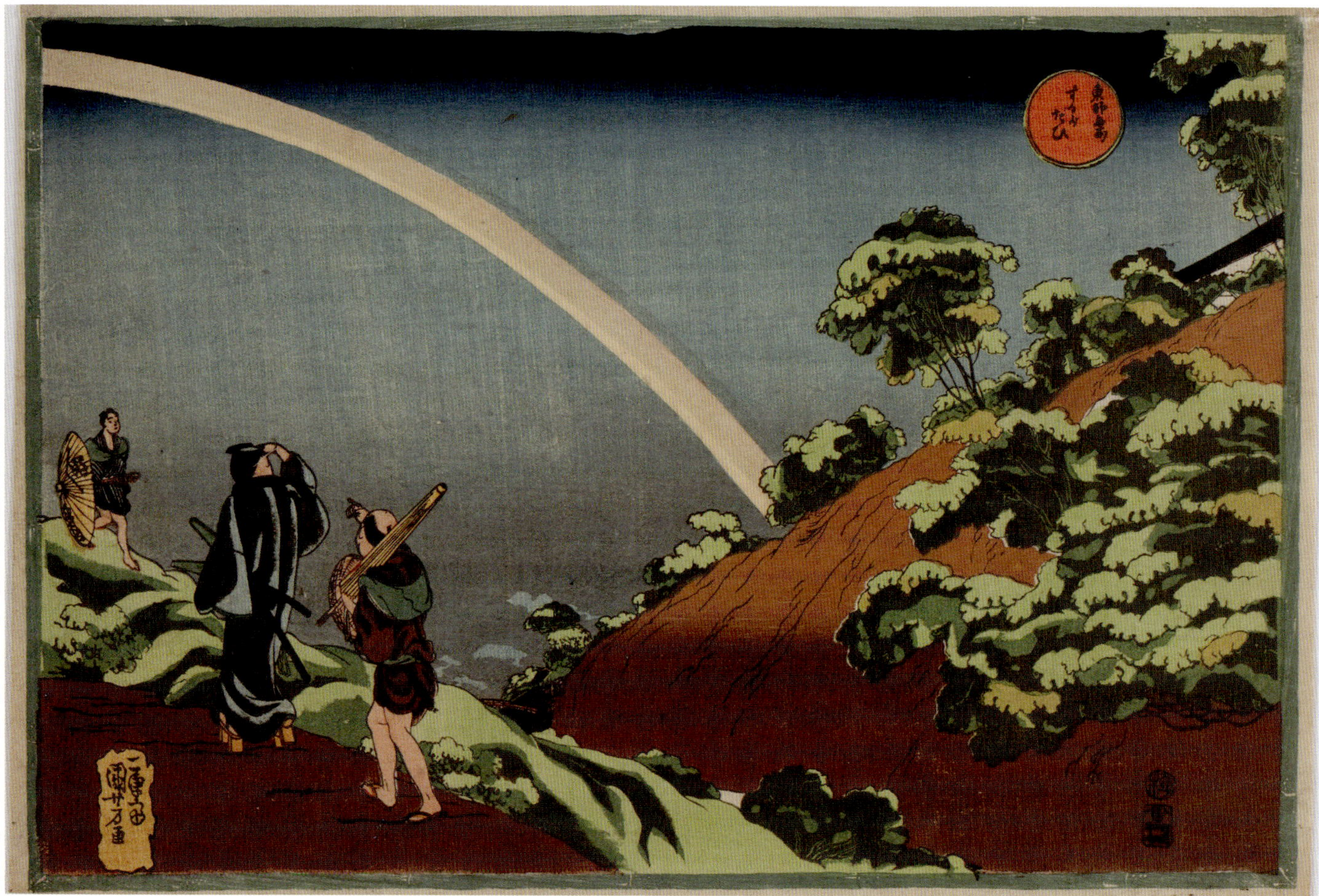

129 (TOP)   Utagawa Kuniyoshi, 1797–1861, "View of Mt. Fuji from Beneath the Shin Ōhashi Bridge," from the series *Thirty-six Views of Mt. Fuji Seen from the Eastern Capital*;

130 (BOTTOM)   Utagawa Kuniyoshi, 1797–1861, "Suruga Hill" (*Surugadai*), from the series *Famous Places in the Eastern Capital*

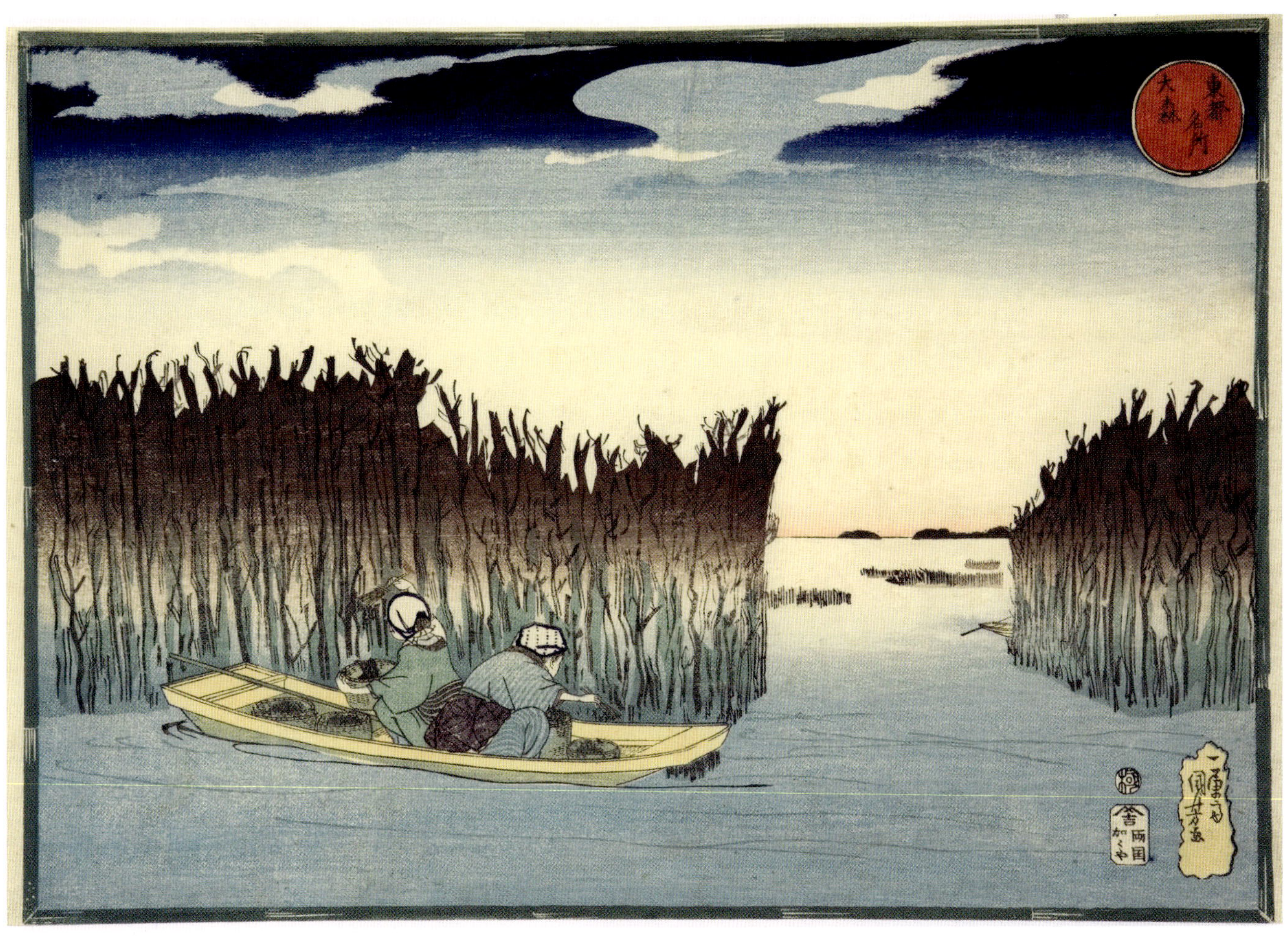

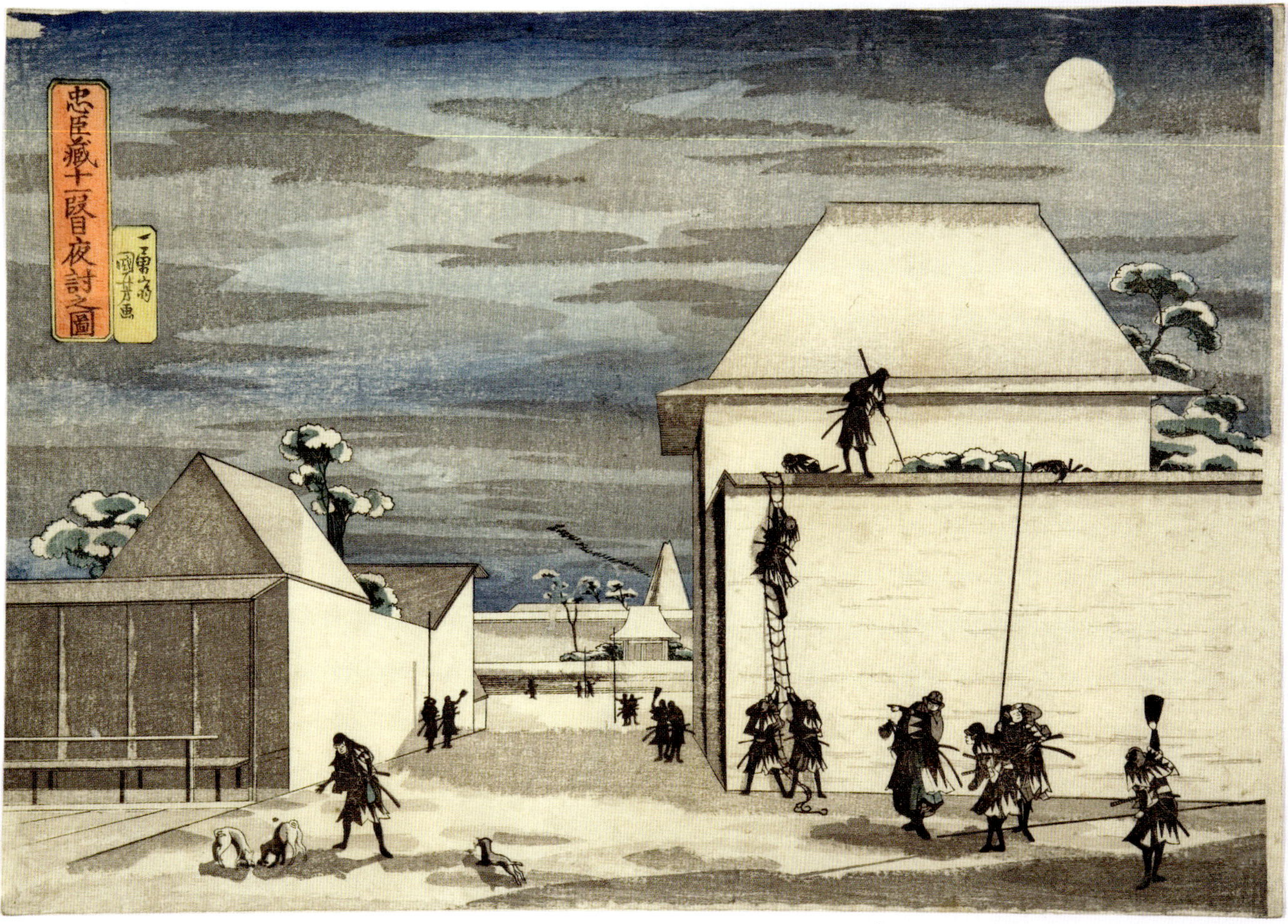

131 (TOP)   Utagawa Kuniyoshi, 1797–1861, "[Gathering seaweed at] Ōmori,"
from the series *Famous Places in the Eastern Capital*;
132 (BOTTOM)   Utagawa Kuniyoshi, 1797–1861, "*Chūshingura*, Act XI: Night Attack"

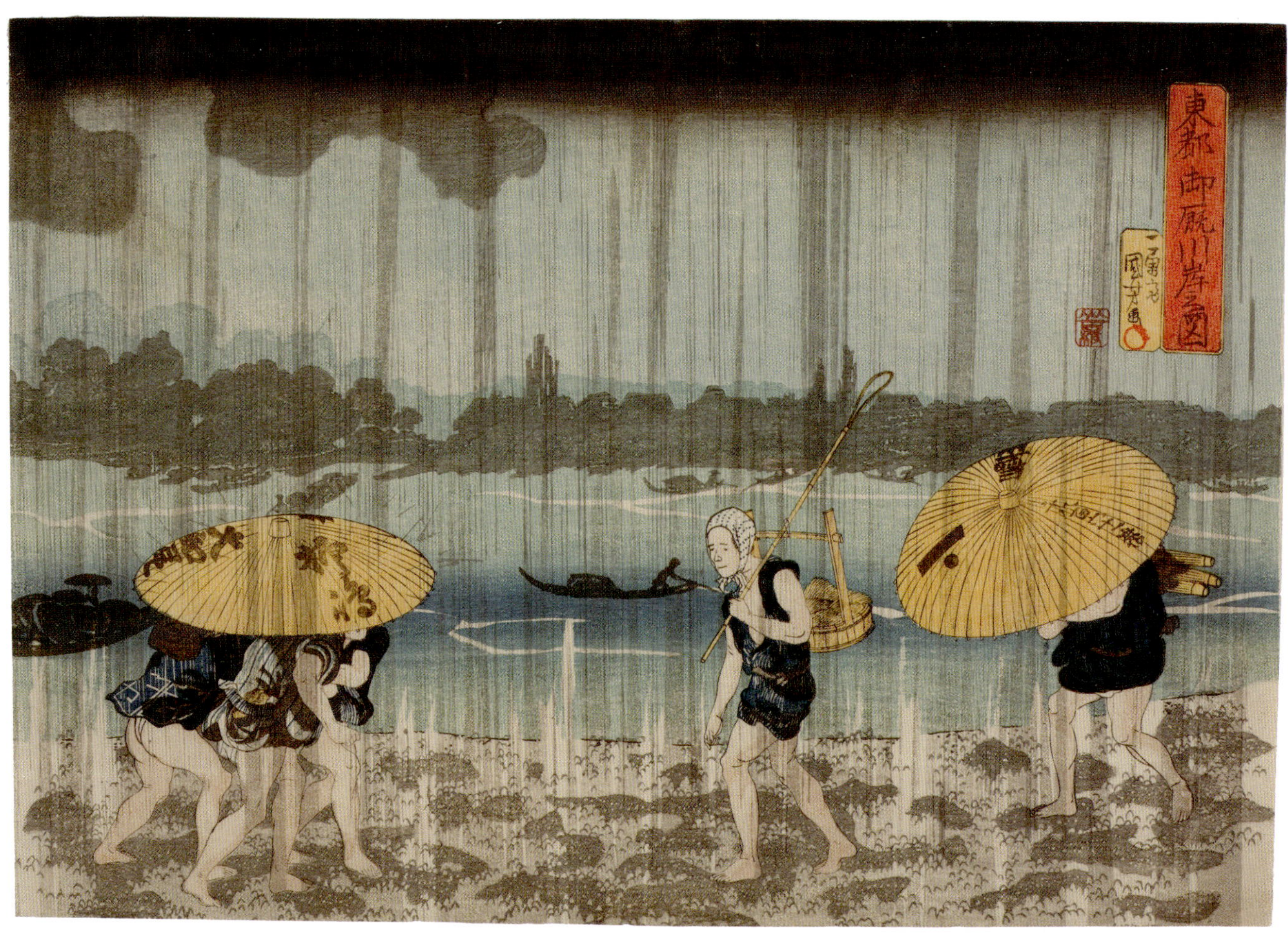

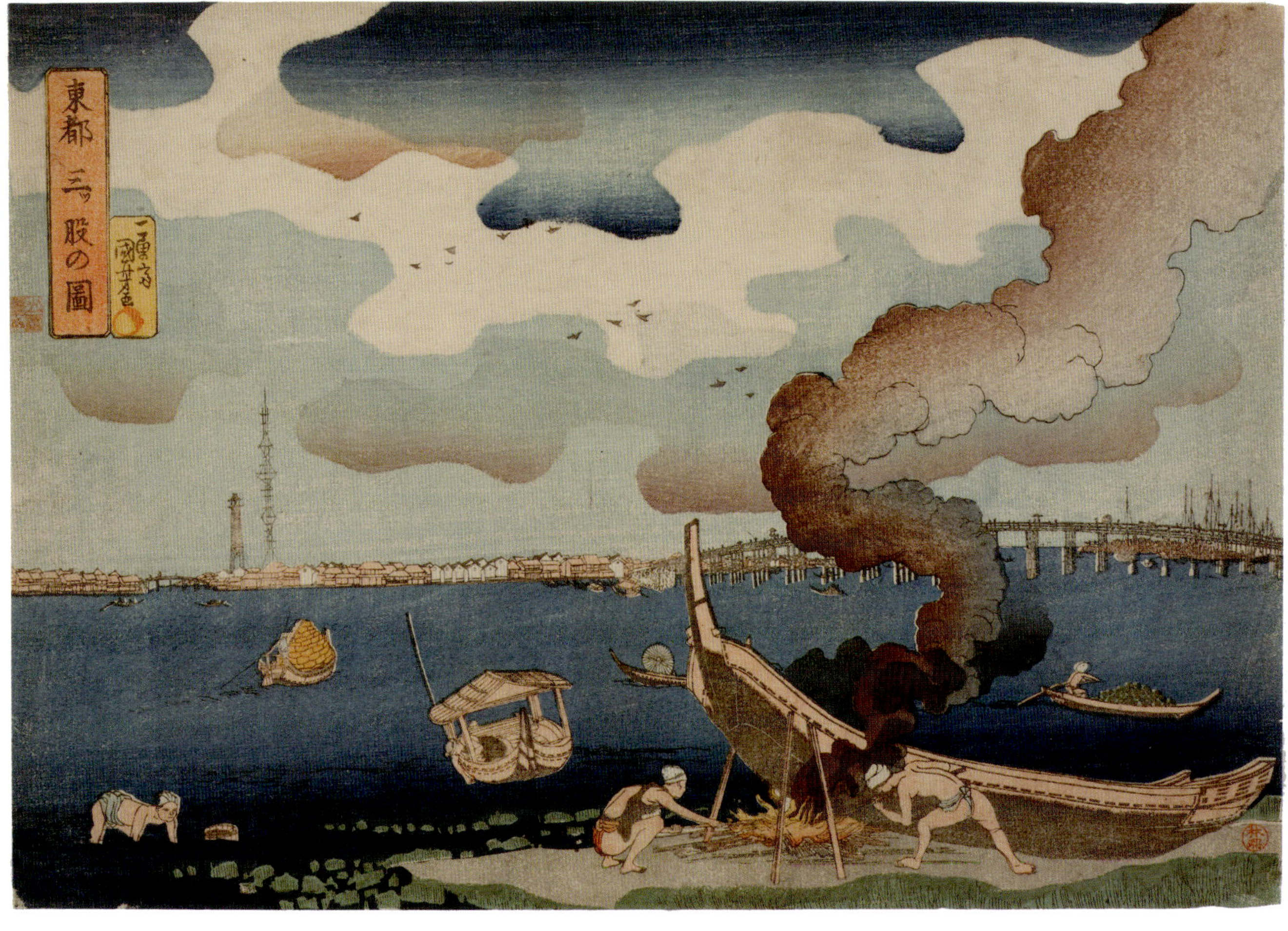

133 (TOP)   Utagawa Kuniyoshi, 1797–1861, "Onmaya Embankment," from the series *The Eastern Capital*;

134 (BOTTOM)   Utagawa Kuniyoshi, 1797–1861, "Mitsumata," from the series *The Eastern Capital*

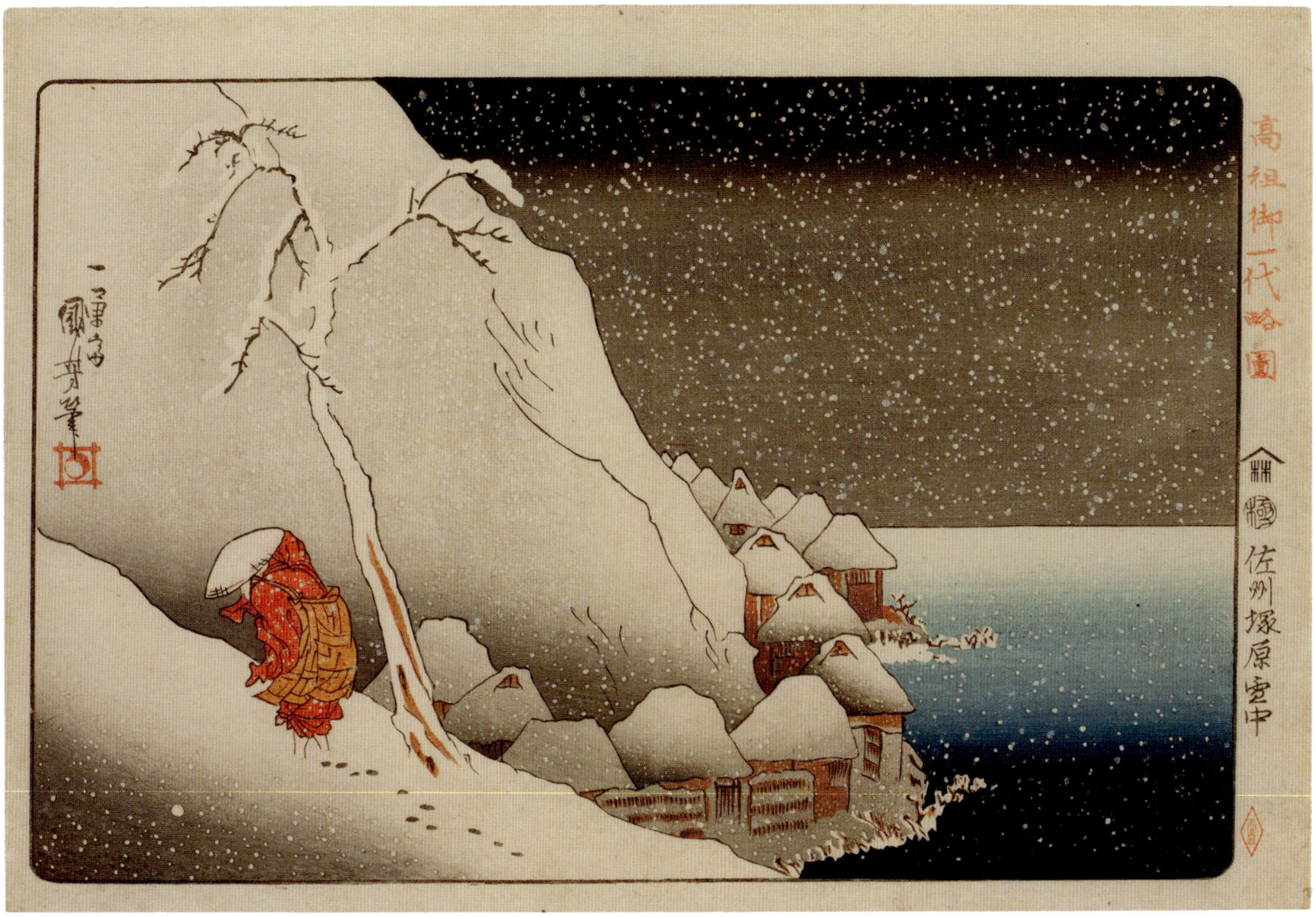

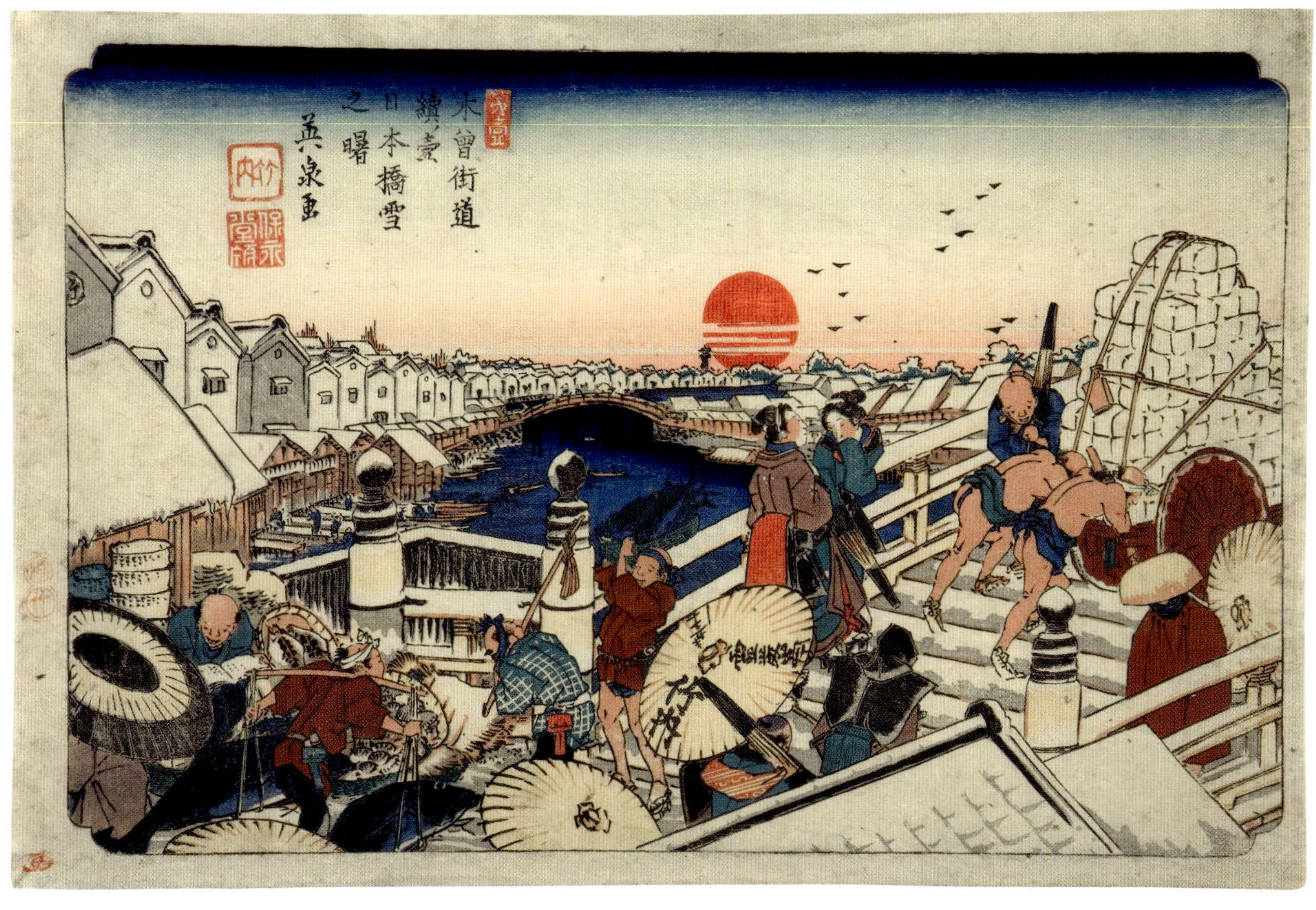

135 (TOP)   Utagawa Kuniyoshi, 1797–1861, "In the Snow at Tsukahara on Sado Island," from the series *Concise Illustrated History of the Founder of the Nichiren Sect*;

136 (BOTTOM)   Keisai Eisen, 1790–1848, "Station No. 1, Snowy Dawn at Nihonbashi," from the series *Kisokaidō*

Entries

1　伝杉村治兵衛　端午子供絵
Attributed to SUGIMURA JIHEI, active c. 1681–1698
A Boys' Day outing
Woodblock print (*tan-e*)
Ō-ōban, 23½. x 11¾ in., 59.7 cm x 29.8 cm
Selected other impressions: WAM, cited in Narazaki (1980), 124
Published: FP 4; UM 8; US 173; ZNS 1; GC 1; DFP fig. 17
Collectors' seals: Edwin and Marjorie Grabhorn; 白爾叟
　　Hakujisō or *Berusō*?
2005.100.1

A festive outing on Boys' Day — the fifth day of the fifth lunar
month — forms the subject of this early hand-colored print. The two
youngest members of the party point up at colorful banners flying
above a low wall with geometric cutouts.[1] One boy has a pair of toy
swords tucked into his waistband, while the other rides on the shoulder of a dandy with a flowered robe and short-cropped hairstyle.
His companion is an attractive young man, or *wakashū,* his long
hair arranged around the shaved top of his head, and with a sword
hanging at his side (the hilt is just visible in front of his fan). His
wide obi (sash) and elongated sleeves — on a robe with chic vertical
stripes — give him a youthful, androgynous appeal. A maid follows
the entourage, sheltering the smaller boy's head with a parasol.

Unsigned, the print has been attributed to Sugimura Jihei on
stylistic grounds. Jihei was a student of Hishikawa Moronobu,
considered the founder of ukiyo-e. Research by David Waterhouse
indicates that buyers could choose to order early prints like this
one with or without hand-coloring, and that some buyers added
color to the print after purchasing them. LA

2　伝鳥居清信　役者紋模様の立美人
Attributed to TORII KIYONOBU I, 1664–1729
A courtesan wearing a robe decorated with actors' crests
C. 1715
Woodblock print (*sumizuri-e*)
Ō-ōban: 22¾ in. x 12½ in., 57.8 cm x 31.7 cm
Published: FP 8; UM 17; US 41 (B/W); GC 2
Collectors' seals: 白爾叟 *Hakujisō* or *Berusō*? (verso)
2005.100.2

This unsigned print of a statuesque beauty presents several problems of identification. Linked stylistically to Torii Kiyonobu I, it
features the sweeping calligraphic outlines and bold decorative
patterns characteristic of works created around 1715. The woman's
front-tied obi tell us that she is a courtesan, and we can surmise
that she is a fan of Kabuki theater, as actors' crests fill the bean-
shaped reserves on her garment, a *kosode* or robe with narrow

sleeve openings. Several of the crests refer to known players of the
time; for example, the triple-gingko-leaf crest of actor Matsumoto
Kōshirō I occupies a prominent position on one sleeve, and the leaf
and comma-swirl (*tomoe*) crest associated with Yamanaka Heikurō
I is shown at her knee, but others are less readily identifiable. More
puzzling is the isolated paulownia crest on her shoulder and hairpin. This could be interpreted as the courtesan's personal crest, but
it also raises another possibility—that the person portrayed might
in fact be an *onnagata,* a Kabuki actor playing a female character
in a play. An example of this kind — an actor dressed as a courtesan, with his own crest on hairpin and sleeve — is Torii Kiyomasu
I's portrait of Fujimura Handayū as Ōiso Tora, in the Museum of
Fine Arts, Boston collection (54.216). LA

3　伝鳥居清倍　源氏物語あかしを読む娘
Attributed to TORII KIYOMASU I, active c. 1696–1716
Woman reading the "Akashi" chapter of *The Tale of Genji*
C. 1710–1720
Woodblock print (*tan-e*)
Ō-ōban: 21½ in. x 12½ in., 54 cm x 31.7 cm
Selected other impressions: BMFA (06.1334, signed *Torii Kiyo-
　　masu*)
Published: US 179; Ukiyo-e 1; GC 3
2005.100.3

This large, hand-colored print is a *mitate,* a contemporary reworking of a classic literary theme, sometimes described as a parody.
A beauty sits before a writing table with a book titled "Akashi" in
one hand. Both pose and title refer to the eleventh-century novel
The Tale of Genji and its author, Murasaki Shikibu, who is said to
have been inspired to write the book's thirteenth chapter, titled
"Akashi," while gazing at a full moon at Ishiyamadera Temple,
located near Lake Biwa. Paintings of Murasaki often show her in
wide-sleeved court-style robes, posed before her desk with a moon
visible outside, but the print takes liberties with that iconography:
instead of the moon there is a round stone basin full of water,
and both the narrow sleeve openings on the woman's outer robe
(*uchikake*) and the decorative comb in her hair distinguish her as a
contemporary beauty of the Edo period. Arranged behind her are
an incense burner in the shape of a lion, a cloth-wrapped article
(possibly an incense container), and a stack of volumes labeled
"Genji." The paper on the desk before her is inscribed with the last
two lines of a *waka* poem by Koshikibu Naishi, another celebrated
Heian period poet: "not yet have I trod there, nor letter seen, from
Amanohashidate" (*mada fumi mo mizu Amanohashidate*).[2]

The Museum of Fine Arts, Boston owns a version of this print
that is signed Torii Kiyomasu I with the seal of publisher Igaya
Kan'emon. Other variations between the two prints suggest that
the Grabhorn version may be a somewhat later edition of Kiyomasu's design, from which the signature and other marks were
removed. LA

1　Narazaki Muneshige has suggested that the wall and two-story tower,
　　though possibly parts of a real castle, might represent painted props
　　constructed for the occasion. *Ukiyo-e shūka,* vol. 10, 136.

2　For the complete poem in Japanese and English, see Mostow, 319.

4 鳥居清倍　太夫と二人の禿
TORII KIYOMASU I, active c. 1696–1716
Courtesan parading with two child attendants
C. 1715
Woodblock print (*tan-e*)
Ō-ōban: 24 in. x 12 in., 61 cm x 30.5 cm
Signature: 鳥居氏清倍圖 *Torii-uji Kiyomasu zu*
Artist's seal: 清倍 *Kiyomasu*
Publisher's mark: 元浜町　伊賀屋　板元 *Motohama-chō Igaya hanmoto*
Publisher and firm name: 伊賀屋勘衛門 *Igaya Kan'emon;* 文亀堂 *Bunkidō*
Published: FP 9; UM 20; US 176; GC 4
Collector's seal: 白爾叟 *Hakujisō* or *Berusō*? (verso)
2005.100.4

A beauty glances down at a black and white cat, perched on the shoulder of one of her two *kamuro*, or child attendants. The beauty's robe is worn off one shoulder with one hand pulled inside the right sleeve of her underrobe, and it is secured with a front-tied obi, in a style familiar from other pictures of high-ranking courtesans on parade (see no. 6). A pattern of four balance toys (*yajirobee*) on her underrobe sleeve might suggest something about her character—is she a fickle lover?—or it might refer to the instability of romantic life in the floating world. Scattered writing (*chirashigaki*) decorates her robe with a mix of bold kanji characters and more delicate cursive *kana* scripts. Two phrases are legible: *ukiyo banare* (removed to the "floating world"), on her sleeve, suggests indifference to customary attitudes, while *hana arashi* (storm of flowers), describes the blossoms swept from trees by an early spring wind — a metaphor for impermanence, or the obstacles that arise in life. Together these sentiments remind viewers to seize the ephemeral pleasures of life. LA

5 懐月堂度繁　猫と戯れる遊女
KAIGETSUDŌ DOHAN, active c. 1704–1716
Courtesan playing with a cat
C. 1705–1715
Woodblock print (*sumizuri-e*)
Ō-ōban: 22 in. x 12¼ in., 55.9 cm x 31.1 cm
Signature: 日本戯畫懐月末葉度繁圖 *Nihon giga Kaigestu matsuyō Dohan zu*
Artist's seal: 度繁 *Dohan*
Publisher's mark: 元浜町　伊賀屋　板元 *Motohama-chō Igaya Hanmoto*
Publisher and firm name: 伊賀屋勘衛門 *Igaya Kan'emon;* 文亀堂 *Bunkidō*
Selected other impressions: CHI (1925.1740); Vever, cited in Hillier (1976), cat. 21
Published: FP 5; UM 42; US 40 (B/W); GC 6
Collector's seal: Edwin and Marjorie Grabhorn
Ex-collection: Charles Morse
2005.100.6

A courtesan playfully dangles a tie-dyed hand towel, teasing the

cat at her feet. This charming scene contains a sophisticated bit of product placement: the box on which she sits is labeled with the name of a confectionary shop, Masaruya, and its address in Asakusa Komagata-chō. Half-hidden behind her legs is the image of a Japanese macaque, the monkey (*masaru*) that is the shop's emblem.

Most of Dohan's prints are of standing courtesans, their forms defined by sweeping curves, calligraphic outlines, and bold patterns. Here, not only is the composition more complex but the three-dimensional rendering of the box lends the figure, balanced at its edge, an unusual degree of solidity. The costume too is especially gorgeous, patterned as it is with a swirling design of flowering myoga ginger and arabesques.

Two other copies of this print are known, one formerly in the Vever Collection, the other in the Art Institute of Chicago. The Chicago version has hand-coloring. LA

6 奥村政信　遊里路上風景
OKUMURA MASANOBU, 1686–1764
Street scene in the pleasure quarter
C. 1705–1715
Woodblock print (*tan-e*)
Ō-ōban: 22½ in. x 12¼ in., 57.1 cm x 31.1 cm
Signature: 奥村政信圖 *Okumura Masanobu zu*
Artist's seal: 政信 *Masanobu*
Publisher's mark: 浅草　菊屋　駒形町 *Asakusa Kikuya Komagata-chō*
Published: US 181; Ukiyo-e 2; G-J vol. 6, 117; GC 7
2005.100.7

It is late afternoon on a street in the Yoshiwara, Edo's licensed prostitution district. An old man leans on a cane as he listens to the sound of a shamisen, the stringed instrument played by one of two prostitutes seated in a latticed window display (*harimise*). Nearby, a notions vendor kneels beside a carrying case stacked with boxes, as a maid places her order near the brothel's entrance. Out in the street, the procession of a sumptuously attired *tayū* (a high-ranking courtesan) and two *kamuro* halts for a moment before a potential customer, a disguised samurai, his features hidden by a deep straw hat. The attendant who follows keeps a close eye on the man bowing at his side, possibly a male entertainer (*taiko*) trying to solicit the samurai's business. Completing this picture of commerce in the pleasure quarter is a second vendor, who lifts a fan-shaped object from the box held at his waist. A label on the box identifies his wares as *goraigō*: toys made from a bamboo tube with a small clay, paper, or wood Buddha inside. When the tube is lowered, a hidden Buddha pops up, surrounded by a folded paper mandorla. This charming toy equates the Yoshiwara's myriad pleasures with the excitement of being welcomed to paradise (*raigō*) by the Buddha Amitabha. LA

7 奥村政信　見立芦葉達磨
OKUMURA MASANOBU, 1686–1764
Mitate of Bodhidharma crossing the Yangzi River on a reed
Woodblock print (*tan-e*)
Ō-ōban (trimmed): 19¼ in. x 12½ in., 48.9 cm x 31.7 cm

Signature: 奥村政信圖 *Okumura Masanobu zu*
Artist's seal: 政信 *Masanobu*
Published: US 182; Ukiyo-e 3; G-J vol. 6, 119; GC 8; DFP fig. 37
2005.100.8

Masanobu's *mitate* wittily evokes an episode known as "Bodhidharma crossing the Yangzi River on a reed" (*Royō Daruma*). According to legend, the river crossing occurred en route to the Shaolin monastery, where Bodhidharma sat facing a wall for nine years without speaking. While serious interpretations abound in Chinese and Japanese paintings, popular prints of the Edo period often playfully substituted a beautiful woman for the monk. This parodic version was reportedly invented in response to a courtesan's comment that she was more enlightened than Bodhidharma because she had spent *ten* years sitting, on display in a brothel.

Other representations of the theme show a beauty who impersonates Bodhidharma by riding on a reed, on a knotted love letter, or even a *shamisen*. Here Masanobu makes her gracefully pole a reed carrying Bodhidharma, rendering his form with a surprisingly direct allusion to the erotic nature of the courtesan's profession.

The river bank ends abruptly at the top edge, and the dimensions of the print indicate that more than an inch of paper is now missing. LA

8　奥村政信　「源氏浮船」
OKUMURA MASANOBU, 1686–1764
"'Ukifune' [chapter] from *The Tale of Genji*" [*Mitate* with the actor
　Sanogawa Ichimatsu I] (*Genji Ukifune*)
C. 1741–1744
Woodblock print (*beni-e*)
Ōban: 12¾ in. x 17¼ in., 32.4 cm x 43.8 cm
Signature: 芳月堂丹鳥齋奥村文角政信画 *Hōgetsudō*
　Tanchōsai Okumura Bunkaku Masanobu ga
Artist's seal: 丹鳥齋 *Tanchōsai*
Selected other impressions: BMFA (06.385, 21.6868); LOC (no.
　1810)
Published: FP 17; UM 49; ZNS, no. 37; US 180; G-J vol. 4, 174;
　GC 9; DFP fig. 52
Collector's seal: Edwin Grabhorn
2005.100.9

A boat bearing an attractive couple drifts along by the light of a waning moon, in a tongue-in-cheek *mitate* rendering of a famous episode from *The Tale of Genji*. The novel relates that in an effort to win the beautiful Ukifune's affections, Genji's grandson Niou takes her one wintry day on an excursion to the Isle of Oranges. The Ukifune scene is typically depicted with snow or the orange trees on the island, and Ukifune usually sits upright facing Niou in the boat.

Masanobu's offers instead a more languid scene, in which the Kabuki actor Sanogawa Ichimatsu I, nattily attired in a checked jacket and stylish coiffure, taps a hand drum for a reclining courtesan who rests on one elbow with snacks and sake close at hand. The words of a love song hang in the air:

Yuki ya yuki ya
mi wa ukibune
ni tsumoru koi

Heavy snow,
settling in a drifting boat
my heart is filled with longing[3]

Sanogawa Ichimatsu had recently made his debut on the Edo stage when this print was made, rapidly rising to the status of matinee idol.[4] His adoring fans would have enjoyed seeing him thus imagined in a romantic scene from a literary classic. LA

9　奥村政信　朝鮮人曲馬の図
OKUMURA MASANOBU, 1686–1764
Korean acrobatic rider writing the character "tiger"
C. 1748
Woodblock print (*beni-e*)
Hashira-e: 28¼ in. x 6⅝ in., 71.8 cm x 16.8 cm
Signature: 芳月堂正名 奥村文角政信正筆 *Hōgetsudō shōmei*
　Okumura Bunkaku Masanobu shōhitsu
Artist's seal: 丹鳥齋 *Tanchōsai*
Publisher: 奥村屋源六 *Okumuraya Genroku*
Selected other impressions: Yale (1950.562); TIK (p-u 1422, PH 22)
Published: FP 20; G-J vol. 6, 130; GC 10; DFP fig. 47
2005.100.10

Each of the dozen Korean embassy delegations that visited Japan during the Edo period brought excitement to the capital. Some five hundred musicians, archers, riders, and other entertainers led sensational processions that drew the attention and admiration of Japanese writers and painters. This example by Okumura Masanobu, dated to the time of the 1748 embassy, shows an exotically costumed rider displaying his skill by brushing the character for tiger (*tora*) while standing in the stirrups of a black and white horse.

Masanobu was an innovator, said to have been the first to employ the narrow *hashira-e* (pillar-print) format. By cutting off the figure at both sides, he creates the effect of a rider galloping past the viewer. Among his other prints of Korean embassy processions is an *uki-e* (perspective picture) showing the Korean embassy's progress through the streets of Edo (Tokyo National Museum collection, A-10569_434), based on a painting by Hanegawa Tōei (active 1735–1750). Another example is a 1711 series of twelve prints of a Korean procession, ten of which are in the British Museum collection (1926,04190.40.1–10), which includes a horseman wearing headgear similar to the black horsehair hat with feathers seen on the rider in this print. LA

10　奥村政信　『二十四孝』「大舜」
OKUMURA MASANOBU, 1686–1764
"Dashun" (*Taishun*)
From *Twenty-four Paragons of Filial Piety* (*Nijūshikō*)

3　Trans. Thompson, 76.
4　Narazaki 1980, no. 37.

Woodblock print (*urushi-e* with brass filings)
Hosoban: 12½ in. x 6¼ in., 31.7 cm x 15.9 cm
Signature: 日本画工奥村政信正筆 *Nihon gakō Okumura Masanobu shōhitsu*
Publisher's mark: 絵問屋通塩町奥村屋 *Etoiya Tōrishiochō Okumuraya*
Publisher and firm name: 奥村政信 *Okumura Masanobu*; 鶴寿堂 *Kakujudō*
Published: GC 11
Collectors' seals: Edwin Grabhorn; 白爾叟 *Hakujisō* or *Berusō*? (verso)
2005.100.11

The series title *Twenty-four Paragons of Filial Piety* refers to a work said to have been composed by the Yuan dynasty (1279–1368) Chinese scholar Guo Jujing. The subject of this print is a virtuous young man known as Dashun (or simply Shun), who never deviated from proper respect toward his family despite harsh treatment from his father, his cruel stepmother, and her jealous son. When scolded or beaten, he simply escaped outside, cultivating the family fields alone. Noting his filial devotion, creatures emerged from the nearby mountains to help: in spring, elephants came to plow the furrows, and in summer birds flocked to pull weeds. When the emperor heard this tale, he stepped in and guided the young man, until eventually Shun assumed the throne himself and became a virtuous ruler.

Wearing a Chinese costume with large floral roundels, Shun strikes the ground with a large mattock. Behind him two birds and a pair of kindly elephants help out with the fieldwork. The thatched roof above the field was embellished with brass filings that glitter when they catch the light. A cartouche running in a band across the bottom of the print identifies Okumura Masanobu as both artist and publisher. LA

11　奥村政信　『二十四孝』「孟荘」（孟宗）
OKUMURA MASANOBU, 1686–1764
"Meng Zong" (*Mōsō*)
From *Twenty-four Paragons of Filial Piety* (Nijūshikō)
Woodblock print (*urushi-e* with brass filings)
Hosoban: 12½ in. x 6¼ in., 31.7 cm x 15.9 cm
Signature: 日本画工奥村政信正筆 *Nihon gakō Okumura Masanobu shōhitsu*
Publisher's mark: 通塩町奥村屋 *Tōrishiochō Okumuraya*
Publisher and firm name: 奥村政信 *Okumura Masanobu*; 鶴寿堂 *Kakujudō*
Published: G.Land 1; GC 12
Collector's seal: Edwin Grabhorn
2005.100.12

Like no. 10, this print comes from the series *Twenty-four Paragons of Filial Piety*. These Chinese tales had a long history in Japan, and more than one eighteenth-century artist took up the popular story of Meng Zong, called Mōsō in Japanese, shown here (for example, see no. 31, by Harunobu). Mōsō's poignant story describes his unswerving devotion to his widowed mother. One winter, his mother fell seriously ill and began to crave a broth of bamboo shoots, which normally sprout only in spring. Mōsō braved heavy snows and cold in search of the shoots without success. Finally, in tears, his prayers were answered as he stumbled upon a few miraculous plants. The broth made from the shoots cured his mother's illness, and Mōsō's story was lauded far and wide as an example of courage and filial regard.

As in the previous example, the scene unfolds within a simple landscape setting. A stream courses over nearby hills as Mōsō drops his mattock in a stand of snow-covered bamboo. Lunging forward, he reaches with both hands for the shoots that will save his mother's life. Over his Chinese-style shoes and robe he wears a large straw hat and straw coat, embellished with brass filings of the type commonly used in Japanese prints of the 1720s and 1730s. LA

12　奥村利信　扇売り
OKUMURA TOSHINOBU, active c. 1718–1749
Fan vendor
C. 1720s
Woodblock print (*urushi-e* with brass filings)
Hosoban: 13 in. x 5⅞ in., 33 cm x 14.9 cm
Signature: 大和畫工奥村利信筆 *Yamato gakō Okumura Toshinobu hitsu*
Artist's seal: unidentified
Published: FP 18; GC 13
Collectors' seals: two unknown collector's seals (verso)
Ex-collection: Frank Lloyd Wright
2005.100.13

Vendors of all kinds plied the streets of Edo, and they are a common subject of both Kabuki and ukiyo-e in the early 1700s. This print portrays a fan vendor, possibly a character familiar from a contemporary Kabuki play. The trailing sleeves of her *furisode* bear a crest with the kanji for "camellia" (*tsubaki*) on a black background above an elaborate design of combs and other hair ornaments interspersed with the characters for geese (*kari*) and good fortune (*kichi*). Stepping forward, she raises one hand to steady the heavy case on her back, labeled with the shop name, Mieidō. Boxes holding pre-cut paper and bamboo ribs for making fans are piled above her head, while folded and open fans inserted at the top and sides help to advertise her wares, as does the round butterfly crest fan she holds in one hand.

In this *urushi-e*, or lacquer picture, a mixture of ink and glue create a lustrous surface effect, making the black sleeves of the garment in this print stand out against the other hand-applied pigments. The front of the robe is further embellished with brass filings. LA

13　奥村利信　『三ぶくつい』「右　江戸もとゆひ」
OKUMURA TOSHINOBU, active 1718–1749
"Right, Hair Tie from Edo" (*Migi, Edo Motoyui*)
From *Triptych* [Beauties of the three cities] (Sanbuku tsui)
C. 1720s
Woodblock print (*urushi-e* with brass filings)
Hosoban: 6⅜ in. x 13½ in., 16.2 cm x 34.3 cm

Signature: 大和画工奥村利信筆 *Yamato gakō Okumura Toshi-nobu hitsu*
Publisher's mark: うき世絵版元絵そうし問屋 ゑ 湯島天神女坂下小松屋伝四朗 *Ukiyoe hanmoto esōshi toiya, E, Yushima Tenjin Onnazaka-shita Komatsuya Denshirō*
Publisher: 小松屋伝四朗 *Komatsuya Denshirō*
Published: Ukiyoe 4; G-J vol. 6, 151; GC 14
2005.100.14

This elegantly dressed courtesan represents Edo within a trio of beauties from Japan's leading cities. As one sheet of a larger triptych, she once stood beside rivals from Osaka and Kyoto. A large roundel on her shoulder identifies her home city, and the words *Edo Motoyui* appear in a title cartouche shaped as a woman's sleeve dangling from a pine branch. The word *motoyui*, which may also be the courtesan's name, refers to a paper hair tie, a special product of Edo at the time this print was made.[5]

The beauty's hairstyle, called *nesagari hyōgo*, is knotted at the neck and adorned with a single large comb. Feathers decorate her black *uchikake* outer robe—phoenix wings on her shoulders and long tail feathers fanned over her body. By applying ink mixed with glue to the outer robe, the printer gave it a lustrous black finish akin to satin — a characteristic of *urushi-e* prints. Gathered at one side, this opulent garment covers the front knot of a tortoise shell–patterned obi and a *kosode* adorned with red autumn leaves. Brass filings add sparkle to the obi, tail feathers, and pine.

The other two sheets of the triptych are "*Osaka Kōbai* [red plum]" (Honolulu Academy of Arts, 16081) and "*Kyoto Oshiroi* [white makeup]" (Museum of Fine Arts, Boston, 11.19121). The design of three beauties is modeled on a prototype created by Okumura Masanobu, Toshinobu's teacher. LA

---

14   二代鳥居清倍 『七小町』「二　雨ごひ小町」
TORII KIYOMASU II, 1706–1763
"No. 2, Komachi Praying for Rain" (*Ni, Amagoi Komachi*)
From *Seven Scenes from the Life of Ono Komachi* (Nana Komachi)
C. 1735–1740
Woodblock print (*beni-e*)
Hosoban: 13 in. x 6¼ in., 33 cm x 15.9 cm
Signature: 絵師鳥居清倍筆 *Eshi Torii Kiyomasu hitsu*
Publisher's mark: ゑ 元濱町伊賀屋板 *E, Motohama-chō Igaya han*
Publisher: 伊賀屋勘衛門 *Igaya Kan'emon*
Selected other impressions: Schindler, cited in Nihon Keizai Shinbunsha, 1985, no. 9
Published: G. Land 2; US 42 (B/W); G-J vol. 6, 113; GC 15
Collector's seal: 白爾叟 *Hakujisō* or *Berusō*? (verso)
2005.100.15

The *Nana Komachi* series portrays seven legends from the life of the celebrated ninth-century poet Ono Komachi. In this scene, titled *Amagoi Komachi,* or Komachi praying for rain, she stands

with three male attendants beside a pond in the Shinsen'en garden at the Heian imperial palace. Slanting rain pours from the sky in response to a prayer Komachi offers in the form of a poem. The verse is inscribed in the cloud-shaped cartouche above:

Kotowari ya
hi no moto nareba
teri mo seme
sari tote wa mata
ame ga shita to wa

True indeed
That the sun should shine
This being "Japan: Origin of the Sun"
Yet are we not also
"beneath the heavens—beneath the rain?"[6]

In the poem, the term *ama ga shita,* "under heaven," cleverly pivots to a second meaning, "under rain" through the homophones *ama* (heaven) and *ame* (rain); to emphasize this point, the pronunciation "*ame*" (rain) is printed next to the character for heaven, *ama*. On an island in the pond stands a shrine to the female dragon deity Zennyo Ryūō, whose divine help Komachi enlists in ending the drought.

The legend of Komachi, a renowned beauty, became the subject of a cycle of seven Noh plays in the medieval period. As the *Nana Komachi* theme was absorbed into Edo popular culture, several renowned beauties of the period took her name as a sobriquet. In contrast to other reworkings in *mitate* form, Kiyomasu takes a classicizing approach based loosely on the style of Tosa school artists affiliated with the imperial court. This is the only known impression of this print, luxurious in its use of vibrant hand-applied colors, mist bands created by blowing pigment across a stencil, and rocks and other details picked out in shiny black ink mixed with glue. LA

---

15   勝河輝重 吉澤菖蒲花傘踊り
KATSUKAWA TERUSHIGE, active c. 1716–1736
The Actor Yoshizawa Ayame I dancing with a flower-decorated umbrella
Woodblock print (*beni-e* with brass filings)
Hosoban: 13¼ in. x 6¼ in., 33.7 cm x 15.9 cm
Signature: 勝河輝重 *Katsukawa Terushige*
Publisher's mark: したしはんぎやあさくさのみつけひげかどうぼう丁 *Shitashi hangiya Asakusa no Mitsuke Hikage Dōbōchō*
Publisher: 和谷屋権四郎 *Izumiya Gonshirō*
Published: FP 15; UM 68; US 184; GC 16
Collector's seal: 白爾叟 *Hakujisō* or *Berusō*? (verso)
2005.100.16

This print appears to depict a girl dancer holding a parasol adorned with cherry blossoms and bells. She seems to be playing the role of

---

5   The sleeve dangling from the pine branch may allude to the Noh play *Hagoromo* (The Feather Mantle), in which a fisherman discovers a celestial feathered robe hanging from a pine at Miho no Matsubara.

6   Trans. Kimbrough, 20. In the print the two final syllables appear to be *to wa* rather than *ka wa* as in Kimbrough's transcription.

a samurai, with two swords tucked into her obi. In fact, the youthful dancer is most likely a male Kabuki actor playing the role of a female imitating a samurai or a young dandy. The large paulownia crests on his sleeves tell us that this is likely the famous *onnagata* Yoshizawa Ayame I.

The dancer's robe has wide sleeve openings tied with tasseled cords (*sasage*), and decoration of grasses—a motif associated with the broad plain of Musashi—and stirrups (*abumi*). The combination resonates with a series of poems referring to the Musashi stirrups included in the ninth-century *Tales of Ise*.[7] The design on the lower hem shows a horse under a thatched roof, a sword crossed with a halberd, a helmet and armored sleeve guards, and what appears to be a potted pine. The dancer's role has not been identified.

This rare surviving example of Terushige's work is hand colored with orange-red, purple, yellow, and green. Metallic filings embellish the umbrella stretchers. MR

16　石川豊信　傘持つ美人
ISHIKAWA TOYONOBU, 1711–1785
Woman holding an umbrella
C. 1740s
Woodblock print (*beni-e*)
Habahiro hashira-e: 28 in. x 6⅛ in., 71.1 cm x 15.6 cm
Signature: 咀篠堂石川秀葩豊信圖 *Tanjōdō Ishikawa Shūha Toyonobu zu*
Artist's seal: 石川氏 Ishikawa uji; 豊信 *Toyonobu*
Publisher's mark: mark of Urokogataya
Publisher and firm name: 鱗形屋孫兵衛 *Urokogataya Magobei*
Selected other impressions: HMA (23307), CHI (1925.2249)
Published: GC 17
2005.100.17

The narrow pillar print, or *hashira-e*, format is used to advantage in this work not only to showcase the subject's figure and beautiful face but also to display her fashionable attire and hairstyle. A broad-faced beauty with heavy, sensual expression stands delicately on flaring "ginko leaf" *geta* (wooden clogs), revealing tiny bare toes. Her hair is done up fashionably with an upper section wound at the back in a figure eight around a distinctly patterned tortoiseshell hair bar (*kōgai*), then further adorned with a matching tortoiseshell comb and a double crane lozenge–shaped openwork hairpin (*kanzashi*). The most unusual aspect of this print is the woman's ivy-patterned raincoat, with its standing collar, cord fasteners, and bow-tied sleeves. This kind of sleeved raincoat (*sodekappa*) may have been derived from the coats of Portuguese missionaries and traders, and altered to fit the shape of traditional Japanese clothing. The woman's sultry expression, the glimpses of flesh, and the massive, protruding snake-eye umbrella (*janome*) give this print a latent eroticism that is heightened by its compressed vertical format. MR

7　McCullough 78–79

17　石川豊信　風呂上り
ISHIKAWA TOYONOBU, 1711–1785
Woman coming out of the bath
Woodblock print (*benizuri-e* with later hand coloring)
Hashira-e: 26⅝ in. x 3⅞ in., 67.6 cm x 9.8 cm
Signature: 咀篠堂石川秀葩画 *Tanjōdō Ishikawa Shūha ga*
Publisher's mark: 板元 *hanmoto,* with mark of publisher Urokogataya
Publisher and firm name: 鱗形屋孫兵衛 Urokogataya Magobei
Published: GC 18
Collector's seal: Hayashi Tadamasa
2005.100.18

Within the slim vertical format of a *hashira-e*, a beauty reinserts hairpins after her bath. Her naked figure is hastily covered with a chrysanthemum-patterned bathrobe (*yokui* or *yukata*), echoing the autumnal theme of the haiku verse inscribed above her head:

*Omokage ni
momiji terisō
furo agari*

A vision,
glowing with the blush of autumn foliage,
fresh from her bath

The voyeuristic exposure of the upper body and leg, and the precariously covered lower abdomen place this print into the category of *abuna-e*, or "dangerous pictures." After the Kyōhō Reforms of 1722 banned the production of pornographic prints (*shunga*), printmakers adopted alternative means of pleasing their clientele. Instead of explicit representations of sexual acts they depicted partially exposed bodies and sensual facial expressions.

The blue color on the robe in this print appears to have been hand applied at a later time. MR

18　石川豊信　「瀬川吉次　八才_而　相勤申候」
ISHIKAWA TOYONOBU, 1711–1785
"The Actor Segawa Kichiji Performing at Age Eight" (*Segawa Kichiji hassai ni shikōshite aitsutomu mōshi sōrō*)
1750.9
Woodblock print (two-color *benizuri-e*)
Ōban: 17 in. x 12¼ in., 43.2 cm x 31.1 cm
Signature: 咀篠堂石川秀葩豊信圖 *Tanjōdō Ishikawa Shūha Toyonobu zu*
Artist's seal: 石川氏 *Ishikawa uji*; 豊信 *Toyonobu*
Publisher's mark: 板元 *hanmoto,* with mark of publisher Urokogataya
Publisher and firm name: 鱗形屋孫兵衛 *Urokogataya Magobei*
Selected other impressions: ŌTA, cited in ŌTA 1988, no. 55.
Published: US 189; Ukiyoe 6; GC 19
2005.100.19

A young Kabuki actor in a robe patterned with chrysanthemums and Chinese-style treasures dances with two lion puppets on his hands—one with a red face and one with a long pale mane. The actor seems to have jumped off a footed stand holding a large display of peonies. Butterflies flit overhead. This dance is clearly a *Shakkyō mono*—a category of lion dances derived from the Noh play *Shakkyō* (Stone Bridge), in which a Buddhist priest meets a boy woodcutter while on a pilgrimage near a stone bridge in China. The child later reappears as a lion (or two lions) to perform an auspicious dance amid the peonies. Such dances were frequently performed on the Kabuki stage in the eighteenth century.

The inscription and the actors' crests—roundels with bundled cotton rovings—tell us that this is the legendary actor Segawa Kichiji, better known by his later name Kikunojō II (1741–1773). This print depicts his stage debut in the dance *Aki no chō katami no tsubasa,* performed as part of the program *Kanadehon shijūshichi ji* at the Nakamura Theater in Edo in the ninth month of 1750. This was a memorial performance on the first anniversary of the death of his adpoted father Segawa Kikunojō I. At this time, Kichiji would have been ten by the traditional method of calculating age, despite the fact that the inscription on this print records him as eight years old. The pinwheels at his feet—likely used as props in the dance—also emphasize his youth.

The predominance of red (*beni*) and the fact that its color is printed instead of being hand applied place this print into the category of *benizuri-e*. MR

19　鳥居清重　「女文字平家物語　四ばん續　渡部滝口競　市川海老蔵」

TORII KIYOSHIGE, active c. 1716–1764
"The Actor Ichikawa Ebizō II as Imperial Guard Watanabe Kisō in the four-act play *Onna moji Heike monogatari*" (*Onna moji Heike monogatari yonban tsuzuki Watanabe Takiguchi Gisō Ichikawa Ebizō*)
1748
Woodblock print (*sumizuri-e* with hand coloring)
Ōban (trimmed): 13⅞ in. x 10¾ in., 35.2 cm x 27.3 cm
Selected other impressions: Riese (no. 5)
Published: FP 11; GC 5
Collectors' seals: Edwin Grabhorn; 白爾叟 *Hakujisō* or *Berusō*? (verso)
2005.100.5

Ichikawa Ebizō II lived from 1688 until 1758. Son of the first Ichikawa Danjūrō, he took the stage name Ebizō in 1735. His role here is identified as Watanabe Kisō in the play *Onna moji Heike monogatari*. Performed at Nakamura Theater as the opening performance of the season (*kaomise*) in the eleventh month of 1748, the play celebrated the arrival in Edo of Nakamura Kumetarō I, a star of the Kyoto stage. Ebizō is dressed for the spectacular *shibaraku* scene, a specialty of the Danjūrō line. His distinctive red robe conceals a warrior's armor, and swords cross the hero's body beneath voluminous sleeves emblazoned with the *mimasu* crest of nested measuring boxes. Crossed eyes, a snarling expression, and dramatic makeup help to complete the *mie*, a pose frozen at a moment of high emotional intensity.

The condition of this print reflects a complicated history. Trimmed at the top and sides, it shows a rectangular patch at lower right where a signature might have been removed. The Riese Collection includes a later version with printed colors (*benizuri-e*) signed by Torii Kiyoshige (at the lower right), but lacking the name of the play and the role seen here. Rose Hempel conjectures that the Grabhorn print comes from the first state, and that the Riese impression was from a reissued second state made when Ebizō acted in the role a second time.[8] LA

20　鳥居清重　「市川団十郎」　景清

TORII KIYOSHIGE, active c. 1716–1764
"The Actor Ichikawa Danjūrō IV [as Kagekiyo]" (*Ichikawa Danjūrō*)
1756–1757
Woodblock print (three-color *benizuri-e*)
Hosoban: 7 in. x 16 in., 17.8 cm x 40.6 cm
Signature: 鳥居清重 *Torii Kiyoshige*
Artist's seal: 清重 *Kiyoshige*
Publisher's mark: 山 本版 *Yamamoto han*
Publisher: 丸屋九左衛門 *Maruya Kuzaemon*
Published: UM 17; GC 20
Provenance: Satō Shōtarō
2005.100.20

A verse, inscribed above the figure, identifies him as one in a famous line of actors who took the name Ichikawa Danjūrō:

Kage kiyoki
mizu
ni gebi nashi
yamazakura
　Sanjō

In shade pure water,
without vulgarity,
mountain cherry blossoms
　Three Measures

The term "Three Measures" at the end of the inscription refers to the crest of three nested measuring boxes used by actors of the Danjūrō line, which is shown on the shoulders of the actor's robe in this print. The poem puns on the name Kagekiyo (literally, "shade pure"), a famous Taira clan warrior from *The Tale of the Heike*. In the print the actor's face is painted in the distinctive striated makeup typical of the Kabuki role of Kagekiyo, for which the actor Ichikawa Danjūrō IV was particularly famed. We know that Danjūrō IV appeared as Kagekiyo in a play entitled *Nippon zutsumi tori no ne Soga*, staged in the first month of 1757; this print may be a record of that performance. His robes cover what seems to be a chain mail undergarment with the character for "west" on the chest, and he wears armored gauntlets and greaves, or shin guards. Raising the cord-wrapped scabbard of his sword into the air, he strikes a stylized pose (*mie*) that marks a dramatic highpoint in the play.

Its resemblance to other actor prints made by Kiyoshige in 1756

8　Hempel, no. 6.

and 1757 (for example, Museum of Fine Arts, Boston, 21.5671 and 21.5670) suggests that this one may have been part of a triptych. MR

---

21 初代鳥居清満 「さんかつ　姉川大吉　半七　坂東彦三郎」

TORII KIYOMITSU I, 1735–1785

"The Actors Anegawa Daikichi as Sankatsu and Bandō
    Hikosaburō II as Hanshichi" (*Sankatsu Anegawa Daikichi,
    Hanshichi Bandō Hikosaburō*)

C. 1760

Woodblock print (three-color *benizuri-e*)

Hosoban: 15⅝ in. x 7 in., 39.7 cm x 17.8 cm

Signature: 鳥居清満画 *Torii Kiyomitsu ga*

Artist's seal: 清満 *Kiyomitsu*

Publisher's mark: 弥　松村 *Ya, Matsumura*

Publisher: 松村屋弥兵衛 *Matsumura Yahei*

Published: US 190; GC 21

2005.100.21

This print depicts a scene from a Kabuki play based on the real-life love suicide of the courtesan Minoya Sankatsu and her married lover, sake merchant Akaneya Hanshichi. This event, which took place in Osaka's Sennichi cemetery on a winter night in 1695, became famous as the subject of numerous puppet and Kabuki plays. Here, the two lovers stand with their hands clasped, just before they depart for the cemetery in the final scene. Hanshichi wears a merchant's ledger hung from his obi, and he carries a brush, with which he seems to have written a verse on Sankatsu's cloud-patterned inner sleeve. Above the two figures are the actors' names and roles as well as the verse:

Aisode ya
fude ni kokoro wo
fukumu sumi

Sleeves meeting;
In the brush
Is heart-filled ink

The second part of the poem refers to Hanshichi's suicide note, which is read in an emotional scene late in the play.

Crests also identify the actors: Hanshichi wears the crane roundel of Bandō Hikosaburō II and Sankatsu the ivy crest of Anegawa Daikichi. While the exact title of the play shown here is unknown, a clue exists in a closely related design by Kiyomitsu in the Museum of Fine Arts, Boston (11.18999). There a possible play title—*Au yo no meoto boshi* (Night Meeting of the Star-Crossed Lovers)—is provided in place of the verse in the Grabhorn example, and the actors' crests appear above their names. MR

---

22 初代鳥居清満 「かまや武兵　中村仲蔵」

TORII KIYOMITSU I, 1735–1785

"The Actor Nakamura Nakazō as Kamaya Takebei" (*Kamaya Take-
    bei Nakamura Nakazō*)

C. 1760s

Woodblock print (*nishiki-e*)

Hosoban: 12¼ in. x 5¼ in., 31.1 cm x 13.3 cm

Signature: 鳥居清満画 *Torii Kiyomitsu ga*

Publisher's mark: さかい町　善 *Sakai-chō Zen*

Publisher: Unknown

Selected other impressions: CHI (1925.2008)

Published: GC 22

Ex-collection: Tod and Freeman Ford

2005.100.22

Kamaya Takebei, the character depicted here, was the sole witness to a 1683 fire started by the teenage beauty Yaoya Oshichi (1667–1683), daughter of a greengrocer. Oshichi's dramatic crime and punishment became the subject of numerous ballads, puppet plays, and Kabuki dramas. In most versions, a fire in Edo leads Oshichi to take refuge at a temple, where she meets and falls in love with a handsome acolyte. Later she returns home, but desperate to be reunited with her lover at the temple, she sets another fire. In the version of the story upon which this print was based, Takebei witnesses the arson and turns Oshichi in, leading to her arrest and execution.

Takebei, here played by Nakamura Nakazō I, is shown in a jaunty checked jacket (*haori*) emblazoned with the actor's crest. Beneath it he wears a *kosode* whose dayflower blue pigment has now turned to yellow, and a sword worn through his striped obi. He looks suspiciously back over his shoulder through a Shinto shrine gate (its plaque is a standard one for Inari shrines: Shōichii Inari Daimyōjin). This scene is thought to have occurred at the beginning of a play in which Oshichi (played by Segawa Kikunojō) falls in love with a masterless samurai named Kichisa (Bandō Hikosaburō) at Masaki Inari Shrine. MR

---

23 初代鳥居清満 「柳屋娘〆　瀬川菊之丞」

TORII KIYOMITSU I, 1735–1785

"The Actor Segawa Kikunojō as the Young Woman of the Yana-
    giya" (*Yanagiya musume Segawa Kikunojō*)

1769.3

Woodblock print (*nishiki-e*)

Hosoban: 5⅝ in. x 12¼ in., 14.3 cm x 31.1 cm

Signature: 鳥居清満画 *Torii Kiyomitsu ga*

Publisher's mark: 馬喰町　西村　弐丁目板元 *Bakurochō
    Nishimura Nichōme hanmoto*

Publisher and firm name: 西村屋与八 Nishimuraya Yohachi; 永
    寿堂 *Eijudō*

Published: FP 22; GC 23

Collector's seal: 白爾叟 *Hakujisō* or *Berusō*?

2005.100.23

A beautiful young woman stands under a ginkgo tree, whose leaves are just beginning to turn yellow. Wearing flared high "ginkgo" *geta*, a chic striped obi, and a minimally decorated *kosode*, she epitomizes the Edo brand of understated chic known as *iki*. Next to her is a tobacco box containing a small brazier and bamboo ashtray, into which she will presumably empty the contents of the long, elegant pipe she holds.

An inscription and the bundled silk roving actor's crest tell us that this is the actor Segawa Kikunojō II. The role is Ofuji, a young woman who worked at the toothpick store Yanagiya, located under a ginkgo tree in the Asakusa section of Edo. Known as one of the three famous beauties of the Meiwa era (1764–1771), Ofuji was the subject of numerous Kabuki plays as well as ukiyo-e prints. This one has been identified as a scene from the second act of the play *Soga moyō aigo no wakamatsu*, performed in the third month of 1769 at the Nakamura Theater in Edo. In the play, contemporary celebrities stand in for characters from the past: here Ofuji is actually Tora Gozen of Ōiso, a courtesan in the warrior epic *The Tale of the Soga Brothers* (Soga monogatari), set in the twelfth century.

Segawa Kikunojō II (1741–1773) is the same actor shown in his boyhood stage debut in no. 19. He took this name in 1756, and became one of the most famous actors specializing in young female roles (*waka onnagata*). Popular not only with male connoisseurs but also with female patrons, he was imitated for everything from his hairstyle and hair accessories to his signature color and the method he used to tie his obi. MR

---

24 橘岷江　『狐廼嫁以李』　「見初め」
TACHIBANA MINKŌ, active c. 1764–1772
"The First Meeting" (*Misome*)
From *The Foxes' Wedding* (Kitsune no yomeiri)
1765
Woodblock print (*nishiki-e*)
Chūban: 7⅝ in. x 10⅞ in., 19.4 cm x 27.6 cm
Connoisseur's seal: 蟠桃　*Hantō*
Selected other impressions: Dr. Harlow Higinbotham; Baron Walter von Heymel (1878-1914)
Published: G.Land 4; GC 24a
Collector's seal: 白爾叟　*Hakujisō* or *Berusō*? (verso)
2005.100.24.1

---

25 橘岷江　『狐廼嫁以李』　「結納」
TACHIBANA MINKŌ, active c. 1764–1772
"Betrothal Gifts" (*Yuinō*)
From *The Foxes' Wedding* (Kitsune no yomeiri)
1765
Woodblock print (*nishiki-e*)
Chūban: 7⅝ in. x 10⅞ in., 19.4 cm x 27.6 cm
Connoisseur's seal: 稚竜　*Chiryū*
Selected other impressions: Dr. Harlow Higinbotham; Baron Walter von Heymel (1878–1914)
Published: GC 24b
Collector's seal: 白爾叟　*Hakujisō* or *Berusō*? (verso)
2005.100.24.2

---

26 橘岷江　『狐廼嫁以李』　「日照り雨」
TACHIBANA MINKŌ, active c. 1764–1772
"Rain When the Sun Is Shining" (*Hideri ame*)
From *The Foxes' Wedding* (Kitsune no yomeiri)
1765
Woodblock print (*nishiki-e*)
Chūban: 7⅝ in. x 10⅞ in., 19.4 cm x 27.6 cm

Connoisseur's/artist's seal: 岷江　*Minkō*
Selected other impressions: Dr. Harlow Higinbotham; Baron Walter von Heymel (1878–1914); CHI, cited in Gentles, no. 1
Published: GC 24c
Collector's seal: 白爾叟　*Hakujisō* or *Berusō*? (verso)
2005.100.24.3

---

27 橘岷江　『狐廼嫁以李』　「盃事」
TACHIBANA MINKŌ, active c. 1764–1772
"Nuptial Sake Cup Ceremony" (*Sakazuki goto*)
From *The Foxes' Wedding* (Kitsune no yomeiri)
1765
Woodblock print (*nishiki-e*)
Chūban: 7⅝ in. x 10⅞ in., 19.4 cm x 27.6 cm
Connoisseur's seal: 柳枝　*Ryūshi*
Selected other impressions: Dr. Harlow Higinbotham; Baron Walter von Heymel (1878–1914)
Published: GC 24d
Collector's seal: 白爾叟　*Hakujisō* or *Berusō*? (verso)
2005.100.24.4

---

28 橘岷江　『狐廼嫁以李』　「産湯」
TACHIBANA MINKŌ, active c. 1764–1772
"First Bathing [of the Infant]" (*Ubuyu*)
From *The Foxes' Wedding* (Kitsune no yomeiri)
1765
Woodblock print (*nishiki-e*)
Chūban: 7⅝ in. x 10⅞ in., 19.4 cm x 27.6 cm
Connoisseur's seal: 亀仙之印　*Kisen in*
Selected other impressions: Dr. Harlow Higinbotham; Baron Walter von Heymel (1878–1914)
Published: G-J vol. 5, 521; GC 24e
2005.100.24.5
according to the 10-vol dict.; #5

---

29 橘岷江　『狐廼嫁以李』　「宮参り」
TACHIBANA MINKŌ, active c. 1764–1772
"Visit to the Shrine" (*Miya mairi*)
From *The Foxes' Wedding* (Kitsune no yomeiri)
1765
Woodblock print (*nishiki-e*)
Chūban: 7⅝ in. x 10⅞ in., 19.4 cm x 27.6 cm
Connoisseur's seal: 翠葉　*Suiyō*
Selected other impressions: Dr. Harlow Higinbotham; Baron Walter von Heymel (1878–1914)
Published: G-J vol. 5, 523; GC 24f
2005.100.24.6

---

30 鈴木春信　『風流諷八景』　「松風の秋月」
SUZUKI HARUNOBU, 1725?–1770
"Autumn Moon of Matsukaze" (*Matsukaze no shūgetsu*)
From *Fashionable Eight Views of Noh Chants* (Fūryū utai hakkei)
1768–1769

Woodblock print (*nishiki-e*)
Hosoban: 12½ in. x 5¾ in., 31.7 cm x 14.6 cm
Signature: 鈴木春信画 *Suzuki Harunobu ga*
Selected other impressions: MIA (74.1.94); V&A (E.81-1969);
    BMFA (46.1406); ŌTA, cited in ŌTA 1988, no. 61.
Published: GC 25
Collector's seal: 白爾叟 *Hakujisō* or *Berusō*?(verso)
2005.100.25

Two women dressed in the long-sleeved *furisode* of unmarried
women are shown on an undulating shoreline. A pine tree behind
them partially screens a full moon. The standing figure, wearing a
design of plovers flying over a pine-lined shore and sails, holds the
cap (*eboshi*) and robe of an aristocrat. The other woman kneels on
the shore. She wears a dark obi decorated with tie-dyed pine bark
lozenges (*matsukawabishi*) over an autumnal morning glory–patterned *furisode*.

Despite the distinctly eighteenth-century character of the dress
and hairstyles, viewers of Harunobu's time would have instantly
recognized this print as a scene from the classic Noh play *Matsukaze* (Wind in the Pines), which is associated with Heian-period
(794–1185) Japan. The play revolves around two sisters, Matsukaze
and Murasame, who work as brine maidens, carrying the seaweed
used to make salt in Suma. The play tells us that both sisters had
love affairs with courtier and poet Ariwara Yukihira (818–893)
during his period of exile to Suma, a reference drawn from a well-
known poem in the anthology *Kokin wakashū*, as well as from a
later reference in *The Tale of Genji*. In the Noh play, the ghosts of
the sisters wait on the beach for Yukihira's return, with only his hat
and cloak as reminders.

This print comes from a series of eight, each of which depicts a
scene from a classical Noh play in an eighteenth-century reinterpretation. MR

---

31   鈴木春信　見立孟宗
SUZUKI HARUNOBU, 1725?–1770
Mitate of Meng Zong (Mōsō), one of the Twenty-four Paragons of
    Filial Piety
1765
Woodblock print (*nishiki-e*)
Chūban: 11½ in. x 8¼ in., 29.2 cm x 21 cm
Selected other impressions: BMFA (21.4600); MIA (74.164);
    CHIBA (2994002); CHI (25.2034); MET (JP2439); Vever,
    cited in Hillier 1974, nos. 95, 96
Published: Hillier 1970, 19; GC 26
Collectors' seals: Edwin and Marjorie Grabhorn, 白爾叟
    Hakujisō or *Berusō*? (both verso)
2005.100.26

Dressed in a wide sedge hat and a straw cape, a beautiful woman
prepares to dig a bamboo shoot out of the deep snow. Her bare feet
and hands, holding a mattock, are pure white against her brilliantly
colored *furisode* robe. The pattern on her robe is of undulating
shorelines lined with bracken and threeleaf arrowhead, the first a
symbol of spring and the second of summer.

Digging bamboo in the snow is standard iconography for the

story of Meng Zong (Mōsō), one of the Chinese Twenty-four
Paragons of Filial Piety (*Nijūshikō*). According to legend, Meng
Zong's sick mother asked him to find bamboo shoots to make a
medicinal broth. He went out in the snowy winter to look, but to
no avail. Then, amazingly, his prayers and tears seemed to produce
bamboo shoots rising up from the frozen ground (see no. 11 for an
earlier version, by Okumura Masanobu). The story was retold in
Japan in various forms, including moral instruction. In this print,
the undertones seem to be more erotic than pious. The imagery
of protruding shoots makes this story an obvious candidate for a
mitate reworking of the theme with a beautiful woman in place of
Meng Zong.

As detailed in David Waterhouse's essay (p. 21), this impression
has been identified as the second state for a calendar print (*egoyomi*) for the year 1765. An earlier version had the numbers of the
long months for that year hidden in the bamboo leaves. Because
this version removes the dating, it was produced after 1765, probably the following year. MR

---

32   鈴木春信　見立琴高仙人
SUZUKI HARUNOBU, 1725?–1770
Mitate of the Chinese immortal Qin Gao (Kinkō Sennin)
Woodblock print (*nishiki-e*)
Chūban: 11¼ in. x 8¼ in., 28.6 cm x 21 cm
Artist's signature:春信画 *Harunobu ga*
Published: US 154; GC 27
Collectors' seals: Edwin and Marjorie Grabhorn, 白爾叟
    Hakujisō or *Berusō*? (both verso)
Ex-collection: Tod and Freeman Ford
Provenance: Judson D. Metzgar
2005.100.27

The story of Qin Gao (Kinkō Sennin), a legendary Taoist immortal reportedly of the Warring States period (c. 480–221 BCE) is a
Chinese narrative with an established presence in Japanese visual
imagery. According to Qin Gao's biography in the *Biographies of Ex-
emplary Immortals* (*Liexian zhuan*, attributed to Liu Xiang, 79–78
BCE), the immortal was known for mastery of the zither (Chinese:
qin, which forms the first character of the immortal's name). After
studying the secrets of immortality and travelling for two hundred
years, he jumped into Lake Zhou in search of dragons. He returned
later to meet his disciples, rising out of the water on a giant red carp.

Harunobu replaces Qin Gao with a beautiful courtesan who
reads a love letter while riding a carp. Wearing an overgarment
with snow-laden pines on top of a red *kosode* with a border design
of bracken, she perches atop a fish that looks for all the world like a
Boys' Day carp banner (*koi nobori*). It is a mark of Harunobu's brilliance as a designer that he successfully marries these elements of
stylization and naturalism into a cohesive whole. MR

---

33   鈴木春信　見立太田道灌
SUZUKI HARUNOBU, 1725?–1770
Mitate of the story of Ōta Dōkan
1766–1767
Chūban: 11 in. x 8 in., 27.9 cm x 20.3 cm

Selected other impressions: BMFA (11.19444; 21.4615); HMA
(14486); MIA (74.1.69); CHI (44.431); BM (1937,0710,0.282);
TNM (A-10569_1278); HU (1933.4.2647)
Published: GC 28
2005.100.28

A young woman in an iris-patterned *furisode,* jauntily tied
obi, and black lacquered *geta* steps out of the rope-curtained entrance to a rustic building bordered by a brushwood fence. The sky
is streaked with clouds and driving rain. She wears a gently smiling
but inscrutable expression as she holds out a branch of flowering
yellow kerria rose (*yamabuki*) in her right hand. Like many other
designs by Harunobu, this image is a *mitate,* using a figure dressed
in contemporary fashions to evoke a much older legend or literary
episode.

Though untitled, the scene would have been recognized by its
Edo-period viewers as a reference to an episode in the life of Ōta
Dōkan (1432–1486), a warrior famous as the architect of Edo
Castle. Once, visiting the countryside, he was caught in a rainfall
and ran to a local residence to borrow a straw raincoat (*mino*).
Instead of providing a raincoat, the young woman who answered
the door wordlessly handed her visitor a branch of double-blos-
soming kerria. Dōkan flew into a rage until he was later reminded
of the double meaning of a *waka* poem in the 1086 anthology
Goshūi wakashū:

*Nanae yae
hana wa sakedomo
yamabuki no
mi no hitotsu dani
naki zo kanashiki*

Though it blossoms
in myriad layers,
the kerria rose,
sadly, bears
not a single fruit

In an alternate reading of the poem, the lines "not a single fruit"
can be interpreted as "not a single raincoat." Realizing that, far from
being rude, the woman's gesture had been an authentic and elegant expression of regret for being unable to grant his wish, Dōkan vowed to
devote himself to the study of *waka,* later becoming a Buddhist priest.

Other impressions of this design have variations in the blocks
used for the wooden door posts and clouds. According to David
Waterhouse (see p. 22), this impression was made in the nineteenth
century using the original keyblock and recarved color blocks.[9] MR

34　鈴木春信　蛍狩り
SUZUKI HARUNOBU, 1725?–1770
Hunting for fireflies
1767–1768

9　Jack Hillier identified the Grabhorn impression as a second state (Hillier
　　1970, no. 112).

Woodblock print (*nishiki-e*)
Chūban: 10½ in. x 8 in., 26.7 cm x 20.3 cm
Signature: 春信画　*Harunobu ga*
Selected other impressions: TIK (P-U 38); CHI (1925.2108);
Vever, cited in Sotheby (1978), no. 57; cited in Kobayashi 2002:
TNM, Hiraki
Published: Hillier 1970, 95; US 157; GC 29
Collectors' seals: 白爾叟　*Berusō?* (verso)
2005.100.29

On a hot summer night, fireflies glow above a winding stream
edged by summer plants — threeleaf arrowhead (*omadaka*), irises,
and reeds. Into this evocative natural scene have stepped a young
couple — a boy and girl engaged in firefly hunting (*hotaru gari*),
one of the traditional leisure pastimes of summer evenings. Their
pale white faces and exposed necks, hands, legs, and feet stand
out against the inky black sky, the bright green of the embankment, and the pale blue water (colored with fleeting dayflower
pigment).

Both are slight of figure and exude youthful innocence, even
while hinting at other pleasures. The boy wears a striped cotton
hand towel tied under his chin—a style often worn to cover one's
identity during elicit activities. His summer robe bears a geometric design known as *kuruwa tsunagi* (a phrase with the double
meaning of "joined curved circles" and "joined pleasure quarters"). This motif was often found on garments handed out by
special tea houses (*hikite jaya*) near the entrance of the pleasure
quarters, which provided introductions to brothels. His companion wears a wood grain–patterned obi over a diaphanous purple
furisode patterned above the hem and on the lower portion of
the sleeves with white bracken (*warabi*)—fern shoots rising out
of the earth. The use of paste-resist white patterns on a dark
background was the epitome of understated chic in Edo during
second half of the eighteenth century.

At least two states of this print are known, with variations in
the man's footwear, the cage, and the net.[10] MR

35　鈴木春信　笠森鍵屋お仙
SUZUKI HARUNOBU, 1725?–1770
Osen of the Kagiya serving tea in front of Kasamori Shrine
1768–1769
Woodblock print (*nishiki-e*)
Chūban: 11¼ in. x 8¼ in., 28.6 cm x 21 cm
Signature: 春信画　Harunobu ga
Selected other impressions: TNM (A-10569_1319); BMFA
(21.4977); BM (1937,0710,0.6); MET (JP2445); HMA
(14486); TSH (春信　1)
Published: GC 30
Collector's seal: Edwin and Marjorie Grabhorn
2005.100.30

At an outdoor teahouse (*mizujaya*) near the gate of a shrine, a
lithe young woman serves tea to a man resting on a wide bench.

10　See Hillier, 1970, 162, and David Waterhouse in the present volume, 23

With one sandal casually kicked off, he holds a pipe in his hand as he gazes at her. His head is sheathed in a wide black hood (*zukin*), presumably of lined silk crepe—a style that was especially popular in the 1700s among samurai from Kyoto and Osaka when visiting the pleasure quarters in Edo. He indeed wears the double swords of a warrior-class man, though the natty vertical stripes are more closely associated with fashionable commoners. Next to the man lies a smoking box containing a small brazier and cylindrical bamboo ashtray; but his main interest is his server — the famed beauty Osen (1751–1857), who worked at the Kagiya teahouse outside the Kasamori Inari Shrine in present-day Taninaka, Taito-ku, Tokyo.

Osen—along with Ofuji of Yanagiya (see no. 23) and Oyoshi of Tsutaya—was renowned as one of the three beauties of the Meiwa era (1764–1772). Said to have drawn customers from across Edo, she was the frequent subject of artists. Harunobu, perhaps the first ukiyo-e artist to depict ordinary women as objects of desire, featured Osen in several prints. The composition of this one is particularly effective, with the verticality of the two figures echoed by the pillar of the shrine gate and the dark tree trunk, juxtaposed with the strong diagonal lines of the wide pathway and benches.

The latent eroticism of this scene is revealed more explicitly in another, similar Harunobu print of Osen and a patron—a copy of which is owned by the University Art Museum, Tokyo University of the Arts. In that version, the patron pulls Osen's wrist forward with one hand, while he slips the other between her thighs. MR

36　鈴木春信　桜狩
SUZUKI HARUNOBU, 1725?–1770
Hunting cherry blossoms
Woodblock print (*nishiki-e*)
Chūban: 10⅞ in. x 8 in., 27.6 cm x 20.3 cm
Signature: 春信画　*Harunobu ga*
Selected other impressions: MET (JP2771)
Published: GC 31
Collectors' seals: Edwin and Marjorie Grabhorn, 白爾叟
　　Hakujisō or *Berusō*? (both verso)
2005.100.31

Having come for a day of leisure under the cherry blossoms, a young couple hurriedly rise to shield themselves from a sudden downpour. Inscribed in the clouds is an anonymous poem from the anthology *Shūi wakashū* (completed c. 1006), which imbues the print with classical associations. In a famous episode, the courtier poet Fujiwara Sanekata (d. 999) supposedly recited this poem while allowing his silken robes to become rain-soaked at a blossom viewing party—an act the other guests found to be startlingly elegant.

> *Sakuragari*
> *ame wa furikinu*
> *onajiku wa*
> *nuru to mo hana no*
> *kage ni kakuren*

Hunting cherry blooms,
the rain comes tumbling down: but
all the same, even
if we get drenched, we may take
shelter in the flowers' shade.[11]

Harunobu incorporates subtly erotic undertones into the skillful composition. The two-lobed curves of the maiden's sleeve arching gracefully over her head are echoed in the tree branches, clouds, and her lover's curved back and tied-up outer robe. The young man holds out a stiffly protruding "snake eye" (*janome*) umbrella parallel to the embankment and to the red felt rug, and perpendicular to the driving rain and the traveler's chest (*hasamibako*)—which was probably used to carry the rug and other furnishings for the picnic. MR

37　鈴木春信　『風流六哥仙』「在原業平」
SUZUKI HARUNOBU, 1725?–1770
"Ariwara Narihira"
From *Fashionable Six Poetic Immortals* (Fūryū rokkasen)
1768–1769
Woodblock print (*nishiki-e*)
Chūban: 10⅞ in. x 8⅛ in., 27.6 cm x 20.6 cm
Signature: 春信画　*Harunobu ga*
Selected other impressions: HMA (14486)
Published: US 194; GC 32
Collectors' seals: Edwin and Marjorie Grabhorn, 白爾叟
　　Hakujisō or *Berusō*? (both verso)
2005.100.32

On a spring evening, a young beauty leans on a sill to gaze at the moon, shining on cherry blossoms above a meandering stream. Beneath her on the veranda is a vase of red plum blossoms, whose scent must fill the air. She dangles her long pipe from one sleeve of a *kosode* decorated with fawn-spotted purple clouds and three-leaf arrowhead. A long obi of hexagonal diaper pattern with spider tie-dying hangs from her back. In the room behind her a two-panel folding screen painted with peonies and gold clouds bears the signature, "painted by Harunobu," cleverly identifying the print's artist.

Above the young lady's head a cloud-form cartouche contains an inscription that reveals the subject matter. One from a series of six prints entitled *Fashionable Six Poetic Immortals,* this print features a young woman who is an avatar of the emotions of ninth-century courtier-poet Ariwara Narihira (825–880), known for his dashing looks and romantic exploits. The scene before us is a contemporary manifestation of one of his most famous *waka* poems:

> *Tsuki ya aranu*
> *haru ya mukashi no*
> *haru naran*
> *waga mi hitotsu*
> *ha moto mi ni shite*

11　Trans. David Waterhouse. See p. 23.

The moon is not the same.
Is the spring the spring of old?
Only this body of mine is the same body … [12]

In this verse, Narihira laments the changing of the seasons, and perhaps the absence of his love, feeling that he himself is the one lonely constant.

According to David Waterhouse, this may be a later reprint using the original keyblock. MR

38　鈴木春信　「大中臣能信朝臣」
SUZUKI HARUNOBU, 1725?–1770
"Ōnakatomi Yoshinobu Ason"
From an untitled series of Thirty-six Poetic Immortals
1767–1768
Woodblock print (*nishiki-e*)
Chūban: 11¼ in. x 8⅜ in., 28.6 cm x 21.3 cm
Signature: 春信画　Harunobu ga
Published: FP 27; GC 33; Hillier 1970, 83
Collectors' seals: Edwin and Marjorie Grabhorn, 白爾叟
　　Hakujisō or *Berusō*? (both verso)
2005.100.33

This print comes from a series based on poems by the Thirty-six Poetic Immortals (*Sanjūrokkasen*), a group selected in the mid Heian period by Fujiwara Kintō (966–1041) and reproduced in portrait paintings and poetry groupings for centuries to follow. The poet featured here is Ōnakatomi Yoshinobu (921–991), whose poem from the anthology *Shūi wakashū* and its commentary informs the imagery:

Chitose made
kagireru matsu mo
kyō yori wa
kimi ni hikarete
yorozuyo ya hen

A thousand years may
be its limit, but the pine
that is picked out by
my lord, from today shall see
ten thousand ages pass by! [13]

The *Shūi wakashū* commentary tells us that this poem was written when the shrine maiden (*miko*) Nyūdō Shikibu performed the rites for the first "Day of the Rat" after the New Year, a time when it is customary to dig up pine seedlings with their roots still attached. Harunobu depicts this subject matter with two beauties as *miko* in red trousers (*hakama*), their hair worn long. Outside the room a plum tree is in bloom. The woman on the right holds a Shinto offering tray laden with pine seedlings. The other *miko* crouches to brush a poem on a

12　Trans. Helen Craig McCullough (McCullough 1968, 71). See also p. 24.
13　Trans. David Waterhouse. See p. 22.

poetry slip (*tanzaku*). A box with writing implements lies beside her on the mat, next to a bamboo basket full of pine seedlings.

Pines are an auspicious symbol of longevity used for decoration at New Year's. The word for the pulled roots (*ne*) of the seedlings is homophonous with the word for rat (*ne*), thus the association with the "Day of the Rat." The floating world undertone of this print comes from the double entendre of the word "pulled roots" (*nebeki*), which could also imply the purchasing of services from a prostitute in the pleasure quarters. MR

39　鈴木春信　『座敷八景』「手拭掛帰帆」
SUZUKI HARUNOBU, 1725?–1770
"Returning Sails of the Towel Rack" (*Tenuguikake kihan*)
From *Eight Parlor Views* (Zashiki hakkei)
1766
Woodblock print (*nishiki-e*)
Chūban: 11⅛ in. x 8½ in., 28.3 cm x 21.6 cm
Publisher firm name: 松鶴堂　*Shōkakudō*
Selected other impressions: CHI (1928.901); MET (JP155); V&A
　　(E.55-1955); BRU, cited in Nagata (2008), no. 15
Published: GC 34
Collectors' seals: Edwin and Marjorie Grabhorn, 白爾叟
　　Hakujisō or *Berusō*? (both verso)
2005.100.34

Two courtesans share a private moment in a room overlooking a veranda and small interior garden. In this quiet scene of domestic activity, one of the women sits on the tatami inside the room stitching a garment — the fabric held taut by a bamboo stretcher attached to the tatami with a curved metal hook. Her sewing box with a red pincushion rests on the doorframe beside her. A round fan and pillow lie just inside the door, hinting at the heat of the room and their leisurely intimacy. The other woman, dressed in a *kosode* with a starch-resist-dyed pattern of white arrowheads and flowing water and a wood-grain–patterned obi, scoops water from a basin to wash her hands. Next to her is a bamboo curtain, presumably leading to the toilet from which she has just emerged. On the veranda beside her a hand towel (*tenugui*) hangs from a rack, ready for use. The towel flutters in the breeze, hinting at this print's hidden subject matter.

Though there is no printed title, this image is known to be one of a series of eight prints produced by Harunobu on request of the haikai poet Okubo Kyosen (Jinshirō, 1722–1777). The prints, considered among Harunobu's masterworks, are *mitate* playing on the Chinese-derived traditional painting motif of "Eight Views of the Xiao and Xiang Rivers," later adapted by Japanese artists as the "Eight Views of Ōmi" (Lake Biwa). This print playfully reworks the theme "Returning Sails off Yabase," substituting the hand towel on its rack for the sailboats usually shown. The idea of appropriating these iconic, sophisticated themes in an intimate scene of mundane pastimes was not invented by Harunobu and Kyosen, but the elite poetry-circle clientele for which they were produced would have appreciated their sophisticated approach to the subject matter.

Scholars have identified three states for this series, the first bearing Kyosen's seal and the third adding Harunobu's signature. As this impression has neither, it is presumed to belong to the second state, reissued for commercial distribution. MR

---

40 鈴木春信 相撲遊び
SUZUKI HARUNOBU, 1725?–1770
Boys sumo wrestling (*Sumō asobi*)
c. 1769
Woodblock print (*nishiki-e*)
Hosoban: 12⅝ in. x 5¾ in., 32.1 cm x 14.6 cm
Signature: 春信画 *Harunobu ga*
Published: GC 35
2005.100.35

Two young boys engage in a sumo wrestling match in front of a mound sprouting autumnal bush clover and miscanthus grass. They wear tie-dyed or red loincloths wrapped to resemble the *mawashi* worn by professional wrestlers. Behind them, a boy umpire who has stripped down to his gray and red bib (*haragake*) gestures with a folding fan. His "poppy" (*keshi*) hairstyle is associated with children of three or four years of age.

Along with the auspicious subject matter of boys growing up plump and strong, this print contains Kabuki-related imagery. The "three measures" (*mimasu*) crest on the fan is associated with the Ichikawa Danjūrō actor lineage, known for the swashbuckling acting style known as *aragoto* (literally, "rough stuff"). The spiral pattern (*Kamezō komon*) on the bib is one made popular by the contemporary Kabuki actor Ichimura Kamezō (Ichimura Uzaemon IX).

Harunobu produced at least five different compositions of sumo wrestling boys. This is the only known impression of this print, which originally had a gradient blue sky colored with fleeting dayflower pigment. It is closest in composition to a print found in the British Museum and other collections. MR

---

41 鈴木春信 『風俗六玉川』「調布の玉川 むさしの名所」
SUZUKI HARUNOBU, 1725?–1770
"Chōfu Jewel River, a Famous Place in Musashi Province" (*Chōfu no Tamagawa, Musashi no meisho*)
From *Six Jewel Rivers in Popular Customs* (Fūzoku mu Tamagawa)
1769–1770
Woodblock print (*nishiki-e*)
Hashira-e: 27⅛ in. x 4¾ in., 68.9 cm x 12.1 cm
Signature: 鈴木春信画 Suzuki Harunobu ga
Selected other impressions: HU (1933.4.1259); BMFA (06.1294); NAM (32-143/49)
Published: GC 36
Collector's seal: 白爾叟 *Hakujisō or Berusō?*
2005.100.36

The Six Jewel Rivers (*Mu Tamagawa*) were among the geographic locations (*utamakura*) commonly cited in early *waka* poetry. One of the rivers was the Chōfu (previously pronounced Tazukuri) Tamagawa, which flows through present-day Tokyo. At the top of this print is a portrait of the master poet Fukiwara Teika (Sadaie, 1162–1241) and an inscription reading "The Jewel River of Chōfu, one of the famous lo-

cales in Musashi Province." On the right side of the print is inscribed one of Teika's poems about this spot, from the anthology *Shūi gūsō*.

*Tazukuri ya
sarasu kakine no
asa tsuyu wo
tsuranuki tomenu
Tamagawa no sato*

The hand-woven hemp
cloth drying on the hedge holds
morning dew like gems
strung on threads: this truly is
the Jewel River Village![14]

The bleached cloth referred to is *sarashi*—handmade plain-weave cloth of fine hemp or ramie, which was cleaned in the cold, flowing water of the river and stretched to dry and whiten in the sun.

The scene chosen by Harunobu to depict this classical imagery appears on the surface to be an innocent scene of a mother—perhaps one of the washerwomen—holding a length of cloth as she looks down at the child at her feet, dressed only in a bib. In fact, the print hints at an underlying eroticism: the woman's front-tied obi (suggesting she may be a courtesan), her exposed breasts and legs — in danger of further exposure from the child's pulling — and even the "octopus leg" tie-dyed pattern of the cloth she holds evoke sexual associations. MR

---

42 鈴木春信 『風俗六玉川』「擣衣の玉川 摂津国の名所」
SUZUKI HARUNOBU, 1725?–1770
"The Cloth-Fulling Jewel River, a Famous Place in Settsu Province" (*Tōi no Tamagawa, Settsu kuni no meisho*)
From *Six Jewel Rivers in Popular Customs* (Fūzoku mu Tamagawa)
1769–1770
Woodblock print (*nishiki-e*)
Hashira-e: 27 in. x 4½ in., 68.6 cm x 11.4 cm
Signature: 春信画 *Harunobu ga*
Selected other impressions: BM (1907, 0531,0.351)
Published: GC 37
Ex-collection: Tod and Freeman Ford
Provenance: Judson D. Metzgar
2005.100.37

---

43 磯田湖龍斎 『雛形若菜の初模様』「大ひしや内みつはな」
ISODA KORYŪSAI, active 1764–1788
"Mitsuhana of the Ōhishiya" (*Ōhishiya uchi Mitsuhana*)
From *Models for Fashion: New Year Designs as Fresh as Young Leaves* (*Hinagata wakana no hatsumoyō*)
C. 1777–1778

---

14   Trans. David Waterhouse. See p. 24.

Woodblock print (*nishiki-e*)
Ōban: 10¼ in. x 15 in., 26 cm x 38.1 cm
Signature: 湖龍齋画 *Koryūsai ga*
Publisher's mark: 永寿板 *Eiju han*
Publisher and firm name: 西村屋与八 *Nishimuraya Yohachi;* 永
　寿堂 *Eijudō*
Selected other impressions: TNM (A-10569_2242); BMFA
　(11.14631); NYPL (I/+-I431); TTCT (0793-C6)
Published: Ukiyo-e 9; GC 38
2005.100.38

Koryūsai designed prints for this series over a six-year period, from
1776 until 1781. The large number of designs—140 in all—attests
to its enduring popularity. In a new departure for prints, Koryūsai
identifies the courtesans by name, and presents them as celebrity
models for the latest textile designs. This combination enhanced
the designs' commercial value, as fashion guides for stylish women,
and as advertisements for courtesans and brothels. It is possible
that clothing manufacturers, perhaps in collaboration with brothel
owners, may have underwritten the publication of the series. This
kind of cross-promotion was one means of buoying the fortunes of
the Yoshiwara and related businesses.

　Mitsuhana and her attendants fill the large frame of this *ōban*-
size sheet, as if passing just inches from the viewer. The imposing
figure of a male attendant shown from the rear fills almost half the
page. By contrast, two *kamuro* are barely visible past Mitsuhana's
sumptuous padded robe and obi, which is decorated with an em-
broidered dragon design. Underneath an outer robe adorned with
fans and cherry blossoms are five more layers, three with resist and
tie-dyed patterns. LA

44　磯田湖龍斎　『雛形若菜初模様』　「中あふみや内万
　太夫」
ISODA KORYŪSAI, active 1764–1788
"Mandayū of the Nakaōmiya" (*Nakaōmiya uchi Mandayū*)
From *Models for Fashion: New Year Designs as Fresh as Young
　Leaves* (Hinagata wakana hatsumoyō)
C. 1777–1778
Woodblock print (*nishiki-e*)
Ōban: 10¼ in. x 14¾ in., 26 cm x 37.5 cm
Signature: 湖龍画 *Koryū ga,* with unidentified *kaō*
Publisher's mark: 永寿板 *Eiju han*
Publisher and firm name: 西村屋与八 *Nishimuraya Yohachi;* 永
　寿堂 *Eijudō*
Selected other impressions: TNM (A-10569_2246); V&A (E.579-1903)
Published: GC 39
Collector's seal: Edwin Grabhorn
Ex-collection: Mrs. Tobin Clark
2005.100.39

This second print from the *Models for Fashion* series offers an in-
door view of three beauties at New Year's. A courtesan identified as
Mandayū of the Nakaōmiya relaxes with one elbow resting on stacked
go and *shōgi* boards. Tobacco pipe in one hand, she looks on as two *kamuro* play *sugoroku*, a game similar to backgammon, against the back-
drop of a folding screen decorated with bush clover and butterflies.
The *kamuro* wear festive New Year's garb, with pine bough–shaped

accessories in their hair and snow-covered pines decorating their *furisode*. The near figure is shown from behind, providing details of her
elaborate hairstyle and showing off her fashionably tied obi. Mandayū
herself is resplendent in a crane-patterned outer robe, stylish vertical
striped obi, and an inner robe patterned with a hexagonal diaper pattern filled with spiders, in pink on white. In an intimate gesture common to other depictions of courtesans, she draws one hand up to her
chin from within the folds of her innermost garment. LA

45　磯田湖龍斎　『風流品川八景』　「夜雨」
ISODA KORYŪSAI, active 1764–1788
"Night Rain" (*Yau*)
From *Fashionable Eight Views of Shinagawa* (Fūryū Shinagawa hakkei)
1776–1781
Woodblock print (*nishiki-e*)
Ōban: 14¾ in. x 10 in., 37.5 cm x 25.4 cm
Signature: 湖龍齋画 *Koryūsai ga*
Published: FP 30; UM 40; GC 40
2005.100.40

The "eight views," or *hakkei*, theme is distantly derived from the
Chinese literary subject "Eight Views of the Xiao and Xiang Rivers." Japanese versions appear as early as the seventeenth century, in
the popular set of "Eight Views of Ōmi" (*Ōmi hakkei*), and in 1765,
Harunobu transposed the eight views to Yoshiwara brothels in the
mitate series *Eight Parlor Views* (see no. 39). The rage for sets like
these continued until around 1780, as the formula was applied to
other locales in and around Edo. Koryūsai alone produced forty-
one "eight views" series during this period.

　Only two prints survive from his *Fashionable Eight Views of
Shinagawa*, which features unlicensed prostitutes from an area
down the coast from Edo. In "Night Rain," a seated figure wearing
a simple but chic gauze checked robe over a red lining reads a love
letter from a long paper scroll. Her standing companion models
more formal attire: her *kosode*, decorated with butterflies hovering
above slender iris stalks, is tied with a stylish obi of cut velvet fabric
decorated with motifs from the Chinese "eight treasures." Paper
crumpled carelessly in a heap between the women suggests displea-
sure with their correspondents. LA

46　磯田湖龍斎　雪中相合傘
ISODA KORYŪSAI, active 1764–1788
Lovers sharing an umbrella, with poem by Bashō
From an untitled series, with haiku poems
1770–1772
Woodblock print (*nishiki-e*)
Chūban: 10½ in. x 7¾ in., 26.7 cm x 19.7 cm
Signature: 湖龍斎画 *Koryūsai ga*
Selected other impressions: CHI (35.403)
Published: Ukiyo-e 8; GC 41
2005.100.41

Koryūsai included three poems by Bashō in his untitled haiku
series of 1770–1772. The verse written here comes from the poetry
anthology *Hakusenshū*:

Iza saraba
yukimi ni korobu
tokoro made

Well then,
let's go snow-viewing
until we tumble over [15]

Koryūsai's rendition shows young lovers out on a wintry day.
Though in no apparent danger of "tumbling," the girl tightens
the sash on her layered robes to prevent them from trailing in the
snow. Her companion, bundled in a hood and full-length coat,
shelters her with a large umbrella. The pressure of the baren (a
printing tool applied to the back of the paper) has left circular
striations in the pale gray sky, suggesting swirling snow. Overall,
the design is strongly reminiscent of Harunobu, calling to mind in
particular one of his most famous prints, a design of lovers posed
beneath a snow-covered willow. A similar figure in hood and long
coat appears in "Ki Tomonori," from Harunobu's untitled series of
Thirty-six Poetic Immortals (*Sanjūrokkasen*). LA

47　磯田湖龍斎　『風流十二節』　盆
ISODA KORYŪSAI, active 1764–1788
Bon Festival
From *Fashionable Twelve Times of the Year* (Fūryū jūnisetsu)
1770–1772
Woodblock print (*nishiki-e*)
Chūban: 10¼ in. x 7¾ in., 26 cm x 19.7 cm
Signature: 湖龍画　*Koryū ga*
Selected other impressions: CHI (25.2202); Van Vleck (1980.2564)
Published: GC 42
Collector's seal: Edwin and Marjorie Grabhorn (verso)
2005.100.42

An attractive young man steers a beauty down the street, a proprie-
tary arm across her shoulders. The manservant at his side lights the
way with a lantern inscribed "Matsuya." All three wear lightweight,
casual robes, for it is a warm night in mid-summer. Inside the
structure behind them two objects round out the scene: a paper-
covered lamp stand and a novelty item, an automaton shaped as a
kankodori — a drum with a cockerel perched on top. [16]

The combination of drum and cockerel comes from China,
where, it is said, a "drum of admonition" was set up outside the
palace gates to enable criticisms of the government. Under wise
rulers, the drum was never used, meaning that birds could rest atop
it without being startled. In Japan, the word *kankodori* was sometimes used to evoke a peaceful reign, but because it can be also be
written with kanji meaning "cuckoo," a summer bird, it is linked to
that season. Carved *kankodori* were placed atop floats (*dashi*) during the great Sannō and Kanda festivals in Edo. These connotations
may be among the reasons that it appears here, in a print related to
Obon, the summer festival honoring ancestor spirits.

15　Trans. Shirane 1998, 337, fn. 24.
16　The mechanism would have been hidden inside the drum body and
　　stand. David Waterhouse generously explained the meaning of the
　　kankodori and provided this translation of the poem.

Further wordplay is contained in the poem written in the moon-
shaped cartouche at the upper right:

Bon no tōro
tsuki wa kumanaku
hanazakari

A lantern for the Bon festival
a moon with no clouds,
and flowers in full bloom!

Written with different characters the word for lantern, *tōro*, can
also mean "visiting a brothel"— an apt double entendre for this
scene. The final word, *hanazakari,* means flowers in full bloom,
but also refers to women at the peak of their beauty. Appropriately
enough, the courtesan's obi is patterned with peonies, a well-
known symbol of female beauty and sexual allure. LA

48　磯田湖龍斎　鷹図
ISODA KORYŪSAI, active 1764–1788
Falcon on its perch
Woodblock print (*nishiki-e*)
Chūban: 11⅜ in. x 8⅜ in., 28.9 cm x 21.3 cm
Signature: 湖龍画　*Koryū ga*
Selected other impressions: BMFA (68.747)
Published: G.Land. no. 6; GC 43
Collector's seal: Edwin and Marjorie Grabhorn (verso)
Provenance: Matsuki Kihachirō
2005.100.43

Jack Hillier expressed his admiration for this print by Koryūsai in
the 1960 Grabhorn Collection catalogue, *Landscape Prints of Old
Japan*:

> Falconry was an aristocratic sport in Japan as it was in Europe,
> and many great painters of the Kano school were noted for their
> depictions of this proud bird, symbolic, almost, of the pride and
> hauteur of the nobleman. Here Koryusai challenged compari-
> son—for all the plebian medium—with the finest classical exem-
> plars, and by counterbalancing the alert but chained ferocity of
> the falcon with the heaviness of the trappings of his perch, gave
> his print a vitality that was sometimes lacking from the work of
> the revered masters he rivalled. [17]

Koryūsai was one of several artists to explore the use of bird-
and-flower genre in the 1770s and 1780s. To the extent that they
quoted upper-class painting traditions, bird-and-flower prints
gave a gloss of cultural legitimacy to ukiyo-e, an art form whose
primary audience was commoners. Another design by Koryūsai
combines the falcon with Mt. Fuji and an eggplant, a trio said to
bring good fortune as the subject of the first New Year's dream.

A version of this print in the Museum of Fine Arts, Boston has
a narrow band of clouds at the top, and may be an earlier state. LA

17　Grabhorn 1960, no. 6.

49　一筆齋文調　市川弁蔵の経若丸と中村仲蔵の教経の
　　亡霊
IPPITSUSAI BUNCHŌ, active 1765–1792
The actors Ichikawa Benzō I as Tsunewakamaru and Nakamura
　　Nakazō I as the ghost of Noritsune
Woodblock print (*nishiki-e*)
Chūban: 8⅜ in. x 11¼ in., 21.3 cm x 28.6 cm
Signature: 一筆齋文調画 *Ippitsusai Bunchō ga*
Artist's seal: 守氏 *Mori uji*
Published: GC 44
Collector's seal: Edwin and Marjorie Grabhorn (verso)
Provenance: Satō Shōtarō
2005.100.44

Little is known about the life of Bunchō, except that he was a
prolific designer of actor and beauty prints during the late 1760s
and early 1770s. Bunchō's dynamic stage compositions often
feature somewhat stocky male figures, as demonstrated here. On
the left, Nakamura Nakazō I is identifiable by a crest of tridents
centered by the character *naka* (仲). His fellow actor, Ichikawa
Benzō I, wears a robe decorated with *mimasu* (the crest of nested
measuring boxes associated with the Ichikawa line) around the
character *ben* (弁). Nakazō, wearing dramatic stage makeup
and long, trailing hair, is thought to be playing the ghost of
Taira Noritsune, a warrior of the classic battle saga *The Tale of
the Heike*. He appears to have the upper hand over the kneeling Benzō, who plays the young Minamoto warrior Yoshitsune,
known in his youth as Tsunewakamaru. Nakazō's once-purple
jacket has faded to beige. LA

50　一筆齋文調　山下金作の伊藤九郎女房
IPPITSUSAI BUNCHŌ, active 1765–1792
The actor Yamashita Kinsaku II as the wife of Itō Kurō
1765–1771
Woodblock print (*nishiki-e*)
Hosoban: 12½ in. x 5¾ in., 31.7 cm x 14.6 cm
Signature: 一筆齋文調画 *Ippitsusai Bunchō ga*
Artist's seal: 守氏 *Mori uji*
Publisher's mark: 西村 *Nishimura*
Publisher: 西村屋与八 *Nishimuraya Yohachi;* 永寿
　　堂 *Eijudō*
Published: GC 45
Provence: R. E. Lewis
2005.100.45

The *onnagata* Yamashita Kinsaku II here plays a delicate beauty
bundling her child against the snow, in a role tentatively identified as "the wife of Itō Kurō." The winter setting is defined by a
bamboo fence and gate with nandina, a winter berry; snowflakes
speckle the gray background. Her *kosode,* decorated with snow-
covered bamboo, is drawn over one shoulder to reveal an inner
layer patterned with octupi, and the child's robe is adorned
with treasure wheels and arabesques. Bunchō's *onnagata* recall
Harunobu's youthful female figures, while appearing somehow

less delicate. Similarly, his setting is reminiscent of Harunobu's
famous snow scenes, but the fence and gate confine the figure in a
shallow, stagelike space appropriate for a theatrical subject.
　　Born in Osaka, Yamashita Kinsaku alternated between the
Kamigata stages of Osaka and Kyoto and the theaters of Edo.
He appears in several other *hosoban*-size prints by Bunchō made
around 1769–1771. Small holes along the right edge of this print
indicate that it was once bound into an album. LA

51　一筆齋文調　二代目市川雷蔵の石橋
IPPITSUSAI BUNCHŌ, active 1765–1792
The actor Ichikawa Raizō II performing the Shakkyō Lion Dance
Woodblock print (*nishiki-e*)
Hosoban: 11⅝ in. x 5⅜ in., 29.5 cm x 13.7 cm
Signature: 一筆齋文調画 *Ippitsusai Bunchō ga*
Artist's seal: 守氏 *Mori uji*
Selected other impressions: ROM (926.18.239)
Published: GC 46
Provenance: Judson D. Metzgar
2005.100.46

Ichikawa Raizō II raises a carved lion's head mask on a stage set
with hanging metal lanterns of the type found at Buddhist temples.
The mask was used as part of a "lion dance" known as *Shakkyō*
("Stone Bridge"), derived from the Noh play by that name. In the
play, based on an ancient Buddhist legend, a monk on a pilgrimage
encounters a boy woodcutter. Later the youth appears to the monk
as a lion (or two lions), performing a dance among peonies. Kabuki versions, popular in the eighteenth century, reenact the "lion
dance" through the use of masks and peonies, the lion's favorite
flower — shown here decorating the actor's outer robe.
　　Born in 1754, Raizō II would have been in his late teens at the
time this print was made. This sheet of the "lion dance" probably
once formed the left half of a diptych, where it was likely paired
with an image of an actor dancing in a female role from the same
performance. LA

52　一筆齋文調　『三十六花撰』　「ゑちぜんやもろこし」
IPPITSUSAI BUNCHŌ, active 1765–1792
"Morokoshi of the Echizenya" (*Echizenya Morokoshi*)
From *The Thirty-six Poetic Immortals as Selected Flowers*
　　(*Sanjūrokkasen*)
Woodblock print (*nishiki-e*)
Chūban: 10¼ in. x 7½ in., 26 cm x 19 cm
Signature: 一筆齋文調画 *Ippitsusai Bunchō ga*
Artist's seal: 守氏 *Mori uji*
Published: US 198; GC 47
Collector's seal: Hayashi Tadamasa; Edwin and Marjorie Grab-
　　horn (verso)
Provenance: Harry Packard
2005.100.47

This print is from a series that references *waka,* or classical poetry, by
members of the "Thirty-six Poetic Immortals" (*Sanjūrokkasen*) to

comment on the emotional and quotidian life of the Yoshiwara prostitute. The poem written in the cloud-shaped panel at the top is from the "Love" section of the imperial anthology *Shūi wakashū*. Attributed to the courtier Fujiwara Asatada (910–966), it describes the disillusionment of a lover who foresees the inevitable ending of an affair:

Afu koto mo
taete shi naku wa
nakanaka ni
hito wo mo mi wo mo
uramizaramashi

Though for rendezvous
Every hope were to vanish
Oh, banish despair—
For she and I would thus be spared
The rancor sure to come [18]

Bunchō's design playfully comments on the poem by showing a man leading Morokoshi, a courtesan attached to the Echizenya brothel, away from a teahouse or restaurant. The late hour is indicated by the presence of a large paper lantern decorated with a crane and cherry blossom logo. An illicit air pervades the scene: she wears bedclothes, secured only with a soft sash, and glances back inside as they steal away; a cloth half-concealing his features, the man reaches inside her sleeve to guide her; the young person at his side looks back along the street, as if checking for observers. Although Bunchō is best known for his actor prints, this image shows his aptitude for the type of intimate scenes associated with life inside the pleasure quarters. LA

53　勝川春章　三代目瀬川菊之丞の傾城たかむらと二代
　　目市川八百蔵の四位の少将
KATSUKAWA SHUNSHŌ, 1726–1792
The actors Segawa Kikunojō III as the courtesan Takamura and
　　Ichikawa Yaozō II as Shii no Shōshō
1776.11
Woodblock print (*nishiki-e*)
Chūban: 12⅜ in. x 8¾ in., 30.5 cm x 22.2 cm
Signature: 勝春章画　*Katsu Shunshō ga*
Published: US 50 (B/W); GC 48
2005.100.48

Ichikawa Yaozō II plays Shii no Shōshō opposite Segawa Kikunojō III as the courtesan Takamura in this scene from the play *Sugata no hana yuki no Kuronushi*. Performed at the Ichimura Theater in the eleventh month of 1776, the play was loosely based on one of seven famous episodes from the life of legendary poet and beauty Ono Komachi. Earlier Noh adaptations of the episode, known as *Kayoi Komachi*, describe a monk's encounter with the ghosts of Komachi and a suitor, Captain Fukakusa (also known as Shii Shōshō), who

purportedly died after spending a hundred nights trying to win her affection. Using the double identities common in Kabuki, the 1776 performance turned the tale into a love triangle between a courtesan named Takamura (in reality Komachi), Shii Shōshō (Captain Fukakusa), and an umbrella vendor named Rokurobei (in reality Ōtomo Kuronushi, also a classical poet), played by Ichimura Uzaemon IX. LA

54　勝川春章　四代目市川団蔵の暫
KATSUKAWA SHUNSHŌ, 1726–1792
The actor Ichikawa Danzō IV in a Shibaraku role
Woodblock print (*nishiki-e*)
Hosoban: 12⅝ in. x 6 in., 32.1 cm x 15.2 cm
Signature: 勝春章画　*Katsu Shunshō ga*
Published: Ukiyo-e 18; GC 49
Provenance: R. E. Lewis
2005.100.49

Ichikawa Danzō IV appears here in the *shibaraku* role, among the most flamboyant and popular of Kabuki's set pieces. It shows off to best effect the "rough style" (*aragoto*) acting that was the specialty of the line of actors bearing the Ichikawa name. During his career Shunshō created several *shibaraku* prints, varying the arrangement of the distinctive deep red costume associated with the role and emphasizing the actor's stage makeup and contorted face. Here Danzō's eyes are crossed in a moment of high dramatic intensity; his mouth curved eloquently downward, his lips open in a terrifying grimace. Head sunk between the stiff upraised shoulders of his costume, Danzō sweeps his broad, geometric sleeves to the front of his body, displaying the dramatic *mimasu* crest of nested measuring boxes. A folding fan at his chest provides a visual counterweight to the upright curve of the sword at his back.

As in no. 50, binding holes at the right edge of this print indicate that it was once mounted in an album. LA

55　勝川春章　三代目沢村宗十郎の髪結い次郎吉
KATSUKAWA SHUNSHŌ, 1726–1792
The actor Sawamura Sōjūrō III as the hairdresser Jirōkichi
1781.8
Woodblock print (*nishiki-e*)
Hosoban: 12¾ in. x 5¾ in., 32.4 cm x 14.6 cm
Signature: 春章画　*Shunshō ga*
Selected other impressions: BMFA (11.18835); CHI (1939.772)
Published: GC 50
2005.100.50

Sawamura Sōjūrō III was a renowned *tachiyaku*, or specialist in male roles. A fixture of the stage for some thirty years, from 1771 until 1801, Sōjūrō excelled at portraying gentle romantic leads (*wagotoshi*), warriors (*budōgoto*), and men of good character (*jitsugotoshi*). In this sheet, the left side of a diptych, Sōjūrō plays a character of the first type, a young hairdresser named Jirokichi. The play is *Shinoda chōjabashira*, performed at the Nakamura Theater in the eighth month of 1781. Shunshō's complete diptych paired Sōjūrō with the

---

18　Trans. Cranston, vol 2, pt. 1, 337.

onnagata Iwai Hanshirō IV in the role of Mitsuōgiya Usugumo. An impression of the diptych's right half is preserved in the Buckingham Collection of The Art Institute of Chicago (1925.2459).

The Grabhorn print is exceptionally well preserved. Sōjūrō wears a simple black robe secured with a wide, striped sash, and feminine pink liners show at his hem and sleeve openings. The case over his shoulder presumably contains the tools of his trade, covered by a cloth printed in dayflower blue pigment. LA

56　勝川春章　三代目瀬川菊之丞の鷺娘
KATSUKAWA SHUNSHŌ, 1726–1792
The actor Segawa Kikunojō III as the Heron Maiden (*Sagi Musume*)
Woodblock print (*nishiki-e*)
Hosoban: 5⅞ in. x 13 in., 14.9 cm x 33 cm
Signature: 春章画　*Shunshō ga*
Published: Ukiyo-e 19; GC 51
Provenance: R. E. Lewis
2005.100.51

Bundled against the cold, the Heron Maiden (*Sagi Musume*) stands beside a pond amid falling snow. Her role requires great skill, for the dance transforms the actor from heron to young maiden and back again, expressing emotions ranging from radiant love to utter despair. First staged in 1762, the Heron Maiden soon became a specialty of the female impersonator Segawa Kikunojō II. His bundled silk roving crest appears on the *furisode* in this print, but the girl's hairstyle with its winglike side locks was one favored by that actor's successor, Kikunojō III, after he assumed the name in 1774. One of the most celebrated *onnagata* in Kabuki history, Kikunojō III appears in three prints by Shunshō from the Grabhorn Collection (nos. 53, 56, 57). According to Edwin Grabhorn's notes in *Ukiyo-e: The Floating World,* this print and Shunsō's portrait of Ichikawa Danzō IV (no. 54) came from the same album, assembled in Edo in 1860. LA

57　勝川春章　鏡を見る三代目瀬川菊之丞
KATSUKAWA SHUNSHŌ, 1726–1792
The Actor Segawa Kikunojō III in a female role, looking in a mirror
Woodblock print (*nishiki-e*)
Hosoban: 13 in. x 5⅞ in., 33 cm x 14.9 cm
Signature: 春章画　*Shunshō ga*
Published: GC 52
Provenance: R. E. Lewis
2005.100.52

This print features Segawa Kikunojō III, one of the most celebrated *onnagata* actors of the Edo period. Here his female character strikes an elegant pose, gazing down at a hand mirror on a lacquered dressing case, with her folded arms displaying to advantage the dramatic pattern of "eightfold" plank bridges (*yatsuhashi*) and irises on the long sleeves of her *furisode*. In gestures familiar from other *onnagata* portraits by Shunsō, her head is twisted to one side to reveal the nape of her neck, and one delicate, feminine hand rests on her outstretched arm. The colors are unusually well preserved, with lush

purple and pink, touches of blue in the crest and hems, and oxidized orange in the bridge planks and mirror stand. Like the previous example, this print is signed in the distinctive manner Shunshō used around 1772–1774. The first character, *shun*, has an extended right-hand stroke, and the third character, read *ga* (painted by), has the appearance of one square within another.[19] LA

58　勝川春章　「東方　うずがふち　小野川」
KATSUKAWA SHUNSHŌ, 1726–1792
[Sumo Wrestlers of the] Eastern Section, Uzugafuchi and Onogawa (*Higashikata Uzugafuchi Onogawa*)
1783-1784
Woodblock print (*nishiki-e*)
Ōban: 14½ in. x 9¾ in., 36.9 cm x 24.8 cm
Signature: 春章画　*Shunshō ga*
Publisher: 松村弥兵衛　Matsumura Yahei
Published: GC 53
2005.100.53

Katsukawa Shunshō was the first print artist to undertake the serious depiction of sumo wrestlers. This print is one of a set showing wrestlers from the Eastern and Western Sections, published between 1783 and 1784. Onogawa of Osaka, shown on the left, was one of the leading wrestlers of his day. Shunshō depicts him as a towering figure with white skin, a square, flat face and a focused, determined expression. He stands in contrast to the ruddy figure of Uzugafuchi, whose large angular face is shaded by a five-o'clock shadow. Both men wear colorful aprons over their bare bodies: Onogawa's bears a linked-circles pattern known as "linked pleasure quarters" (*kuruwa tsunagi*), and Uzugafuchi has dragons and flaming jewels amid clouds on his apron. The background, now faded to brown, was originally colored blue with fleeting dayflower pigment. MR

59　勝川春英　三代目坂東彦三郎の大星由良之助
KATSUKAWA SHUN'EI, 1762–1819
The actor Bandō Hikosaburō III as Ōboshi Yuranosuke
Woodblock print (*nishiki-e*)
1795.4
Ōban: 15 in. x 10 in., 38.1 cm x 25.4 cm
Signature: 春英画　*Shun'ei ga*
Publisher's mark: 岩　*Iwa*
Publisher: 岩戸屋喜三郎　*Iwatoya Kisaburō*
Selected other impressions: BMFA (11.22301; 21.7325); Vever, cited in Hillier 1976, no. 315
Published: FP 45; GC 54
2005.100.54

This standing portrait features the actor Bandō Hikosaburō III in his best-known role, Ōboshi Yuranosuke. The scene has been identified as belonging to a performance of *Kanadehon Chūshingura* at the Miyako Theater in the fourth month of 1795. Viewers of the time would have been able to recognize this as a moment from the

---

19　Clark 1994, 203.

seventh act, set at the Ichiriki teahouse. Clues include the actor's fashionable hairstyle, known as *honda mage*—shaved far back at the top and sides, with only a narrow topknot projecting forward—and his costume, which consists of a long jacket (*haori*) worn with two swords, one tucked into his sash, the other held in one hand.[20]

This is the right-hand sheet of a triptych, a complete example of which is preserved in the Museum of Fine Arts, Boston collection (21.7314–21.7316). LA

60　勝川春英　二代目中村仲蔵の荒巻耳四郎と二代目中村野塩の貫之息女此花

KATSUKAWA SHUN'EI, 1762–1819

The actors Nakamura Nakazō II as Aramaki Mimishirō and Nakamura Noshio II as Konohana, daughter of Ki Tsurayuki

1794.11

Woodblock print (*nishiki-e*)

Aiban: 12¾ in. x 9¼ in., 32.4 cm x 23.5 cm

Signature: 春英画 *Shun'ei ga*

Publisher's mark: 麻布 *Azabu*

Published: US 206; GC 55

Collector's seal: Irma Grabhorn

2005.100.55

This print is an example of the *ōkubi-e* ("large head") style of actor portrait, which originated with artists of the Katsukawa school in the late 1780s (see no. 61, by Shunkō). This double portrait depicts a moment in the "Ōshukubai koi no hatsune" scene of the Kabuki play *Uruōtoshi meika no homare*, which was performed in the eleventh month of 1794 at the Miyako Theater in Edo. The performance, which dealt with historical power struggles preceding the enthronement of Emperor Seiwa (850–880), was the subject of a number of prints by Tōshūsai Sharaku and other artists. The actor Nakamura Nakazō II wore a plain cloth cap for the role of Aramaki Mimishirō Kanetora disguised as Saizō Saiwaka. The *onnagata* actor Nakamura Noshio plays the role of Konohana, the daughter of the poet Ki Tsurayuki. This print, the only known surviving impression, retains outstanding color, including purples, pinks, and the delicate dayflower blue background. MR

61　勝川春好　三代目市川高麗蔵の足軽三平

KATSUKAWA SHUNKŌ, 1743–1812

The actor Ichikawa Komazō III as Ashigaru Sanpei

Woodblock print (*nishiki-e*)

Ōban: 14⅝ in. x 10 in., 37.1 cm x 25.4 cm

Signature: 春好画 *Shunkō ga*

Published: US 207; GC 56

2005.100.56

This print is thought to depict the actor Ichikawa Komazō III as he appeared during the Kabuki play *Komachi mura shibai no shōgatsu*, performed in the eleventh month of 1789 at the Nakamura Theater in Edo. Komazō's distinctive prominent nose would identify him

to fans, who would also recognize the crest of nested boxes (*mimasu*) surrounding the character *taka* (高, high) on the shoulder of his robe. Wearing gauntlets, Komazō looks diagonally up to his right, capturing the essence of a dramatic moment in the play.

Katsukawa Shunkō, a founder of the Katsukawa school, was well known for developing the "large head" (*ōkubi-e*) format of actor portraits. All of his prints in this format are thought to date to a single thirteen-month period, spanning the eleventh month of 1788 through the eleventh month of 1789.[21] This is one of two depicting Komazō III. A rare surviving impression, it retains outstanding color, though the fleeting dayflower blue background is faded around the edges where it was likely pasted into an album. MR

62　勝川春好　『横綱ノ圖』　谷風

KATSUKAWA SHUNKŌ, 1743–1812

The Sumo Wrestler Tanikaze

From *Yokozuna* (Yokozuna zu)

Early 1790s

Woodblock print (*nishiki-e*)

Ōban: 14½ in. x 10⅛ in., 36.8 cm x 25.7 cm

Signature: 春好画 *Shunkō ga*

Publisher's mark: 豊 *Toyo*

Publisher and firm name: 豊島屋文治右衛門 *Toyoshimaya Bunjiemon*; 文錦堂 *Bunkindō*

Selected other impressions: BRU, cited in Nagata 2008, no. 73

Published: GC 57

2005.100.57

This print by Katsukawa Shunkō—a disciple of Shunshō, the originator of the sumo wrestler print genre—depicts the legendary *yokozuna* Tanikaze Kajinosuke entering the ring. *Yokozuna* is the elusive highest rank in the sumo world, and Tanikaze was only the fourth wrestler in history to be awarded the title. He maintained an unparalleled winning streak until he was beaten by Onogawa of Osaka (depicted in no. 58) in the second month of 1782. Tanikaze and Onogawa were granted the *yokozuna* license on the same day in 1789, and originally this portrait of Tanikaze was paired with a print of Onogawa in his regalia as part of a larger set commemorating past champions.[22] Here, Tanikaze is depicted as a corpulent, muscular figure whose eyes disappear into the puffy flesh of his cheeks. He wears a red-fringed apron emblazoned with the first character of his name, *tani* (谷, valley). The twisted rope (*shimenawa*) around his waist is the symbol of a *yokozuna* (literally, "horizontal rope"). His attendant carries a sword, which is used in a special ring-entering ceremony to denote the *yokozuna*'s elevated status. LA

63　勝川春好　「東前頭　鶴ヶ滝　行司木村庄之助　西前頭秀ノ山改　伊達ヶ関」

KATSUKAWA SHUNKŌ, 1743–1812

"The Sumo Wrestler Tsurugataki, Maegashira of the Eastern Section, the Referee Kimura Shōnosuke, and the Sumo Wrestler Hide-

---

20　*Shindorā Korekushon* 1985, no. 42.

21　Clark 1994, 340, 342.
22　Nagata 2008, no. 73.

noyama, Renamed Dategaseki, Maegashira of the Western Section" (*Higashi Maegashira Tsurugataki Gyōji Kimura Shōnosuke Nishi Maegashira Hidenoyama aratame Dategaseki*)
Early 1790s
Woodblock print (*nishiki-e*)
Ōban: 14½ in. x 10¼ in., 36.8 cm x 26 cm
Signature: 春好画 *Shunkō ga*
Publisher's mark: 豊 *Toyo*
Publisher and firm name: 豊島屋文治右衛門 *Toyoshimaya Bunjiemon*; 文錦堂 *Bunkindō*
Selected other impressions: BRU, cited in Nagata 2008, no. 72
Published: GC 58
Provenance: O. P. Reed, Jr.
2005.100.58

Eighteenth-century sumo wrestlers (*rikishi*) were identified according to various categories. Associated with either the Eastern or the Western Side, their rank would change depending on their wins and losses in two annual tournaments. At the top of the hierarchy were the three upper-class (*jōi*) ranks of *ōzeki, sekiwake,* and *komusubi,* followed by *maegashira,* the highest of the upper-level (*jōdan*) ranks. The two wrestlers in this commemorative print are identified as *maegashira*. Standing to the left is Dategaseki—formerly known as Hidenoyama—of the Western side, with Tsurugataki of the Eastern side squatting next to him. The wrestlers are supervised by the referee (*tachi gyōji*) Kimura Shōnosuke, who wields a lowered fan (*gunbai*). Records of the time indicate that Tsurugataki held the rank of *maegashira* in 1786 and 1788, but that by the time Dategashira achieved the title in 1791 Tsurugataki's standing had declined. LA

64　歌川豊春　琴棋書画　「琴」
UTAGAWA TOYOHARU, 1735–1814
"Music" (*Kin*)
From an untitled series of the Four Accomplishments (*Kinkishoga*)
Woodblock print (*nishiki-e*)
Ōbaiban: 19 in. x 14¼ in., 48.3 cm x 36.2 cm
Signature: 哥川豊春画 *Utagawa Toyoharu ga*
Artist's seal: 豊春 *Toyoharu*
Publisher's mark: 鱗形屋孫兵衛 *Urokogataya Magobei*
Publisher firm name: 鶴鱗堂 *Kakurindō*
Selected other impressions: BMFA (11.21213)
Published: US 208; GC 59
Ex-collection: Tod and Freeman Ford
2005.100.59

Three girls in an elegantly appointed room play music in a *shakyo* ensemble. The *kokyū*, on the left, is a stringed instrument played with a bow; it joins two more familiar instruments, the *shamisen* and *koto*. At the top right the character *kin* (also read *koto*) identifies the scene as "Music" from a set of the Four Accomplishments (*kinkishoga*), a theme, common in earlier paintings, that alludes to the Chinese gentlemanly pursuits of music, strategy games, calligraphy, and painting. Here Toyoharu follows a tradition of Edo period artists who reenvisioned the theme by substituting beauties in modern costume for Chinese scholars.

References to contemporary fashion include chic wardrobe items like the *kokyū* player's striped, *ikat*-dyed obi.

This elegant design was printed on thick paper in the largest size used for ukiyo-e prints. Special permission would have been required to bypass government restrictions on paper size, indicating that this was a private commission. We cannot be sure that it is the case here, but luxury prints of this type have been found mounted in albums made for daimyo or other high-ranking samurai collectors. Of this rare set the Grabhorn Collection has a second print, "Painting" (no. 65); the Tokyo National Museum has "Painting" and "Calligraphy"; and the Museum of Fine Arts, Boston has a full set plus two other impressions of "Strategy Games." LA

65　歌川豊春　琴棋書画　「画」
UTAGAWA TOYOHARU, 1735–1814
"Painting" (*Ga*)
From an untitled series of the Four Accomplishments (*Kinkishōga*)
1772–1775
Woodblock print (*nishiki-e*)
Ōbaiban: 18¼ in. x 13⅞ in., 46.4 cm x 35.2 cm
Signature: 哥川豊春画 *Utagawa Toyoharu ga*
Artist's seal: 豊春 *Toyoharu*
Publisher's mark: 鱗形屋孫兵衛 *Urokogataya Magobei*
Publisher firm name: 鶴鱗堂 *Kakurindō*
Selected other impressions: BMFA (11.21215); TNM (A-10569_830)
Published: US 48 (B/W); GC 60
2005.100.60

Two girls inspect a painting of an *onnagata* actor in this second print from the Four Accomplishments (*kinkishoga*) series by Toyoharu (see no. 64). On the floor are arranged brushes, a set of mineral pigments, and scrolls of paper; a set of smoking utensils rests on the floor behind them. A third girl holds up the painting in which the actor Segawa Kikunojō is identifiable by the bundled roving crest on one sleeve. Bush clover (*hagi*) blossoming in the garden beside a stone basin indicates that it is autumn, when the major Kabuki theaters staged their opening performances of the season.

Founder of the Utagawa school, Toyoharu studied in the workshop of a professional Kano-school painter. This training may have contributed to his confident use of classical themes like the Four Accomplishments. Although Toyoharu is best known for architectural and landscape prints featuring Western perspective, the elegant figures and interior settings in this print recall the work of Suzuki Harunobu, who died in 1770, a few years prior to the production of this series. LA

66　北尾重政　紅梅下の馬
KITAO SHIGEMASA, 1739–1820
Horses beneath a flowering plum tree
C. 1770s
Woodblock print (*nishiki-e*)
Chūban: 8½ in. x 11 in., 21.6 cm x 27.9 cm
Signature: 北尾重政画 *Kitao Shigemasa ga*

Published: FP 29; US 160; GC 61
Collector's seal: Edwin and Marjorie Grabhorn (verso)
Provenance: Matsuki Kihachirō
2005.100.61

A black, a white, and a spotted horse stand at the edge of a stream, beneath a flowering plum tree. In pointed contrast to the detailed drawing of the tree, the horses are printed in reserve, without outlines. Internal definition is achieved by means of *karazuri*, sometimes known as "blind-printing" or "gauffrage." In this technique, blank areas of the design are pressed on the carved block to create low relief embossed patterns without the use of color. The mane and tail of the white horse have the most *karazuri*, but there are embossed details on all three animals.

Shigemasa was founder of the Kitao school, whose members included Kubo Shunman (nos. 99, 100) and Kitao Masanobu, also known as Santō Kyōden (no. 68). Over the course of his career, Shigemasa designed more than 250 illustrated books in addition to many single sheet prints. This deluxe, experimental print was probably created at the bequest of a private patron, or possibly members of a poetry circle. Stylistically, the print belongs to the 1770s, so if it was made as a calendar print (*egoyomi*) for a "horse" year it could be dated to 1774. LA

---

67   北尾重政　『東西南北之美人』　「東方の美人　仲町
　　　於仲　おしま」
KITAO SHIGEMASA, 1739–1820
Beauties of the Eastern Quarter: Onaka and Oshima of the Nakamachi (*Tōhō no bijin: Nakamachi Onaka, Oshima*)
From *Beauties of the East, West, South, and North* (*Tōzai nanboku no bijin*)
C. 1775–1777
Woodblock print (*nishiki-e*)
Ōban: 15½ in. x 10 ¼ in., 39.4 cm x 26 cm
Selected other impressions: BMFA (11.14978; 21.5858); MIA (P.75.51.653); HMA (21758); TNM (A-10569_180); MET (JP194); BM (1924,0327,0.7)
Published: GC 62
Ex-collection: Charles Morse
2005.100.62

This print comes from a set of four representing beauties from the four directions—referring to four different prostitution districts in Edo. Nakachō was an area in the Fukugawa, the unlicenced pleasure quarters in the eastern part of Edo, where female musical performers known as *tatsumi geisha* were renowned for their cool attitudes and fashionable chic.

There are many impressions of this print; the Grabhorn version identifies the two women by name as Onaka (right) and Oshima (left). Both wear luxurious, cutting-edge fashions. Their *kosode* robes are decorated—with orchids or bamboo—only around the hems and lower front edges as was newly in vogue in the second half of the eighteenth century. Their hair is done in the popular *marumage* style—relatively flat in front with stiff, broad sidelocks and a large puffed topknot behind. Oshima's obi appears to be of a type of chintz (*sarasa*) made on India's Coromandel Coast for the Indonesian market and

imported into Japan during the eighteenth century on Dutch ships.[23] Onaka's obi is imprinted in gold at one end. Their black collars—Oshima's of luxurious and fashionable velvet—and their bare feet suggest the women are geisha. (Proud *tatsumi geisha* were known to wear bare feet year round.) Their skewed hair combs and prominently displayed folded tissue paper give a hint of eroticism.

Other prints in the series show beauties from the western quarter of Sakaichō, the southern quarter of Shinagawa, and the northern quarter of Yoshiwara. MR

---

68   北尾政演　初郭公
KITAO MASANOBU, 1761–1816
Listening to the first cuckoo on a late spring outing
Woodblock print (*nishiki-e*)
Ōbaiban: 15 in. x 21 in., 38.1 cm x 53.3 cm
Signature: 政演画　*Masanobu ga*
Selected other impressions: BMFA (21.5709); Vever, cited in Hillier 1976, no. 503
Published: Ukiyo-e 12; GC 63
2005.100.63

The *hototogisu*, or cuckoo, was traditionally considered a harbinger of summer. At the start of the fifth month, as the weather warmed up, fashionable Edoites would venture to locations attractive to the bird: Hakusan in Koishikawa, Negishi, Surugadai, Nezu, and the Sumida River. Here a group is gathered at the edge of a pond where irises and a budding willow mark the season. A girl in an elegant *furisode* and brocade obi lowers her parasol as she catches sight of a *hototogisu*, while on a bench nearby, an attractive couple in stylish attire relaxes, chatting and smoking, seemingly uninterested in bird watching. Ignored by all, a boy dances about in excitement, having spotted a large frog or toad on the landing.

Kitao Masanobu was the sobriquet of a printmaker and illustrator who trained under Kitao Shigemasa (see no. 67). Later in his career he assumed the pen name Santō Kyōden, writing the light fiction that made him a taste-maker among fashionable habitués of the Edo pleasure quarters. This large *ōbaiban*, or double *ōban* print, exists in only two other copies; one in the Museum of Fine Arts, Boston the other formerly in the Vever collection (present whereabouts unknown). Popular in the 1780s, the *ōbaiban* size was also the format used by Masanobu for a sumptuous album, *New Beauties of the Yoshiwara in the Mirror of Their Own Script* (*Yoshiwara keisei shin bijin awase jihitsu kagami*). LA

---

69   鳥居清長　『風俗東之錦』　娘と侍女二人
TORII KIYONAGA, 1752–1815
Woman on an outing with two female attendants
From *Current Manners in Eastern Brocade* (*Fūzoku azuma no nishiki*)
1783
Woodblock print (*nishiki-e*)

---

23   See Ishida Chihiro, "Edo jidai no sarasa yunyū: Oranda sen no hakusaihin o chūshin toshite" in *Nezu Bijutsukan* (1993).

Ōban: 15½ in. x 10½ in., 39.4 cm x 26.7 cm
Signature: 清長画 *Kiyonaga ga*
Selected other impressions: BMFA (11.13946; 21.5489); MET
    (JP1719); HU (1933.4.2829); LEI (1353–1808); Van Vleck
    (1980.2522)
Published: GC 64
Collector's seal: Edwin and Marjorie Grabhorn (verso)
Provenance: Matsuki Kihachirō
2005.100.64

Kiyonaga was an especially acute observer of fashion in the city of
Edo. This print comes from his celebrated series *Current Manners
in Eastern Brocade*, of which twenty surviving designs are known.
The term "eastern brocade" (*azuma no nishiki*) refers to the full-
color prints of Edo — suggesting that they are as sumptuous and
colorful as the luxurious woven textiles made in Western Japan,
particularly Kyoto. The prints' subject matter also elevates the
series above the common themes of ukiyo-e by portraying respect-
able women of various classes with their female and sometimes
male attendants, rather than denizens of the pleasure quarters.

This print shows an unmarried woman of the samurai class
dressed in a woven bamboo sun hat (*sugegasa*), an underrobe of
red and white cherry blossoms and a sheer ramie or silk gauze
furisode patterned around the hem with a paste-resist-dyed white
decoration. Now brown, the robe was likely originally blue or
purple. Her two attendants, similarly dressed in unlined *kosode*,
carry a parasol to protect their skin from the sun. All three wear
soft sashes (*shigoki obi*) below their main obi to hike up the excess
length while they are outside. Kiyonaga depicts the fine summer garments with exquisite ripples of fabric, draping over the
women's bare feet. MR

70　鳥居清長　『当世遊里美人合』「橘中妓」
TORII KIYONAGA, 1752–1815
"Geisha from Tachibana-chō" (*Kitchūgi*)
From *Contest of Modern Beauties of the Pleasure Quarters* (Tōsei
    yūri bijin awase)
Woodblock print (*nishiki-e*)
1782
Ōban: 10⅛ in. x 15¼ in., 25.7 cm x 38.7 cm
Signature: 清長画 *Kiyonaga ga*
Selected other impressions: BM (1930,0510,0.5); MIA (81.133.190)
Published: FP 31; UM 200; GC 65
Collector's seal: Edwin and Marjorie Grabhorn (verso)
2005.100.65

This print comes from a series of twenty-one designs, five of which
are diptychs, portraying amusements of the various pleasure quarters in Edo. The title, *Kitchūgi* (literally, "geisha from the Tachibana [district]") refers to an area west of the Ryōgoku Bridge along
the Hamamachi Canal, where many prostitutes lived while waiting
to be called to the pleasure quarters in Ryōgoku. The word *kitchūgi*
also shares pronunciation with the phrase "playing chess inside a
mandarin orange." According to Chie Hirano, this play on words
alludes to the Chinese legend of a man who finds an enormous
mandarin in his orchard with two old men playing chess inside the

narrow space.[24] The men say that they are having as much fun as if
they were on Mt. Shang, where the four sages lived in retirement.
Because the geographic name "Tachibana" means "mandarin," the
title plays on the idea that this district is a "narrow place in which
you can enjoy yourself." The two women in the front run into the
wind, followed by their maid carrying an umbrella. Their attempt
to preserve their appearance in the heavy wind is only partially successful, as their robes fly open exposing red and white underrobes
that ripple tantalizingly around their bare legs. Equally impressive
is the show of textiles: a *kosode* with pattern known as *sayagata* and
a paste-resist-dyed *furisode* with paulownia motifs around the hem,
lower front flaps, and sleeves, worn with an exotic obi of imported
Indian chintz (*sarasa*). MR

71　鳥居清長　『当世遊里美人合』「南駅景」
TORII KIYONAGA, 1752–1815
"Courtesans of the South Station" (*Nan'eki no kei*)
From *Contest of Modern Beauties of the Pleasure Quarters* (Tōsei
    yūri bijin awase)
1783
Woodblock print (*nishiki-e*)
Ōban: 10¼ in. x 15¼ in., 26 cm x 38.7 cm
Signature: 清長画 *Kiyonaga ga*
Selected other impressions: BMFA (06.1268; 21.5641)
Published: GC 66
Collector's seal: Hayashi Tadamasa
2005.100.66

This is one of a series of twenty-one known prints depicting beautiful
courtesans from the various pleasure quarters in Edo. Nan'eki (literally "southern station") is one name for the Shinagawa district, where
the two courtesans and young attendant shown here presumably live.
In the series, Kiyonaga presents the distinctive styles and customs
associated with each district. This print shows the women wearing
costumes boldly patterned with various auspicious images—gaudier
and less elegant, perhaps, than those of their loftier counterparts in
the Yoshiwara. The woman holding a pipe wears a cherry blossom-
patterned *kosode* under a shell-patterned obi. The other wears a
white *kosode* figured with red floral roundels and tied with a chic
green velvet obi; her *uchikake* is dramatically decorated with sails
and pines. The kneeling attendant wears a *furisode* with cranes and
sandbanks and a black obi with floral cloud motif. She uses a cloth
to hold a telescope, its preciousness further indicated by the high-
quality lacquered box from which it has been removed. MR

72　鳥居清長　『当世遊里美人合』　花下酔美人
TORII KIYONAGA, 1752–1815
A drunken beauty beneath cherry blossoms
From *Contest of Modern Beauties of the Pleasure Quarters* (Tōsei
    yūri bijin awase)
1783
Woodblock print (*nishiki-e*)

24　Hirano, 263.

Ōban diptych: 15¼ in. x 10¼ in., 38.7 cm x 26 cm (each)
Signature: 清長画 *Kiyonaga ga*
Selected other impressions: BMFA (11.13969-70; 21.7425-6)
Published: GC67
Collector's seal: Edwin and Marjorie Grabhorn (right only, verso)
2005.100.67.1-.2

An excursion to view cherry blossoms forms the subject of this charming diptych, from the series *Contest of Modern Beauties of the Pleasure Quarters* (see nos. 70, 71). The scene pits a genteel middle-class beauty with two companions, against an inebriated courtesan whose unfettered antics are being kept under check by an entourage of three. Kiyonaga's beauties are uniformly tall, slender, and stylish, lined up in a row as if posing for a fashion spread in *Vogue*. Since they are out walking, each woman has a soft sash, known as a *shigeki* obi, tied around her hips to prevent her hem from trailing on the ground. Otherwise the costumes of the two main figures announce their differences in station. The demure girl on the right sports a pale yellow obi with a delicate arabesque pattern, and shells and sea plants decorate the long, trailing sleeves and skirt of her youthful violet (now brown) *furisode*. By contrast, the courtesan's dramatic black *kosode* flaps open to reveal the bare white flesh of her chest and legs. Loosely tied at the front of her body, her strumpet's obi bears a bold hexagonal pattern. LA

73　鳥居清長　洗張り
TORII KIYONAGA, 1752–1815
Washday
1788
Woodblock print (*nishiki-e*)
Ōban triptych: 15 in. x 10 in., 38 cm x 25.4 cm (each)
Signature: 清長画 *Kiyonaga ga*
Publisher's mark: 蔦屋重三郎 *Tsutaya Jūzaburō*
Publisher firm name: 耕書堂 *Kōshodō*
Selected other impressions: BMFA (21.7350-52); CHI (1925.2335); Van Vleck (1980.2528ab)
Published: GC 68
Collectors' seals: 受益書庫之印 *Jūeki bunko no in*; Edwin and Marjorie Grabhorn (three sheets, verso)
Provenance: Judson D. Metzgar
2005.100.68.1-.3

In a wide, three-sheet composition, Kiyonaga depicts beauties of the pleasure quarters in their off-duty hours. At the right four courtesans relax and attend to their toilettes as their clothes are washed outside. It is a warm summer day, judging from the morning glories growing on a lattice nearby. Stretched out to dry between two trees is a long bolt of cloth. The cloth is a silk kimono that has been prepared for washing by being taken apart at the seams and basted together into its original textile format. It was then kneaded by hand in water, sometimes using the starchy washwater of rice or the skin of the soapberry fruit (*Sapindus mukurossi*, or *mukurōji*) as detergent. We see this step at the left: a maid, her sleeves tied up with a cord, draws water from a well and pours it into a washbasin. Another maid sits on a tiny stool washing in the adjacent basin, a white towel covering her hair. In the garden

proper two women attend to the stretched bolt of silk, which has a dappled tie-dyed pattern. The woman on the left holds up a bamboo stretcher (*shinshibari*) as a second beauty reaches across to fasten the pin of her stretcher into the fabric's selvedge. MR

74, 75　鳥居清長　三囲神社向島春遊
TORII KIYONAGA, 1752–1815
A spring excursion to Mimeguri Shrine at Mukōjima
C. 1787
Woodblock print (*nishiki-e*)
Ōban triptych: 15⅜ in. x 10 in., 39.1 cm x 25.4 cm (each)
Signature: 清長画 *Kiyonaga ga*
Publisher's mark: 高津版 *Kōzu han*
Publisher and firm name: 高津屋伊助 *Kōzuya Isuke*; 慶雲堂 *Keiundō*
Selected other impressions: BMFA (left: 06.1044; left & center: 21.7429-30); V&A (E.392-1895); TNM (center: A-10569-1221)
Published: US 213–215; GC 69
Collector's seal: Hayashi Tadamasa
2005.100.69.1-.3

A parade of elegantly dressed beauties passes along an embankment near the Sumida River in the Mukōjima district of Edo. Nearby fields are yellow with rape blossoms and green with vegetation—possibly rice seedlings—so the season must be late spring or summer. In the distance at the left a path leads down from the riverbank toward the gate of Mimeguri Shrine, and at the far right a few people are gathered in the doorway of a local eatery known for its specialty carp cuisine. The river's opposite shore is lined with a string of famous local sites: from right, Imadō Bridge, spanning the Sanya Canal (entrypoint to the Yoshiwara); the shrine at Matsuchiyama; the pagoda of Sensōji Temple; Azuma Bridge; and the lumberyard beyond it.

Kiyonaga created at least twenty-four triptychs during his career, most between 1786 and 1788, using the format to set his figures within detailed panoramic landscapes. The women in his triptychs model the latest fashions, including the loosely tied obis seen here in several variations.

A second version of the right-hand sheet survives in two impressions, in the Victoria and Albert Museum and Art Institute of Chicago collections. In the variant a maid bends over to collect herbs as her mistress touches her hat brim, and a boy is half hidden behind her. LA

76　鳥居清長　釣り舟の男女
TORII KIYONAGA, 1752–1815
A fishing party
1784
Woodblock print (*nishiki-e*)
Hashira-e: 26⅞ in. x 4¾ in., 68.3 cm x 12.1 cm
Signature: 清長画 *Kiyonaga ga*
Publisher's mark: 永寿板 *Eiju han*
Publisher and firm name: 西村屋与八 *Nishimuraya Yohachi*; 永寿堂 *Eijudō*
Selected other impressions: ROM (926.18.264)

Published: GC 70
Collector's seal: 白爾叟 *Hakujisō* or *Berusō*? (verso)
Ex-collection: Tod and Freeman Ford
2005.100.70

A fishing boat on a bay carries three figures: a slender standing beauty, a youth with fishing pole and head cloth, and a second woman, crouched behind the fisherman with one hand resting on his shoulder. Across the water, the snow-covered peak of Mt. Fuji rises above coastal scenery dotted with autumn leaves. Above this charming scene a verse reads:

> *Tsuri meisho*
> *momiji gasane no*
> *Fuji mo ari*

> Oh, this famous place for fishing!
> Mr. Fuji with its skirt adorned
> with colored maples
> also can be seen from here [25]

Kiyonaga's mastery of the narrow *hashira-e* format is apparent in figures and scenic elements arranged like puzzle pieces: the pyramidal form of the seated pair echoes Mt. Fuji's conical peak, and the lifted obi and erect figure of the beauty repeat the upturned prow and tall mast of the sailboat floating on the bay. Only one other specimen of this print is known, in the Royal Ontario Museum collection. LA

77　喜多川歌麿　『青楼仁和嘉女芸者部』　「獅子　たま屋　おいと」
KITAGAWA UTAMARO, 1754–1806
"Lion Dance: Oito of the Tamaya" (*Shishi Tamaya Oito*)
From *The Female Geisha Section of the Niwaka Festival in the Yoshiwara* (Seirō niwaka onna geisha no bu)
1783
Woodblock print (*nishiki-e*)
Ōban: 15¼ in. x 10¼ in., 38.7 cm x 26 cm
Signature: 哥麿画 *Utamaro ga*
Publisher: 蔦屋重三郎 *Tsutaya Jūzaburō*
Selected other impressions: TNM (A-10569_1803); Vever, cited in Hillier 1976, no. 386; Scheiwe, cited by Asano, no. 80
Published: US 161; GC 71
Collector's seal: unidentified (verso)
2005.100.71

This print is part of a series of at least five that depict female geisha dressed in the dynamic costumes worn for the Niwaka Kyōgen performances held in the Yoshiwara each year during the eighth month. The geisha in this case is identified as Tamaya Oito. Shown in full regalia for her role in a Lion Dance, she wears a fringed apron with a threatening spider web motif and a black robe with couched gold thread over an underrobe with a black cut-velvet

collar and design of a carp swimming upstream. Instead of dancing, she is shown during a moment of leisure casually drinking sake at a teahouse called Minatoya. The peony lantern by her side is inscribed with her name, Ito. Two *kamuro* attendants in elaborate floral headdresses excitedly exclaim over her costume as the teahouse's proprietress—smoking a long pipe—looks on. Scholars have suggested that this series was published by Tsutaya Jūzaburō to commemorate the establishment of his business in Toriaburamachi in 1783. MR

78　喜多川歌麿　『歌撰恋之部』　「稀二逢恋」
KITAGAWA UTAMARO, 1754–1806
"Love That Rarely Meets" (*Mare ni au koi*)
From *Anthology of Poems: The Love Section* (Kasen koi no bu)
C. 1793–1794
Woodblock print (*nishiki-e*)
Ōban: 15 in. x 10¼ in., 38.1 cm x 26 cm
Signature: 哥麿筆 *Utamaro hitsu*
Publisher's mark: ivy-leaf mark of Tsutaya Jūzaburō 蔦屋重三郎 *Tsutaya Jūzaburō*
Publisher firm name: 耕書堂 *Kōshodō*
Selected other impressions: BMFA (11.14324; 34.257); BM (1906.1220,0.331)
Published: FP 34; GC 72
Ex-collection: Tod and Freeman Ford
Provenance: Judson D. Metzgar
2005.100.72

This image comes from a series of five close-up portraits expressing moods of ordinary women in love.[26] Here, on a luxurious apricot mica background, a young girl who has perhaps just discovered love for the first time gazes into the distance. Her white fingers are partially concealed within her kimono sleeve, lifting it coyly to chin level. Her head is charmingly decked out in a Shimada hairstyle with a variety of *kanzashi* pins—including the paired floral ornaments (*ryōten*) fashionable in the late 1700s.

Written with the characters for poem (*ka*) and selection (*sen*), the series title has been translated "Anthology of Poems," but it also puns on the word for "poetic immortal" (*kasen*, written with a different character for *sen*), as well as the phrase "Uta[maro]'s selection" (an alternate reading for *ka* is *uta*). The second part of the title, "Love Section" (*koi no bu*), is followed by a subtitle similar to the kind found in *kyōka* poetry anthologies: "Love That Rarely Meets." The British Museum has an impression in which the girl's *kosode*, here faded to brown, retains its original vibrant purple color. The Museum of Fine Arts, Boston has the only other known copy, as well as a later printing lacking the title. MR

79　喜多川歌麿　『北国五色墨』　「藝妓」
KITAGAWA UTAMARO, 1754–1806
"Geisha" (*Geigi*)

---

25 Trans. Hirano, no. 674.

26 Asano (*Kaisetsu hen*), 130.

From *Five Shades of Ink in the Northern Quarter* (Hokkoku
    goshiki-zumi)
C. 1794–1795
Woodblock print (*nishiki-e*)
Ōban: 10¼ in. x 15⅛ in., 26 cm x 38.4 cm
Signature: 哥麿筆 *Utamaro hitsu*
Publisher's mark: 山可 *Yamaka*
Publisher: 伊勢屋孫兵衛 *Iseya Magobei*
Published: MPJ 118; UM 238; US 162; Ukiyo-e 16; GC 73
Collector's seal: Hayashi Tadamasa
Provenance: Cartier sale, Paris, 1962 (cited in Ukiyo-e, 16)
2005.100.73

This rare print comes from the series *Five Shades of Ink in the
Northern Quarter*, created around 1795 when Utamaro was at
the height of his powers. Each print from the series has a dif-
ferently colored cartouche shaped as an ink stick (in this case,
black), and each compares a shade of ink to one of five occupations for women working in the "north country" or Yoshiwara
(located north of Edo castle). Because the word *sumi*, or ink,
can have the meaning "to reside" when written with another
character, the series title also can be interpreted as "five types of
Yoshiwara residents."

   Geigi, shown here, is the most elevated of the five ranks portrayed. The others are *kashi* (low-class prostitutes who operated
at the rear of the Yoshiwara near the moat), *tetsubo* (literally,
"gun," as they were at risk of being "shot down" by venereal dis-
ease), *setsu no musume* (prostitutes whose services could be purchased at a set rate), and *oiran* (highest-ranking courtesans). *Geigi*, also known as geisha, were trained entertainers—dancers and
musicians who performed for guests in banquet or private party
settings. The subject of the print is young but poised, dressed in
an unpatterned gauze *kosode* with ivy crests and the white collar
worn by geisha. The rich yellow ground and mica used for her
obi and hair ornaments mark this as a luxury production. As she
leans back from her conversational partner, this *geigi* exposes the
nape of her neck and the fanned-out layers of her costume. The
lines at her collar in turn brilliantly lead the eye to her bare fore-
arm and delicate upraised hand gesture—a masterful composition. MR

---

80   喜多川歌麿　髪結
KITAGAWA UTAMARO, 1754–1806
Dressing the hair
C. 1794–1795
Woodblock print (*nishiki-e*)
Ōban: 15 in. x 10 in., 38.1 cm x 25.4 cm
Signature: 哥麿筆 *Utamaro hitsu*
Publisher's mark: 上村 *Uemura*
Publisher: 上村与兵衛 *Uemura Yohei*
Selected other impressions: NYPL (416397); BMFA (21.6379);
    Vever, cited in Hiller 1976, no. 445
Published: Ukiyo-e 13; GC 74
2005.100.74

In this print two women prepare for the evening by arranging

their hair with the aid of mirrors. The intimacy and implied
sensuality of the scene is expressed in the women's bare fore-
arms, the exposed knees of the first figure, and the nape of the
second woman's neck. It belongs to a set of prints with yellow
backgrounds published by Uemura Yohei around 1794 to 1795.
Mica is used for the mirrors' reflective surfaces, and printed
glue (ink mixed with animal-based glue, called *nikawa*) im-
parts a lustrous surface to the lacquered mirror stand and
frames. MR

---

81   喜多川歌麿　『青楼十二時 續』「丑ノ刻」
KITAGAWA UTAMARO, 1754–1806
"Hour of the Ox" (*Ushi no koku*)
From *The Twelve Hours of the Yoshiwara* (Seirō jūni toki tsuzuki)
C. 1794
Woodblock print (*nishiki-e*)
Ōban: 10¼ in. x 15½ in., 26 cm x 39.4 cm
Signature: 哥麿筆 *Utamaro hitsu*
Publisher's mark: 蔦屋重三郎 *Tsutaya Jūzaburō*
Publisher firm name: 耕書堂 *Kōshodō*
Censor's mark: 極 *kiwame*
Selected other impressions: BMFA (11.14566; 21.6607); BM
    (1909,0618,0.69); BRU (2); CHI (1925.3051); MET (JP977);
    TNM (A-10569_3527?); cited in Asano no. 151: Berès, JUM
Published: FP 35; GC 75
2005.100.75

One of the most overtly sexual prints in the collection, this image
shows a courtesan rising from her bed, tissues in hand, on her way
to the toilet. It is from a set of twelve prints showing the daily life
of *oiran,* the highest-ranking courtesans of the Yoshiwara. Each of
the prints corresponds to one of twelve two-hour intervals, beginning with the so-called "Hour of the Rat" around midnight. The
hours are designated in the bell at the top of each print's clock-
shaped cartouche.

   The hour of the ox, shown here, is about two in the morning. Even in her dishabille, the courtesan presents an elegant
figure, dressed in what appears to be a gauze-weave silk robe
with chrysanthemum crests and morning glories around the
hem. Her gown is fastened in the front with a soft sash, as was
typically worn for sleeping. She carries folded paper tissues
(*kaishi*) in one hand as she lights her way with a match-like
sliver of pine soaked in oil (*shisoku*). Slipping on one sandal,
she reveals a white leg set in alluring contrast to her red under-
kimono (*juban*). An amulet bag and hand towel rest on the
edge of a nearby folding screen—presumably her client is asleep
on the other side.

   This print shows signs of having been tipped into an album. It
may have been part of a set issued in that format. MR

---

82   喜多川歌麿　『美人花合』「喜瀬川　おなみ　めなみ」
KITAGAWA UTAMARO, 1754–1806
Kisegawa (*kamuro* Onami and Menami) (*Kisegawa Onami
    Menami*)
From *Beauties Compared to Flowers* (Bijin hana awase)

C. 1795–1796
Woodblock print (*nishiki-e*)
Ōban: 15 in. x 10 in., 38.1 cm x 25.4 cm
Signature: 正銘哥麿筆 *Shōmei Utamaro hitsu*
Artist's seal: 本家 *honke*
Publisher's mark: 本、近江屋 *Hon, Ōmiya*
Publisher and firm name: 近江屋権九朗 *Ōmiya Gonkurō*; 聚宝
　堂 *Shūhōdō*
Selected other impressions: TIK (P-U 186); BMFA (21.6451); CHI
　(1952.390); ŌTA, cited in ŌTA 1988, no. 82; cited in Asano
　no. 232: TNM, ASH, BER
Published: GC 76
Provenance: Satō Shōtarō
2005.100.76

In this print from a series of five featuring famous beauties of Edo,
a woman looks coquettishly to one side, her left fingers caught under her chin while her right hand holds a tassled round paper fan
(*uchiwa*). Her hair is arranged with multiple hairpins (*kanzashi*)
in the "hanging lantern sideburns" (*tōrōbin*) style, in which bow-
shaped whalebone is used to extend wings of hair out to either side
of the head. A morning glory vine on her fan suggests the late summer season.

The round cartouche at the upper right corner contains the
yellow-flowered kerria rose, to which the courtesan is likened.
In the other cartouche, at the upper left, we learn the identity
of this figure, Kisegawa, as well as the names of her *kamuro* attendants, Onami and Menami. Kisegawa was the name used by
an acclaimed courtesan of the Matsubaya, a renowned Yoshiwara
brothel.

The publisher Ōmiya Gonkurō reused the five portraits
from this set three times. They were found first in a series
titled *Comparing the Charms of Five Beauties* (*Gonin bijin aikyō
kurabe*), where rebuses (visual puns) supplied clues to their
names. A second, retitled version substituted flowers for the
rebuses and, as in this print, a third version supplied the courtesan's names. MR

83　喜多川歌麿　『近代七才女詩歌』「美濃正子女」
KITAGAWA UTAMARO, 1754–1806
"Masako of Mino [Prefecture]" (*Mino Masako jo*)
From *Chinese and Japanese Poems by Seven Talented Women of the
　Present Day* (*Kindai shichisaijo shika*)
C. 1801–1804
Woodblock print (*nishiki-e*)
Naga-ōban: 21 in. x 9½ in., 53.3 cm x 24.1 cm
Signature: 哥麿筆 *Utamaro hitsu*
Publisher and firm name: 村田屋次朗兵衛 *Murataya Jirōbei*; 栄
　邑堂 *Eiyūdō*
Censor's mark: 極 *kiwame*
Selected other impressions: BMFA (21.6346); MIA (P.13,964)
Published: US 227; GC 77
Collector's seal: 白爾叟 *Hakujisō* or *Berusō*? (verso)
2005.100.77

The elongated format of this print is well suited for the image of a

courtesan in her sleepwear carrying an infant on her shoulder. At
her feet, a young attendant (*kamuro*) entertains the child. The inscription on the right edge of the print gives the name of the series
from which it comes: seemingly seven prints with poetry by seven
famous women poets. Although not all of these have been identified, each print seems to have contained a poetic inscription and a
private scene of daily life.

This print features the poet Yabe Masako (1745–1773), who was
born in Mino Province and died before the age of thirty. On the left
side of the print is inscribed one of her better-known *waka* poems,
entitled "Love Associated with Clothing" (*Kinu ni yosuru koi*)—included in the 1790 directory of notable eccentrics *Kinsei kijin den*
(volume 4), as well as in the love section of Masako's own poetry
anthology *Yabe Shōshi shōshū*. MR

*Omou sono
hito ni wa kiseshi
tsukikusa no
hana surikoromo
utsurō ga uki*

It wafts by,
the fading scent of the
moonflower-rubbed robe
that was worn
by the man I love

84　喜多川歌麿　『當世美人三遊』「北国」
KITAGAWA UTAMARO, 1754–1806
"Northern Quarter" (*Hokkoku*)
From *Three Amusements of Modern Beauties* (*Tōsei bijin sanyū*)
C. 1800
Woodblock print (*nishiki-e*)
Naga-ōban: 20½ in. x 9½ in., 52.1 cm x 24.1 cm
Signature: 哥麿筆 *Utamaro hitsu*
Publisher's mark: 村 *Mura*
Publisher and firm name: 村田屋次朗兵衛 *Murataya Jirōbei*; 栄
　邑堂 *Eiyūdō*
Censor's mark: 極 *kiwame*
Selected other impressions: BMFA (21.6542); CIA (PA 211, no.
　343); HMA (15575); HU (1933.4.603); TNM (A-10569_1940)
Published: US 225; GC 78
Collector's seal: 白爾叟 *Hakujisō* or *Berusō*? (verso)
2005.100.78

85　喜多川歌麿　母と子ののぞき遊び
KITAGAWA UTAMARO, 1754–1806
Mother peeping at her baby
C. 1799–1800
Woodblock print (*nishiki-e*)
Ōban: 15 in. x 9¾ in., 38.1 cm x 24.8 cm
Signature: 哥麿筆 *Utamaro hitsu*
Publisher's mark: 本、近江屋 *Hon, Ōmiya*
Publisher and firm name: 近江屋権九朗 *Ōmiya Gonkurō*; 聚宝
　堂　*Shūhōdō*

Selected other impressions: MET (JP1526); BMFA (1999.229;
    18.310); cited in Asano no. 364: Berès, BRU, JUM, TNM, BN
Published: US 163; GC 79
2005.100.79

86　喜多川歌麿　藤花下の二美人
KITAGAWA UTAMARO, 1754–1806
Two women under wisteria flowers
C. 1804
Woodblock print (*nishiki-e*)
Ōban: 14¼ in. x 10 in., 36.2 cm x 25.4 cm
Signature: 哥麿筆　*Utamaro hitsu*
Publisher's mark: 若　*Waka*
Publisher and firm name: 若作狭屋與市　*Wakasaya Yoichi;* 若林
    堂　*Jakurindō*
Selected other impressions: KANS (1928.7870)
Published: US 164; GC 80
2005.100.80

This print in Utamaro's later style shows an extraordinary state
of preservation, its pale pink background, purple robes, and
red underrobes retaining their original brilliance. A courtesan
and her attendant pause during a walk to turn back and look
at something or someone behind them. The wisteria blossoms
above their heads, the beauty of the two women's faces, and the
sense of familiarity between them add to the charm of this scene.
The courtesan wears a high-arched "hanging lantern sideburn"
(*tōrōbin*) hairstyle adorned with floral and fan-decorated hairpins, bows, and ribbons. Her robe of sheer purple silk patterned
with chrysanthemums reveals the red and white robe beneath.
Her attendant's hair is inserted with simpler pins, and she wears a
kosode of simple but chic checked silk. MR

87　喜多川歌麿　『女職蚕手業草』「壱」
KITAGAWA UTAMARO, 1754–1806
"Number One" (*Ichi*)
From *Women Engaged in the Sericulture Industry* (Joshoku kaiko
    tewaza-kusa)
C. 1798–1800
Woodblock print (*nishiki-e*)
Set of 12 *ōban*: approx. 15⅜ in. x 10¼ in., 39.1 cm x 26 cm (each)
Signature: 哥麿筆　Utamaro hitsu (each)
Publisher's mark: Crane mark of 鶴屋喜右衛門　Tsuruya Kiemon
    (each)
Publisher and firm name: 鶴屋喜右衛門　Tsuruya Kiemon; 仙鶴
    堂　Senkakudō
Selected other impressions: BMFA (19.147; 21.7321; 34.241); Van
    Vleck (1980.3227); CHI (1925.3246)
Published: TWP I; US 224; GC 81
Collector's seal: Edwin Grabhorn (each)
2005.100.81.1

88　喜多川歌麿　『女職蚕手業草』「弐」
KITAGAWA UTAMARO, 1754–1806

"Number Two" (*Ni*)
From *Women Engaged in the Sericulture Industry* (Joshoku kaiko
    tewaza-kusa)
C. 1798–1800
Woodblock print (*nishiki-e*)
Selected other impressions: BMFA (19.148; 21.7322; 34.242); Van
    Vleck (1980.3228); CHI (1925.3247)
Published: TWP II; GC 82
2005.100.81.2

89　喜多川歌麿　『女職蚕手業草』「三」
KITAGAWA UTAMARO, 1754–1806
"Number Three" (*San*)
From *Women Engaged in the Sericulture Industry* (Joshoku kaiko
    tewaza-kusa)
C. 1798–1800
Woodblock print (*nishiki-e*)
Selected other impressions: BMFA (19.149; 21.7323; 34.243); Van
    Vleck (1980.3229); CHI (1925.3248)
Published: TWP III; GC 83
2005.100.81.3

90　喜多川歌麿　『女職蚕手業草』「四」
KITAGAWA UTAMARO, 1754–1806
"Number Four" (*Shi*)
From *Women Engaged in the Sericulture Industry* (Joshoku kaiko
    tewaza-kusa)
C. 1798–1800
Woodblock print (*nishiki-e*)
Selected other impressions: BMFA (19.150; 21.7324; 34.244); Van
    Vleck (1980.3230); CHI (1925.3249)
Published: TWP IV; GC 84
2005.100.81.4

91　喜多川歌麿　『女職蚕手業草』「五」
KITAGAWA UTAMARO, 1754–1806
"Number Five" (*Go*)
From *Women Engaged in the Sericulture Industry* (Joshoku kaiko
    tewaza-kusa)
C. 1798–1800
Woodblock print (*nishiki-e*)
Selected other impressions: BMFA (19.151; 21.7325; 34.245); Van
    Vleck (1980.3231); CHI (1925.3250)
Published: TWP V; GC 85
2005.100.81.5

92　喜多川歌麿　『女職蚕手業草』「六」
KITAGAWA UTAMARO, 1754–1806
"Number Six" (*Roku*)
From *Women Engaged in the Sericulture Industry* (Joshoku kaiko
    tewaza-kusa)
C. 1798–1800
Woodblock print (*nishiki-e*)

Selected other impressions: complete set: BMFA (19.152; 21.7326; 34.246); Van Vleck (1980.3232); CHI (1925.3251)
Published: TWP VI; GC 86
2005.100.81.6

93　喜多川歌麿　『女職蚕手業草』「七」
KITAGAWA UTAMARO, 1754–1806
"Number Seven" (*Shichi*)
From *Women Engaged in the Sericulture Industry* (Joshoku kaiko tewaza-kusa)
C. 1798–1800
Woodblock print (*nishiki-e*)
Selected other impressions: complete set: BMFA (19.153; 21.7327; 34.247); Van Vleck (1980.3233); CHI (1925.3252)
Published: TWP VII; GC 87
2005.100.81.7

94　喜多川歌麿　『女職蚕手業草』「八」
KITAGAWA UTAMARO, 1754–1806
"Number Eight" (*Hachi*)
From *Women Engaged in the Sericulture Industry* (Joshoku kaiko tewaza-kusa)
C. 1798–1800
Woodblock print (*nishiki-e*)
Selected other impressions: BMFA (19.154; 21.7328; 34.248); Van Vleck (1980.3234); CHI (1925.3253)
Published: TWP VIII; GC 88
2005.100.81.8

95　喜多川歌麿　『女職蚕手業草』「九」
KITAGAWA UTAMARO, 1754–1806
"Number Nine" (*Kyū*)
From *Women Engaged in the Sericulture Industry* (Joshoku kaiko tewaza-kusa)
C. 1798–1800
Woodblock print (*nishiki-e*)
Selected other impressions: BMFA (19.155; 21.7329; 34.249); Van Vleck (1980.3235); CHI (1925.3254)
Published: TWP IX; GC 89
2005.100.81.9

96　喜多川歌麿　『女職蚕手業草』「十」
KITAGAWA UTAMARO, 1754–1806
"Number Ten" (*Jū*)
From *Women Engaged in the Sericulture Industry* (Joshoku kaiko tewaza-kusa)
C. 1798–1800
Woodblock print (*nishiki-e*)
Selected other impressions: BMFA (19.156; 21.7330; 34.250); Van Vleck (1980.3236); CHI (1925.3255)
Published: TWP X; GC 90
2005.100.81.10

97　喜多川歌麿　『女職蚕手業草』「十一」
KITAGAWA UTAMARO, 1754–1806
"Number Eleven" (*Jū-ichi*)
From *Women Engaged in the Sericulture Industry* (Joshoku kaiko tewaza-kusa)
C. 1798–1800
Woodblock print (*nishiki-e*)
Selected other impressions: BMFA (19.157; 21.7331; 34.251); Van Vleck (1980.3237); CHI (1925.3256)
Published: TWP XI; GC 91
2005.100.81.11

98　喜多川歌麿　『女職蚕手業草』「十二終」
KITAGAWA UTAMARO, 1754–1806
"Number Twelve, The End" (*Jū-ni owari*)
From *Women Engaged in the Sericulture Industry* (Joshoku kaiko tewaza-kusa)
C. 1798–1800
Woodblock print (*nishiki-e*)
Selected other impressions: BMFA (19.158; 21.7332; 34.252); Van Vleck (1980.3238); CHI (1925.3257)
Published: TWP XII; GC 92
2005.100.81.12

99　窪俊満　宇治茶摘み
KUBO SHUNMAN, 1757–1820
Picking tea in Uji
Late 1780s
Woodblock print (*nishiki-e*)
Aiban triptych: 12½ in. x 8¾ in., 31.7 cm x 22.2 cm (each)
Signature: 窪俊満画 *Kubo Shunman ga* (left sheet)
Selected other impressions: BMFA (11.14944, right sheet only)
Published: G.Land 13; UM 279; US 218–220; GC 100
2005.100.82.1-.3

Writing in the 1960 catalogue of the Grabhorn Collection *Landscape Prints of Old Japan*, Jack Hillier commented, "Is it possible that tea-pickers wore such lovely clothes, or, more to the point, wore them with such grace? Of course, it is all a delightful pastoral make-believe, such as Melchior created in Dresden china, or Bustelli in Nymphenburg."[27] Indeed, the costumes of the tea pickers on the left side of this triptych seem to the modern eye every bit as lovely as those worn by the two fashionable women at right, visitors to the famous tea-growing region of Uji. Though the workers are distinguished by their poses (hoisting tea or baskets of leaves) and costumes (aprons, tied-up sleeves, simple straw sandals), their up-to-date obi and hairstyles seem to playfully transpose the attributes of pleasure quarters style to the world of rural labor.

The setting for these figures comes from an illustration of the village of Uji in a 1780 guidebook, *Pictures of Famous Places in the Capital*

27　Hillier 1960, no. 13.

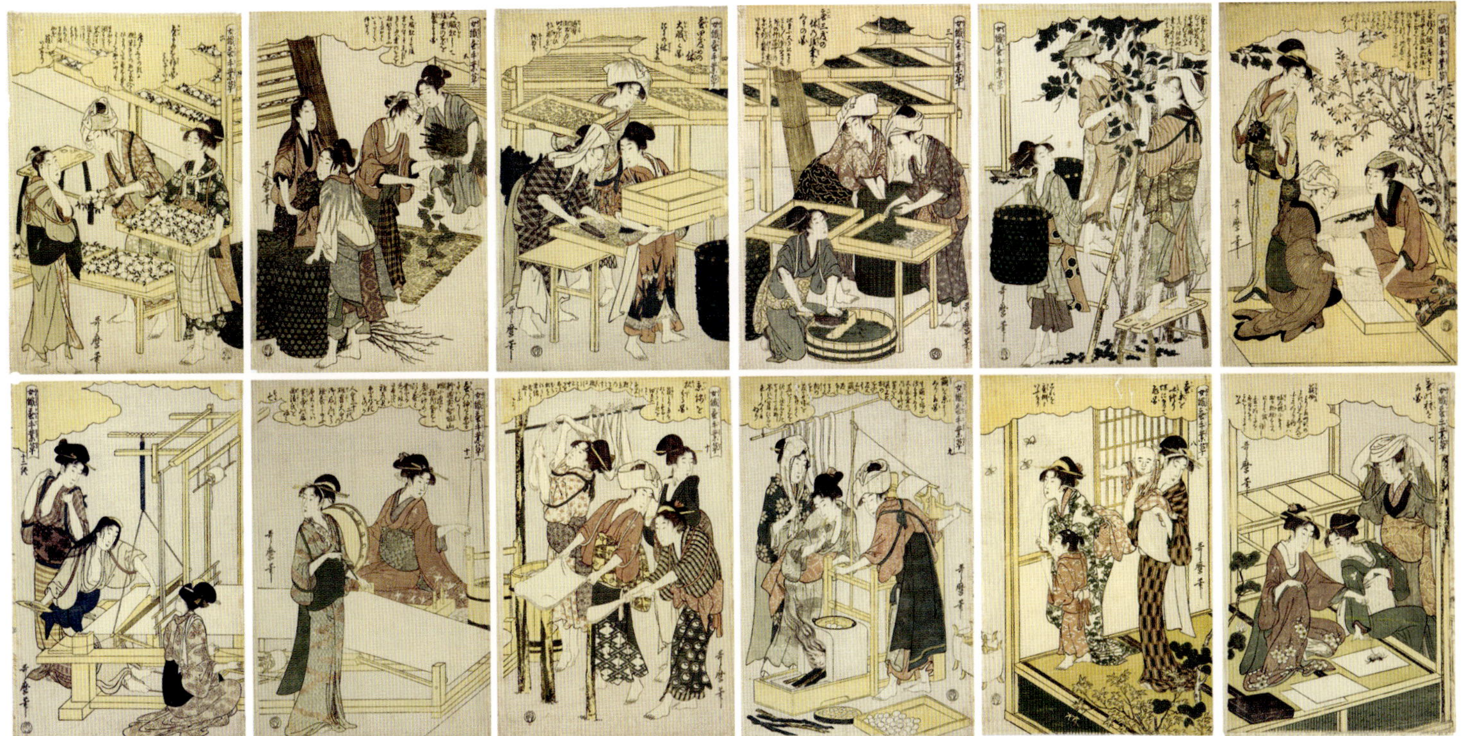

Nos. 87–98, showing the order of the prints, beginning top row right to left and continuing bottom row right to left.

(*Miyako meisho zukai*). The influence of Kitao Shigemasa and Torii Ki-yonaga is also evident in the figures and composition of the tea-picking scene, which was published a year or two before Shunman's great masterpiece, the hexaptych "Six Jewel Rivers." Somewhat faded today, the limited palette of this rare triptych is characteristic of an experimental phase in printmaking during the 1780s. LA

stops by a house one day asking for the loan of a raincoat. The young woman who lives there offers him a flowering branch of kerria rose (*yamabuki*), but no raincoat. Angered by this response, Dōkan returns home, only to realize that the flowers were meant not as an insult, but as an elegant reference to a *waka*, or classical poem (see no. 33 for Harunobu's rendition of this theme). LA

100　窪俊満　柳下美人
KUBO SHUNMAN, 1757–1820
Young woman under a willow tree
Woodblock print (*nishiki-e*)
Hashira-e: 25¾ in. x 4⅝ in., 65.4 cm x 11.7 cm
Signature: 俊満画 *Shunman ga*
Selected other impressions: BMFA (11.22006; 21.6195)
Published: GC 101
Ex-collection: Tod and Freeman Ford
Provenance: Judson D. Metzgar
2005.100.83

In this early pillar print (*hashira-e*) by Shunman, a beauty stands beneath the dangling branches of a willow, the trailing sleeves of her *furisode* patterned with meandering streams and asters. Through the narrow frame of the print we see her hold up a spray of flowers while shyly covering her mouth with one upraised sleeve.

　How are we to read this picture? Is she simply a beauty enjoying nature on a warm spring day, or does her gesture signify something in particular? One possibility is that it alludes to a famous story about Ōta Dōkan, the celebrated warrior and poet credited with building Edo Castle in the seventeenth century. In this tale, Ōta

---

101　栄松斎長喜　四季の美人　初日の出
EISHŌSAI CHŌKI, 1775–1825
Sunrise on New Year's morning
From an untitled series of beautiful women in the four seasons
Woodblock print (*nishiki-e*)
Ōban: 15 in. x 9⅞ in., 38.1 cm x 25.1 cm
Signature: 長喜画 *Chōki ga*
Publisher's mark: 蔦屋重三郎 *Tsutaya Jūzaburō*
Publisher firm name: 耕書堂 *Kōshodō*
Censor's seal: 極 *kiwame*
Selected other impressions: BMFA (21.4780); TNM (A-10569_630); BAUR (G97); BM (1927,0613,0.5); Riese (no. 22)
Published: FP 38; MPJ 250; GC 97; DFP 2
Ex-collection: Gaston Migeon
Provenance: Aoyama Saburō
2005.100.84

With its nearly perfect color preservation, this print is arguably the best surviving impression of one of Eishōsai Chōki's masterworks. It comes from a rare, luxurious series featuring beauties in the four seasons of the year and incorporating blown mica. Scholars have identified two states of this print, of which this is believed to be the second due to the lack of outline around the ocean sandbanks.

Comb and hairpins precariously askew, a lean beauty pauses next to a washbasin to glance back across the sea to a brilliant red sunrise. With her right hand tucked warmly inside her robes, she reaches the other out from within her inner robe in order to pull her collar against the cold air. The mica-sheen emitting from the black sky and brightness of the water at the top of the print evoke the iridescence of the early morning light. The blossoming pheasant's eye (*fukujusō*) plant next to the dipper on the basin signals that this is the auspicious first sunrise of New Year's.

We can tell that this woman has come directly from her bed from the disarray of her robes and her soft sash, loosely tied in front for sleeping. Her garments, in elegant stripes, well represent the tastes of the Kansei era (1789–1801) at which time this print was made. Vertical striped textiles, inspired by South and Southeast Asian imports, became increasingly popular in mid to late eighteenth century Edo, partially in response to repeated sumptuary laws banning ostentation in dress, hair ornaments, and even hairstyles. Here her subdued but exotic-looking multistriped inner robe (over a red tie-dyed undergarment) and her simple pinstriped outer robe represent the essence of understated Edo chic. MR

102　栄松斎長喜　「おさん　茂兵衛」
EISHŌSAI CHŌKI, 1775–1825
"[The Tragic Lovers] Osan and Mohei" (*Osan Mohei*)
Woodblock print (*nishiki-e*)
Ōban: 15 in. x 10⅛ in., 38.1 cm x 25.7 cm
Signature: 子興画　*Shikō ga*
Publisher's mark: 本　Hon
Publisher and firm name: 近江屋権九朗　*Ōmiya Gonkurō;* 聚宝堂　*Shūhōdō*
Selected other impressions: TNM (A-10569_3327)
Published: US 223; GC 99
2005.100.85

The characters Osan and Mohei were well known to Edo audiences from plays for the puppet and Kabuki stage. Osan, daughter of a poor family, was married to a well-to-do almanac maker in Kyoto. Desperate to ease her parent's poverty, she asked her husband's steward Mohei for help. From this point on, the lovers became embroiled in a chain of dramatic events leading to their arrest and crucifixion in 1683. Fiction writer Ihara Saikaku (1642–1693) adapted these sensational events as one of the erotic tales in *Five Women Who Loved Love* (*Koshoku gonin onna*, 1686), and in 1715 Chikamatsu Monzaemon (1653–1725) wrote a puppet play about the lovers called *Daikyōshi mukashi goyomi.* Chikamatsu's adaptation was also staged again and again as a Kabuki play in the 1700s.

The tale's enduring popularity is evident from the number of prints made to depict the couple, but Chōki's version is especially poignant. The red cord (*tasuki*) over Osan's shoulders indicates that she is posing as the household's maid, Otama, as part of a plan to reveal her husband's infidelity. In a plot twist of the type thrilling to Edo audiences, Mohei enters the room at night and makes love to Osan, thinking she is Otama. Realizing their mistake, the lovers are instantly filled with remorse at having inadvertently consummated their affair. Here Mohei,

wearing a simple checked robe open at the waist, wipes away tears as Osan, her hair in disarray, expresses her anguish by biting a tightly gripped cloth. LA

103　栄松斎長喜　『東風俗五節句合』　七夕
EISHŌSAI CHŌKI, 1775–1825
Tanabata Festival
From *Comparison of the Customs of the Five Festivals in Eastern Japan* (Azuma fūzoku gosekku awase)
C. 1796
Woodblock print (*nishiki-e*)
Ōban: 15¼ in. x 10 in., 38.7 cm x 25.4 cm
Signature: 子興画　*Shikō ga*
Publisher's mark: 松安　*Matsuyasu*
Selected other impressions: BMFA (21.5893)
Published: GC 98; US 222
Collector's seal: Hamilton Easter Field
2005.100.86

104　鳥文斎栄之　『若菜初衣裳』「松葉屋染之助　わかき　わかば」
CHŌBUNSAI EISHI, 1756–1829
"Somenosuke of the Matsubaya with [*kamuro*] Wakaki and Wakaba" (*Matsubaya Somenosuke Wakaki Wakaba*)
From *New Year Fashions as Fresh as Young Leaves* (Wakana hatsu ishō)
Woodblock print (*nishiki-e*)
Ōban: 15 in. x 10 in., 38.1 cm x 25.4 cm
C. 1795–1796
Signature: 栄之圖　*Eishi zu*
Publisher's mark: 永寿板　*Eiju han*
Publisher and firm name: 西村屋与八　*Nishimuraya Yohachi;* 永寿堂　*Eijudō*
Censor's mark: 極　*kiwame*
Selected other impressions: BM (1948, 0410, 0.25); BMFA (11.14082)
Published: Ukiyo-e 17; GC 102
Ex-collection: Tod and Freeman Ford
Provenance: Judson D. Metzgar
2005.100.87

Eishi was one of the leading artists of the 1790s, rivaling Utamaro in elegant depictions of contemporary beauties. This series is devoted to top-ranking courtesans and the sumptuous garments they wore during the first procession of the New Year. The name of this particular beauty—Somenosuke—is given at the top of the print, along with those of her brothel, Matsubaya, and her two *kamuro* attendants, Wakaki and Wakaba. Her multilayered outer garment, patterned with flying birds, is worn over a pink *kosode* bearing her crest of crossed hawk feathers on the shoulder. A lacquered rack holds a black obi decorated with larger crests and a festive outer robe with a hawk swooping across a background of aster flower sprays. On the floor before her is a potted adonis plant (*fukujusō*), the symbol of good fortune in the New Year that appears also in Chōki's print of sunrise on New Year's morning (no. 101).

While other prints in the series feature fan-shaped cartouches, this one sports a miniature version of Somenosuke's robe (top right). She must have created quite a stir when parading through the streets in this spectacular attire, the height of her slender figure enhanced by an extravagant *hyōgo* chignon with two towering topknots. LA

---

105   鳥文斎栄之　『七賢人略美人新造揃』「てうじや内　とき哥」

CHŌBUNSAI EISHI, 1756–1829
"Tokiuta of the Chōjiya" (*Chōjiya uchi Tokiuta*)
From *An Array of Beautiful Apprenctice Courtesans as the Seven Sages of the Bamboo Grove* (Shichi kenjin yatsushi bijin shinzō zoroe)
C. 1795
Woodblock print (*nishiki-e*)
Ōban: 15 in. x 10 in., 38.1 cm x 25.4 cm
Signature: 栄之圖　*Eishi zu*
Publisher's mark: 岩　*Iwa*
Publisher and firm name: 岩戸屋喜三郎　*Iwatoya Kisaburō;* 栄林堂　*Eirindō*
Censor's mark: 極　*kiwame*
Selected other impressions: CHI (1925.3109)
Published: FP 39; US 216; GC 104
Ex-collection: Tod and Freeman Ford
Provenance: Judson D. Metzgar
2005.100.88

The two lovely girls of this yellow-ground print are attendants to a courtesan of the Chōjiya brothel. Tokiuta, on the right, is a *shinzō*, or apprentice courtesan; her companion is a younger, unnamed *kamuro* attendant. Seated indoors, they smile happily as they read "yellow-cover books" (*kibyōshi*), a type of light fiction popular in the late 1700s. Like modern comic books, the yellow-cover books were plentifully illustrated (see the open book in Tokiuta's lap), and full of witty commentary on contemporary life.

This charming scene is part of a set in which Eishi playfully compares seven *shinzō* of his day to the "Seven Sages of the Bamboo Grove," scholarly figures from ancient Chinese lore noted for their literary and intellectual attainments. Underlining the parody are the girl's genteel activities — reading, writing, and playing music — and folding screens painted with bamboo, set up behind the figures (the Chinese sages are usually shown standing or sitting within an actual grove).

Tokiuta appears to be dressed for New Year's: she wears pine and plum ornaments in her hair, and her robe is decorated with snow-covered pine branches and what appear to be auspicious plaques. As in other prints from the series, the girls wear special decorated hair combs, here with a crane-shaped roundel, repeated on Tokiuta's robe. LA

---

106   鳥文斎栄之　『六歌仙』「喜撰法師」

CHŌBUNSAI EISHI, 1756–1829
"Monk Kisen" (*Kisen Hōshi*)
From *Six Poetic Immortals* (Rokkasen)
Woodblock print (*nishiki-e*)

Ōban: 15 in. x 9⅞ in., 38.1 cm x 25.1 cm
Signature: 栄之画　*Eishi ga*
Selected other impressions: CHI (1952.399); BM (1906,1220,0.261)
Published: GC 103
2005.100.89

Eishi created other series likening modern beauties to the "Six Poetic Immortals," but in this sophisticated set he pairs groups of figures with famous verses and creates settings linked to the imagery of the poems. Here a middle-class young lady appears on an excursion to Uji, a district renowned for its beautiful autumn foliage. The *waka* poem written above is by the ninth-century Buddhist monk and poet Kisen:

Wago io wa
miyako no tatsumi
shika zo sumu
yo o Ujiyama to
hito wa iu nari

To the southeast of the capital
I live in my thatched hut.
The world is bleak, they say,
Gloomy as the name of these Uji hills.[28]

The poem plays on the similarity of the place name *Uji* to the word *ushi*, "gloomy" or "bleak." The imagery evokes a solitary life of reclusion — to which Eishi's much cheerier scene provides a sharp contrast. In this modern reworking the visitor's youthful costume consists of a *furisode* with cherry blossom decoration and an obi patterned with peony sprays. Holding a small tobacco pipe tied with a red bow, she turns back to converse with two companions, a young girl and a maid, both wearing simple striped *kosode*. A few landscape details provide the appropriate setting: a maple tree, scattering its leaves; a stream coursing over some rocks; and two deer, another symbol of autumn, posed on hills across a mist-filled expanse. LA

---

107   鳥高斎栄昌　『郭中美人競』「扇屋滝川」

CHŌKŌSAI EISHŌ, active 1780–1800
"Takigawa of the Ōgiya" (*Ōgiya Takigawa*)
From *Contest of Beauties in the Pleasure Quarters* (Kakuchū bijin kurabe)
Woodblock print (*nishiki-e*)
Ōban: 15⅛ in. x 10⅛ in., 38.4 cm x 25.7 cm
Signature: 鳥高齋栄昌畫　*Chōkōsai Eishō ga*
Selected other impressions: TNM (A-10569_2679)
Published: GC 105
Ex-collection: Lila Perry
Provenance: Harry Nail
2005.100.90

Yamaguchi Chūemon published some two dozen prints in the

---

28   Trans. Shirane 1987, 186.

series *Contest of Beauties in the Pleasure Quarters*. At least nineteen are designs by Eishō, with three others by Eiri and one by Eichō. Together, this grand series portrays courtesans from the ten top-ranked Ōmagaki brothels in the Yoshiwara district and four from the Hanmagaki houses, ranked a level below. The beauties are shown in the *ōkubi-e* format of close-up portraits, first used for female subjects by Utamaro during the early 1790s.

Eisho's teacher, Chōbunsai Eishi, moved the *ōkubi-e* in a subtly new direction by emphasizing the smiling or laughing countenances of beauties. Like his teacher, Eishō was adept at projecting images of carefree pleasure. Here, Takigawa of the prosperous Ōgiya brothel lifts a cup of sake—she is shown in the midst of drinking with a client. Her raised brows and open mouth express her tipsy delight, while the knuckles of one hand are raised to her chin in a coquettish gesture. Adding energy to the scene are her boldly patterned robes, the collar of her inner garment, which stands stiffly to attention at her neck, and bristling hair ornaments that jut across the title cartouche to the right.

Though worn, the background in this print shows traces of its original blue coloring. LA

108　鳥橋斎栄里　雷雨
CHŌKYŌSAI EIRI (active c. 1781–1818)
Beauty in a rainstorm
Woodblock print (*nishiki-e*)
Hashira-e: 25 in. x 4⅝ in., 63.5 cm x 11.7 cm
C. 1790s
Signature: 栄里画　*Eiri ga*
Publisher's mark: 永寿板　*Eiju han*
Publisher and firm name: 西村屋与八　*Nishimuraya Yohachi;* 永寿堂　*Eijudō*
Censor's mark: 極　*kiwame*
Selected other impressions: KANS (1928.7813)
Published: GC 106
Collector's seal: 白爾叟　*Hakujisō* or *Berusō?* (verso)
2005.100.91

A young woman scrambles to open her umbrella while keeping her garments from flapping open as she battles the wind and rain. The expression on her face and the dramatic appearance of the Thunder God riding on swirling black clouds above her head, however, do not bode well for her. She grasps her geometric patterned ikat (*kasuri*) unlined robe close to her, inadvertently allowing one white thigh to peek out from beneath her red underrobe. Her umbrella retains most of the fleeting dayflower blue pigment with which it was originally colored. David Waterhouse notes that the design is related to one found in an earlier print by Harunobu.[29]

According to Yoshida Teruji, the signature on this print was employed by the artist in the first part of his career, when he was known by the sobriquets Chōkyōsai and Shikyūsai. The artist used several different characters for the name Eiri in later years, in conjunction with alternative names. MR

29　E-mail communication. See Waterhouse 2013, no. 53.

109　東洲斎写楽　尾上松助の松下造酒之進
TŌSHŪSAI SHARAKU, active 1794–1795
The Actor Onoe Matsusuke I as Matsushita Mikinoshin
1794.5
Woodblock print (*nishiki-e*)
Ōban: 9¾ in. x 14½ in., 24.8 cm x 36.8 cm
Signature: 東洲斎寫樂画　*Tōshūsai Sharaku ga*
Publisher's mark: 蔦屋重三郎　*Tsutaya Jūzaburō*
Publisher firm name: 耕書堂　*Kōshodō*
Censor's mark: 極　*kiwame*
Selected other impressions: BMFA (21.7247); Nelson (158); TNM (A-10569_469; A-8593); BM (1909,0618,0.42); TIK (P-U 159); Guimet, cited in ŌTA 2007, no. 116; Vever, cited in Hillier 1976, no. 595),
Published: FP 48; GC 94
2005.100.92

Sharaku's portrait of Onoe Matsusuke I corresponds to a scene from *Katakiuchi noriyai banashi*, a Kabuki play performed in the fifth month of 1794 at the Kiri Theater. In the story two sisters named Miyagino and Shinobu exact revenge on the villain who has killed their father, Matsushita Mikinoshin. (A second print by Sharaku shows the villain, Shiga Daishichi, about to unsheathe his sword.) Onoe Matsusuke played Mikinoshin, a masterless samurai (*rōnin*) impoverished by illness. His successful depiction of Mikinoshin's poor health is noted in a review of the play in the 1794 *Mirror of Actor's Physiognomy* (Yakusha ninsō kagami). The print shows just how this reduced state was conveyed by the actor: a wild thatch of thinning hair sprouts from the shaved portion of his pate; his topknot (*mage*) is askew; pale gray shadows rim his eyes and mouth; and hunched forward anxiously, he grasps a folded fan in one upraised hand—powerless to defend himself from his imminent death at the hands of Daishichi. LA

110　東洲斎写楽　四代目市川鰕蔵の竹村定之進
TŌSHŪSAI SHARAKU, active 1794–1795
The Actor Ichikawa Ebizō IV as Takemura Sadanoshin
1794.5
Woodblock print (*nishiki-e*)
Ōban: 15 in. x 10 in., 38.1 cm x 25.4 cm
Signature: 東洲齋寫樂画　*Tōshūsai Sharaku ga*
Publisher's mark: 蔦屋重三郎　*Tsutaya Jūzaburō*
Publisher firm name: 耕書堂　*Kōshodō*
Censor's mark: 極　*kiwame*
Selected other impressions: BMFA (11.14677); HMA (20656); Rijksmuseum (RP-P-1956-586); TNM (A-10569_470); MET (JP2650, JP3114); BM (1906,1220,0.201); CHI (1925.2733); CLV (1930.205); HU (1933.4.505); BRK (42.85); LOC (FP 2-JPD, no. 60); Vever, cited in Hillier 1976, no. 598
Published: Ukiyo-e 22; US 52 (B/W); GC 93
Provenance: Judson D. Metzgar
2005.100.93

Ichikawa Danjūrō V was among the most acclaimed actors of Edo in 1791 when he passed his name to his successor and became known as Ebizō IV. He appears here in the role Takemura Sadanoshin in the play *Koi nyōbō somewake tazuna*, performed at the Kawarazaki Theater in the fifth month of 1794. His family crest of *mimasu* or nested measuring boxes appears on his robe and on the stiff-shouldered vest that denotes his profession as Noh dancer. A transient dayflower blue colors the vest, the robe is colored orange, and a trace of red shows between his slightly parted lips.

Adapted from a puppet play by Chikamatsu (1653–1724), the play's story featured Sadanoshin as a father driven to commit suicide to atone for the misdeeds of his daughter, Shigenoi. Sharaku suggests Ebizō's substantial stage presence through hulking shoulders, a prominent nose and jaw. His facial features distorted in anguish, with brows lifted and eyes open wide, the actor clasps his hands in front of his chest. Though open to interpretation, this supplicating gesture suggests that he may be pleading for Shigenoi's release from imprisonment. Asano Shūgō argues that Sharaku depicts either the moment just prior to Sadanoshin's suicide, or the moment, known as *kagebara* (literally "shadow stomach"), when Sadanoshin signals his imminent death by announcing to the audience that he has administered a deadly cut to his belly. LA

111　東洲斎写楽　四代目岩井半四郎の信濃屋お半と三代
　　　目坂東彦三郎の帯屋長右衛門

TŌSHŪSAI SHARAKU, active 1794–1795
The actors Iwai Hanshirō IV as Shinanoya Ohan and Bandō
　　　Hikosaburō III as Obiya Chōemon
1794.8
Woodblock print (*nishiki-e*)
Ōban: 14⅞ in. x 9¾ in., 37.8 cm x 24.8 cm
Signature: 東洲齋寫樂画　*Tōshūsai Sharaku ga*
Publisher's mark: 蔦屋重三郎　*Tsutaya Jūzaburō*
Publisher firm name: 耕書堂　*Kōshodō*
Censor's mark: 極　*kiwame*
Selected other impressions: MET (JP 3119); CHI (1935.60)
Published: FP 50; US 229; GC 95
Provenance: Satō Shōtarō
2005.100.94

Ohan, a girl in her late teens, meets and falls in love with Obiya Chōemon, a married man nearing fifty. Wracked by guilt, which worsens once Ohan becomes pregnant, the couple pledges to commit double suicide. The subject comes from the second half of the play *Nihonmatsu michinoku sodachi*, staged at the Kawarazaki Theater in the eighth month of 1794. The costumes of the two actors confirm this identification: Chōemon's plain striped *kosode*—here hiked up with his sash—and Ohan's diamond-patterned *furisode* robe match those in an illustration for the play from a contemporary playbill. Two renowned actors of the day, Bandō Hikosaburō III and the celebrated *onnagata* Iwai Hanshirō IV play the roles of Chōemon and Ohan. Sharaku's print depicts the couple's *michiyuki*, or travel scene, in this case a final journey to the Katsura River. At the end of the play, Chōemon carries his lover on his back into the water to drown, in the sort of tragic death scene beloved by Edo audiences. LA

112　東洲斎写楽　山科四郎十郎の名護屋三左衛門

TŌSHŪSAI SHARAKU, active 1794–1795
The actor Yamashina Shirōjurō as Nagoya Sanzaemon
1794.7
Woodblock print (*nishiki-e*)
Hosoban: 12 in. x 6 in., 30.5 cm x 15.2 cm
Signature: 東洲齋寫樂画　*Tōshūsai Sharaku ga*
Publisher's mark: 蔦屋重三郎　*Tsutaya Jūzaburō*
Publisher firm name: 耕書堂　*Kōshodō*
Censor's mark: 極　*kiwame*
Selected other impressions: MET (JP1520); CHI (1934.227)
Published: FP 49; US 53 (B/W); GC 96
Provenance: Harry Packard
2005.100.95

This print appeared as part of a triptych of three actors in a scene from the Kabuki play *Keisei sanbon karakasa*. The play was performed at the Miyako Theater in Edo in the seventh month of 1794. Asano Shūgō places this sheet, showing the actor Yamashina Shirōjurō as Nagoya Sanzaemon, at the center of the triptych, facing Fuwa no Bansaku to the left and Bansaku's wife Sekinoto to the right. (The sheet with Senkinoto is known today only through black and white photographs.[30]) The roles of Bansaku and Sekinoto were played by Ichikawa Danjūrō VI and Sanogawa Ichimatsu III respectively. Here, Shirōjurō adopts a confrontational pose, his face contorted in a grimace as his character receives the news that his lord, the shogun Higashiyama Yoshiteru, has been driven out of Kyoto. The print has been trimmed slightly along the top edge, cutting off the area above the signature. LA

113　歌川豊国　『役者舞台之姿絵』「はま村や」（三代
　　　目瀬川菊之丞の大和万歳実は都九条の白拍子久かた）

UTAGAWA TOYOKUNI, 1769–1825
"Hamamuraya" (The actor Segawa Kikunojō III as Yamato Manzai,
　　　actually Shirabyōshi Hisakata of Miyako Kujō) (*Hamamuraya*)
From *Portraits of Actors on Stage* (Yakusha butai no sugata-e)
1794.11
Woodblock print (*nishiki-e*)
Ōban: 15¼ in. x 10¼ in., 38.7 cm x 26 cm
Signature: 豊国画　*Toyokuni ga*
Publisher's mark: 泉市版　*Sen'ichi han*
Publisher and firm name: 泉屋市兵衛　*Izumiya Ichibei*; 甘泉
　　　堂　*Kansendō*
Censor's mark: 極　*kiwame*
Selected other impressions: BMFA (21.6830); CHI (1942.117);
　　　Vever, cited in Hillier 1976, no. 627
Published: GC 146
2005.100.96

A celebrated specialist in female roles (*onnagata*), Segawa Kikunojō III is identified in the title cartouche by his actor guild name, Hamamuraya. His distinctive crest, shaped as a bundle of

---

30　See Tōkyō Kokuritsu Hakubutsukan 2011, 132–133, for pictures of all
　　　three prints.

silk rovings (*yuiwata*), would have been instantly recognizable to Edo fans. As is often the case in Kabuki, Kikunojō plays a contemporary figure who harbors a double identity. Here he appears as the performer Yamato Manzai, in reality the *shirabyōshi* Hisakata of Kujō Street in Kyoto. A *shirabyōshi*, a female entertainer who performs in the costume of a nobleman, Kikunojō wears a courtier's lacquered hat (*eboshi*), tied under the chin, and carries a man's folding fan. An outer garment with *tachibana* (an inedible citrus) and oak leaf roundels on a yellow ground partially conceals a womanly *furisode* patterned with bold chysanthemum blossoms. His gesture—one arm raised, the other long sleeve swept forward—conveys a sense of dancelike motion.

The portrait commemorates a dance entitled "Ōshukubai koi no hatsune," performed during the Kabuki play *Uruōtoshi meika no homare* at the Miyako Theater in the eleventh month of 1794. Designed as the right half of a diptych, the print was paired with an image of Nakamura Nakazō II as Saizō Saiwaka, in reality Aramaki Mimishiro Kanetora. For a related work, based on the same play, see Shun'ei's double portrait, no. 60. LA

114　歌川豊国　『役者舞台之姿絵』　「わた屋」　（二代目小左川常世の中﨟尾上）

UTAGAWA TOYOKUNI, 1769–1825

"Wataya" (The actor Osagawa Tsuneyo II as Chūrō Onoe) (*Wataya*)

From *Portraits of Actors on Stage* (Yakusha butai no sugata-e)

1795.1

Woodblock print (*nishiki-e*)

Ōban: H 15½ in. x 10½ in., 39.4 cm x 26.7 cm

Signature: 豊國画　*Toyokuni ga*

Publisher's mark: 泉市版　*Sen'ichi han*

Publisher and firm name: 泉屋市兵衛　*Izumiya Ichibei*; 甘泉堂　*Kansendō*

Selected other impressions: Muzeum Narodowe w Krakowie, cited in Suzuki, no. 35

Published: US 232; GC 148

2005.100.97

The statuesque figure depicted here is the *onnagata* actor Osagawa Tsuneyo II. Standing beneath a blossoming cherry tree, he holds up an orange amulet pouch, normally an item worn under one's clothing. Tsuneyo appears here in the role of Chūrō Onoue, during a performance of *Shimekazari kichirei Soga* at the Kawarazaki Theater during the first month of 1795. An oblong slip of paper used for inscribing poetry dangles from a branch, providing the series title, followed by the actor's guild, Wataya. Originally this print was the left-hand sheet of a triptych with the actors Onoe Matsusuke I at right and Iwai Hanshirō IV at center.

Tsuneyo is dressed in the style of a lady-in-waiting for an elite household. A magnificent outer robe patterned with purple bush clover on a pale gray ground bears the actor's crest of three ivy leaves on its sleeve. A pink sash, tied at the hips, matches the headdress, called *agebōshi*, worn to protect her coiffure. Superbly printed, with embossed cherry blossoms, this impression is exceptionally well preserved.

Completed over the course of two years, from 1794 through 1796,

the prints of the *Actors on the Stage* series bear comparison with the best of Sharaku's *hosoban* actor portraits from the same period. LA

115　歌川豊国　『役者舞台之姿絵』　「あふみや」　（初代中山富三郎のさざ浪辰五郎女房おひで実は安倍貞任宗任妹てりは）

UTAGAWA TOYOKUNI, 1769–1825

"Ōmiya" [The actor Nakayama Tomisaburō I as Ohide, wife of Sazanami Tatsugorō, actually Teriha, younger sister of Abe Sadatō and Abe Munetō] (*Ōmiya*)

From *Portraits of Actors on Stage* (Yakusha butai no sugata-e)

1794.11

Woodblock print (*nishiki-e*)

Ōban: 14¾ in. x 10 in., 37.5 cm x 25.4 cm

Signature: 豊國画　*Toyokuni ga*

Publisher's mark: 泉市版　*Sen'ichi han*

Publisher and firm name: 泉屋市兵衛　*Izumiya Ichibei*; 甘泉堂　*Kansendō*

Censor's mark: 極　*kiwame*

Published: US 167; GC 147

2005.100.98

In this third print from the series *Actors on the Stage*, the *onnagata* actor Nakayama Tomisaburō I plays Ohide, the wife of Sazanami Tatsugorō. As is common in Kabuki, this character has a double identity; in the play she is revealed to be Teriha, younger sister of the twelfth-century warriors Abe Munetō and Abe Sadatō. The play, *Otokoyama o-Edo no ishizue*, was the season's opening performance (*kaomise*) at the Kiri Theater in the eleventh month of 1794.

Toyokuni designed some fifty prints for this series, which was published by Izumiya Ichibei over two years, from 1794 to early 1796. Here, the actors' guild name—in this case Ōmiya—follows the series title in a cartouche at the left. Tomisaburō is identified by the paulownia crest on his bright yellow robe, as well as by his distinctive prominent nose and jutting chin. As in other prints from the series, the figure is highlighted against a pale gray ground, patterned with swirling marks made by the *baren*, a round printing tool applied to the back of the paper.

Sharaku depicted the actor in the same role in a bust portrait print in the Tokyo National Museum collection (LA-11718). LA

116　歌川豊国　三代目坂東彦三郎の富士太郎と二代目中村野塩の今様唄比丘尼

UTAGAWA TOYOKUNI, 1769–1825

The actors Bandō Hikosaburō III as Fujitarō and Nakamura Noshio II as Imayō Utabikuni

1796.9

Woodblock print (*nishiki-e*)

Ōban: 15¼ in. x 10¼ in., 38.7 cm x 26 cm

Signature: 豊國画　*Toyokuni ga*

Publisher's mark: 伝　*den*

Publisher and firm name: unknown

Published: US 57 (B/W); GC 149

2005.100.99

This print, from Toyokuni's series of seven double actor portraits, depicts characters from *Saru nitemo Fuji no utsushie*, a play performed in the ninth month of 1796 at the Miyako Theater. The samurai who holds aloft a wood and paper lantern is Bandō Hikosaburō III in the role of Fujitarō, and his companion is Nakamura Noshio II, playing Imayō Utabikuni, in reality the bodhisattva Samantabhadra. The lantern and Noshio's sedge hat suggest they are travelling by night, so the scene may represent a *michiyuki*—the dance interlude used to depict the journey of a romantically linked couple. Toyokuni captures the moment's drama by showing the couple leaning close together, juxtaposing Hikosaburō's massive form and intense expression with Noshio's sweet face and feminine pose. The colors in this impression are exceptionally well preserved. LA

117　歌川豊国　『風流 芸者身振姿絵』「とらや　虎丸」
UTAGAWA TOYOKUNI, 1769–1825
"Toramaru of the Toraya" (*Toraya Toramaru*)
From *Portraits of Fashionable Geisha Imitating Actors* (*Fūryū geisha miburi sugata-e*)
C. 1798
Woodblock print (*nishiki-e*)
Ōban: 15 in. x 10 in., 38.1 cm x 25.
Signature: 豊國画 *Toyokuni ga*
Publisher's mark: 蔦屋重三郎 *Tsutaya Jūzaburō*
Publisher firm name: 耕書堂 *Kōshodō*
Censor's mark: 極 *kiwame*
Published: GC 150
2005.100.100

This rare print comes from a series with a novel theme: *geisha* impersonating famous Kabuki actors. The player is identified in the square cartouche at upper left as "Toraya" and "Toramaru," both pseudonyms associated with Arashi Ryūzō II (the first is a guild name, or *yago*, the second a poetic name, or *haigo*). Ryūzō II, who died in the eleventh month of 1798, specialized in villain roles. The geisha who entertains an unseen client with her impression plays the role with panache. Pushing up one sleeve, she thrusts her left arm down with fingers splayed, in a gesture that would have been familiar to Ryūzō's many fans. Toyokuni's own *Actors on the Stage* series depicts Ryūzō as Ukiyo Matabei with one out-thrust arm, as do Sharaku's portraits of him as Matabei, and as another character, Otomo Sukune. A well-known *okubi-e* portrait by Sharaku shows Ryūzō with the same signature gesture, roughly pushing up one sleeve in the role of the moneylender Ishibe Kinkichi.

In Toyokuni's playful rendering, the geisha's face mimics Arashi's characteristic features, and her hairpin and comb bear a version of his crest. Her performance is accompanied by a seated geisha playing a *tsutsumi* drum. The pale gray background and standing lamp suggest a nighttime scene in which she performs before a private audience. LA

118　歌川豊国　風呂場
UTAGAWA TOYOKUNI, 1769–1825
The bathhouse
Woodblock print (*nishiki-e*)

Ōban: 15½ in. x 10 in., 39.4 cm x 25.4 cm
Signature: 豊国画 *Toyokuni ga*
Publisher's mark: 鶴屋金助 *Tsuruya Kinsuke*
Publisher firm name: 雙鶴堂 *Sōkakudō*
Selected other impressions: BMFA (21.7747-9); TNM (right: A-10569_5028)
Published: FP 52; US 168–70; GC 152
Ex-collection: Tod and Freeman Ford
Provenance: Judson D. Metzgar
2005.100.101.1-.3

119　歌川豊国　「江戸芝居三階之圖」
UTAGAWA TOYOKUNI, 1769–1825
"The Third Floor of a Theater in Edo" (*Edo shibai sankai no zu*)
Woodblock print (*nishiki-e*)
Ōban: 14⅝ in. x 10 in., 37.1 cm x 25.4 cm
Signature: 豊國画 *Toyokuni ga*
Publisher's mark: 三 *Mi*
Publisher name: 三河屋清右衛門 *Mikawaya Seiemon*
Censor's mark: 極 *kiwame*
Selected other impressions: TNM (A-10569_2468); TSH (豊国 34)
Published: GC 151
2005.100.102.1-.3

Edo period theaters were subject to size restrictions, with most exteriors limited to two stories. Inside, however, the space was divided into first floor, second-floor mezzanine, and a third floor of dressing rooms, including a large communal space that could be used for gatherings of the type shown here.

The eleven actors represented in this triptych are all celebrities of the late 1790s. They have been identified as: (from right) Sawamura Gennosuke I (Sōjūrō IV), writing on a fan; Sawamura Tōzō I, holding a pipe; Ichikawa Omezō I, holding a Western-style wine glass; the *onnagata* actor Iwai Kumesaburō I (Hanshirō V), also with a pipe; Bandō Hikosaburō III, gesturing to his right; Bandō Mitsugorō III, standing with an unidentified actor behind him; Ichikawa Danjūrō VII, the short man; Onoe Eizaburō I (Kikugorō III), seated with a scroll; Matsumoto Kōshirō V, wearing a checked robe; and Nakayama Tomisaburō I, costumed as a female character.[31]

A variety of accessories completes this behind-the-scenes view, including two lines of makeup mirrors on wooden stands, with braziers, covered basins, makeup jars, and brushes. A wig on a stand, covered swords, and robes also hang ready to hand. At the right a red lacquered tray holds the makings of a meal for the actors — a platter of fish and noodles ready to be simmered in a broth-filled pot. LA

120　歌川豊広　ほととぎすを聞く美人
UTAGAWA TOYOHIRO, 1773-1828
Woman listening to a cuckoo
Woodblock print (*nishiki-e*)
Vertical *ōban* diptych: 29¾ in. x 9¾ in., 75.6 cm x 24.8 cm
Signature: 豊廣画 *Toyohiro ga*

31　Hiraki, 9.

Published: G-J vol. 3, 78; GC 153
Collector's seal: 白爾叟 *Hakujisō* or *Berusō*? (verso)
2005.100.103

A slender beauty pauses on a balcony, round fan in one hand, as a cuckoo wings through the air. In classical court poetry the cuckoo is a harbinger of summer, its distinctive cry heard first in the fifth month of the year. Here the cuckoo appears with its beak open in song, amid what appears to be an early-morning mist. Wearing her nightclothes, the beauty is either on her way to bed or has just arisen. The warmth of the day is suggested by her fan, and by her unlined blue robe, decorated with delicate white orchid sprigs showered over the hem. This sheer fabric is layered over a plain white layer and loosely tied with a wide red sash tie-dyed with a pattern of small white circles.

The composition is spread over two upright sheets of *ōban*-sized paper, a format newly popular in the early nineteenth century. Toyohiro produced just a few such upright diptychs of beauties, two examples of which may be found in the Museum of Fine Arts, Boston collection (one shows a woman boarding a roofed boat and the other a woman carrying a candle). The Grabhorn print has some horizontal creases, suggesting that it may once have been mounted as a hanging scroll, but it still preserves much of its original brilliant color. LA

---

121   昇亭北寿 『東都』 「両国之風景」
SHŌTEI HOKUJU, active 1789–1818
"View of Ryōgoku Bridge" (*Ryōgoku no fūkei*)
From *The Eastern Capital* (Tōto)
Woodblock print (*nishiki-e*)
Ōban: 10⅜ in. x 15¼ in., 26.4 cm x 38.7 cm
Signature: 昇亭北寿画 *Shōtei Hokuju ga*
Publisher's mark: 永寿板 *Eiju han*
Publisher and firm name: 西村屋与八 *Nishimuraya Yohachi;* 永寿堂 *Eijudō*
Censor's mark: 極 *kiwame*
Selected other impressions: BMFA (11.2277, RES.54.183); MET (JP1409); BM (1926,0616,0.1); LEI (3930-15); TS, cited in Naito 2009, no. 219
Published: G.Land 27; GC 142
2005.100.104

Prints of the famous sites of Edo became popular among print buyers in the first decades of the nineteenth century. This urban landscape shows a view from the west bank of the Sumida River across the Ryōgoku Bridge. The towering structure in the foreground is a mat-covered stall used for side-shows including exotic animals, curiosities, circus performances, and acrobats. A second tower appears on the far side of the river, beside the roof of Ekō'in, a memorial temple dedicated to those who perished in the Great Meireki Fire of 1657 — and also the site of sumo matches in the Edo period. A bustling crowd fills the shopping and entertainment district at the base of the bridge, while pleasure boats float past on the river. Here and there parasols ward off the heat of a summer afternoon.

A student of Hokusai, Hokuju was active during the Bunka

era (1804–1817). Several aspects of the print point to his familiarity with Western copperplate engravings available in Japan at that time: the low horizon; the expansive, mist-streaked sky and puffy white clouds; his use of two-point perspective (in the bridge); the shadows cast by the buildings, boats, and figures; and the scratchy parallel lines of the stall roofs, which imitate the look of cross-hatching and engraved lines.

Printed in relief against a pale blue sky, the clouds here are unusually well defined relative to other impressions, such as those in the British Museum and Museum of Fine Arts, Boston. This may be an instance of a later state using recarved blocks. LA

---

122   柳々居辰斎 『近江八景』 「唐崎夜雨」
RYŪRYŪKYO SHINSAI, 1764?–1820
"Night Rain at Karazaki" (*Karazaki no yau*)
From *Eight Views of Ōmi* (Ōmi hakkei)
Woodblock print (*nishiki-e*)
Ōban: 10 in. x 14½ in., 25.4 cm x 36.8 cm
Signature: 柳々居辰齋寫 *Ryūryūkyo shinsai utsusu*
Censor's mark: 極 *kiwame*
Published: GC 143
2005.100.105

The Karasaki pine appears like a verdant mountain, rising on wooden stilts from the waters of Lake Biwa. A slender peninsula leads a traveler to this marvel, where a Shinto shrine gateway and wooden fence mark the sanctity of the ancient tree. As appropriate for the theme, "Night Rain at Karasaki," storm clouds and slanting rain stand out against a pale gray sky.

The series title *Eight Views of Ōmi* refers to eight scenic places in Ōmi Province, today known as Shiga Prefecture. The set emerged as a poetic theme by the early seventeenth century, and was a popular print subject throughout the rest of the Edo period. Shinsai's *Ōmi hakkei* series is one of several published in the 1810s and 1820s using techniques learned from imported European engravings. Western elements include the low, rounded horizon, which suggests the curvature of the earth; the sense of recession along the curving shore; the use of shading; the layered clouds in the sky; the distinctive shapes of the foreground trees; and the picture frame at the margins of the print. While acknowledging Western custom, Shinsai adapts the picture frame to Japanese taste with a decoration of scattered cherry blossoms. LA

---

123   八島岳亭 『浪華名所天保山勝景一覧』 「大阪天保山夕立の景」
YASHIMA GAKUTEI, 1786?–1868
"View of an Afternoon Downpour at Mt. Tenpō in Osaka" (*Ōsaka Tenpōzan yūdachi no kei*)
From *Famous Places in Osaka: Scenic Views of Mt. Tenpō* (Naniwa meisho Tenpōzan shōkei ichiran)
1834
Woodblock print (*nishiki-e*)
Ōban: 9⅞ in. x 14½ in., 25.1 cm x 36.8 cm

Signature: 五岳　Gogaku
Publisher and firm name: 塩屋喜助　*Shioya Kisuke;* 興文
堂　*Kyōbundō*
Selected other impressions: BM (1931,0427,0.10); Oberlin
(1950.485); TIK (P-U 286); HMA (22048); Vever, cited in
Hillier 1976, cat. 792
Published: G.Land 30; GC 144
2005.100.106

Gakutei trained under Totoya Hokkei (1780–1850), one of
Katsukisha Hokusai's best students, and he may also have studied
for a time under Hokusai himself. Best known for his designs
for the privately published prints known as *surimono*, and as the
author of light verse and fiction, Gakutei's sole excursion into
landscape is the remarkable series *Scenic Views of Mt. Tenpō.*
Published in Osaka in 1834, the series celebrated a new regional
showplace for the area. Three years earlier, Mt. Tenpō came into
being when workers dredging the Aji River for flood preven-
tion and improved access started to create an artificial mountain
above the harbor. Planted with pine and cherry trees, and boast-
ing teahouses and other attractions, the area quickly became a
popular holiday destination.

Mt. Tenpō's tripartite peak, nicknamed "Landmark Mountain,"
rises in the print above a long breakwater lined with pine trees.
Dark storm clouds emit a driving rain, as a rough sea threatens to
engulf a ship identified as the Daitō Maru. Heaving on the full sail,
the sailors on board steer the ship to safety. In its tightly ordered
composition and theatrical intensity, this scene rivals Hokusai's
best efforts.

The print has been trimmed at the left, right, and bottom edges. LA

___

124　八島岳亭　『浪華名所天保山勝景一覧』　「天保山末
広橋月夜の図」
YASHIMA GAKUTEI, 1786?–1868
"Moonlit night at the Suehiro Bridge at Mt. Tenpō" (*Tenpōzan
Suehirobashi tsukiyo no zu*)
From *Famous Places in Osaka: Scenic Views of Mt. Tenpō* (*Naniwa
meisho Tenpōzan shōkei ichiran*)
1834
Woodblock print (*nishiki-e*)
Ōban: 10 in. x 14½ in., 25.4 cm x 36.8 cm
Publisher and firm name: 塩屋喜助　*Shioya Kisuke;* 興文
堂　*Kyōbundō*
Selected other impressions: MET (JP1412); BM (1907,1018,0.243);
KANS (1928.7595); Honolulu (14545)
Published: GC 145
2005.100.107

In this second print from the series *Scenic Views of Mt. Tenpō*
(see no. 123), Gakutei offers a close-up view of merrymakers on
their way to sample the delights of Osaka's newest entertainment district. The river is calm, and an enormous full moon
rises in the night sky, as a roofed pleasure boat bearing a man
and two female companions is poled beneath Suehiro Bridge.
Gnarled pine branches frame the scene, enhancing the dramatic
perspective of the sharply rising prow and the curving timbers

underneath the bridge. A simple palette of bright yellow, green,
brown, and gray effectively unifies these elements, which fit
together like the pieces of an interlocking puzzle.

The Suehiro Bridge marked the northern entry into a network
of channels surrounding Mt. Tenpō. According to Timothy Clark,
the 1835 illustrated gazetteer *Famous Views of Mt. Tenpō* (*Tenpōan
meisho zue*) commented on its unusual construction, which apparently lacked the supporting pillars shown in this print.[32] LA

___

125　歌川国貞　『役者はんじもの』　五代目岩井半四郎
UTAGAWA KUNISADA, 1786–1865
Iwai Hanshirō V
From *Actor Rebuses* (Yakusha hanjimono)
1812.6
Woodblock print (*nishiki-e*)
Ōban: 15½ in. x 10¼ in., 39.4 cm x 26 cm
Signature: 五渡亭國貞画　*Gototei Kunisada ga*
Publisher's mark: mark of 西村屋与八　*Nishimuraya Yohachi*
Publisher firm name: 永寿堂　*Eijudō*
Censor's mark: 極　*kiwame* and 山口　*Yamaguchi* (山口屋藤兵
衛　Yamaguchiya Tōbei)
Selected other impressions: BMFA (11.22316, 11.42329)
Published: GC 162
2005.100.109

The Grabhorn Collection includes two examples from Kunisada's
early series of actor portraits with rebuses (visual puns). Above a bust
portrait of the *onnagata* star Iwai Hanshirō V in the role of a maid, a
pink bean-shaped cartouche contains a three-part rebus identifying
the actor. The first part of the actor's name, *Iwai*, is rendered as a girl
riding on a man's shoulder in the *obitoki iwai*, a ceremony celebrat-
ing the girl's first wearing of an obi around age seven. To the left is a
hanko, or signature seal, supplying the sound *han*, and a white (*shiro*)
rabbit provides the two final syllables, *shi* and *ro*. For good measure,
only half the rabbit is shown: in Japanese *han* also means "half."

To the left of the cartouche is a money box with the word
kinsenryō (1,000 gold *ryō* coins) written on its lid. Not coinciden-
tally, *senryō* (1,000 *ryō*) was a term used during the Edo period to
denote the most popular actors, whose salary was said to exceed
1,000 *ryō* per year. Edo urbanites took great pleasure in decipher-
ing clever visual puns of the sort provided by this print. LA

___

126　歌川国貞　『役者はんじもの』　三代目坂東三津五郎
UTAGAWA KUNISADA, 1786–1865
Bandō Mitsugorō III
From *Actor Rebuses* (Yakusha hanjimono)
1812.6
Woodblock print (*nishiki-e*)
Ōban: 10⅜ in. x 15¼ in., 26.4 cm x 38.7 cm
Signature: 五渡亭國貞画　*Gototei Kunisada ga*
Publisher's mark: 西村屋与八　*Nishimuraya Yohachi*
Publisher firm name: 永寿堂　*Eijudō*

___

32　www.britishmuseum.org (webpage for 1907,1018,0.243).

Censor's mark: 極 *kiwame* and 山口 *Yamaguchi* (山口屋藤兵衛 *Yamaguchiya Tōbei*)
Selected other impressions: BMFA (11.22314, 11.42327)
Published: GC 163
2005.100.110

In this second print from the *Actor Rebuses* series, Kunsiada presents the actor Bandō Mitsugorō III in the role of Kudō Saemon Suketsune in the play *Haru no komaikioi Soga*. The cartouche shows a clerk, or *bantō* working an abacus, and two dots (*dakuten*) above his shoulder denote the correct reading, changing *bantō* to *bandō*, the first part of this actor's name. To the left are crests of flowering quince, the emblem of Soga brothers Gorō and Jūrō, heroic twelfth-century warriors and Suketsune's cousins. Further narrowing the reading are butterflies, specifically associated with Gorō. Since there are three (*mitsu*) of these Gorō emblems, this part of the rebus can be read as Mitsugorō. As in the previous example, a box with the words "1,000 gold *ryō* (coins)" points to the high salaries achieved by such popular actors during the Edo period. In the print Mitsugorō wears a warrior's formal attire, consisting of a vest with wing-like shoulders (*kataginu*) and a magnificent peacock-feather pattern, worn over a cloud-patterned *kosode*. LA

---

127   歌川豊重　『名勝八景』「大山夜雨　従前不動頂上の圖」
UTAGAWA TOYOSHIGE (Toyokuni II, 1777–1835)
"Night Rain over Ōyama: View of the Summit of the Former Fudō Temple" (*Ōyama yau juzen Fudō chōjō no kei*)
From *Eight Views of Scenic Places* (Meishō hakkei)
C. 1833–1834
Woodblock print (*nishiki-e*)
Ōban: 9⅝ in. x 14½ in., 24.4 cm x 36.8 cm
Signature: 豊國筆 *Toyokuni hitsu*
Artist's seal: 歌川 *Utagawa*
Publisher's mark: 林 *Iseya Rihan; Kinjudō Hayashi*
Publisher and firm name: 伊勢屋利兵衛 *Iseya Rihei*; 錦樹堂 *Kinjudō*
Censor's mark: 極 *kiwame*
Selected other impressions: MET (JP1416); BM (1907,0531,0,514); Oberlin (1950.507)
Published: G.Land 131; GC 154
Ex-collection: Tod and Freeman Ford
Provenance: Judson D. Metzgar
2005.100.108

Toyokuni II's memorable "Night Rain over Ōyama: View of the Summit of the Former Fudō Temple" is one of a set of eight prints depicting famous places in Kanagawa Prefecture. Mt. Ōyama lies at the southwest end of the Tanzawa mountain range, where frequent rain and mist conferred on it the nickname "Rainfall Mountain" (Afuriyama). An ancient sacred site, Ōyama has both a Buddhist temple at its base, and a Shinto shrine atop the summit. Steep stone stairways lead from Ōyama-dera, dedicated to the esoteric Buddhist deity Fudō Myōō, to Afuri Jinja, where the Shinto deity Sekison Daigongen is enshrined.

A popular pilgrimage site throughout the Edo period, the mountain was thronged with religious devotees during the three-month period each year when climbing to the peak was permitted. In the print, Ōyama is shown in the midst of a torrential downpour. A few hardy pilgrims have already ascended to a point above the rooftop of the temple gate; farther up a few others, led by a man carrying a symbolic wooden sword (*ōkitachi*), climb toward the lower shrine. The main shrine buildings are just visible at the top of the mountain, high above. At the left, shrouded in mist, is the familiar conical peak of Mt. Fuji. LA

---

128   歌川国貞　「二見浦曙の圖」
UTAGAWA KUNISADA, 1786–1865
"Dawn at Futamigaura" (*Futamigaura akebono no zu*)
From an untitled series of landscapes
C. 1832
Woodblock print (*nishiki-e*)
Ōban: 10¼ in. x 15 in., 26 cm x 38.1 cm
Signature: 香蝶國貞画 *Kōchō Kunisada ga*
Artist's seal: 五渡亭 *Gototei*; 国貞 *Kunisada*
Publisher's mark: ト *To*
Publisher and firm name: 山口屋藤兵衛 *Yamaguchiya Tōbei*; 錦耕堂 *Kinkōdō*
Censor's mark: 極 *kiwame*
Selected other impressions: BMFA (06. 2539, 46.1400); HMA (14446); MET (JP1497); KANS (1928.7755); BAUR (G275)
Published: G-J vol. 9, no. 2; GC 164
2005.100.111

The "wedded rocks" of Futamigaura, in Mie Prefecture, are identified with Izanagi and Izanami, the progenitor couple in Japanese mythology. Joining them is the thick straw rope, or *shimenawa*, used to demarcate a Shinto sacred space. Thus connected, the rocks form a gateway to nearby Futami Okitama Shrine. In Kunisada's somewhat fanciful rendering of the scene, the rocks tower above the beach at low tide, dwarfing several travelers who have arrived just in time to see the famous sight of the sun rising between them. Two palanquins rest at the taller rock's base, and lanterns mark their journey through the night. Farther along the shore to the right, two silhoutted figures gesture toward the sunrise.

Kunisada's study of Western engravings is evident in several aspects of the design: the rays of the sun, reserved against the dark night sky and fanned out in one-point perspective; the low horizon line; and the parallel strokes used to shade the rocks and distant hills. The print is from an untitled seres of ten published by Yamaguchiya Tōbei around 1832, at a time of great popularity for landscape prints. Designed in related pairs, the series includes an image of abalone divers at Ise, a site located close by Futamigaura. LA

---

129   歌川国芳　『東都富士見三十六景』「新大はし橋下の眺望」
UTAGAWA KUNIYOSHI, 1797–1861
"View of Mt. Fuji from Beneath the Shin Ōhashi Bridge" (*Shin Ōhashi kyōka no chōbō*)
From *Thirty-six Views of Mt. Fuji Seen from the Eastern Capital* (Tōto Fujimi sanjūrokkei)

C. 1844
Woodblock print (*nishiki-e*)
Ōban: 9⅝ in. x 14⅜ in., 24.4 cm x 36.5 cm
Signature: 一勇齋國芳画 *Ichiyūsai Kuniyoshi ga*
Artist's seal: arabesque
Publisher's mark: 村田 *Murata*
Publisher and firm name: 村田屋次郎兵衛 *Murataya Jirōbei;* 栄
邑堂 *Eiyūdō*
Censor's mark: 極 *kiwame*
Selected other impressions: BMFA (11.24947); HMA (16437);
TNM (A-10569_852); Oberlin (1950.571); V&A (E.2266-
1909); ŌTA, cited in ŌTA 1988, no. 116.
Published: GC 155
2005.100.112

The success of Katsushika Hokusai's series *Thirty-six Views of
Mt. Fuji* in the 1830s led to the publication of several other sets
featuring novel views of the iconic peak. Kuniyoshi's entry in this
category, entitled *Thirty-six Views of Mt. Fuji Seen from the Eastern Capital,* was begun in 1844, but only five of the prints were
completed. This one features a view from the Sumida River, where
the mountain peak is dwarfed by the enormous supporting piers
of Shin Ōhashi bridge. A small barge floats underneath the bridge,
heading downstream toward Eitai Bridge, just visible at far left.
Focused on their work, neither boatman seems to notice Fuji. One
stands lookout over a man-made "mountain" of cargo while the
other guides the boat through the narrow channel. Beyond dense
reeds is a glimpse of the white-walled warehouses that line the opposite shore.

This impression lacks two birds and a *kyōka* verse by Banshōtei
Gyokuga (or Tamaka), found in the sky in most other published
examples. The European-style title cartouche Kuniyoshi used
for the series is based on the emblem held by an angel in "Batavia" from Johan Nieuhof's *Voyages and Travels to the East Indies*
(*Gedenkwaerdige zee en lantreize door de voornaemste landschappen
van West-en Oostindiën*). This popular scientific book published in
Amsterdam in 1682 was imported to Japan in the 1700s. LA

---

130   歌川国芳　『東都名所』「するがだひ」
UTAGAWA KUNIYOSHI, 1797–1861
"Suruga Hill" (*Surugadai*)
From *Famous Places in the Eastern Capital* (*Tōto meisho*)
Early 1830s
Woodblock print (*nishiki-e*)
Ōban: 9¾ in. x 14½ in., 24.8 cm x 36.8 cm
Signature: 一勇斉国芳画 *Ichiyūsai Kuniyoshi ga*
Publisher's mark: 吉, 両国, 加ゞ屋 *Kichi, Ryōgoku, Kagaya*
Publisher and firm name: 加賀屋吉右衛門 *Kagaya Kichiemon;*
青盛堂 *Seiseidō*
Censor's mark: 極 *kiwame*
Selected other impressions: BMFA (11.16010), HMA (14253,
16429), BM (2008,3037.03603), Oberlin (1950.532)
Published: GC 156
2005.100.113

This scene from a series of eight views of the "Eastern Capital"

(Edo) shows the hilly district of Surugadai, home during the Edo
period to many samurai officials. One such resident walks along
an embankment above the Kanda River, wearing a long raincoat at
the end of the rainshower. His attendant rests a folded umbrella on
his shoulder, and an approaching youth tilts his umbrella to shed
drops of water. Surrounded by scenery that glows in the late afternoon light, all three figures gaze at a rainbow that arcs across the
river valley. Local details that enhance the sense of place include
the Kanda aqueduct, spanning the river at one end, and the outer
wall of Yushima Seidō, a worship hall dedicated to Confucius, visible at the top of the hill on the right.

Western elements include the shading used to model the figure's
costumes and the grassy slope, and the green bamboo frame drawn
around the picture. This impression lacks a distinctive crack mark in
the gray block used for the sky, found in many other examples, and
the vibrant coloring of the foliage, in four shades of green, is also
unusual. Only faint traces of color remain in the rainbow. LA

---

131   歌川国芳　『東都名所』「大森」
UTAGAWA KUNIYOSHI, 1797–1861
[Gathering seaweed at] "Ōmori" (*Ōmori*)
From *Famous Places in the Eastern Capital* (*Tōto meisho*)
Early 1830s
Woodblock print (*nishiki-e*)
Ōban: 9¾ in. x 14⅝ in., 24.8 cm x 37.1 cm
Signature: 一勇齋國芳画 *Ichiyūsai Kuniyoshi ga*
Publisher's mark: 吉, 両国, 加ゞ屋 *Kichi, Ryōgoku, Kagaya*
Publisher and firm name: 加賀屋吉右衛門 *Kagaya Kichiemon;*
青盛堂 *Seiseidō*
Censor's mark: 極 *kiwame*
Selected other impressions: BMFA (11.16004); MET (JP2857);
BM (2008,3037.03601; 1914,0217,0.4?); Oberlin (1950.533);
TNM (A-10569_2533); CLV (1985.335); KANS (1928.0995);
BRU, cited in Nagata 2008, no. 258; Guimet, cited in ŌTA
2007, no. 170); Vever, cited in Hillier 1976, no. 830
Published: GC 157
2005.100.114

Kuniyoshi was at the height of his powers when he designed
the eight landscapes of the series "Famous Places in the Eastern
Capital." Each design evokes a particular mood, time of day, and
place in scenes combining skillful two-dimensional designs with
perspective techniques adapted from European engravings. Here
he takes us out on Edo Bay at Ōmori, south of Shinagawa, where
a skiff holding two women floats beside a bed of upright branches.
Inserted into the bay's gentle current, the branches were used to
cultivate the seaweed that was harvested in winter, then dried to
make *Asakusa nori*, a famous Edo product. One of the women
plucks seaweed from a branch with special chopsticks, as the other
uses a rake to gently lift strands into a basket. Another boat is just
visible beyond a second cultivation bed on the right. In the chill
morning air, a band of pink dawn light lingers at the horizon.
Wispy clouds are printed in layers using the *ita bokashi* method, in
which the edges of the block are softened through abrasion then
applied with pigment to achieve gradations of color. The reeds are
printed in green and black linear patterns over an area shaded from

pale tan to brown. Together with the distant horizon and floating clouds, they help to convey a sense of deep space. LA

---

132 歌川国芳 「忠臣蔵十一段目夜討之圖」
UTAGAWA KUNIYOSHI, 1797–1861
Chūshingura, Act XI: Night Attack (Chūshingura *jūichi danme youchi no zu*)
Early 1830s
Woodblock print (*nishiki-e*)
Ōban: 10½ in. x 15 in., 26.7 cm x 38.1 cm
Signature: 一勇齋國芳画 *Ichiyūsai Kuniyoshi ga*
Selected other impressions: HMA (16426); YALE (38130); Oberlin (1950.545); TNM (A-10569_2542); TIK (P-U 310); V&A (E.2590-1962); Riese (no. 32); Guimet, cited in ŌTA 2007, no. 168
Published: G.Land 35; GC 160
2005.100.115

One of the most popular Kabuki plays of all time, *Chūshingura* was based on the story of a vendetta from the early 1700s. The tale concerns a group of loyal retainers who set out to avenge the forced suicide of their lord. Because of censorship laws banning current events from the stage, the play, which debuted in 1748, was set in a much earlier era, and the names of the warriors were changed. The moment shown here is the penultimate one in the play, when, after years of plotting and waiting, the retainers sneak into the mansion of Kō Moronō, the man they hold responsible for their lord's death. On a silent night, their footsteps muffled by snow, the men are directed by Ōboshi Yuranosuke to scale the wall and enter the compound. A full moon lights their way.

Of the many versions of this scene created in the nineteenth century, this is perhaps the most unusual. Kuniyoshi based his design closely on an illustration of houses in Batavia in Johan Nieuhof's *Voyages and Travels to the East Indies* (*Gedenkwaerdige zee en lant-reize door de voornamste landschappen van West en Oostindien*), a scientific book published in Amsterdam in 1682. Kuniyoshi borrowed not only the shape and linear perspective of the buildings, but also the pose of Yuranosuke, the form of a running dog, and the shadows cast upon the ground by these and other figures. This is the second state, lacking the red light beam that shines from the lantern held at right in some versions. LA

---

133 歌川国芳 『東都』 「御厩川岸之図」
UTAGAWA KUNIYOSHI, 1797–1861
"Onmaya Embankment" (*Onmayagashi no zu*)
From *The Eastern Capital* (Tōto)
early 1830s
Woodblock print (*nishiki-e*)
Ōban: 10⅛ in. x 14½ in., 25.7 cm x 36.8 cm
Signature: 一勇齋國芳画 *Ichiyūsai Kuniyoshi ga*
Artist's seal: *toshidama*
Publisher's mark: 山口版 *Yamaguchi han*
Publisher and firm name: 山口屋藤兵衛 *Yamaguchiya Tōbei;* 錦耕堂 *Kinkōdō*
Selected other impressions: BMFA (45.650); HMA (14554);

TNM (A-10569_850); Oberlin (1950.547); LOC FP 2 – JDP, no. 50; Vever, cited in Hillier, no. 825
Published: G.Land 34; GC 158
2005.100.116

The Onmaya riverbank is the scene of a torrential afternoon downpour. Sheets of rain hit the ground with percussive force, filling the road with mud; drops of water ricochet off the umbrella at the left. So dense is the mist that only silhouettes are visible on the opposite shore.

Of the five men who make their way along the embankment, only the man at the center seems resigned to the weather. A metal hoop on the end of his pole tells us that he is an eel catcher. A second man to the right carries a large umbrella emblazoned with the insignia of the print's publisher, Yamaguchiya Tōbei. Written on it is the number 1,861, which some scholars interpret as a boastful claim about the number of Yamaguchiya's publications. Given that the man carries three more folded umbrellas under his arm, he may be the agent of an umbrella rental firm hurrying to make a delivery.

At left, three more men huddle together under a single umbrella, the sandals of one tucked into his sash, safe from the mud below. Their umbrella advertises a second business, the Yamatoya, located in Yanagishima. A ferry is silhouetted in the water at the left, so the men may be coming and going from the landing.

Like the puffy clouds and the realistic effect of rain striking the ground, the heavily shaded robes and tangled, muscular limbs of figures at the left show the artist's inspired adaptation of Western models. A second state of this print lacks the darker *bokashi* band seen here across the middle of the river. LA

---

134 歌川国芳 『東都』 「三つ股の圖」
UTAGAWA KUNIYOSHI, 1797–1861
"Mitsumata" (*Mitsumata no zu*)
From *The Eastern Capital* (Tōto)
Early 1830s
Woodblock print (*nishiki-e*)
Ōban: 10⅛ in. x 14½ in., 25.7cm x 36.8 cm
Signature: 一勇齋國芳画 *Ichiyūsai Kuniyoshi ga*
Artist's seal: *toshidama*
Publisher's mark: 山口版 *Yamaguchi han*
Publisher and firm name: 山口屋藤兵衛 *Yamaguchiya Tōbei;* 錦耕堂 *Kinkōdō*
Selected other impressions: BMFA (11.2266); BMFA (54.308); MET (JP2858); Guimet, cited in ŌTA 2007, no. 171; HMA (23307)
Published: GC 159
2005.100.117

A smoke plume rises from the fire that two carpenters use to scorch the wooden hull of a fishing boat. Called *funatade,* the treatment helps to safeguard the timbers from decay and insect infestations. Carefully shaded brown smoke plumes wafting across the sky skillfully evoke the effect of vapor dispersed by a breeze.

The setting for this charming scene is Mitsumata, where the Onagi tributary joins the Sumida River. Past Eitai Bridge, at the right, are the masts of boats at the Tsukadajima fishing port in Edo Bay. The tiny scale of the Mannen Bridge, houses, and warehouses lining the opposite shore conveys a sense of the river's breadth.

For all that this is local scenery, familiar to residents of Edo, this picture is also infused with Western elements: thin even outlines defining the smoke, free-form floating clouds layered above a low horizon line, and a foreshortened view of the fishing boat to left of center reveal the artist's experimental use of techniques acquired through study of Western engravings. LA

135　歌川国芳　『高祖御一代略圖』「佐州塚原雪中」
UTAGAWA KUNIYOSHI, 1797–1861
"In the Snow at Tsukahara on Sado Island" (*Sashū Tsukahara setchū*)
From *Concise Illustrated History of the Founder of the Nichiren Sect* (*Kōso goichidai ryakuzu*)
C. 1835
Woodblock print (*nishiki-e*)
Ōban: 9⅝ in. x 14⅜ in., 24.4 cm x 36.5 cm
Signature: 一勇齋國芳画　*Ichiyūsai Kuniyoshi ga*
Artist's seal: *toshidama* (within a square)
Publisher's mark: 林　*Hayashi*
Publisher and firm name: 伊勢屋利兵衛　*Iseya Rihei*; 錦樹堂　*Kinjudō*
Censor's mark: 極　*kiwame*
Selected other impressions: BM (2008,3037.12110; 1908,0616,0.175); BAUR (G365); V&A (E.2590-1962); Vever, cited in Hillier 1976, no. 836
Published: GC 161
Collector's seal: unidentified (*Unki?*)
2005.100.118

A monk in red struggles up a steep slope, sinking with each step deep into the snow. Next to him a bare tree, twisted by the weather, echoes his solitary perseverance. By contrast the houses lining the nearby shore seem huddled together for warmth, as a heavy snow fills the evening sky. The printer's art is evident in both the subtle shading of the water, hills, and sky, and in the snowflakes, which combine printed dots and specks of *gofun* (ground shell) spattered from a brush.

The subject of this remarkable design is Nichiren (1222–1282), founder of the Buddhist sect bearing his name. Kuniyoshi, himself a fervent follower, created a series of ten prints commemorating the founder's life for the 550th anniversary of his death. This scene shows Nichiren in Tsukahara on Sado Island, where he spent the years from 1271 to 1274 in exile. Nichiren's isolation on the desolate hillside alludes to a period when he was abandoned by most of his followers; his steadfast pose echoes the strength he summoned to compose an important treatise, *Kaimokusho*, at Konponji temple in Tsukuhara.

Two versions of this print exist, with and without a horizon line. Scholars disagree as to which is the first state. Robert Schaap notes that a break in the outline at the left edge of the print is often filled in later, as is the case in this impression.[33] LA

33　Schaap, 188.

136　渓斎英泉　『木曽街道』「續ノ壹　日本橋雪之曙」
"Station No. 1, Snowy Dawn at Nihonbashi" (*Tsuzuki no ichi Nihonbashi yuki no akebono*)
From *Kisokaidō* (Kisokaidō)
Woodblock print (*nishiki-e*)
Ōban: 9½ in. x 14⅜ in., 24.1 cm x 36.5 cm
1835
Signature: 英泉画　*Eisen ga*
Publisher's mark: 竹内　*Takenouchi*; 保永堂版　*Hōeidō han*
Publisher and firm name: 竹内孫八　*Takenouchi Magohachi*; 保永堂　*Hōeidō*
Selected other impressions: BMFA (11.25640, 21.4792, 21.4793); HMA (15586, 15587); BM (1906,1220,0.957); Oberlin (1950.849); KANS (1928.7835); LEI (2751-1); ŌTA, cited in ŌTA 1988, no. 113
Published: GC 179
2005.100.119

Eisen deftly captures the bustling atmosphere of a cold winter morning on Nihonbashi Bridge in the center of Edo. Two red-cheeked women stop to converse as the sun rises over the river, which is lined on both sides with a succession of snow-covered warehouses. Stripped almost bare to heave a towering cart across the bridge, two laborers provide a striking contrast to travelers—a monk and samurai among others—who are bundled against the frigid air. At the bridge's base, the morning fish market is in full swing: a porter hefts a basket of horse mackerel to his shoulder, another man balances two giant tuna on a pole, and a clerk peers at his ledge amid baskets piled with flounder and shellfish.

Eisen and Utagawa Hiroshige (1797–1858) both contributed prints to the *Kisokaidō* series, which documents sights along the northern route between Edo and Kyoto. (Eisen made twenty-four prints, Hiroshige the other forty-six, for a complete set of seventy.) It was released on the heels of Hiroshige's success with the *53 Stations of the Tōkaidō Road* series, also published by Takenouchi Magohachi (Hōeidō). Takenouchi took the opportunity to advertise his role by putting his name and address on the umbrella at the center of this opening print of the *Kisokaidō* series (see detail below). LA

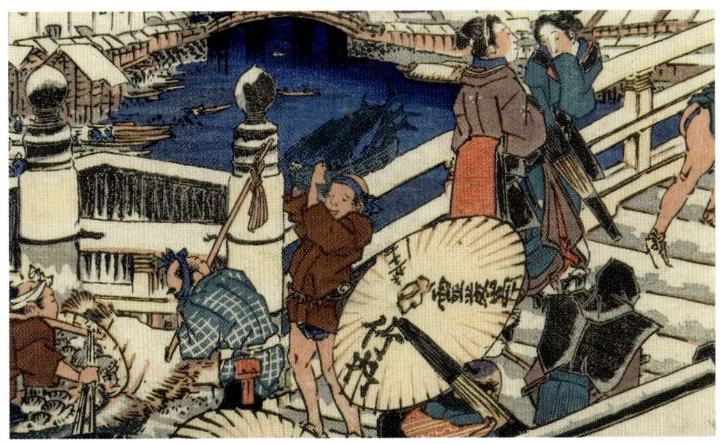

Abbreviations

*These abbreviations appear in the "Selected Impressions" and
"Published" fields in the catalogue entries, beginning on p. 150.*

COLLECTIONS

ASH: Ashmolean Museum of Art & Archaeology, University of Oxford
BAUR: Baur Foundation, Museum of Far Eastern Art, Geneva
BER: Museum für Ostasiatische Kunst, Berlin
BM: British Museum, London
BMFA: Museum of Fine Arts, Boston
BN: Bibliothèque Nationale de France, Paris
BRK: Brooklyn Museum
BRU: Musées Royaux d'Art et d'Histoire, Brussels
CHI: Art Institute of Chicago
CHIBA: Chiba-shi Bijutsukan, Chiba
CLV: Cleveland Museum of Art
Guimet: Musée Guimet, Paris
HMA: Honolulu Museum of Art, Honolulu
HU: Harvard Art Museums, Cambridge, MA
JUM: Japan Ukiyo-e Museum, Matsumoto
KANS: Spencer Museum of Art, University of Kansas, Lawrence, KS
LEI: Museum Volkenkunde, Leiden
LOC: Library of Congress, Washington, DC
LOH: Legion of Honor, Fine Arts Museums of San Francisco
MET: Metropolitan Museum of Art, New York
MIA: Minneapolis Institute of Arts
NAM: Nelson-Atkins Museum of Art, Kansas City
NYPL: New York Public Library
Oberlin: Allen Memorial Art Museum, Oberlin College, Oberlin, OH
ŌTA: Ōta Kinen Bijutsukan, Tokyo
Rieder: Collection Rieder, Basel
ROM: Royal Ontario Museum, Toronto
Schindler: Ex-collection Werner Schindler, Geneva
TTCT: Tōkyō Toritsu Chūō Toshokan (Tokyo Metropolitan Central Library), Tokyo
TIK: Tikotin Museum of Japanese Art, Haifa
TNM: Tōkyō Kokuritsu Hakubutsukan (Tokyo National Museum)
TS: Takahashi Seiichirō Collection, Toyko
TSH: Tabako to Shio no Hakubutsukan, Tokyo
V&A: Victoria & Albert Museum, London
Van Vleck: The E. B. Van Vleck Collection of Japanese Prints, Chazen Museum of Art, University of Wisconsin-Madison, Madison, WI
Vever: Ex-collection Henri Vever, Paris
WAM: Worcester Art Museum, Worcester, MA

PUBLICATIONS

DFP: Meech, Julia, Jane Oliver, and John T. Carpenter. *Designed for Pleasure: The World of Edo Japan in Prints and Printings, 1680–1860.* New York: Asia Society of America, 2008.
FP: Grabhorn, Marjorie, Edwin E. Grabhorn, and Harold P. Stern. *Figure Prints of Old Japan: A Pictorial Pageant of Actors & Courtesans of the Eighteenth Century.* San Francisco: Book Club of California, 1959.
GC: Yamaguchi, Keisaburō, ed. *Gurabuhoon korekushon: Ukiyo-e meihin-ten.* Tokyo: Bun'yūsha, 1995.
G–J: Genshoku Ukiyoe Dai Hyakka Jiten Henshū I'inkai, ed. *Genshoku Ukiyoe dai Hyakka Jiten,* 11 vols. Tōkyō: Taishūkan Shoten, 1980–1982.
G.Land: Grabhorn, Edwin E., Marjorie Grabhorn, and Jack Ronald Hillier. *Landscape Prints of Old Japan: From the Beginning of the Eighteenth Century to the Middle of the Nineteenth Century.* San Francisco: Book Club of California, 1960.
Hillier 1970: Hillier, Jack. *Suzuki Harunobu: An Exhibition of his Colour-Prints and Illustrated Books on the Occasion of the Bicentenary of his Death in 1770.* Philadelphia: The Philadelphia Museum of Art, 1970.
MPJ: Stern, Harold P. and UCLA Art Galleries. *Master Prints of Japan: Ukiyo-e Hanga.* New York: Harry N. Abrams, 1969.
TWP: Grabhorn, Edwin E., and Irma Grabhorn-Engel. *Twelve Wood-Block Prints of Kitagawa Utamaro: Illustrating the Process of Silk Culture.* With an introduction by Jack Hillier. San Francisco: Book Club of California, 1965.
Ukiyo-e: Grabhorn, Edwin and Marjorie. *Ukiyo-e: The Floating World.* San Francisco: Book Club of California, 1962.
UM: Shibui Kiyoshi, Hazama Inosuke, Yoshida Teruji, Suzuki Jūzō, and Oka Isaburō. *Ukiyo-e [Ukiyo-e Masterpieces].* Tokyo: Nihon Keizai Shinbun, 1969.
US: Link, Howard A, Narasaki Muneshige and Yamaguchi Keizaburō. *Honoruru Bijutsukan (& the Edwin and Irma Grabhorn Collection).* Translated by Tobita Shigeo. Vol. 10 of *Ukiyo-e shūka.* Tokyo: Shōgakkan, 1979.
ZNS: Narazaki, Muneshige, Shimada Shujiro, Yamane Yuzo, eds. *Ukiyoe.* Vol. 7 of *Zaigai Nihon no Shihō.* Tokyo: Mainichi Shinbunsha, 1980.

Glossary

ARAGOTO: "rough" style of Kabuki acting—associated with the Ichikawa Danjūrō line—which employs exaggerated poses, gestures, costume, and speech to portray characters of heroic courage and physical strength.

BENI-E: a *sumizuri* print hand colored with safflower red (*beni*), often in combination with yellow, green, and blue.

BENIZURI-E: a print whose primary colors are safflower red (*beni*) and green, in which each color is printed from a separate block.

BOKASHI: shaded or gradated tones achieved by various printing techniques, such as wiping the block with a moistened cloth before applying pigment.

EGOYOMI: "picture calendar," in which symbols for the long and short months of the lunar year are incorporated within the design.

FURISODE: "swinging sleeves," a kimono with long, hanging sleeves, typically worn by young, unmarried women.

GEISHA: an entertainer trained to sing, dance, and play music. Until the mid-1700s the term was used to refer to male musicians working in the pleasure quarters, but later women took up the title as well, outnumbering their male counterparts by 1800.

HAKKEI: "eight views" representing or alluding to the traditional Chinese painting theme of "Eight Views of the Xiao and Xiang Rivers" (for example, the *Ōmi hakkei,* or "Eight Views of Ōmi").

HASHIRA-E: "pillar-picture," a print in a long, narrow, vertical format.

KAMURO: a child attendant to a high-ranking courtesan. *Kamuro* received training in the arts, along with their older counterparts, *shinzō.*

KAOMISE: "showing the faces," the opening performance of the Kabuki season, in which theaters introduced the members of their acting troupes to the public. *Kaomise* took place each year, from the eleventh through early in the twelfth month, and were often promoted and celebrated in prints.

KARAZURI: blind-printing, gauffrage.

KIBYŌSHI: "yellow cover," illustrated books of satiric fiction, popular in the Edo period.

KOSODE: "small sleeves," a kimono robe with narrow wrist openings, worn regularly by all classes of Edo period men and women.

KYŌKA: a form of comic Japanese poetry. Like the classical verse form known as *tanka* or *waka, kyōka* poems are five lines long and consist of thirty-one syllables, arranged in a 5-7-5-7-7 pattern.

MIE: a dramatic pose struck by male actors, to capture the emotional intensity of a moment. For *aragoto* roles, the actor might take a big step forward, open his eyes wide, swing his head, and spread his hands before freezing the action in a powerful gesture.

MIMASU: "three rice measures," the crest of nested boxes or concentric squares associated with the Ichikawa line of actors.

MITATE: a contemporary reworking of a historical or classical literary scene, sometimes described as a parody.

MURASAKI-E: "purple pictures," prints in a limited palette, in some cases using only shades of gray and violet.

NISHIKI-E: "brocade pictures," full-color prints, sometimes using other luxury techniques like embossing (*karazuri*).

OBI: a sash used to secure the *kosode* and prevent it from opening. While both men and women wore narrow obi in the first part of the Edo period, wide obis of brocade and other expensive fabrics became fashionable in the late seventeenth century, growing wider and wider by 1800.

ŌKUBI-E: "big-head pictures," bust-portraits of actors and courtesans, popularized in the late 1780s.

ONNAGATA: an actor specializing in female roles; a female role in a Kabuki play.

SHIBARAKU: "Stop a moment!" A theatrical set piece included during interludes in a Kabuki play or between plays; features the sudden appearance of a hero wearing dramatic red costume and striped stage makeup.

SHINZŌ: an adolescent attendant to a courtesan, typically aged fourteen and older. *Shinzō* received training in the arts, along with their younger counterparts, *kamuro.*

SUMIZURI-E: monochromatic pictures printed in ink (*sumi*).

TAN-E: *sumizuri-e* hand colored with red pigment (*tan*) and one or two other colors.

UCHIKAKE: an outer garment draped unbelted over a *kosode,* often elaborately decorated and with a sweeping, padded hem.

UKIYO-E: "pictures of the floating world," a term used to refer to woodblock prints, paintings, and book illustrations made to depict the actors and courtesans of Edo Japan; for the nineteenth century the term also encompasses other popular print subjects such as landscapes and warriors.

URUSHI, URUSHI-E: "lacquer," "lacquer pictures," hand colored *sumizuri-e* with a mixture of ink (*sumi*) and glue added to black areas for a lustrous, "lacquer-like" effect.

WAKA: a classical poetic form of thirty-one syllables arranged in five lines in a 5-7-5-7-7 pattern.

WAKASHŪ: an adolescent boy or young man; *wakashū* were often physically distinguished by hairstyles with a partially shaved crown and long forelocks. In prints, *wakashū* sometimes have an effeminate appearance and are cast as the objects of homosexual desire.

YOSHIWARA: licensed brothel district in Edo.

Selected Reading

1 WORKS IN WESTERN LANGUAGES

Avitabile, Gunhild. *Early Masters: Ukiyo-e Prints and Paintings from 1680 to 1750.* New York: Japan Society, 1991.

Bickford, Lawrence. *Sumo and the Woodblock Print Masters.* New York: Kodansha, 1994.

Brandt, Klaus J. *Hosoda Eishi 1756–1829: Der Japanische Maler und Holzschnittmeister und seine Schüler.* Stuttgart: K. J. Brandt, 1977.

Breuer, Karin. *Japanesque: The Japanese Print in the Era of Impressionism.* San Francisco: Fine Arts Museums of San Francisco and DelMonico Books/Prestel, 2010.

Calza, Gian Carlo. *Ukiyo-e.* London: Phaidon, 2005.

Chicago Art Institute. *Ukiyo-e Masterpieces from the Art Institute of Chicago: Catalog of an Exhibition, Held 24 Feb.–18 Mar. 1973, at Riccar Art Museum, Tokyo, 24 Mar.–15 Apr. 1973, at the Kyoto National Museum of Modern Art, Kyoto.* Chicago: Art Institute of Chicago, 1973.

Clark, Timothy. *Kuniyoshi from the Arthur R. Miller Collection.* London: Royal Academy of Arts, 2009.

Clark, Timothy, Donald Jenkins, and Osamu Ueda. *The Actor's Image: Print Makers of the Katsukawa School.* Edited by Naomi Noble Richard. Chicago: Art Institute of Chicago in association with Princeton University Press, 1994.

Clark, Timothy, Allen Hockley, Anne Nishimura Morse, and Louise E. Virgin. *The Dawn of the Floating World, 1650–1765: Early Ukiyo-e Treasures from the Museum of Fine Arts, Boston.* London: Royal Academy of Arts, 2001.

Collia-Suzuki, Gina. *The Complete Woodblock Prints of Kitagawa Utamaro: A Descriptive Catalogue.* London: Nezu Press, 2009.

———. *Utamaro Revealed: A Guide to Subjects, Themes & Motifs.* London: Nezu Press, 2008.

Cranston, Edwin A. *A Waka Anthology.* 2 vols. Stanford: Stanford University Press, 1993–2006.

Davis, Julie Nelson. *Utamaro and the Spectacle of Beauty.* Honolulu: University of Hawai'i Press, 2008.

Elvehjem Museum of Art. *The Edward Burr Van Vleck Collection of Japanese Prints.* Madison: University of Wisconsin-Madison, 1990.

Faulker, Rupert, with consultation by B. W. Robinson. *Masterpieces of Japanese Prints: The European Collections; Ukiyo-e from the Victoria and Albert Museum.* Tokyo: Kodansha, 1991.

Forrer, Matthi. *The Baur Collection: Japanese Prints.* 2 vols. Geneva: Collections Baur, 1994.

Gentles, Margaret O. *The Clarence Buckingham Collection of Japanese Prints: Harunobu, Koryūsai, Shigemasa, Their Followers and Contemporaries.* Chicago: Art Institute of Chicago, 1965.

Grabhorn, Edwin E. *A Brief History of Japanese Color Prints and Their Designers: Delivered Before the Members of the Roxburghe Club of San Francisco, Monday Evening, April 4, 1938, by Edwin Grabhorn.* San Francisco: Grabhorn Press, 1938.

———. "An Interview at the Grabhorn Press," typescript interview by Carol Packard, c. 1959, Grabhorn Ukiyo-e Collection archives.

Grabhorn, Edwin E., and Irma Grabhorn-Engel. *Twelve Wood-Block Prints of Kitagawa Utamaro: Illustrating the Process of Silk Culture.* With an introduction by Jack Hillier. San Francisco: Book Club of California, 1965.

Grabhorn, Edwin E., and Jack Hillier. *Landscape Prints of Old Japan: From the Beginning of the Eighteenth Century to the Middle of the Nineteenth Century; Illustrated from Original Prints in the Collection of Edwin and Marjorie Grabhorn.* San Francisco: Book Club of California, 1960.

Grabhorn, Marjorie, and Edwin Grabhorn. *Figure Prints of Old Japan: A Pictorial Pageant of Actors & Courtesans of the Eighteenth Century, Reproduced from the Prints in the Collection of Marjorie & Edwin Grabhorn.* With an introduction by Harold P. Stern. San Francisco: Book Club of California, 1959.

———. *Ukiyo-e: The Floating World. Illustrated by Twenty-eight Rare Examples of Japanese Woodblock Prints by Seventeen Great Masters of the Art.* San Francisco: Book Club of California, 1962.

Graybill, Maribeth, ed. *The Artist's Touch, the Craftsman's Hand: Three Centuries of Japanese Prints from the Portland Art Museum*. Portland: Portland Art Museum, 2011.

Hempel, Rose, and Wolfgang Holler. *Gems of the Floating World: Ukiyo-e Prints from the Dresden Kupferstich-Kabinett*. New York: Japan Society, 1995.

Hillier, Jack. *Japanese Prints and Drawings from the Vever Collection*. 3 vols. London: Sotheby Parke Bernet, 1976.

———. *Suzuki Harunobu: An Exhibition of His Colour-Prints and Illustrated Books on the Occasion of the Bicentenary of His Death in 1770*. Philadelphia: Philadelphia Museum of Art, 1970.

Hirano, Chie. *Kiyonaga: A Study of His Life and Works with a Portfolio of Plates in Color and Collotype*. Cambridge, Mass.: Harvard University Press, 1939.

Izzard, Sebastian J., John T. Carpenter, and Thomas Rimer. *Kunisada's World*. New York: Japan Society, 1993.

Jenkins, Donald. *The Ledoux Heritage: The Collecting of Ukiyo-e Master Prints*. New York: Japan Society, 1973.

———. *Ukiyo-e Prints and Paintings: The Primitive Period, 1680–1745: An Exhibition in Memory of Margaret O. Gentles*. Chicago: Art Institute of Chicago, 1971.

Kimbrough, R. Keller. "Reading the Miraculous Powers of Japanese Poetry: Spells, Truth Acts, and a Medieval Buddhist Poetics of the Supernatural." *Japanese Journal of Religious Studies* 32, no. 1 (2005): 1–33.

Kobayashi, Tadashi. *Utamaro: Portraits from the Floating World*. Translated by Mark A. Harbison. Tokyo: Kodansha, 2000.

Kobayashi, Tadashi, and Howard A. Link. *Edo Beauties in Ukiyo-e: The James A. Michener Collection*. Translated by Juliann Wolfgram. Edited by Carol Shankel. Honolulu: Honolulu Academy of Arts, 1994.

Ledoux, Louis V. *Japanese Prints of the Primitive Period in the Collection of Louis V. Ledoux: Catalogue by the Owner with Twenty Plates in Full Color and Thirty in Halftone*. New York: E. Weyhe, 1942.

Link, Howard A. *The Theatrical Prints of the Torii Masters: A Selection of Seventeenth and Eighteenth-century Ukiyo-e*. Honolulu: Honolulu Academy of Arts, 1977.

Mann, H. George. "Osamu Ueda." *Impressions* 33 (2012): 113–117.

———. "Passionate Pursuit: My Adventures in Ukiyo-e." *Impressions* 25 (2003): 77–91.

Marks, Andreas. *Japanese Woodblock Prints: Artists, Publishers and Masterworks 1680–1900*. Rutland: Tuttle Publishing, 2010.

———. *Publishers of Japanese Woodblock Prints: A Compendium*. Leiden: Hotei Publishing, 2010.

McCullough, Helen Craig, trans. *Tales of Ise: Lyrical Episodes from Tenth-Century Japan*. Stanford: Stanford University Press, 1968.

Meech, Julia. "The Early Years of Japanese Print Collecting in North America." *Impressions* 25 (2003): 14–53.

———. "Edwin Grabhorn: Printer and Print Collector." *Impressions* 25 (2003): 55–69.

———. "Who Was Harry Packard?" *Impressions* 32 (2011): 83–113.

Meech, Julia, and Jane Oliver, eds. *Designed for Pleasure: The World of Edo Japan in Prints and Paintings, 1680–1860*. New York: Asia Society and Japanese Art Society of America, 2008.

Metzgar, Judson D. *Adventures in Japanese Prints*. Los Angeles: Grabhorn Press for Dawson's Book Shop, 1943.

Michener, James A., and Richard Lane. *Japanese Prints from the Early Masters to the Modern*. Tokyo: Charles E. Tuttle Company, 1959.

Mostow, Joshua S. *Pictures of the Heart: The Hyakunin Isshu in Word and Image*. Honolulu: University of Hawai'i Press, 1996.

Narazaki, Muneshige. *Sharaku: The Enigmatic Ukiyo-e Master*. Translated by Bonnie F. Abiko. Tokyo: Kodansha, 1983.

———. *The Japanese Print: Its Evolution and Essence*. Adapted by C. H. Mitchell. Tokyo: Kodansha, 1966.

Pins, Jacob. *The Japanese Pillar Print: Hashira-e*. London: Robert G. Sawers, 1982.

Redesdale, Algernon Bertram Freeman-Mitford. *Tales of Old Japan: With Illustrations Drawn and Cut on Wood by Japanese Artists*. 2 vols. London: Macmillan and Co., 1893.

Reed, O. P. "Appraising the Frank Lloyd Wright Collection: A Personal Memoir." *Impressions* 24 (2002): 92–97.

Sakamoto, Gorō. "Eight Parts Full: A Life in the Tokyo Art Trade." Special issue, *Impressions* (2011).

Schaap, Robert. *Heroes & Ghosts: Japanese Prints by Kuniyoshi 1797–1861*. Leiden: Hotei Publishing, 1998.

Shirane, Haruo. *The Bridge of Dreams: A Poetics of the Tale of Genji*. Stanford: Stanford University Press, 1987.

———. *Traces of Dreams: Landscape, Cultural Memory, and the Poetry of Bashō*. Stanford: Stanford University Press, 1998.

Smyers, Karen A. *The Fox and the Jewel: Shared and Private Meanings in Contemporary Japanese Inari Worship*. Honolulu: University of Hawai'i Press, 1998.

Sotheby & Co. *Highly Important Japanese Prints, Illustrated Books and Drawings, from the Henri Vever Collection*. Part 1. London: Sotheby & Co., 1974.

———. *Highly Important Japanese Prints, Illustrated Books, Drawings and Fan Paintings from the Henri Vever Collection*. Part 2. London: Sotheby & Co., 1975.

Sotheby Parke Bernet & Co. *Highly Important Japanese Prints, Illustrated Books, Drawings and Paintings from the Henri Vever Collection*. Part 3. London: Sotheby Parke Bernet & Co., 1977.

———. *Fine Japanese Prints, Drawings and Paintings: The Property of a Gentleman*. London: Sotheby Parke Bernet & Co., 1978.

Sotheby, Wilkinson & Hodge. *A Choice Collection of Japanese Colour Prints, the Property of Baron Walter von Heymel, of Munich . . . and a Very Important Old Japanese Album Containing Forty Prints by Harunobu, the Property of Mrs. A. M. Litchfield*. London: Sotheby, Wilkinson & Hodge, 2 December 1910.

———. *A Valuable and Extensive Collection of Japanese Colour Prints, Formed by the Late W. O. Danckwerts, Esq., K. C. . . .* London: Sotheby, Wilkinson & Hodge, 21 July 1914.

Stern, Harold P., and UCLA Art Galleries. *Master Prints of Japan: Ukiyo-e Hanga*. New York: Harry N. Abrams, 1969.

Takahashi, Seiichirō. *Masterworks of Ukiyo-e: Harunobu*. Adapted by John Bester. Tokyo: Kodansha, 1968.

———. *Traditional Woodblock Prints of Japan*. Translated by Richard Stanley-Baker, Heibonsha Survey of Japanese Art. Vol. 22, 3rd ed. New York and Tokyo: Weatherhill and Heibonsha, 1976.

Thompson, Sarah E., and Harootunian, H. D. *Undercurrents in the Floating World: Censorship and Japanese Prints*. New York: Asia Society, 1991.

Toby, Ronald P. "Carnival of the Aliens. Korean Embassies in Edo-Period Art and Popular Culture." *Monumenta Nipponica*, 41, no. 4 (1986): 415–456.

Toyama, Usaburō. *The Western-Style Colour Prints in Japan: A Catalogue on Retrospective Works of the Exhibition in Foreign Country, Organised by Nippon Hanga Kyokai / Nihon shoki yōfū hanga shū: kaigai tenrankai zuroku*. Tokyo: Daiichi Shobo, 1936.

Tyler, Royall, trans. *Japanese Nō Dramas*. London: Penguin Books, 1992.

Uther, Hans-Jörg, "The Fox in World Literature: Reflections on a 'Fictional Animal.'" *Asian Folklore Studies* 65, no. 2 (2006), 133–160.

Vergez, Robert. *Early Ukiyo-e Master Okumura Masanobu*. Tokyo: Kodansha, 1983.

Waterhouse, David. *The Harunobu Decade: A Catalogue of Woodcuts by Suzuki Harunobu and His Followers in the Museum of Fine Arts, Boston*. Leiden: Hotei Publishing, forthcoming 2013.

Waterhouse, D. B. *Harunobu and His Age: The Development of Colour Printing in Japan*. London: Trustees of the British Museum, 1964.

———. *Images of Eighteenth-Century Japan: Ukiyo-e Prints from the Sir Edmund Walker Collection*. Toronto: Royal Ontario Museum, 1975.

———. "Korean Music, Trick Horsemanship and Elephants in Tokugawa Japan." In Yoshihiko Tokumaru and Osamu Yamaguchi, *The Oral and the Literate in Music*. Tokyo: Academia Music Ltd., 1986, 353–370.

Welch, Matthew, Yuiko Kimura-Tilford, Shūgō Asano, Minneapolis Institute of Arts, and Shibuya Kuritsu Shōtō Bijutsukan. *Worldly Pleasures, Earthly Delights: Japanese Prints from the Minneapolis Institute of Arts*. Minneapolis: Minneapolis Institute of Arts, 2011.

Wentz, Roby. *The Grabhorn Press: A Biography*. San Francisco: Book Club of California, 1981.

Wheat, Carl I. "Private Presses and Fine Printers of California." *News Notes of California Libraries* 29, no. 3 (July 1934): 94.

Yonemura, Ann. *Masterful Illusions: Japanese Prints in the Anne van Biema Collection*. Washington DC: Smithsonian Institution, 2002.

Yuasa, Yoshiko, and Edward F. Domino. *100 Woodblock Prints of Edo Culture from the Ukiyo-e Collection of the Tobacco and Salt Museum*. Ann Arbor: NPP Books, 2008.

Aoki Shinzaburō. "Kono michi hitosuji ukiyo-e no michi—Kaneko Fusui-shi o shinobu." *Ukiyo-e geijutsu* 58 (Dec. 1978): 22–25.

Asano Shūgo, and Timothy Clark. *Kitagawa Utamaro ten* [The Passionate Art of Utamaro]. 2 vols. Tokyo: Asahi Shinbun-sha, 1995.

Chiba-shi Bijutsukan, ed. *Seishun no ukiyoeshi Suzuki Harunobu: Edo no kararisto tōjō*. Chiba: Chiba-shi Bijutsukan; Hagi: Yamaguchi Kenritsu Hagi Bijutsukan, Uragami Kinenkan, 2002.

Genshoku ukiyo-e dai hyakka jiten. 11 vols. Tokyo: Taishūkan Shoten, 1980–1982.

Ihara Toshirō. *Kabuki nenpyō*. 8 vols. Tokyo: Iwanami Shoten, 1956–1963.

Kano Hiroyuki. *Kiyonaga to nishiki-e*. No. 364 of *Nihon no bijutsu*. Tokyo: Shibundō, 1996.

Kikuchi Sadao. *Toyokuni*. Vol. 6 of *Ukiyo-e hakka*. Tokyo: Heibonsha, 1985.

Kinsei fūzoku zufu. 13 vols. Tokyo: Shōgakkan, 1984.

Kobayashi Tadashi, ed. *Nishiki-e no tanjō: Edo shōmin bunka no kaika*. Tokyo: Tōkyō-to Edo-Tōkyō Hakubutsukan, 1996.

Link, Howard A., Narazaki Muneshige, and Yamaguchi Ōzaburō. *Honoruru Bijutsukan* [Honolulu Academy of Arts and the Edwin *&* Irma Grabhorn Collection]. Translated by Tobita Shigeo. Vol. 10 of *Ukiyo-e shūka*. Tokyo: Shōgakkan, 1979.

Nagata Seiji, ed. *Berugii ōritsu bijutsu rekishi hakubutsukan, Berugii ōritsu toshokan shozō Berugii roiyaru korekushon ten*. Tokyo: Yomiuri Shinbun-sha, 2008.

Naitō Masato and Higuchi Kazutaka. *Yume to tsuioku no Edo: Takahashi Seiichirō korekushon meihin-ten*. Tokyo: Keiō Gijuku, 2009

Nannichi Gimyō. *Inari o tazunete: inari shinkō no yurai to goshintoku*. Ōsaka: Bunshindō, 1981.

Narazaki Muneshige. "Tsuitō Nishi Saijūshi." *Ukiyo-e geijutsu* 119 (May 1996): 16–19.

Narazaki Muneshige, Akiyama Mitsuyasu, Shimada Shūjirō, and Yamane Yūzō, eds. *Ukiyo-e*. Vol. 7 of *Zaigai Nihon no shihō*. Tokyo: Mainichi Shinbun-sha, 1980.

Nihon Keizai Shinbun-sha, ed. *Shikago bijutsukan ukiyo-e meihin-ten*. Tokyo: Nihon Keizai Shinbun sha, 1973.

———. *Shindorā korekushon ukiyo-e meihin-ten*. Tokyo: Nihon Keizai Shinbun-sha, 1985.

Ōhara Rieko. *Kurokami no bunkashi*. Tokyo: Tsukiji Shokan, 1988.

Ōsaka Shiritsu Sumai no Myujiamu, ed. *Kamigata yakusha-e no sekai: Shibai toshi Ōsaka*. Osaka: Ōsaka Shiritsu sumai no Myūjiamu, 2001.

Ōta Kinen Bijutsukan et al., eds. *Ōta Kinen Bijutsukan zō ukiyo-e meihin zuroku*. Tokyo: Ōta Kinen Bijutsukan, 1988.

———. *Gime tōyō bijutsukan shozō ukiyo-e meihinten*. Tokyo: NHK Promotion, 2007.

———. *Kuniyoshi: Botsugo 150-nen kinen:* Tokyo: NHK Promotion, 2011.

Packard, Harry. "Nihon bijutsu shūshūki" (Diary of a collector of Japanese art). *Geijutsu shinchō* 27, no. 2 (Feb. 1976): 139.

Santorii Bijutsukan, ed. *Sono na wa Tsutaya Jūzaburō: Utamaro Sharaku no shikakenin*. Tokyo: Santorii Bijutsukan, 2010.

Shibui Kiyoshi. *Ukiyo-e zuten*. Tokyo: Kazama Shobō, 1964.

Shibui Kiyoshi, Hazama Inosuke, Yoshida Teruji, Suzuki Jūzō, and Oka Isaburō. *Ukiyo-e* [Ukiyo-e Masterpieces]. Tokyo: Nihon Keizai Shinbun, 1969.

Suwa Haruo, ed. *Edo no hana kabukie ten: Kinsei shoki fūzokuga kara bakumatsu ukiyo-e made*. Tokyo: Tōbu Bijutsukan and Yomiuri Shinbun-sha, 1999.

Tabako to Shio no Hakubutsukan, ed. *Ukiyo-e hanga*. 3 vols. Tokyo: Tabako to Shio no Hakubutuskan, 2011.

Takamizawa Takako. *Aru ukiyo-eshi no isan: Takamizawa Enji oboegaki*. Tokyo: Tōsho Sensho, 1978.

Tōkyō Kokuritsu Hakubutsukan, ed. *Sharaku: tokubetsuten*. Tokyo: Tōkyō Kokuritsu Hakubutsukan and Tōkyō Shinbun-sha, 2011.

———. *Tokubetsuten ukiyo-e: Kyū Matsukata korekushon chūshin to shite*. Tokyo: Tōkyō Kokuritsu Hakubutsukan, 1984.

Tsuboi Kyō. "Kaneko Fusui o shinobu." *Kikan ukiyo-e* 75 (Oct. 1978).

Ukiyo-e shūka. 19 vols. Tokyo: Shōgakkan, 1978–1985.

Ukiyo-e taika shūsei. 26 vols. Tokyo: Taihōkaku Shobō, 1931–1934.

Yamaguchi Keizaburō, ed. *Gurabuhoon korekushon: ukiyo-e meihin-ten*. Tokyo: Bun'yūsha, 1995.

Yamato Bunkakan, ed. *Joseizō no keifu: Matsuura byōbu kara Utamaro made*. Nara: Yamato Bunkakan, 2011.

Yoshida Teruji. *Harunobu zenshū*. Tokyo: Takamizawa Mokuhan-sha, 1942.

———. *Ukiyo-e jiten*. 3 vols. Tokyo: Ryokuen Shobō, 1965.

Yura Tetsuji, ed. *Sōgō Nihon ukiyo-e ruikō*. Tokyo: Gabundō, 1979.

Index

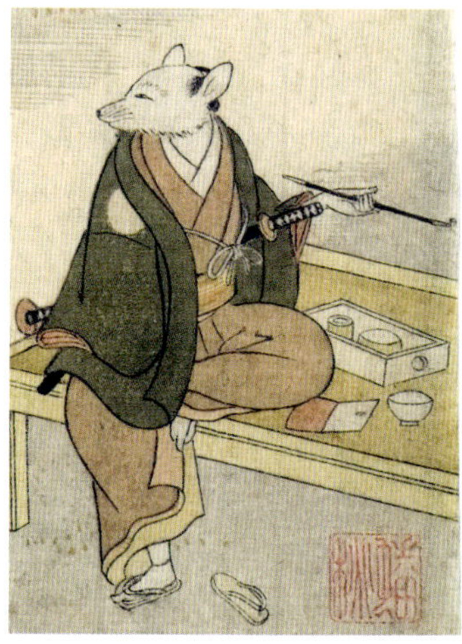

The Printer's Eye: Ukiyo-e from the Grabhorn Collection was produced at the Asian Art Museum, San Francisco; it documents a generous donation of Japanese prints from the estate of Edwin and Irma Grabhorn. Publication was made possible thanks to generous contributions from an Ahmanson Foundation trustee, Lloyd E. Cotsen, and Mrs. Kazuko Imagawa Zolinsky. Jay Xu is the museum's director, Forrest McGill its chief curator. The book's content was directed by Laura W. Allen and Melissa M. Rinne in the museum's Japanese art department. Edited and proofread by Daniel King and Thomas Christensen, it was designed and typeset in Adobe Garamond Premier Pro and indexed by Thomas Christensen. It was printed in Hong Kong by Regal Printing, Ltd.